Tourism Infrastructure Design

Tourism Infrastructure Design

Edited by
Joaquín Alvado Bañón,
Krizsán András,
Pan Youcai

Contents

Preface ··· 6

1 Visitor Center Design ··· 8

Introduction ··· 10

Visitor Center Design Guidelines ··· 12

Planning ··· 12
Criteria for Supporting Visitor Center Proposals ··· 13
Decision Criteria for Proposing a Visitor Center ··· 17
Interpretive Master Planning ··· 19
Site Design ··· 24
Building Design ··· 29

Visitor Center Projects ··· 34

Strømbu Service Center and Rest Area ··· 34
Fogo Island Natural Park Headquarters ··· 42
Visitor Center 'Kasteeltuin Slot Assumburg' ··· 50
Wasit Nature Reserve Visitor Center ··· 56
Yew Dell Botanical Gardens Visitor Center ··· 62
Wild Turkey Bourbon Visitor Center ··· 68
Visitor Center for Architectural Miniatures Park ··· 76
Fazer Visitor Center and Meeting Center ··· 82
Red Rock Canyon Visitor Center ··· 88
Naples Botanical Garden Visitor Center ··· 98
Villers Abbey Visitor Center ··· 104
Coedy Brenin Visitor Center ··· 114
Cabañeros National Park Visitors Center ··· 122
Visitor Center of Mont-Tremblant National Park ··· 132

2 Scenic Overlook Design ··· 140

Introduction ··· 142

Scenic Overlook Design Guidelines ··· 142

The Influencing Factors ··· 143
Minimizing Site Disturbance ··· 144
Sustainable Organization and Appearance ··· 144
A Quality Visitor Experience ··· 145
Circulation ··· 146
Grading ··· 148
Landscaping ··· 149
Public Services ··· 149
Site Furnishings and Amenities ··· 149
Supplemental Facilities/Built Structures ··· 150

Scenic Overlook Projects ··· 152

Aurland Lookout ··· 152
Austin Observation Tower ··· 158
Viewing Platform Trautmansdorff ··· 166
Mountain Peak Platform on Top of Tyrol ··· 170
Quilotoa Crater Overlook ··· 176
Viewpoint from Palm Grove ··· 182
The Pyramid Viewpoint ··· 188
Löyly ··· 194
The Infinite Bridge ··· 200
Sky Walk ··· 204
The World Championship Ski Jump ··· 210

3 Campsite Facilities Design ⋯ 218

Introduction ⋯ 220

Campsite Facilities Design Guidelines ⋯ 222

Campground Layout ⋯ 222

Campground Utilities and Trash ⋯ 223

Campsite Parking Spurs ⋯ 225

Campsite Layout and Components ⋯ 225

Accessible Campsites ⋯ 226

Campground Projects ⋯ 228

International Self-driving and RV Campground at Ranwu Lake ⋯ 228

Xinduqiao RV Campground along No.318 National Road ⋯ 240

Jiange Cuiyunlang RV Campground along No.318 National Road ⋯ 256

Home of Freedom-Mount Huang Qiyun Campground ⋯ 268

Ga-pyeong Glamping ⋯ 286

Parque Tejo ⋯ 294

Index ⋯ 306

Preface

Joaquín Alvado Bañón

Fitting with the title of the book, a broad variety of tourist infrastructure projects and practices are featured here. There are more than 30 architectural projects from all over the world. The touristic development approaches highlighted are unusual and express personal points of view. All these works show the potential of uniting the landscape and the architecture in a single image.

Over the years, a special relationship between architecture and tourism has been developing. Each can be said to depend on the other. Today, we cannot deny the global condition of the architectural practice and the geographical open relations due to touristic experiences. Architecture, in terms of tourism, is now an integral element of designing for cities and their surroundings all over the globe.

In ancient times, architecture, as a touristic site, had a very important role. Temples, theaters, and stadiums were built as public monuments, expressing the culture and the society from which they arouse. Nowadays, they have become attractions for a new era. In many cities throughout Europe (e.g. Paris, Rome, Athens, Venice, Barcelona and many others), tourism relies solely on the culture of monuments, the culture of the society when these monuments were created.

The brand of these cities is their history, but the rapid increase in the consumption of heritage culture destabilizes city centers. The tremendous tourist demand and the problematic relationship between citizens and tourists require rethinking our tourism infrastructure. We needa new cultural perspective and a contemporary approach to tourism that holds a close connection to the landscape. When we talk about landscape, we talk about a creating new identity for the place and a new way of consuming space. This book shows a new veer towards sustainability, a new touristic architectural approach to the natural environment. The viewpoints, sports infrastructure, visitor centers, and RV camps presented in these pages introduce to the reader a new way to understand the landscape, a sustainable approach to the contemporary relation between architecture and tourism.

For examples of this sustainable approach, this book contains plenty: the Aurland Look Out in Norway taking nature as its primary guide in design with architectural considerations playing a secondary role; the Austin Observation Tower in the United

States elegantly integrating efficient use of materials with thoughtful structural design; the Mountain Peak Platform Top of Tyrol in Austria, designed as a spiritual place where even stressed mountaineers can find peace and recuperate enjoying the seemingly endless expanses of mountains; and the Quilotoa Crater Overlook in Ecuador, where architecture creates opportunities for the visitor to see the landscape in different ways than from every position in the crater. In all these examples and in others presented, architecture is designed to highlight, preserve and protect the landscape.

The book is also filled with examples of architecture providing tourist experiences while preserving and interpreting the territory: the Infinity Bridge in Denmark, a footbridge designed toenable visitors to experience the magnificent landscape of the bay and become aware of its relationship with the city; the Sky Walk in the Czech Republic, a piece of architecture that allows visitors an unique experience of walking through the clouds; the World Championship Ski Jump in Oslo, Norway, a design that unifies various amenities into one holistic design; and the Fogo Island Natural Park Headquarters in Fogo, Cape Verde, where the body of the building is made up of a continuous surface, composed of local black masonry block—a mixture of cement and ashes from the volcano. All these works are presented as examples where buildings experiment with nature to instill new meaning for the place and generate economic activities as cultural landscapes for touristic destinations.

This is a compilation of projects concerning how to develop tourism and at the same time preserve a certain set of landscape values. Modern tourism ought to be closely linked to sustainability and the elements of nature itself. The infrastructure depicted here shows that when combined with tourism, architecture gives the landscape certain effects, which further highlights the need for strategies to achieve sustainable development. The architecture presented transforms territory into an attractive landscape to allow a complete experience of nature.

As I have said, contemporary architecture and tourism must find a new direction to sustainability in order to protect and respect the landscape. This book aims to explore how architecture values ecosystems, landscape experiences and its impact on the environment as a basis for developing new practical methods to preserve nature.

1 Visitor Center Design

Introduction

Krizsán András

The ancient Romans believed that all natural or human-made space is inspired and protected. The unique purity of a landscape is always a passionate experience, focused on the climate of the region, the diversity of the environment and the culture of people living there. Through these experiences, people, wherever there is wonder in the world, feel as if being personally addressed. The heavens, the earth, dwellings, and cities are just like human beings. They have their own history, tradition, spatial features and details, which in any case make our orientation easier, allowing us to be more identified by the location. Every inch of a land, a cliff, or a tiny valley has its own character and identity that can hardly be described by personal concepts and experiences. Almost everything may change, but man's aspiration to relate his identity to collecting these experiences do not. Although the civilization of our time tries to conjure up for itself the spirit of universal culture, to merge the landscape and natural features of different continents into a homogenous mass, but these attempts are in vain. Every single piece of the earth has its own character and identity. It is especially true for historical sites or natural attractions, where the spirit of the place is concentrated in the 'genius loci.'

It is not an easy task to design in such a sensitive and intensive environment, at such a concentrated mixture of attractions and experiences, and to construct a new building. To do so, respect for the landscape is essential. Humility for the environment, morphological analysis, and conscious preparatory work is the only way to understand the landscape, the trees, the people, and to carry on what the Creator exalts and blossoms.

When creating buildings, we are part of two complementary processes. In one case we attack, break the existing environment, the balance created by nature and history. However, on the other hand, we are building a new state of balance through construction and giving a new interpretation to the surrounding landscape and countryside. Between our personal self and our environment, architecture, the architect is the mediator, the 'guiding principle,' which is able to give human dimensions to the world around us. Good architecture is healing architecture and a building sacrifice at the same time.

Now, this sensuous attitude, humility to the place's spirit, appears in architecture, especially in designing visitor centers all around the world. Architects think of visitor centers as a reality that attaches particular importance to the specific factors of the construction site, landscape and historical traditions, rejecting the sculpted version of architecture specific in the modern era. Architects today no longer look for 'high-tech' enchantment, but distance themselves from the emotional, formalistic tendencies that are too arbitrary to make a real contact with the landscape. They do not refer neither to stereotypes typical of didactic architecture nor the self-realization of the fine art, emphasizing individuality over all. They try to remain in the background, in the environment, or in the spirit of the place, and they prefer to add a signal to the landscape so that the visitor can have an experience of his or her own. This architecture can understand the beauty of the landscape, its historical sights, and help to renew and further let live the 'genius loci.'

Traditional architectural concepts originated essentially from the importance of tradition and heritage and, as such, visitor centers of historical monuments or antique ruins were designed in historical styles. Their objective was 'telling tales' from the past, didactically summoning the heroes of long-gone eras, utilizing the historical elements in constructing the tourist attraction. However, the natural beauty of the landscape itself would be hidden.

Contemporary architecture, on the other hand, seeks the simplicity of rational, clean interior spaces and shapes in designing a visitor center. Avoid using special forms and uninteresting, unnecessary decorations, but instead shape the architecture around the function. After all, visitor centers are contemporary buildings that deal with contemporary features. Their exterior design, homogeneous façades, and materials from their surroundings—all have their origin in the landscape and place. Their structure can be understood at first glance. The simple generosity of the architectural concept becomes tangible. A good visitor center does not want to compete with the surrounding landscape and attractions, but tries to create its own aura and functional meaning. It is an artwork that creates its own inner intimacy and at the same time opens the gaze and the soul to the attractions.

A visitor center is a multifunctional center where the layout of the building is maximally adapted to functional requirements. It is easy to use, taking advantage of terrain opportunities, providing accessibility access and safe usage. In its internal layout, there is not only a checkpoint, but also information and communication features. An important element and role of today's visitor centers is the organization of exhibitions, screenings and performances that enrich the local knowledge, to provide new experiences and add further programs to local attractions, focusing more on the surrounding landscape and sights in the cultural life of the wider surroundings. In most cases, the social, cultural, and tourist events are grouped around these 'memorial places.' These are such complex building entities, where contemporary interior design, exhibitions, installations, information, lecture and 3D auditoriums together offer attractive and new experiences for visitors.

This book is made up of a diverse collection of visitor centers built over recent years all around the world. The book introduces designs of visitor centers, some adjusted to the natural or historical environment, others created as a counterpoint. The samples presented are examples of contemporary architecture illustrating the inspiration's inexhaustibility. Sometimes, visitor centers are made of special materials and modern design elements, and on the other hand sometimes interpreting centuries-old building traditions. These examples pay close attention to the most important topics in modern construction theory such as sustainability, reuse and recycling.

Visitor centers are such interactive buildings where, through our personal impressions and experiences, we can have a spontaneous dialogue with a location and even become its friend. We can feel the spirit of the place, an unmistakable experience we are allowed to call our own.

Visitor Center Design Guidelines

Visitor centers are a primary type of recreational infrastructure for creating as a dedicated educational space for interpretive displays and programs. Visitor centers generally have support facilities (e.g., parking lots, attractive grounds, outdoor seating, walkways, and vistas) and conveniences for visitors(e.g., toilets, water, maps, literature, telephones, and vending machines).

Visitor centers, which include their associated facilities, services, and programs, serve to:

- Effectively educate the public about the surrounding scenery and tourist-related activities.
- Enhance the tourism opportunities for all visitors, especially those with disabilities.
- Introduce other opportunities and facilities that are available within the project.
- Provide information on the natural, cultural, and historical features of the project area.
- Ensure visitor safety and enjoyment.
- Promote environmental preservation and safety issue.

The designer and other personnel working on the project can use these guidelines to ensure that visitor centers are planned, developed, and managed in accordance with the overall philosophy and goals of sustainable development in an appropriate and cost-effective manner. The guidelines are derived from American Bureau of Reclamation. Reclamation's Visual Identity Program Online Manual; Museum Property Manual and Standards; and other Reclamation manuals will apply when planning, developing, and managing visitor centers.

These guidelines will be re-evaluated and revised as new information, technology, or materials are developed. Designers and engineers should note that site-specific architectural and engineering specifications are beyond the scope of this manual. This book should be shared with all local public agencies and cooperating associations helping to manage visitor centers on project lands.

Planning

There are several levels of planning that influence the development, management, and operation of visitor center facilities. Figure 1 displays the hierarchy of planning involve, which can be referenced for visitor center planning purposes.

Authorizing legislation is the legal foundation for all project operations, facilities, programs, and services. Authorizing legislation provides justification and guidance for visitor centers. Planning and operating with proper authorization is a legal responsibility of project managers.

The Resource Management Plan is the next level of planning for visitor centers. This plan provides comprehensive goals and objectives for project resources and can serve as a decision document to determine if a visitor center is appropriate and suitable.

A visitor center may or may not be an appropriate tool to achieve the project's interpretive goals and objectives. Interpretive master planning is the primary process for assessing if a visitor center is appropriate for a project. If a visitor center is deemed appropriate, the interpretive planning process should also suggest what type of center would be

Figure 1 / Visitor center planning

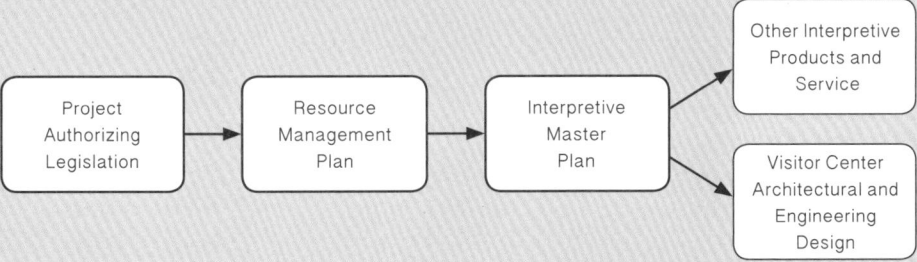

suitable. Interpretive master planning is a process that enables managers to develop a systematic and comprehensive approach to interpretation for the project or site.

If a visitor center is deemed appropriate and suitable, the interpretive master planning process can also serve to define various qualities of the visitor center, such as the project's uniqueness, possible interpretive tools, and central themes. The guidelines outlined in this book briefly describe the interpretive planning process, but do not address the development of specific interpretive media (e.g., exhibits, signs, or brochures).

Architectural and engineering design for the visitor center is the final level of analysis. Detailed guidance and specifications would be provided by the designer and are beyond the scope of this manual. (The principles of Crime Prevention through Environmental Design (CPTED) and Terrorism Prevention Through Environmental Design (TPTED), as outlined in the 'Visitor Center Security' chapter of these guidelines, should be incorporated in the design.)

Criteria for Supporting Visitor Center Proposals

Constructing visitor centers is one method of providing an interpretive program. Developing interpretive programs and products is limited only by one's imagination. Some examples of common interpretive media are: wayside exhibits, kiosks, brochures, videos, displays, guided hikes, nature centers, living history programs, presentations, and visitor participatory projects. Choosing the right interpretive medium depends on the goals of the interpretive program, the needs of the agency, the needs and types of visitors, and the sources available to be interpreted.

Visitor centers are often recommended as the desired interpretive approach before proper consideration has been given to other interpretive options. In the proper environment, a visitor center can be a very effective interpretive approach. However, good interpretive planning is needed to determine if and when a visitor center should be used.

Below are questions that should be answered before a decision can be made as to whether a visitor center is the best interpretive option.

1. Is a visitor center the most effective interpretive medium to use for the specific location, audience, resources, and purpose of the interpretive program?

<u>a. Has an interpretive plan been completed that identifies the interpretive program goals, objectives, and themes?</u>

(1) A visitor center is an expensive interpretive tool and should be chosen only after it is determined to be the most cost-effective means of accomplishing the educational objectives of the project. This decision should be obtained through the development of an interpretive master plan that will help identify the interpretive goals, objectives, and themes for the overall interpretive program. The interpretive master plan should also identify areas, in addition to a visitor center, where interpretive media will be used to accomplish the program's objectives.

(2) Before any design work is started, there should be clear goals, objectives, and themes developed specifically for the visitor center and the entire interpretive program. A facility planning session should be held that includes all the involved domain specialists and potential partners. Everyone should be clear about the purpose of the overall interpretive program and any proposed visitor center as part of that overall program.

(3) Interpretive themes should be coordinated between agencies and other local facilities so as to avoid overlaps in content. Many regions of the United States of America interpret unique topics, such as desert ecology, the Lewis and Clark expedition, southwest Indian culture, the gold rush, and western settlements. Coordination with regional providers will help each facility complement an overall theme so the visitor has a more holistic understanding of the area.

(4) A visitor center can help implement an interpretive program. Visitor centers are very effective in providing a focus for the interpretive programs. Tours and special events are often easier to organize when there is a visitor center. Guides can use many of the visitor center exhibits to help explain concepts and ideas before going out on the trail or taking visitors on a tour. Visitor centers, however, should not be viewed as the interpretive program. They are only one of many strategies for reaching the public with information and education about the project and the agency's mission.

(5) Large visitor center projects often result from a proposal growing beyond its original intent or from an economic development project for a local community. The success of a visitor center as an economic development effort depends on many factors, such as proximity to major travel routes, promotional efforts, the quality of the exhibits and interpretive program, and the potential market for the topics in the visitor center. A market evaluation and cost-benefit analysis should be completed before design work starts on a visitor center that is to serve as an economic development project.

<u>b. Has the Interpretive Master Plan analyzed the potential audiences?</u>

(1) A market analysis or audience analysis regarding the types and diversity of potential visitors is critical to determining the need for a visitor center. (See Haas and Wells, 2006.) Information may be collected using approved visitor survey instruments.

- Demographics: Demographics provide descriptive information about current and potential visitors (e.g., age, gender, nationality, income, disability, group size, how far they travel, as well as various social, physical, cultural, or economic factors of the area).

- Psychographics (interests, opinions, and expectations): Psychographics are used to determine why visitors come to your site and what specific experiences are they seeking (e.g., being with friends and family, getting away from daily stress, and seeking challenging outdoor recreation).

(2) Type, placement, and design of a visitor center depend also on the interests, expectations, and abilities of visitors. Visitor centers can serve both an orientation function and an education function. Therefore, decisions about the best proportion of each function should be made during interpretive planning.

- **Orientation:** Visitor centers are very effective at orienting first-time visitors who are unfamiliar with the area and who wish to learn information about the local facilities, recreation opportunities, and the cultural and natural resources. They are also very effective for repeat or recreational visitors who travel to an area for a specific recreation activity, such as rafting, fishing, or boating. These users typically have their equipment and are ready to start their recreation activity. Their main interest is to gain information on conditions related to their chosen recreation activity, such as where the fish are biting or current river flows.

- **Education:** Visitor centers are also effective in reaching visitors with specific interests. Beyond orientation to a location, visitors are often interested in supplemental educational information about the site, its resources, or its functions. This information can include natural or cultural history; sometimes it will include specific history of the area, specific functions of a historic heritage, special provisions at the site, and so forth. Specific goals and objectives for this level of education should be addressed in an interpretive planning process.

c. Are the visitor and recreational objectives already being served by another facility in the area? Before a visitor center proposal is approved, there should be a thorough survey of other visitor centers and interpretive efforts in the region. This survey should identify whether visitor needs are already being met by other facilities and if the recreational objectives could more easily accomplish their mission by entering into a partnership with any of the existing facility managers. Whenever possible, visitor centers should be inter-agency centers. Visitors do not generally know or care about different agencies. They usually go to a visitor center for orientation information about an area or resource that interests them.

d. Has the interpretive plan determined the best location for a visitor center? The purpose of the interpretive program and visitor center is the main criteria for deciding the best location of a visitor center. Orientation and information visitor centers are best located at places visitors encounter before deciding where to go. If the visitor center was built to reflect a specific regional theme, the best location will probably be near the main access road. Visitors should be able to find the visitor center easily and shortly after they enter the area. In general, poor locations for visitor centers include the end of long dirt roads, more than a few miles off the main road, deep inside the area of interest, or away from the main entrance to a resource.

2. Does the proposed visitor center relate to the tourist mission and management objectives?

a. There should be a direct relationship between the tourist mission, the management objectives of the project, and the interpretive program.

b. An effective visitor center is supported by a resource management plan and is not a separate part of the overall efforts of the visitor services. The goals and objectives of building a visitor center should be clearly identified in planning documents related to the site and interpretive program. These goals include addressing some of the challenges visitor centers bring to an area, such as the potential to concentrate or coordinate visitor use.

c. An important objective of any visitor center is to help the public appreciate and discover the resource diversity and recreational opportunities in the area. In addition, helping visitors feel a sense of ownership and involvement in protecting these resources is important. The visitor center should be supported by an appropriate array of accessible current publications, exhibits, and programs to help visitors discover and appreciate resources on nearby recreation lands.

3. Are there documents showing clear commitment from partners and State or Federal congressional support for the visitor center?

a. A cost analysis should be done showing how the involved partners will share predicted costs. Cost sharing should be realistic, reflecting the true ability of partners to live up to their promises. For instance, if a private group, such as a cooperative association, will staff the project it should be shown that the association is truly prepared and able to take on this responsibility. These partnerships and economic commitments can be used to explain the project to the relevant governmental bodies.

b. The agreement should also clearly identify the responsibilities of each partner, including who is responsible for accessibility retrofits on identified deficiencies, expected in-kind services, as well as procedures for maintaining and canceling the agreement.

c. Congressional members and local legislators should be able to show support for the project, including operations and maintenance funding. However, all congressional support should be consistent with the project management goals and should consider sound fiscal commitment.

d. The scope and magnitude of the project should be clear, so that it does not expand beyond fiscal reach. Often, as more partners get involved, more ideas are adopted and, as a result, the facilities grow bigger to accommodate these ideas. The interpretive plan should include discussion about the specific purpose and scope of the project and should include criteria for making decisions that might affect the scope of the project. The proposed construction project should also be divided into phases to maximize funding options and accountability.

4. Is the operator prepared to accept the long-term commitment that a visitor center requires? Has a cost analysis been prepared that shows the following:

a. Have staffing needs been met?

(1) Visitor centers should be open when public demands are highest. Usually, this means weekends and late hours on Friday and Saturday. It is poor customer service to have the doors closed when visitors expect them open.

(2) Interpretive programs should be well staffed. This is needed, especially by students. Teachers and students are better served when the ratio of students to guides does not exceed 10 to 1.

(3) Presentations should accommodate the general public. Visitors enjoy personal presentations that go beyond the materials in the exhibits and enable them to ask questions. People also have different learning strategies and preferences. Some people learn best by reading the materials, others by listening, others through sign language or alternative formats, and others by experimental involvement. A successful program will use several different interpretive techniques, including those that take into account the needs of persons with sensory or cognitive impairments.

(4) Staff should help in scheduling interpretive events, managing volunteer programs, and coordinating special exhibits and events. Staff should be experienced and prepared to create temporary exhibits covering contemporary issues.

b. Is the operation and maintenance budget for the visitor center complete?

(1) Repairs are needed occasionally for all exhibits, and exhibits should generally be replaced every 10–12 years. This means future funding commitments.

(2) Printed posters, brochures, and other supplies are needed for the interpretive program, tours, and other activities. If there is a cultural theme to the interpretive program, there should be funds for purchasing sample artifacts, replicas, and period attire.

(3) Additional funds are needed in case electronic, technological, or mechanical equipment for the exhibits and interpretive programs wear out or become otherwise unusable. A future funding commitment will be required.

(4) Maintenance is needed for the building and internal facilities, such as lights, heat, audiovisual equipment, assistive listening systems, and special lighting equipment.

c. Should fee collection facilities be considered in the design?

Almost all visitor centers collect revenues, whether they are in the form of donations, program fees, vending machine revenues, or sales.

d. Are there steps for a value engineering review of the project?

Value engineering should be done on all visitor centers to ensure that the proposed design of the building best serves the established goals and objectives of the facility. A value engineering study should address important issues, such as the location of the restrooms and any potential sales area.

e. Has a cost-benefit analysis been completed to show the long-term cost per visitor?

During the first 5 years, there should be only minor repair and maintenance costs for the visitor center. After 5 years, many of the exhibits will need updating, and major repairs may be needed for some of the exhibits and for the building itself.

Decision Criteria for Proposing a Visitor Center

Arbitrary decisions are those made without any principles or reasoning. A list of explicit decision criteria can serve several important functions in proposing and planning a visitor center, such as helping to (a) make the decision process transparent and trackable; (b) develop a full set of reasonable alternatives; (c) ensure a full, fair, adequate, and deliberate evaluation of consequences for alternatives; (d) improve communication and increase meaningful public participation; and (e) create an administrative record.

The decision criteria should fully reflect the circumstances at hand and be commensurate with the potential consequences of the decision to be made. The number of criteria needed to adequately assess development of a visitor center increases as the potential consequences of that decision increase. The following criteria are commonly used when proposing a visitor center.

1. Is a visitor center the most effective interpretive medium for the specific location, audience, and purpose of the interpretive program?

a. Does an interpretive plan or similar document provide specific rationale for why a visitor center is the best interpretive technique for the type of visitor interest and type of use in the area?

> **High**—The interpretive plan provides sound rationale for why a visitor center is appropriate.
>
> **Medium**—The interpretive plan provides some rationale for why a visitor center is one of many techniques that could be used to reach the intended audience, but other media may also be appropriate.
>
> **Low**—No interpretive plan was completed; no proper visitor analysis of the intended audience was conducted; or a plan was completed, and other techniques are more appropriate.

b. Are the visitors' and agency's public information needs being served by other means (e.g., other regional visitor centers or visitor contact stations)?

> **High**—Other centers and stations do not exist.
>
> **Medium**—Other centers or stations are more than a day's drive away.
>
> **Low**—Other centers or stations are within a day's drive.

2. Does the proposed visitor center relate to recreational mission and management objectives?

a. Does the visitor center's purpose relate directly to the mission of Reclamation, its programs, or its legislative mandates?

> **High**—The proposed center strongly relates to recreational mission.
>
> **Medium**—The proposed center generally relates to the project's mission.
>
> **Low**—The proposed center relates only slightly to the project's mission.

b. Does a publicly reviewed resource management plan, plan amendment, or other planning document identify a visitor center as part of the preferred management strategy?

> **High**—Plan(s) recommend building a visitor center.
>
> **Medium**—Plan(s) list a visitor center as a possible approach.
>
> **Low**—Plan(s) state that a visitor center is not necessary or do not consider a visitor center.

3. Is there clear legislative authority and valid commitments from partners showing clear economic and congressional support for the visitor center?

a. Is there support from relevant national and local government agencies?

High—Documentation shows sufficient support from relevant national and local governmental entities.

Medium—Documentation shows some support from relevant national and local governmental entities.

Low—There is no clear commitment to the visitor center.

b. Is there a partnership agreement for operation and maintenance if partners are proposed?

High—A partnership agreement for more than 10 years contains clearly stated responsibilities for staffing and operation and maintenance costs. There are clear provisions for regular review and updating of the agreement.

Medium—A partnership agreement for more than 5 years contains stated responsibilities for staffing and operation and maintenance costs. There are some provisions for regular review and updating of the agreement.

Low—A partnership agreement for no more than 3 years states general responsibilities for staffing and operation and maintenance costs. There are poorly stated or nonexistent provisions for regular review and updating of the agreement.

4. Has the long-term staffing, maintenance, and funding commitment required to support the visitor center been determined?

a. Was a cost analysis completed that considered proper staffing and the operational and maintenance costs related to a visitor center?

High—A cost analysis was conducted. No problems are evident.

Medium—A cost analysis was conducted. Potential problems are evident.

Low—No cost analysis was conducted, or a cost analysis was conducted and problems are certain.

b. Is there a process for conducting a value engineering review?

High—Funding for a value engineering review is available and a review will be conducted.

Medium—A value engineering review is planned, but funding is not yet available.

Low—There is no plan for a value engineering review.

c. Has consideration been given to the benefits of contracting specific services such as maintenance and security?

High—A cost analysis was conducted. Benefits such as cost savings are evident.

Medium—A cost analysis was conducted. Benefits such as cost savings are limited.

Low—A cost analysis was conducted. Benefits such as cost savings do not exist.

Interpretive Master Planning

Interpretive master planning is a strategic process that, in its implementation, provides a plan for achieving management objectives through interpretive media and education.

Interpretive planning analyzes all of the project needs and existing resources then recommends a wide array of interpretive services, facilities, products, and programs to most effectively and efficiently communicate the themes and significance of the recreational resources. This section shall touch upon the objectives and methods of interpretive planning as well as the type of feedback interpretive planning is expected to provide.

Principles of Interpretive Planning

Interpretive planning defines how an organization will handle the task of facilitating interpretive visitor experiences, enjoyment, and learning. Interpretive planning should adhere to the following principles:

- Consider the client (such as tourist, family, senior, person with disabilities, or local school group) and describe the desired visitor experiences at the site.
- Define the location's unique attributes.
- Set up key goals for facilitating visitor learning in concert with management goals.
- Recommend and outline appropriate approaches and strategies for orienting and educating the visitor in ways that communicate the project's most significant and compelling stories while protecting and preserving the integrity of the natural and cultural resources.
- Prescribe the best mix of methods, media, and messages based on current research and reflects knowledge about visitor expectations, demographics, and changing social trends and needs.
- Create a set of guidelines that are flexible, ongoing, interdisciplinary, and responsive to client needs.
- Set a style for interpretive media.
- Consider the timing and financing of programs in the project development.
- Is facilitated by a person or team of people who have an understanding of and have demonstrated competence in interpretive planning.
- Ensure universal accessibility.

Interpretive Planning Process

Interpretive planning is a process of describing an existing situation and need, inventorying and analyzing current resources, identifying major stories or themes, recommending a set of specific interpretive approaches and media, and implementing and evaluating products and services. It is essential for guiding the development of a visitor center that then considers the following processes.

Purpose of Planning

Why is this plan being done? This stage is often referred to as scoping and can include, but is not limited to, the following analysis:

- Existing situation, vision, or mission of the area, resource, site, or project—What does the enabling legislation suggest about the purpose of the project? What is the mission of the tourist project in terms of resource management and visitor services? What is the existing situation that creates a demand for a visitor center or interpretive projects or both?

- Site or project goals—Why do the interpretation at this site? Why is a visitor center considered for this site or facility? What specific goals will the interpretation at this site or visitor center help achieve?

- Background or history of the area, resource, or project—What is the historic, cultural, social, and political context for planning an interpretation at this location?

- Context for planning—Are there funding, staffing, or political considerations that might influence resource management? Are there new or unusual forces exerted on the resource that necessitate interpretive planning?

Resources Inventory

This part of the plan inventories all of the available resources, possible themes for the project, and potential audience. Each of the following sections should include an inventory of the resources. The inventory describes what exists, and why that inventory is important or relevant to planning for interpretation.

Resource Inventory

- Bio-physical—outstanding natural and biological features.

- Socio-cultural—outstanding cultural features or phenomenon.

- Recreational resources or facilities—marinas, boat ramps, campgrounds, picnic areas, trails, etc.

Facilities and Programs Inventory

- Existing infrastructure—roads, bridges, buildings, dams, power plants, canals, fish hatcheries, etc.

- Existing interpretation or education—interpretive exhibits and publications and/or educational collections such as skins, skulls, rocks, artifacts, and plants; library resources; and visitor orientation materials such as kiosks, bulletin boards, and orientation signs.

- Existing accommodations—provisions made for effective communication and equal opportunity to experience for persons with disabilities.

Management Inventory

- Resource management summaries

- Security issues and requirements.

- Existing plans that will affect visitor services and education.

- Any existing and relevant resource management issues (urban-wild land interface and conflicts, user conflicts between personal water craft and anglers, sensitive natural or cultural areas, etc.) that affect the visitor experience and that should be interpreted for the visiting public.

Audience and Stakeholder Inventory

- Current visitors—number of visitors, demographics, motivations, interests, market segments, etc.

- Stakeholders of the area, resource, or site—partners, funders, and interest groups that might have a stake in either the management of the resources of the area or in the education of visitors to the area.

Again, it is not sufficient to just collect this information. Analysis involves deliberate thought, discussion, deliberation, reflection, and judgment. Consider why and how this information is useful for the project, and how this information is helpful for making decisions about the project.

Significant Themes and Visitor Experiences

This section of an interpretive plan summarizes the project's fundamental importance and its relevance to the visitor experience.

Statements of significance, compelling stories, and site-wide themes are all used to describe the distinct qualities of resources at the site, including natural, cultural, scientific, recreational, and inspirational resources. Statements of significance are based on the site's specific legislation and general management plan, and they answer the question: 'What are the major stories, issues, ideas, or characteristics that make this area distinctive and should be conveyed to the visitors?' Statements of significance can be a line, a paragraph, or a page.

Visitor-experience opportunities or desired visitor experiences describe how the interpretive program facilitates physical, social, intellectual, inspirational, and emotional experiences for visitors. These statements include the activities we hope visitors engage in, the facts we hope they learn, the feelings we hope they experience, and the scenery we hope they appreciate. In an interpretive plan, these opportunities are expressed as broad, recreation-related goals that suggest desired visitor experiences. Visitor-experience opportunities can be written as bullets or as narrative descriptions.

Example Visitor Experiences

From the Interpretive Addendum to the Poudre-North Park Scenic and Historic Byway Corridor Management Plan, 1998:

Water/Poudre River: From tundra to plains, the Poudre River reflects the story of water law in the West. The river's water storage and diversion projects are vital to industry, wildlife, agriculture, and recreation. Understanding the river's management and recognizing its uses are important to preserving this natural treasure.

Scenery: The Byway is a significant 'Gateway to the Rockies,' providing travelers a first-hand look at narrow canyons, wild rivers, great gorges, piedmont, high peaks, cirques, and sweeping parks. The Byway's geological richness and scenic beauty should be an integral part of visitor education.

From the North Park Watchable Wildlife Plan, Colorado Division of Wildlife, 1995:

Partnerships: Nearly 75 percent of North Park is publicly owned, requiring a unique partnership between Federal, State, and private landowners to manage and protect its abundant natural resources of wildlife, range, water, forests, minerals, and recreation opportunities.

Lifestyle preservation: The current lifestyles of the citizens of North Park are anintegral part of the area's overall natural and cultural heritage. As such, past and present lifestyles and values should be infused into watchable wildlife interpretation.

From the Blue Ridge Music Center Interpretive Plan, National Park Service:

The park will provide opportunities for visitors to:

- Listen to a wide variety of traditional music of the Blue Ridge, including both live and recorded music.
- Become acquainted with musicians from the region whose backgrounds, life histories, and artistry illustrate important themes in history.
- Participate in informal music and dance activities at the site.
- Have an enjoyable recreational experience without impairing the natural and cultural values of the site.

From the Lakota Tatanka Heritage Plan, National Park Service:

As visitors travel through the park, they are exposed to the vastness of the prairie with an occasional but exciting glimpse of buffalo, elk, and perhaps even a band of Lakota people crossing the prairie. When they arrive at the visitor center, they are exposed to enjoyable learning experiences designed to enrich the minds of all ages and cultural backgrounds. These learning experiences focus on three elements that form the management objectives of the park . . . first, the prairie that nurtures a vast array of plants and animals, second, the Sioux Indians, and last, the park management program itself.

Program, Product, and Service Recommendations

This part of the plan recommends specific programs, products, and services as they relate to the existing resource inventory, statements of significance, and visitor experience opportunities. The recommendations are a strategy or prescription for the best set of programs and services to meet the visitors' needs, while at the same time preserving the site's resource integrity. Often, the best set of programs and services is selected from a set of recommended alternatives using criteria such as those previously described in the 'Decision Criteria for Proposing a Visitor Center' section.

In an interpretive master plan, recommendations are made concerning a variety of accessible media that best meet site or park goals for visitor education. The objective is to select the most appropriate media based on available resources (time, money, personnel, and expertise) and the purposes of the plan. Choices for media recommendations can include any of the following:

Facilities

- Visitor centers
- Kiosks
- Waysides
- Visitor contact stations

Personal Programs

- Guided walks and talks
- Campfire programs
- Storytelling
- Living history programs
- Oral histories
- Demonstrations

- Environmental education activities
- Puppet shows and dramatic presentations
- Roving interpretations
- Visitor information stations

Manufactured or Printed Products

- Publications, including Grade II Braille, audio recordings, and computer disk of text
- Kits and adventure packs
- Discovery boxes and traveling exhibits
- Exhibits, including tactile features, and audio recording or computer disk of feature exhibits
- Signs, including tactile features, and audio recording or computer disk of feature exhibits
- Maps and brochures for self-guided activities, including Grade II Braille, audio recording, or computer disk

Electronic Technology Products

- Web pages with audio description of slides provided
- Audiotape tours with printed script
- Video programs (open or closed caption)
- PowerPoint slide programs
- High-tech programming (animatronics, augmented reality, computer interactive programs, video-equipped microscopes, virtual reality, etc.)

The section of the interpretive plan that specifies final recommendations should also include resources for the successful design, fabrication, and installation of the recommendations, including all personnel, materials and equipment, money, and time.

Site Design

The development of a visitor center design is the process of integrating structure(s), utilities, and visitor circulation at a specific location. The process includes initial site inventory and assessment, alternative analysis, detailed design development, and construction procedures and services. This section begins with guidance for site selection, followed by site access, and utilities and waste systems. The following section continues this discussion related to building design.

Site Selection

Selecting a visitor center site for recreation area may include any of the following: reservoir, lake, beach, river, marine areas, compelling landform, scenic view, cultural resource, canal, dam, and so forth. When sitting visitor facilities, consideration should be given to both natural and cultural features of an area. The site inventory and analysis should clearly identify the quality and extent of these features, possible impacts to the existing environment, and potential mitigation measures that might be necessary.

Possible mitigation measures might include minimizing new disturbance by using existing facilities (such as parking, access roads and graded areas), conducting pre-disturbance surveys on ecological resources (such as water bodies, natural habitats and sensitive species populations), preparing a restoration plan for habitat and the construction site to minimize negative impacts on wildlife, and so on. The characteristics that make an area attractive to visitors may also pose problems. Some attractive areas may be very sensitive to disturbance and unable to withstand impacts of human activity. Other attractive areas may be too remote to justify development for direct visitor use. Some areas may be too close to safety hazards or too developed to be appropriate for visitor center development. Conversely, some degraded areas may, in fact, provide opportunities for development, allowing more options for site preservation and ecological restoration. Some areas may have terrain issues that will increase the cost of compliance with accessibility standards. The site selection process must address the following questions:

- Will the anticipated impact of development on the site be acceptable?
- What inputs (energy, materials, labor, and products) would be necessary to support development and are the required inputs available?
- Can waste outputs (solid waste, sewage effluent, exhaust emissions) be dealt with at acceptable environmental costs?
- Will the terrain increase costs for compliance with accessibility standards (i.e., additional earthwork to meet the slope and cross slope requirements of parking spaces, accessible routes, wheelchair seating spaces in outdoor areas, required clear space at telephones, drinking fountains, waste receptacles, and other facilities)?

The process of site selection for a visitor center is one of identifying, weighing, and balancing the attractiveness (e.g., compelling natural and cultural features, access, and sense of place) of a site against the costs inherent in its development. The characteristics of a region or site should be described spatially (using either conventional or computer-generated maps) to provide a precise geographic inventory. Spatial zones meeting programmatic objectives within acceptable environmental parameters are likely development sites.

The programmatic requirements and environmental characteristics of site development vary greatly, but the following factors should be considered in site selection:

Site compatibility

When deciding the site of a visitor center, consider (a) visual compatibility (will the visitor center look like it belongs in that location?), (b) cultural compatibility (will the visitor center respect local social and cultural history of the site?), and (c) ecological compatibility (will the visitor center honor and/or complement the surrounding geology, vegetation, and water forms?).

Visitor capacity

Every site and/or facility has a capacity for human activity. A detailed site analysis should determine this capacity based on the sensitivity of site resources, the ability of the land to regenerate, and the desired visitor experiences.

Density

When sitting facilities, carefully weigh the relative merits of concentration versus dispersal. Natural landscape values may be easier to maintain if facilities are carefully dispersed. Conversely, concentration of structures leaves more undisturbed natural areas.

Climate

The characteristics of a specific climate should be considered when locating facilities so that human comfort can be maximized, while protecting the facility from climate extremes such as heat, cold, dryness, or volatile and unpredictable weather.

Slopes

In many environments, steep slopes predominate, requiring special sitting of structures and costly construction practices. Building on steep slopes can lead to soil erosion, loss of hillside vegetation, inaccessible walkways and routes, damage to ecosystems, and costly ground surface impacts to provide access to persons with disabilities. Generally, appropriate site selection should locate more intense development on gentle slopes, dispersed development on moderate slopes, and no development on steep slopes.

Views

Views are critical, reinforcing a visitor experience. Site location should maximize desired views of natural features and facilities in order to support visitor experiences (visitor experiences include the perceptions, feelings, and reactions a visitor has in relationship with the surrounding environment).

Natural hazards

When considering site locations, avoid naturally hazardous situations, such as precipitous topography, dangerous animals and plants, and turbulent water areas. Site layout should allow controlled access to these features.

Access to natural and cultural features

Good sitting practices can maximize pedestrian access to the wide variety of onsite and offsite resources and recreational activities. Low-impact development is the key to protecting vital resource areas.

Landscape considerations

Consideration of the natural landscape is important during site selection and planning. It is generally less expensive to care for landscape during construction than to restore a badly degraded landscape after construction. These efforts include carefully defining the construction zone and not 'clearing and grubbing' soil areas unnecessarily. Placement of vegetation requires careful planning to allow growth to maturity without costly maintenance and will not infringe on an accessible route. Natural vegetation can be an important aspect of the visitor experience and should be preserved to the degree possible. If new planting is needed, using native plant species and avoiding or controlling exotic or invasive species in landscape and site design is highly recommended.

Support facilities and public use areas

Safety, visual quality, accessibility, noise, and odor are all factors that need to be considered when sitting support services and facilities. These areas need to be separated from public use and circulation areas. In certain circumstances, utilities, energy systems, and waste systems areas can be a positive part of the visitor experience. For more information, see the 'Utilities and Waste Systems' section further on in the book.

Proximity of goods, services, and housing

Visitor center developments require the input and delivery of numerous goods and services, as well as staffing for normal operation. Sitting facilities should consider the frequency, availability, and nature of these elements and the costs involved in providing them.

Site Access

Site access refers to not only the means of physically entering a development, but also the en-route visitor experience. For example, the en-route experience can dramatize the transitions between origin and destination with obvious sequential gateways and can provide opportunities for interpretation or education along the way.

Designers can consider utilizing corridors to limit the impact to environmental and cultural resources and to control development along the corridor leading to the facility, and providing anticipation and drama by framing views or directing attention to landscape features along the access route.

For a visitor center project, a sense of arrival at the destination is very important. Sense of arrival means an emotional and mental state that accompanies the end of a visitor's travels and the beginning of their visit experience. For some visitors, at a visitor center marks the end of a journey involving both lengthy planning and travel. For some, a sense of arrival is created by the clear opportunity to park their car, and begin their exploration of the site with the assistance of exhibits, signs, guidebooks, trails, shuttle buses, etc. For others, this sense of arrival begins with the first sight of clear way-finding and signage.

Besides the above tips, designers should also consider allowing simplicity of functions to prevail, while respecting basic human needs of comfort, safety, and access for persons with disabilities.

Site access can be achieved by various means of travel, such as by foot, private vehicles, off-highway vehicles, boats, and aircraft. Transportation means that are the least polluting, least noisy, and least intrusive in the natural environment are the most appropriate for a sustainable development. Where environmental or other constraints make physical access impossible, remote video presentation maybe the only way for people to access the site.

Utilities and Waste Systems

With the development of a site comes the need for some level of utilities (e.g., water, waste, energy). Thus when planning the site design of a visitor center project, the layout of utilities and waste systems should also be taken into consideration ahead of time.

Developments that are more elaborate have more extensive systems to provide water, waste treatment, and energy for lighting, heating, cooling, ventilating, etc. The provision of these services and the accessories associated with them may adversely impact the landscape and the functioning of the natural ecosystem. Early in the planning process, utility systems must be identified that will not adversely affect the environment and will work within established natural systems. After appropriate systems are selected, careful site planning and design are required to address secondary impacts, such as soil disturbance and intrusion on the visual setting.

In addition, aim to buffer the noise associated with mechanical equipment and the odors associated with waste treatment by manipulating the landscape through the placement of trees and shrubs.

Utility corridors

Because of the impact created by utility transmission lines, onsite generation and wireless microwave receivers are preferable alternatives in many cases. When utility lines are necessary, they should be buried near other corridor areas that are already disturbed, such as roads and pedestrian paths. Where possible, locate overhead lines away from desirable view sheds and landform crests.

Night lighting

The nighttime sky can be dramatic and contribute to the visitor experience. Light intrusion and the glare from over-lighting can obscure night sky viewing and may disorient migratory birds. Care is required to keep night lighting to the minimum necessary for safety and security. Urban lighting standards do not apply. Low-voltage lighting with photovoltaic collectors should be considered as an energy-efficient alternative. Light fixtures should remain close to the ground to minimize eye level glare. Fixtures should be of a type that directs light downward rather than outward or upward.

Storm drainage

In a modified landscape, consideration must be given to the impact of storm drainage on the existing drainage system and the surrounding structures and systems that will be necessary to handle the new drainage pattern. The main principles in storm drainage control are to regulate runoff in order to provide protection from soil erosion and to avoid directing water into unmanageable channels. Removal of natural vegetation, topsoil, and natural channels that provide drainage control should be avoided to the extent practicable. An alternative is to stabilize soils, capture runoff in depressions (to help recharge groundwater supply), and re-vegetate areas to replicate natural drainage systems.

Irrigation systems

Low-volume irrigation systems are appropriate in most areas as a temporary method to help restore previously disturbed areas. Irrigation piping can be reused on other restoration areas or incorporated into future domestic hydraulic systems. Captured rainwater, recycled gray water, or treated sewage should also be considered for use as irrigation water.

Waste treatment

In modified landscapes, it is often appropriate to attach waste treatment systems to existing municipal systems; however, if it is not possible to attach to a municipal system, it is important to consider treatment technologies that are biological and non-mechanical and that do not involve soil leaching or major soil disturbance. While a septic system can be considered, treatment methods that result in useful products, such as fertilizer and fuels, should be investigated. Constructed biological systems are increasingly being put to use to purify wastewater. They offer the benefits of being environmentally responsive, nonpolluting, and cost effective.

Building Design

Visitor center building design considers the process of facility location, design, materials, and construction. In this process, visitor access and site entry; orientation, information, and visitor comfort needs; and programmatic needs such as educational, interpretive, and sales should all be considered. This section begins with an overview of general building design considerations, which is followed by guidance for visitor flow and floor planning. Finally, a series of environmental, cultural, and sensory considerations are provided as they relate to building design.

Designing for Enhancing Visitors' First Impression

Visitors form initial impressions at the first encounters with the site and related facilities. Their initial reactions can influence their overall visitor experience. In order to enhance visitor experience, considerations for the following factors should be taken during the designing process.

Entry

- Road design should follow natural contours and respect topography and landscapes, reflecting the visitor center's overall theme(s).
- Design should help slow entering vehicles and heighten awareness of surroundings.

Parking

- Parking lot placement should not encroach on the visitor center building and should allow for transitional passage to the center.
- A drop-off loop is often appropriate and should be provided for buses and visitors with mobility issues.
- Service and emergency entrances and pathways should be screened or routed to minimize visual impact.
- Main parking lots should provide natural shading and landscaping that is consistent with landscaping throughout the rest of the site.

Walkways

- Walkways from the parking areas to the visitor center should be visible or clearly indicated. A view of the visitor center is desirable.
- Walkways to the visitor center and around the site need to consider visitor capacity, scale, and other design elements and should meet requirements under the relevant regulations.
- Lighting should be modest; it should provide for safety but avoid light spillover. Lighting should be sufficient to light trails or walkways to and from visitor center and parking areas.
- A view of the visitor center entry should be clear from major walkways.

Information Area or Lobby

- A porch or patio should be provided as an informal or formal meeting place outside the main lobby area.

- The visitor lobby should be large, open, well-lit, and should provide a barrier-free (i.e., include access for wheelchairs and children) entry with grates and floor mats.
- Floors, walls, and ceiling surfaces should be designed to minimize noise.
- The information desk should be brightly illuminated.
- Visitors prefer both personal (a person at a desk) and non-personal (brochures, maps, interactive computers) forms of information.

Comfort Areas

- Restrooms and drinking fountains should be easy for visitors to access upon entering the visitor center.
- Benches or appropriate seating areas should be provided around the building so visitors have several places to rest.
- Food and drink services may be considered.

High-Quality Wayfinding

Visitor experience and satisfactions are directly influenced by the convenience of navigating the visitor center. This means, a high-quality wayfinding system is an important part in the visitor center design. During this process, designers need to take the following elements into consideration.

- After-hours information that is easy to find, well lit, and comprehensive should be provided.
- Telephones should be provided for emergency use. Public telephones should be clearly signed and meet the technical standards for persons with hearing impairments.
- Orientation maps and instructions for site use should be provided.
- Bench seating, bathrooms, and shelter in staging areas where visitors are expected to gather or wait should be provided. These staging areas should also include secure and protected areas for storing program equipment and supplies.
- Wayfinding signs should be placed near the entrance to an area and should be on an accessible route for persons with mobility impairments. Wayfinding signs should incorporate features that aid persons with visual and cognitive impairments, such as the use of tactile characters and symbols, color to separate and clarify themes, pictographs, and pictograms.
- Accessible features of the site should be marked with the International Symbol of Accessibility (wheelchair symbol) on the wayfinding sign.

Cultural Considerations

The value and desire of cultural activities is part of a rich, robust, and rewarding visitor experience. Destinations, particularly urban cities, have an opportunity to showcase cultural activities and provide cultural experiences through the formation of cultural districts.

Archeological Resources

Preserve and interpret archeological features to provide insight into the successes and failures of previous cultural responses to the environment.

Local Architecture

Analyze local historic building styles, systems, and the materials used to find time-tested approaches in harmony with natural systems. Use local building material, craftsmen, and techniques to the greatest extent practicable in the development of new facilities.

Historic Resources

Reuse historic buildings, whenever possible, to assist in their preservation and to contribute to the special quality of the place.

Local Culture

Understand the local culture and the need to avoid the introduction of socially unacceptable or morally offensive practices. Seek the views of the local population as well in order to foster a sense of ownership and acceptance. Include environmentally sound local construction techniques and materials in the development of new facilities.

Incorporate local expressions of art, handiwork, detailing, and, when appropriate, technology into new facility design and interior design. Provide opportunities and space for the demonstration of local crafts and performing arts.

Sensory Considerations

Sensory considerations not only make the visit more interesting and memorable, but they will determine the success or failure of effectively communicating information to visitors (especially those with disabilities). The most effective interpretive methods employ as many of the senses as possible. Increasing the number of senses used in communication dramatically increases the effectiveness of the learning experience.

Visual

Provide visitors, including those with disabilities, with ready access to educational materials to enhance their understanding and appreciation of the local environment and the threats to it. Incorporate views of natural and cultural resources into even routine activities to provide opportunities for contemplation, relaxation, and appreciation. Use design principles of scale, rhythm, proportion, balance, and composition to enhance the complementary integration of facilities into the environmental context. Provide visual surprises within the design of facilities to stimulate the educational experience. Limit the height of development to preserve the visual quality of the natural and cultural landscape. Use muted colors that blend with the natural context unless environmental considerations (reflection/absorption), cultural values (customs/taboos), or safety (needed contrast for persons with visual impairment) dictate otherwise.

Sound

Locate service and maintenance functions away from public areas. Space interpretive stops so that natural or site-specific sounds dominate. Use vegetation to muffle sound between public and private activities and orient openings toward natural sounds such as the lapping of waves, babbling of streams, and rustling of leaves. Limit the volume of unnatural sounds such as those from radio and television.

Touch

Allow visitors to touch and be in touch with the natural and cultural resources of the site. Tactile models, built to scale, offer a full experience to many visitors, including persons with visual disabilities. Vary walking surfaces to give different qualities to different spaces. Use contrasting textures to direct attention to interpretive opportunities.

Smell

Allow natural fragrances of vegetation to be enjoyed. Direct air exhausted from utility areas away from public areas.

Cradle-to-Grave Analysis

Sustainable design also considers building materials. The complete life cycle of resources, energy, and waste implications of possible building materials can be analyzed before building construction. A cradle-to-grave analysis traces a material or product (and its byproducts) from original, raw material sources (plant, animal, or mineral) through extraction, refinement, fabrication, treatment, transportation, use, and eventual reuse or disposal. This analysis includes the tabulation of energy consumed and the environmental impacts of each action and material.

Questions that guide a cradle-to-grave analysis include:

- What is the source of the raw material? Is it renewable? Sustainable? Locally available? Nontoxic?

- How is the raw material extracted? What energy is used in that extraction process? What other impacts result from the extraction (e.g., habitat destruction, erosion, siltation, pollution)?

- How is the material transported? How far does it have to be transported? How much fuel is consumed? How much air is polluted?

- What is involved in processing and manufacturing the material? How much energy is required; what air, water, and/or noise pollution will result from the processing? What type of waste, and how much, is generated in processing and manufacture?

- Are any treatments or additives used in the manufacture of the material? What types of treatments are necessary? Are those treatments hazardous?

- How is the final product used? What type of energy does it require? How long will it last? How does its use affect the environment? How much waste does it generate?

- When the product is obsolete, how is it disposed of? Can it be recycled? Does it contain solid or toxic wastes?

Selection of building materials should consider local materials when possible and materials that require less energy to manufacture, transport, operate, and maintain. Prioritizing materials by source can be helpful for making building material decisions.

- Primary materials are materials found in nature such as stone, earth, and flora (cotton, hemp, jute, reed, wood, and wool). If new lumber is used, consider using only lumber from certified sustainable forests or certified naturally felled trees. Use caution with any associated treatments, additives, or adhesives that may contain toxins or with materials that off-gas volatile organic compounds and thus may contribute to indoor air pollution or atmospheric pollution.

- Secondary materials are materials made from recycled products such as wood, aluminum, cellulose, and plastics. Verify that production of the material does not involve high levels of energy, pollution, or waste. Verify that materials and products salvaged from old buildings are functional and safe to use. Look closely at the composition of recycled products; toxins may still be present. Consider cellulose insulation; ensure that it is fireproof and provides a greater R-value per inch thickness than fiberglass. Utilize the aluminum from recycled materials; recycling aluminum uses 80 percent less energy to produce than initial production. Evaluate the use of products containing recycled hydrocarbon-based products; they may help keep used plastics out of landfills but may do little to reduce production and use of plastic from original resources. Keep alert for new developments; new, environmentally sound materials from recycled goods are appearing on the market every week.

- Tertiary materials are manmade materials (artificial, synthetic, and nonrenewable) such as plywood, plastics, and aluminum that vary in the degrees of their environmental impact. Avoid use of materials and products containing or produced with chlorofluorocarbons or hydro-chlorofluorocarbons because these chemicals deplete the ozone layer. Avoid materials that off-gas volatile organic compounds because they contribute to indoor air pollution and atmospheric pollution. Minimize use of products made from new aluminum and other materials that are resource disruptive during extraction and high-energy consumers during refinement.

References

Recreation Facilities Design Guidelines, U.S. Department of the Interior, Bureau of Reclamation, 2013

Strømbu Service Center and Rest Area

Location / Folldal, Norway
Area / 86,111 square feet (8000 square meters)
Completion / 2009
Architect / Carl-Viggo Hølmebakk AS
Photography / Carl-Viggo Hølmebakk
Client / National Tourist Routes in Norway

The Rondane Tourist Road on the east side of the Rondane Mountains goes 26 miles (42 kilometers) from Enden in the south to Folldal in the north. The center is situated near the midpoint of this route and, besides being a rest stop, the place also serves as a main gateway to Rondane National Park, a popular hiking area for mountain trekkers and other tourists. Placing the two user groups together has been important for the layout, addressing both of their demands. For the car tourists: they can be introduced to nature and the mountains during a few minutes stop. And for the hikers: they can leave or come back to civilization after days in the wilderness. Strømbu is also an information center for several activities in the district and the place is almost entirelyrun and operated by the local parish.

The main building has an area that offers quite different experiences depending from side you look. Towards the parking area, a planted slope with stairs and a ramp leads to a roof terrace, showing a view of the mountains and the nearby mountain river. On the northern end is a quiet room for rest with fireplace, which also provides view to the wooded river terrain. These two areas create a complex organization of kiosk and information area, serving both the outdoor and the indoor. The organization also serves a practical role, since the slope makes room for a large septic tank for the toilets, which would not be possible to position below the ground water level. The toilet facilities are placed in a separate building.

New additions are still being planned by the facilities, both for the buildings themselves and for the surrounding landscape. Today, the warming room is also used for local happenings, and there is a need for expanding the kitchen and dining area. A local cook wants to build a small accommodation building with a restaurant for hikers and car tourists. A new footbridge over the river will replace an old and flooding exposed footbridge. On the path leading up to the mountains, a 350-step staircase will prevent wear on the natural vegetation and terrain.

Site plan
① Dismantled old bridge
② New bridge
③ Atnaelva River
④ Reinforced river bank
⑤ Information center

01 / Exterior view of facilities
02 / Model showing first floor without roofing

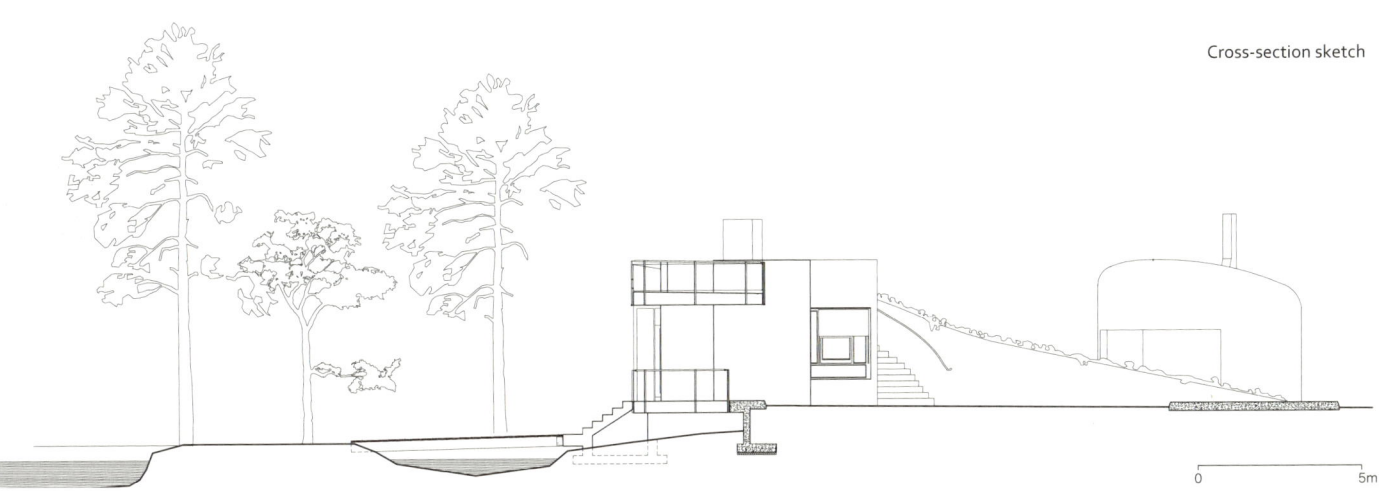

Cross-section sketch

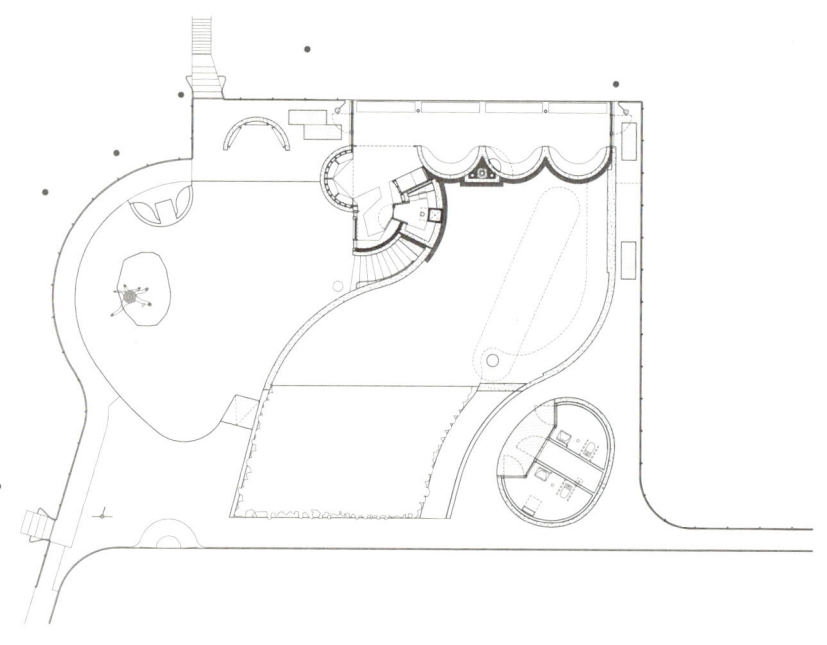

Detailed sketch of site plan

03 / Rear view of warming room
04 / South-facing courtyard
05-06 / Kiosk servicing outside and inside

① Waterproof base
② Wind bracing
③ Recessed flat steel for wind retention
④ Heater
⑤ Window with galvanized ceiling hood
⑥ Main component
⑦ Upside-down component
⑧ Horizontal component
⑨ Handle
⑩ Frame section

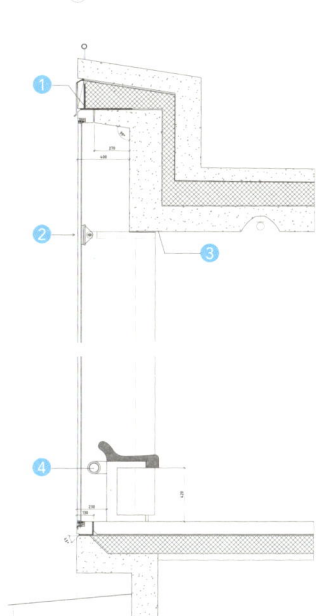

Detailed sketch of floor and cornice

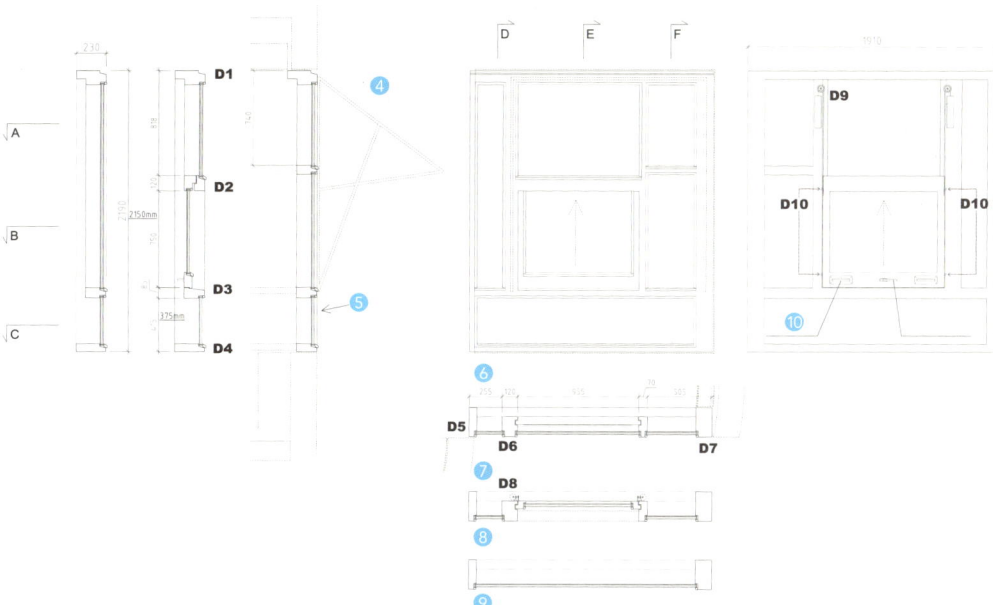

Window schematics for kiosk

07 / Warming room facing west towards Rondane National Park
08 / Restroom
09 / Sitting area in warming room with fireplace in background

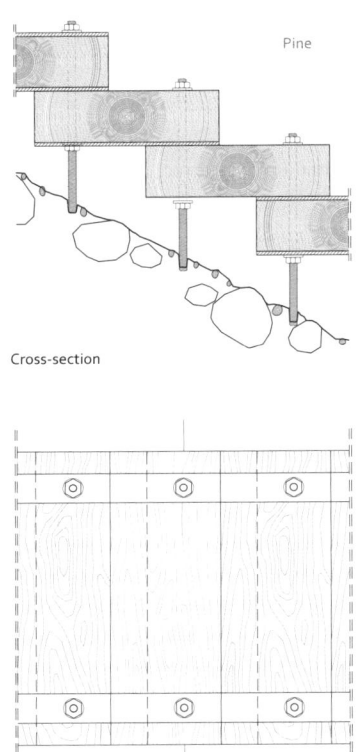
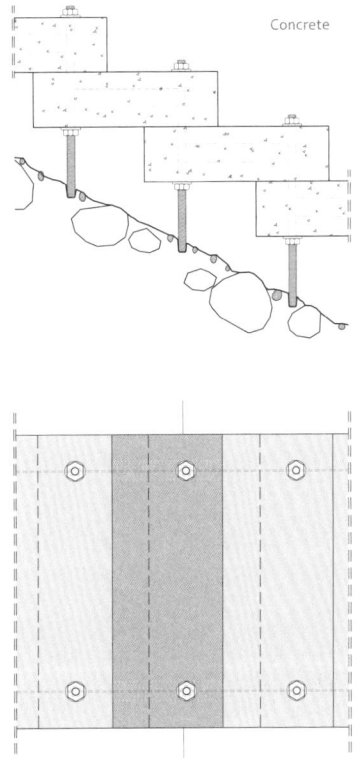
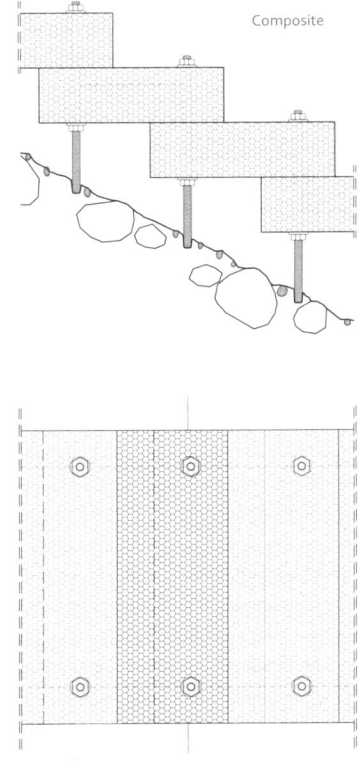

Pine — Concrete — Composite

Cross-section

Plans

Rest area stairway diagrams

10 / Main pathway to restrooms
11 / Entrance to warming room
12 / Another view of south-facing courtyard
13 / Stairway up to Bratteggen

Fogo Island Natural Park Headquarters

Location / Fogo, Cape Verde
Area / 34,445 square feet (3200 square meters)
Completion / 2013
Architect / oto arquitectos
Photography / FG+SG—Fernando Guerra, Sergio Guerra
Client / Cape Verde Ministry of Agriculture

Amidst the crater of the volcano on Fogo Island at an altitude of 5906 feet (1800 meters) lies a village of about 1200 inhabitants who live in one of Cape Verde's poorest regions. The natural landscape, strikingly marked by the volcano and its crater, possesses a unique and rare beauty, with the potential of becoming a world heritage site. The idea was therefore to achieve a balanced solution, where architecture and landscape become accomplices, complementary to each other.

The body of the building is made up of a continuous surface, composed of local black masonry block—a mixture of cement and ashes from the volcano. During daytime, the long walls outline the building and blend with the road, suggesting the existence of spaces through the interplay of shadows. At night, bright light is avoided as a means to protect native birds. To address the lack of any previous infrastructure, the building was thought of as a self-sufficient unit: solar panels and a double-grid water system ensure that the buildings' energy needs are satisfied throughout the year. The building is divided into two main areas: a cultural area, composed of a covered auditorium, an open-air auditorium, library and terrace-café; and an administrative area, which is comprised of meeting rooms, offices, laboratories, and various technical apparatuses.

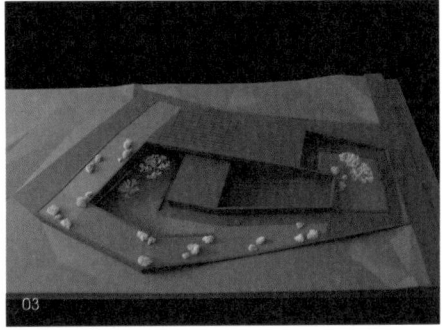

With the headquarter fully operational, the park offers a higher standard experience for visitors, which contributes to enriching the social, cultural, and economic sectors of the island, helping to harmoniously integrate and enhance the island with the surrounding space.

The biggest challenge encountered in this project was maximizing the few local resources available by utilizing a sustainable approach that attempts to 'do more with less' and highlights human beings' role in nature. The main idea in designing the building was that the structure becomes a part of the landscape and that the landscape also becomes a part of the structure, blending all elements together in a symbiotic symphony. Furthermore, the idea also involved extending the volcanic area and subsisting vegetation of the park to the new administrative headquarters. The design attracts visitors and locals to confidently descend to the bottom of the crater through the use of carefully constructed pedestrian paths amid the volcanic rocks. The inclusion of the construction on the surroundings is achieved by using mostly black masonry block, a mixture of cement and axes of the volcano.

Site plan

The building supports administrative and cultural functions. The cultural section (the most significant space) is distributed in three main areas: the exhibition area, the exterior auditorium, and the semi-underground auditorium. The local fauna and flora also make up the existing pedestrian paths exiting onto the green roof.

Particular features were of prominent concern in the design, such as environmental energy and social aspects. The use of the natural resources and the energy

01 / South elevation
02 / Aerial view
03 / Model

Sections

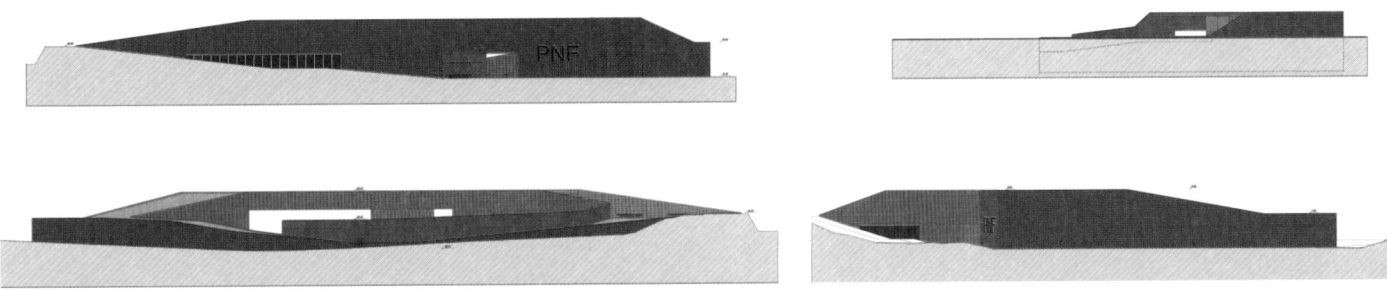

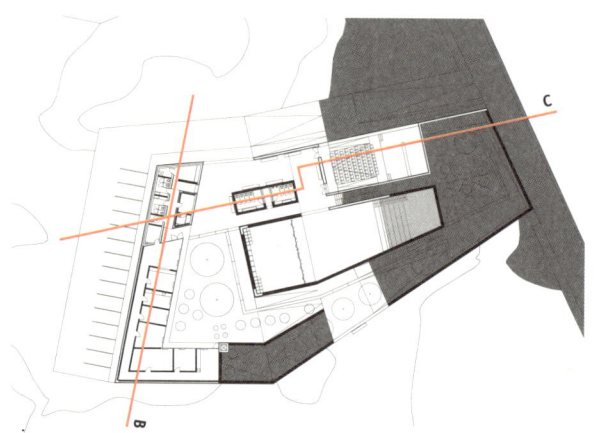

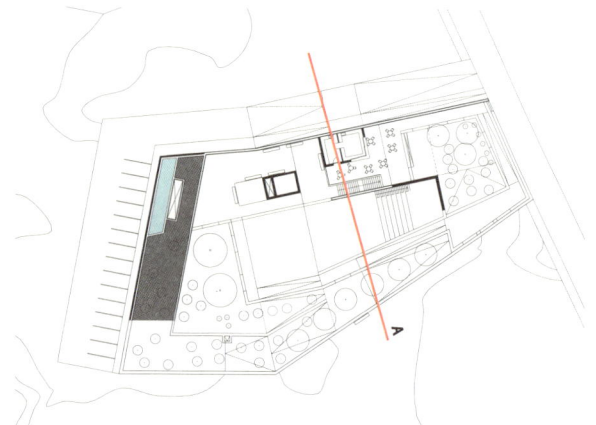 

First-floor plan   Second-floor plan   0   10m

efficiency were a priority in construction. A structure made by the people for the people, employing manual labor as well as making use of local resources with reduced environmental impact. Fogo Island Natural Park Headquarters will gain a completely different edifice. Not only is it a tourist attraction itself, but it also acts as a training center, providing support for all kinds of activities for the local community.

Particular features are highlighted, such as environmental energy and social aspects. A structure made by the people for the people, employing manual labor as well as making use of local resources with reduced environmental impact. Ilha do Fogo's Natural Park Head Office will gain a completely different edifice. Not only is it a tourist attraction itself, but also a training center and support intended for all kinds of activities for the local community.

04 / South road view
05 / Entrance view towards volcano peak
06 / Patio looking towards volcano peak

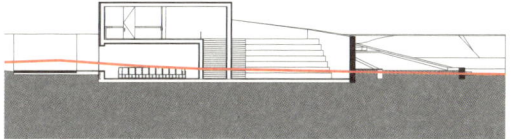
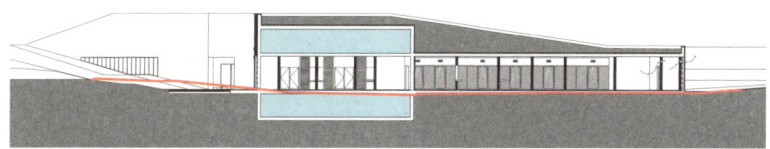
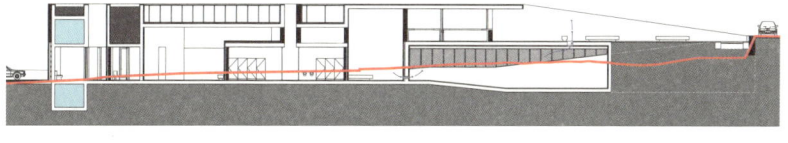

Sections

07-09 / Roof walkways
10 / Solar panels on roof

07

08

09

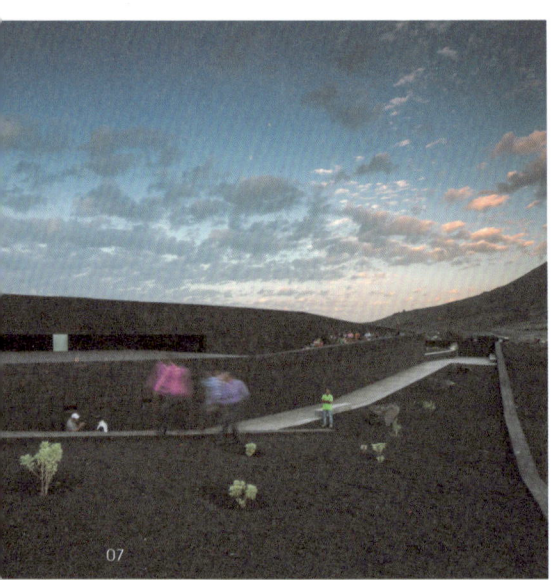

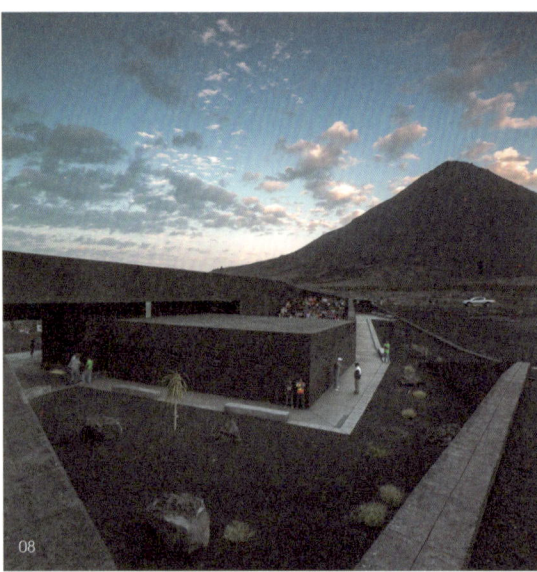

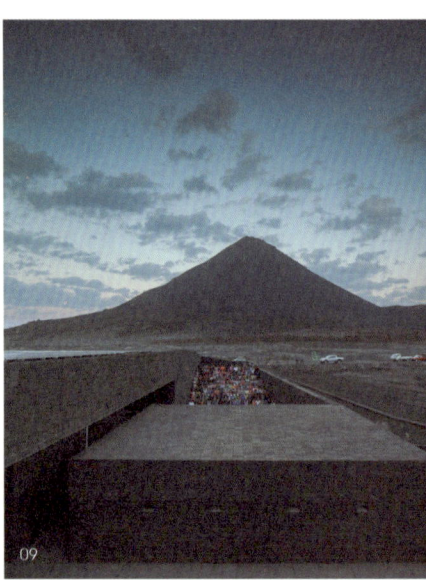

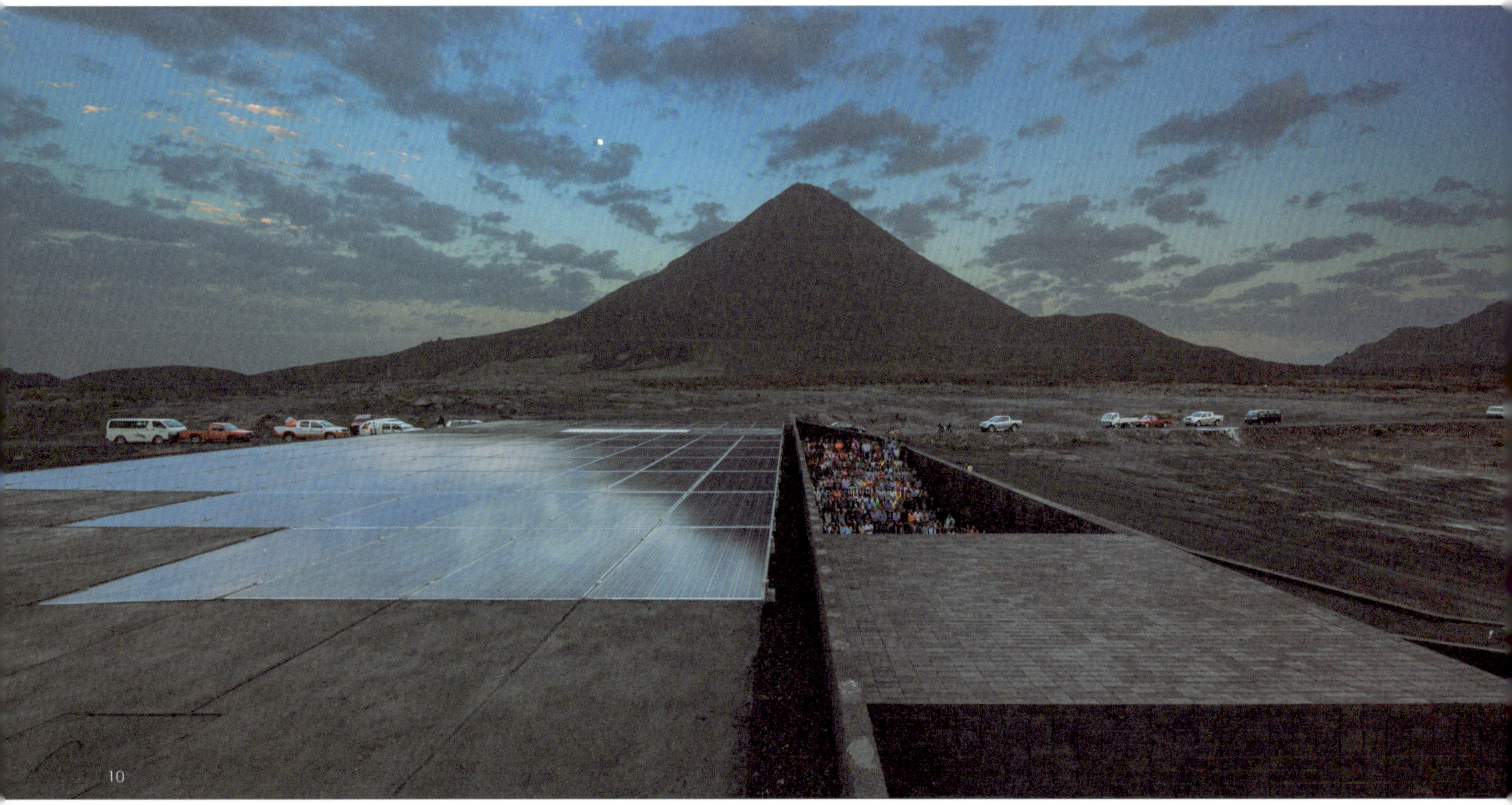

10

Natural ventilation
Integrated façade grid systems allow for passive control of internal temperature, taking advantage of the building's thermal inertia, which allows for heat accumulation during the day and natural ventilation during the night.

Energy production
Photovoltaic roof panels absorb solar energy which is then stored as electricity, covering the needs of the LED-based lighting system.

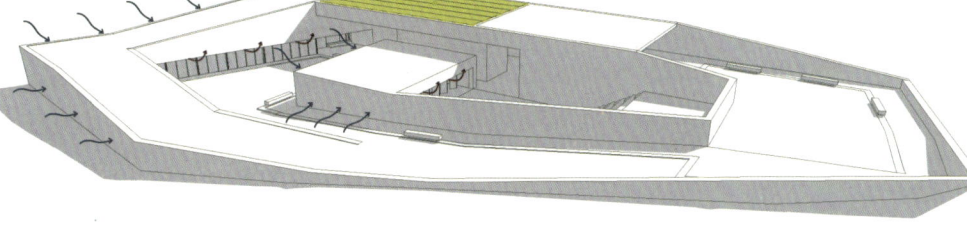

Water collection/waste management
Rainwater is collected and directed along the top of the building to a storage tank, from which it can be used both as irrigation and domestic water. Grey water is recollected, recycled, and pumped back into the system.

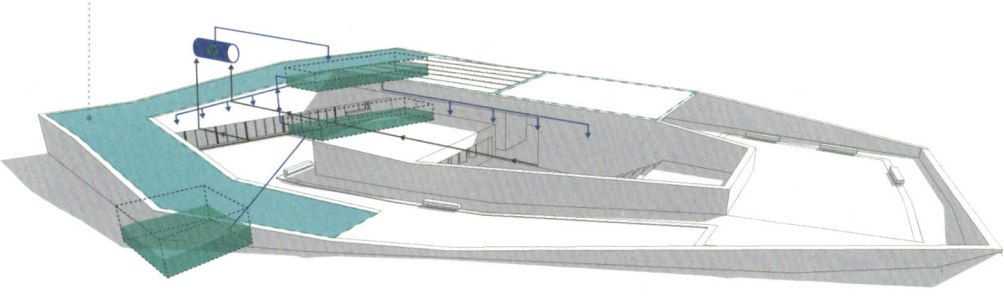

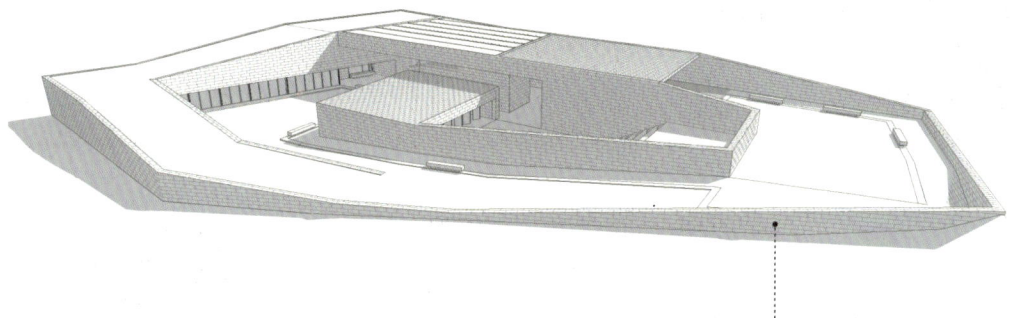

Materiality
Material selection was strongly based on local availability and production: local masonry cement block incorporates ashes from the volcano, acquiring the desired dark tonality, blending building and landscape together.

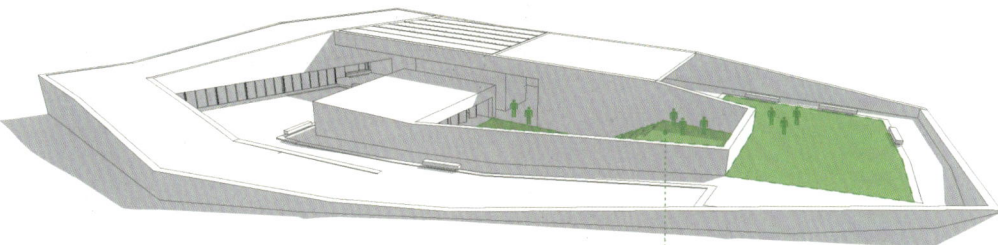

Social interaction
The local community was considered a driving force for the project, which sought to develop adequate spaces for social interaction. The café and auditoriums act as stages for cultural and recreational activities.

Park and outer areas

11 / Entrance view of patio
12 / Entrance hall
13 / Library hall
14 / Library
15 / Office corridor
16 / Laboratory

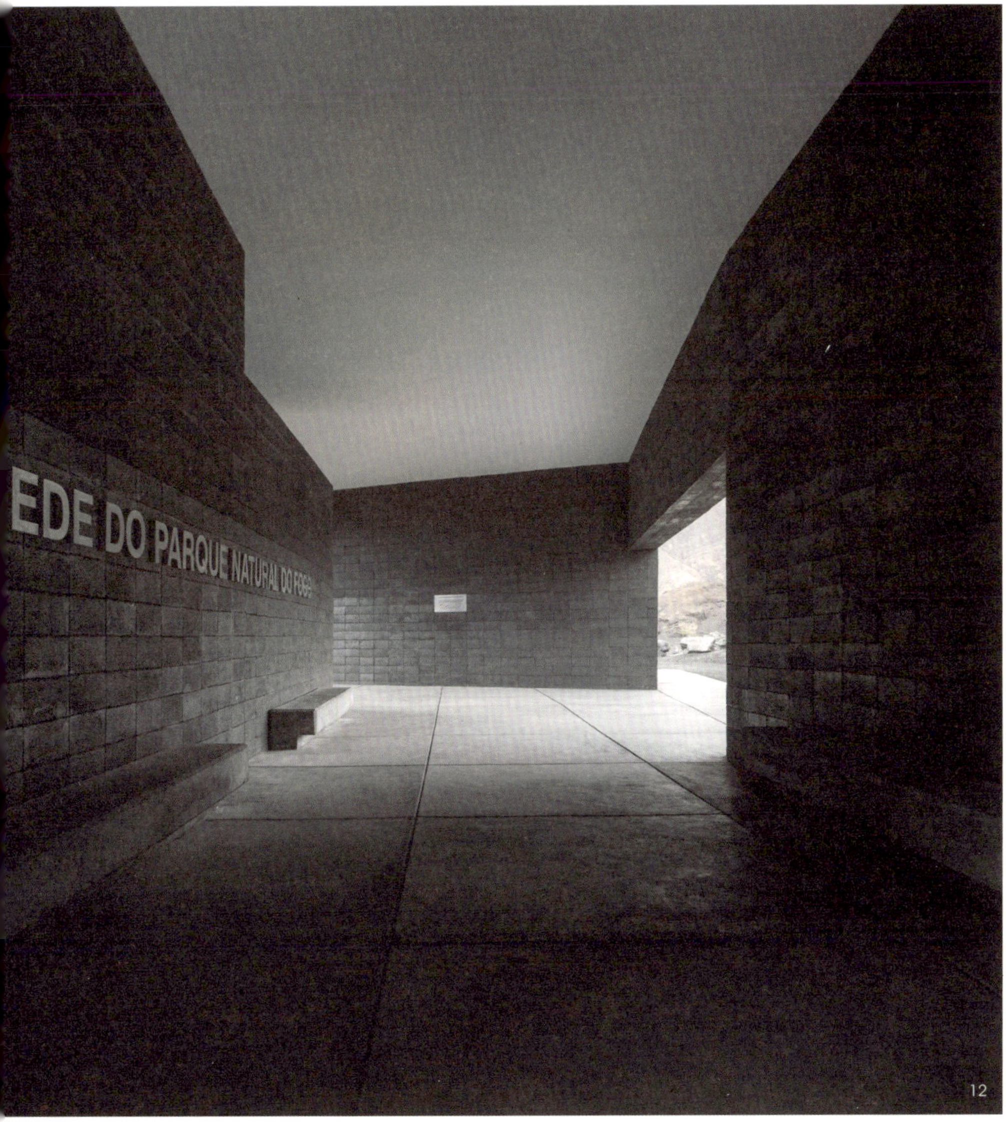

12

15

16

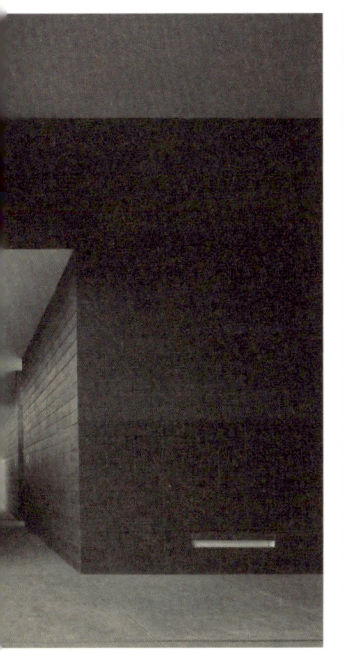

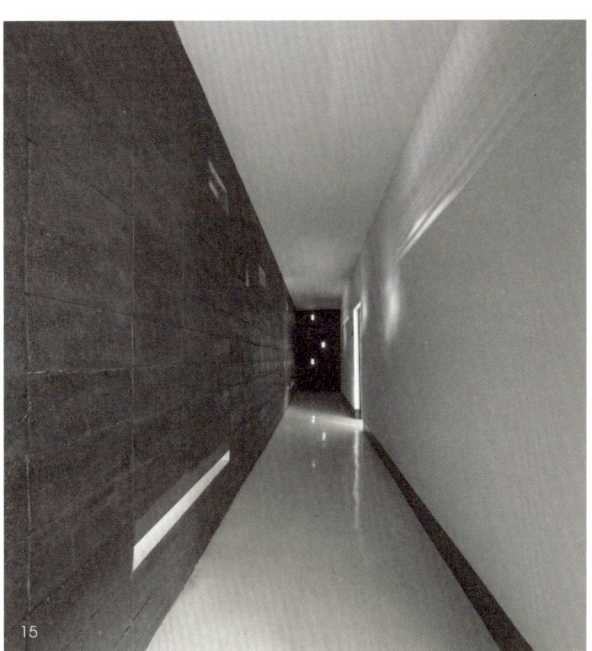

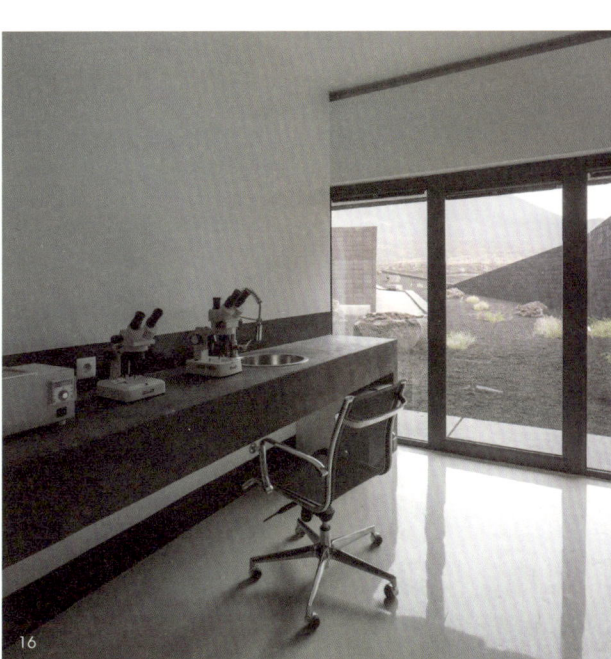

Visitor Center 'Kasteeltuin Slot Assumburg'

Location / Heemskerk, The Netherlands
Completion / 2015
Architect / lab03
Photography / Jeroen Staats
Client / Municipality of Heemskerk

At the end of 2014, in collaboration with contractor Somass, lab03 won the competition for a new visitor center next to the historical castle Assumburg in Heemskerk, a municipality in The Netherlands. The new center became necessary following the reconstruction of the historical castle garden and the subsequent increase in the number of visitors. The building accommodates a general reception area, an office for volunteers, and a workshop.

The design restores the symmetry of the forecourt by positioning the building on the remains of the former stables. In this way, the central axis of the forecourt is again flanked by two functioning service buildings: the orangery and the new visitor center. In time, the openings in the historical wall will be reopened and the visitor center will then be much more effectively connected with the forecourt. With the positioning, the chosen outline and use of material, the building blends into the environment in a natural way. The new addition is set back from the existing monumental wall. By extending the roof over the existing wall, an extra covered outdoor space is created. The new building adds a new layer to the location, while respecting the history of the site.

01 / Visitor center with Assumburg Castle in background
02 / Visitor center next to courtyard

① Orangery
② Forecourt
③ Visitor center
④ Castle
⑤ Historical castle garden

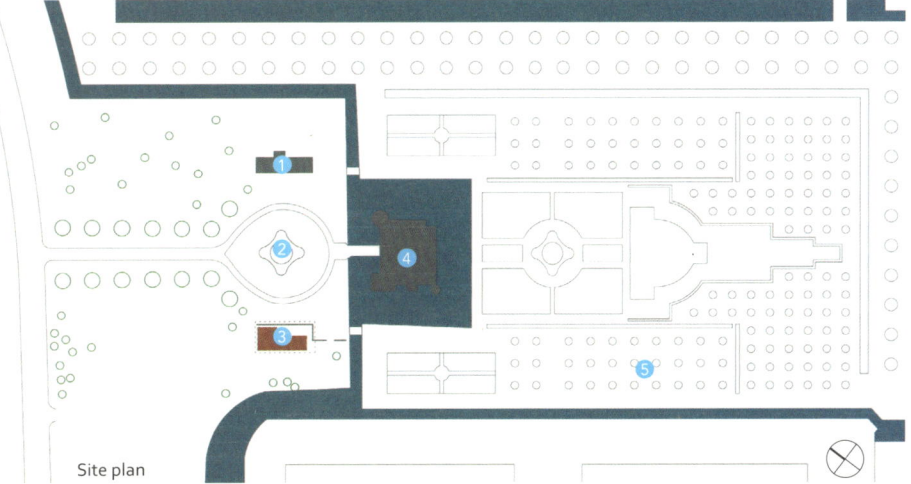

Site plan

03 / New roof connecting former stables with visitor center
04 / Openings in the wall connecting forecourt and visitor center
05 / Entrance
06 / Roof extending over wall to create extra covered outdoor space

The entire public program is located on the ground floor. By separating the reception area and the office spaces, both spaces can be used independently. The workshop is accessible from both the inside and from the outside. Above the workshop, in the attic, there is a space for the storage of fruit and vegetables from the garden. Handcrafted buildings and modern installation techniques are well suited to one another: the larch timber used in the construction was sawn in the wind-powered sawmill Jonge Schaap, nearby at the Zaanse Schans. The visitor center is heated by a pump, therefore making a gas connection unnecessary. The building is intended to be neutral in its energy use. The old glass roof tiles provide extra light for the outdoor space. They light the space in a mysterious way, matching the atmosphere of the ancient castle.

North elevation

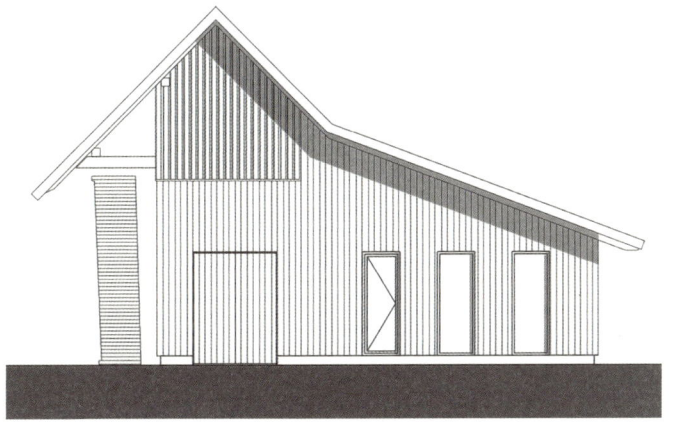

Side section

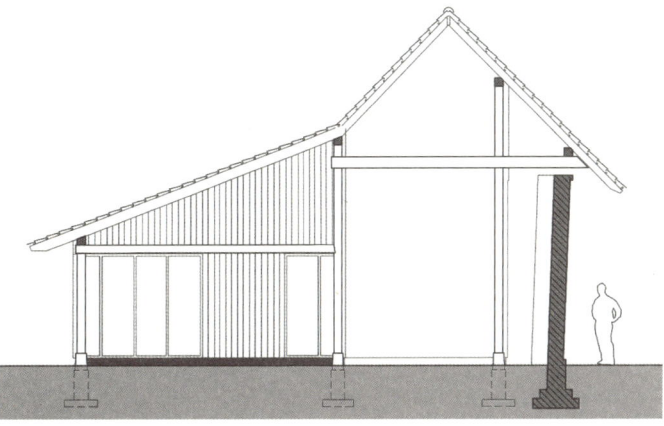

First-floor plan

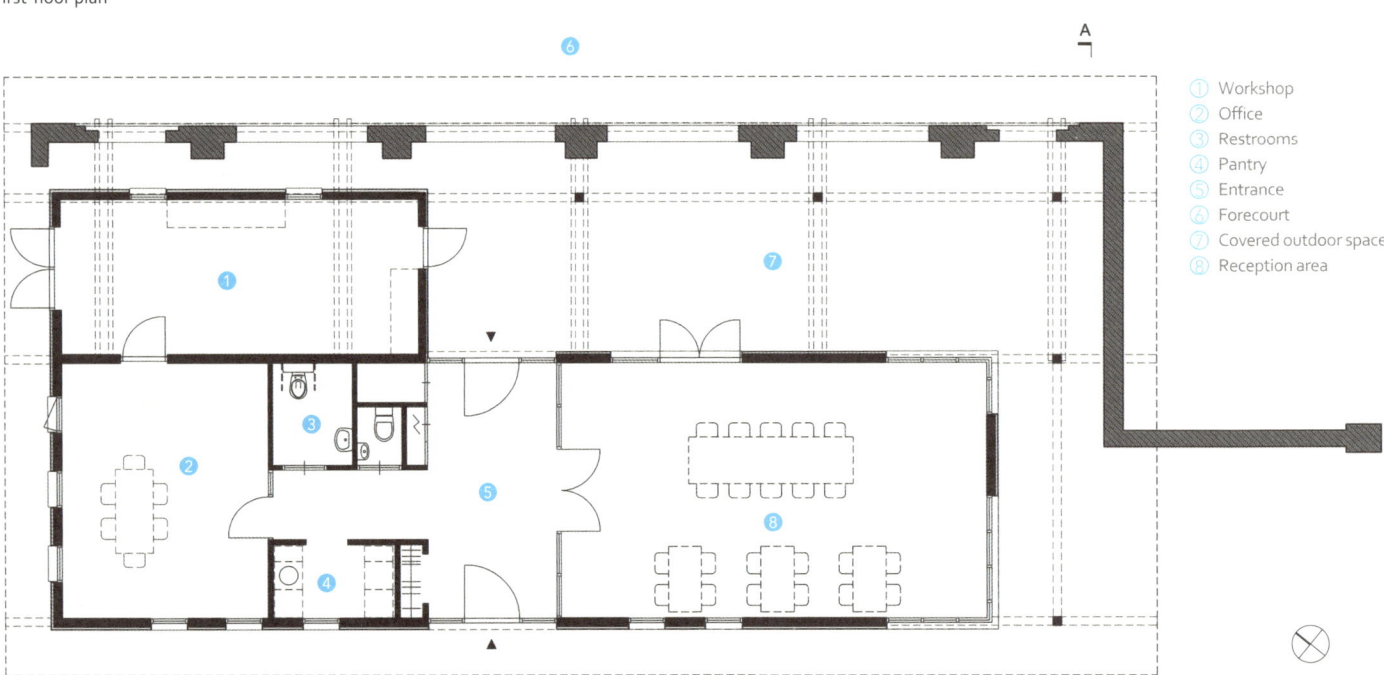

1. Workshop
2. Office
3. Restrooms
4. Pantry
5. Entrance
6. Forecourt
7. Covered outdoor space
8. Reception area

07 / Glass roof tiles providing extra light for outdoor space
08 / Reception area
09 / View of garden from reception area

08

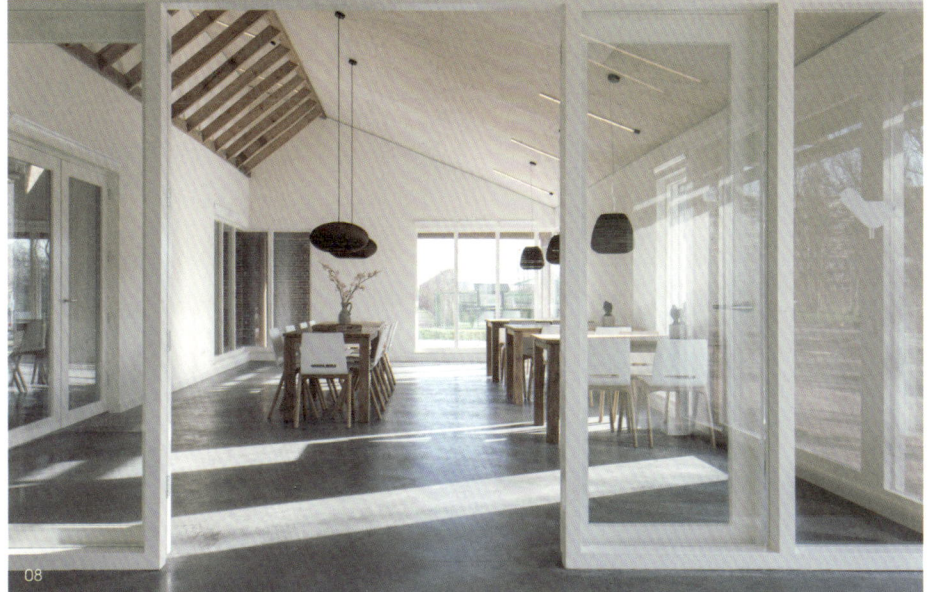

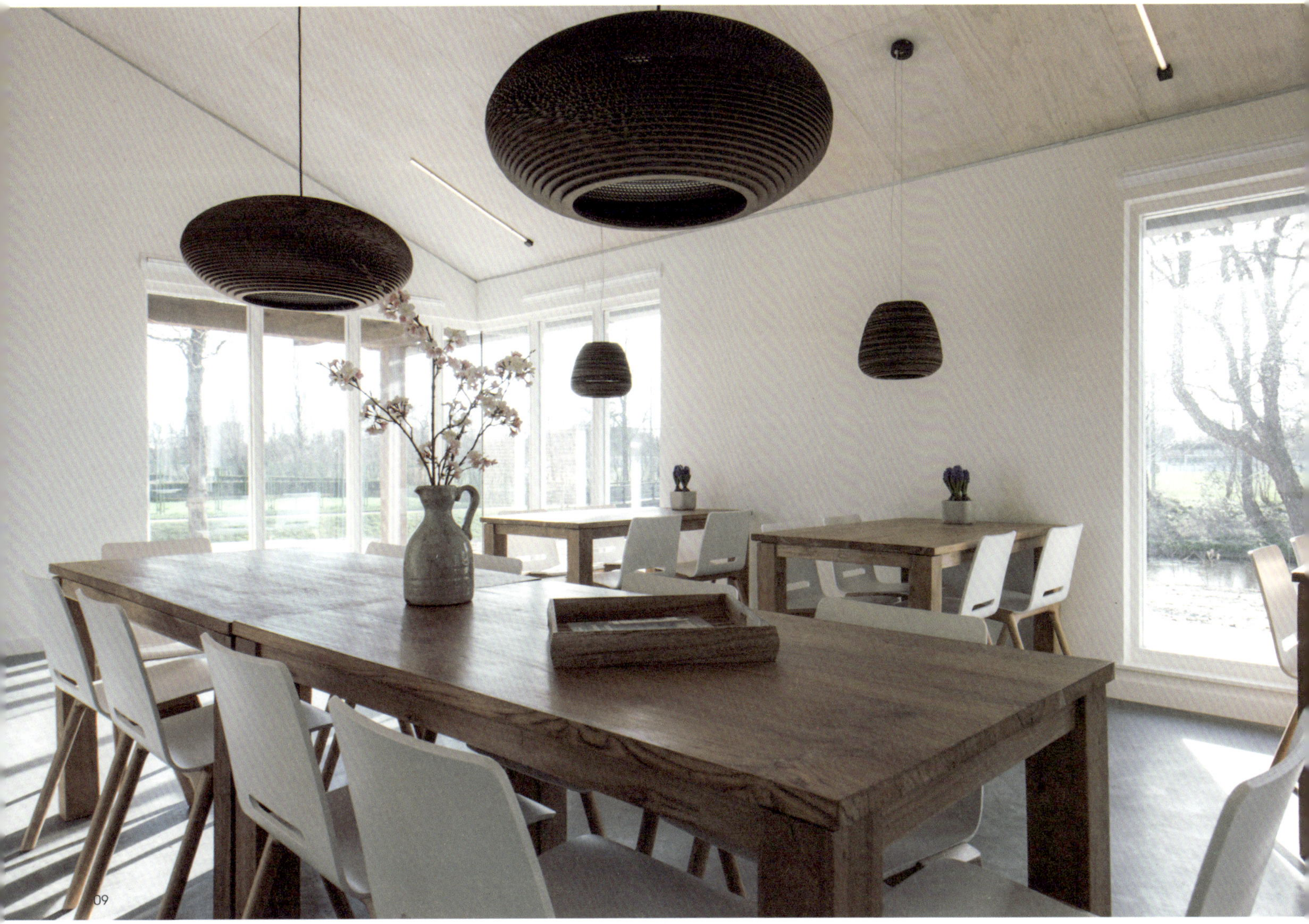
09

Wasit Nature Reserve Visitor Center

Location / Sharjah, UAE
Area / 27,276 square feet (2534 square meters)
Completion / 2015
Architect / X Architects
Photography / Nelson Garrido
Client / EPAA, Environmental and Protected Area Authority

Wasit Natural Reserve (WNR) was originally a wastewater and rubbish dump. The rehabilitation process of the damaged eco-system started in2005. 430,556 square feet (40,000 square meters) of rubbish was removed and 35,000 trees have been re-planted, healing the land from toxic chemicals and conserving the unique salt flats and coastal sand dunes.

After years of efforts to bring the non-migratory birds back to the site, WNR is now home to 350 species of birds, a landing zone for 33,000 migratory birds, and acts as a breathing lung for Sharjah city. A wetland visitor center is established on site in order to continue to protect the natural environment, educate people on the richness of the wetland ecosystem, and provide information about the birds that frequent the area and other wetlands areas of the emirate. The facility has become heaven for bird watchers and researchers.

The architecture of the center blends with its surroundings and uses the existing topography to minimize the visual impact on the natural scene. When visitors arrive, a pathway leads them underground into a viewing area. A fully transparent wall allows the visitors to experience the birds' natural environment and become part of it.

Site plan

01 / Aerial view

① Restroom
② Kitchen
③ Food storage
④ Café
⑤ Viewing gallery
⑥ Office
⑦ Souvenir shop
⑧ Courtyard
⑨ Reception area
⑩ Lecture hall
⑪ Kitchen to prepare food for wildlife
⑫ Garbage disposal
⑬ Aviary
⑭ Ibis rock wall
⑮ Pond
⑯ Water purification plant

Site plan

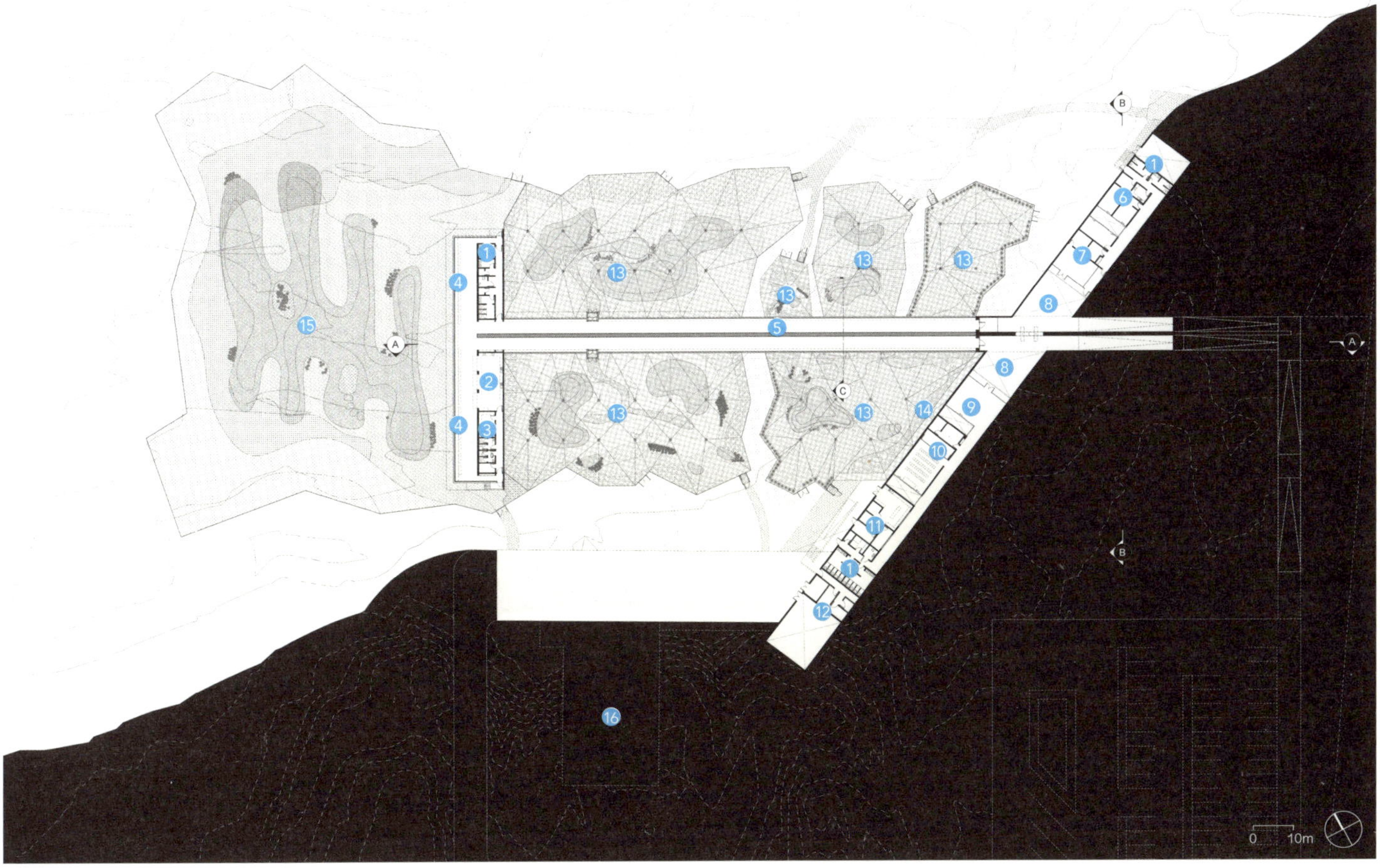

Concept diagram

Sections	Tilting service block against existing wall provides a north-facing wall for ibises	Maximizing visual area between cages and gallery walkway	Maximizing natural scenery from café

Section AA

Section BB

0 5m

02 / Wasit Wetland site
03 / View of nature reserve

03

Program diagram

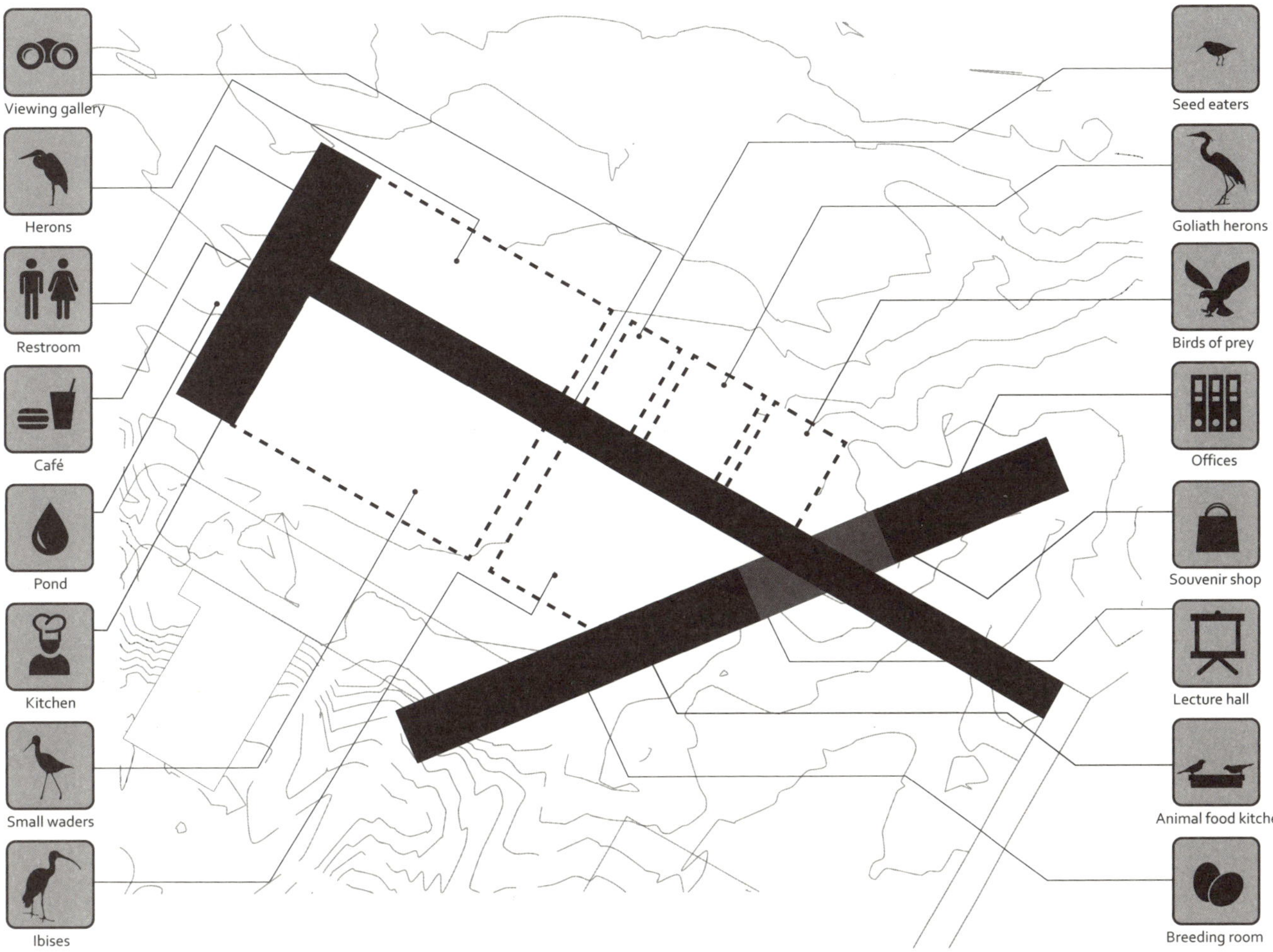

- Viewing gallery
- Herons
- Restroom
- Café
- Pond
- Kitchen
- Small waders
- Ibises
- Seed eaters
- Goliath herons
- Birds of prey
- Offices
- Souvenir shop
- Lecture hall
- Animal food kitchen
- Breeding room

04 / Central courtyard
05 / Landing zone for migrant birds
06 / Bird watching area
07 / Educational center
08 / Interior view of main gallery

Section CC: gallery detail

① Aviary
② Gallery

0   5m

Yew Dell Botanical Gardens Visitor Center

Location / Crestwood, Kentucky, United States
Area / 3003 square feet (279 square meters)
Completion / 2010
Architect / de Leon & Primmer Architecture Workshop
Photography / de Leon & Primmer Architecture Workshop
Client / Yew Dell Botanical Gardens
Budget / $150,000

The Yew Dell Botanical Gardens Visitor Center is a new 1842 square feet (171 square meters) facility for a property founded in 1943 by horticulturalist and nurseryman Theodore Klein. The historic property, recognized for its unique collection of themed structures and gardens, is part of the Garden Conservancy, a national organization dedicated to saving and preserving America's exceptional gardens. Funded in its entirety by a private donor, the project entails the rehabilitation of an existing tobacco barn situated near the property entry. The program includes: reception area with information and ticket sales, gift shop, plant sale area, group tour meeting zone, internet sales office, and storage.

Preserving the exterior iconic image of the tobacco barn structure, the new facility is designed as a 'building-within-a-building.' For economy and energy efficiency, the project utilizes the shell of the existing barn as an independent shade structure, leaving it essentially unaltered with the exception of minor framing stabilization. Working with existing structural bay modules, new conditioned interior spaces are consolidated to one side of the barn interior while unconditioned spaces are designed as covered flexible-use areas.

During low-humidity spring and fall seasons, frameless glass doors can be left open to merge both halves of the barn. Following state historic preservation guidelines, new construction is clearly differentiated from the existing structure through light-colored interior wood plank surfaces and material contrasts.

The use of light—both natural and artificial—is a key design element that transforms the facility throughout the day, affecting the transparency and visibility of the various programmatic components while amplifying the rustic characteristics of the existing tobacco barn. Acting as either a mirror or a transparent boundary depending on the viewing angle, tempered glass walls reflect and refract sunlight, views, and outer barn walls, emphasizing a sense of spaciousness while allowing the original barn to visually register within interior spaces. During the evening, the facility becomes

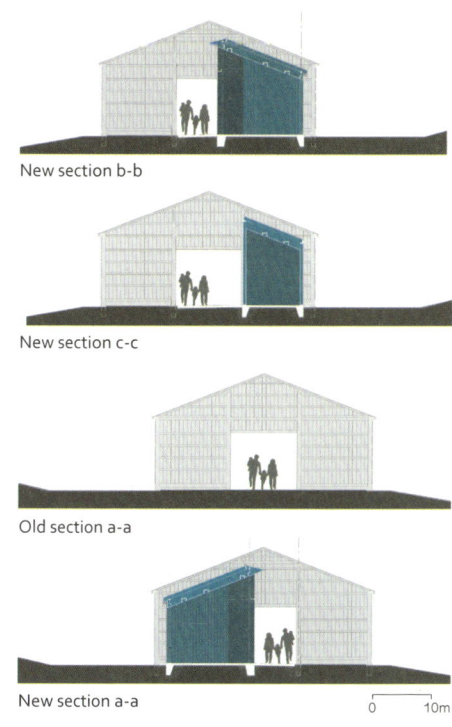

New section b-b

New section c-c

Old section a-a

New section a-a   0   10m

01 / Nighttime view of garden entrance

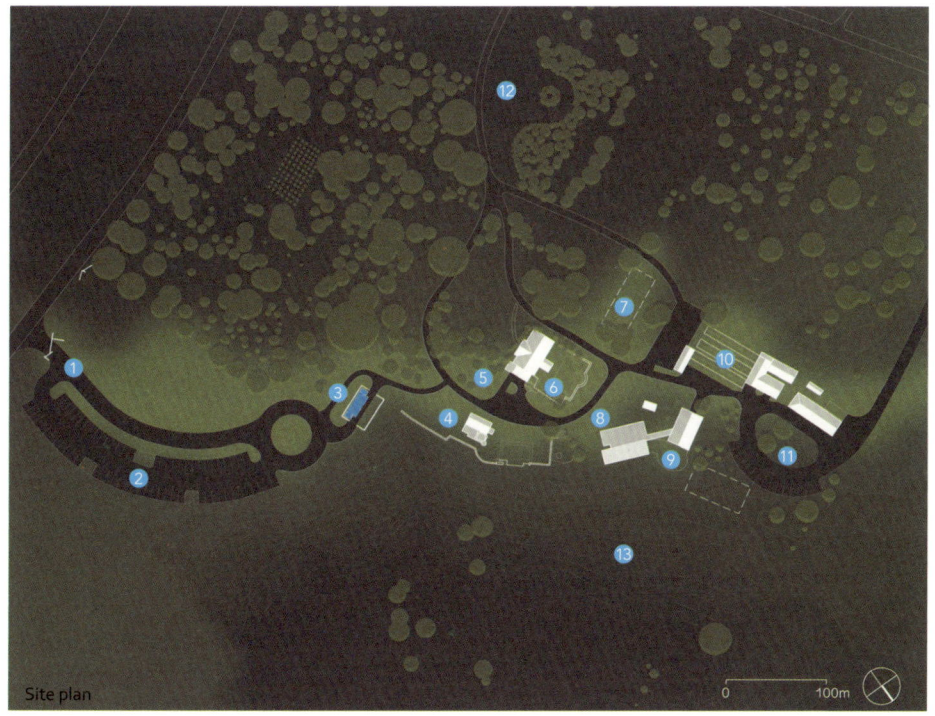

Site plan   0   100m

① Main entrance
② Parking
③ Visitor center
④ Castle
⑤ Offices
⑥ Walled garden
⑦ Allée
⑧ Event pavilion and barn
⑨ Terrace
⑩ Greenhouses
⑪ Service court
⑫ Gardens
⑬ Meadow

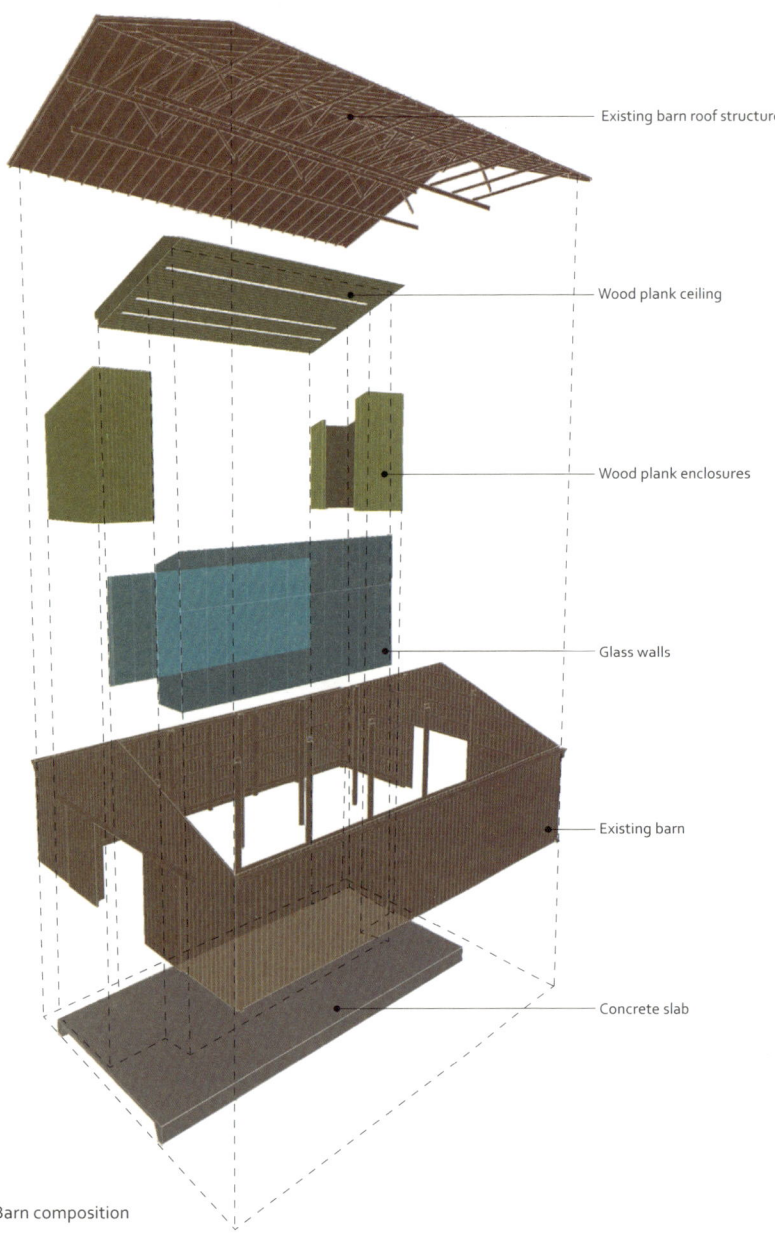

- Existing barn roof structure
- Wood plank ceiling
- Wood plank enclosures
- Glass walls
- Existing barn
- Concrete slab

Barn composition

02

03

04

a glowing lantern within the gardens, with the outer barn shell expressed though interior light filtering through gaps between the wood siding. A conventional palette of materials, including milk-painted tongue and groove wood siding, tempered glass, and sealed concrete floors, is detailed with simplicity and precision.

02 / Night view of gardens
03 / Side view of visitor center entryway
04 / Side view of visitor center facing gardens

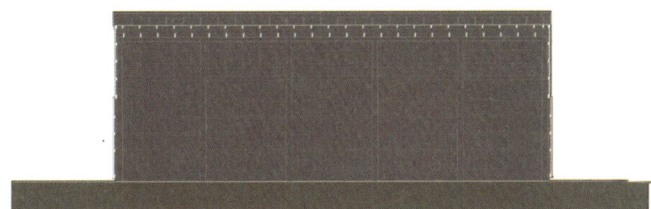

Old section d-d

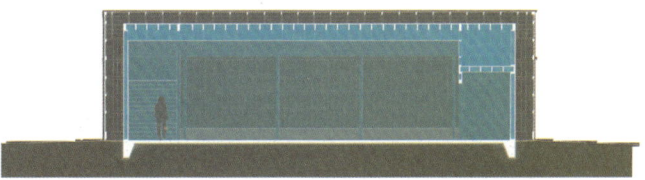

New section e-e

0   10m

05 / View of reception area and gift shop
06 / Entrance to reception area and gift shop
07 / Interior view of reception and gift shop

67

Wild Turkey Bourbon Visitor Center

Location / Lawrenceburg, Kentucky, United States
Area / 9139 square feet (849 square meters)
Completion / 2013
Architect / de Leon & Primmer Architecture Workshop
Photography / de Leon & Primmer Architecture Workshop
Client / Gruppo Campari (USA-Campari America)
Budget / $4,000,000 (includes exhibits and site development)

Located on a bluff overlooking the Kentucky River, the visitor center is then newest component of recent additions & expansions to the Wild Turkey Distillery Complex, one of seven original member distilleries of the Kentucky Bourbon Trail. The 9,140 square feet (849 square meters) facility houses interactive exhibits, a gift shop, event venues, a tasting room, and ancillary support spaces.

Utilizing a simple barn silhouette (an interpretation of Kentucky tobacco obarns common to the area), the building presents a clear & recognizable marker at the scale of the landscape. Clad in a custom chevron pattern of stained wood siding, the simplicity of the barn form is contrasted by the intricacy of the building skin at closer range, creating a shifting sense of scale and tactility that is deliberately both simple and complex. Alternating areas of light-filtering lattice blur the boundaries between inside/out and light/dark. By night, the solidity of the dark structure transforms into a delicate, glowing lantern of filigree perched above the river.

Public circulation and movement is an important component used to prolong and amplify the visitor experience and begins with a descending road that gradually reveals the visitor center building and river bluff edge. Internally, the building is organized along a ramped, split-level public promenade that culminates in an elevated tasting room overlooking the Kentucky River, the bourbon's base water source. Referencing the nearby bridges spanning the river, a wooden trestle element provides a physical spine from which the various programmatic elements are reached.

The project employs forms, materials and patterns that are common to the region and to the bourbon-making process, but are expressed in unexpected ways. While the building evokes a traditional tobacco barn with its black pitch coating, the proportions (particularly the roof outline) are exaggerated and relate more to the monumental scale of the nearby bourbon-agin grick houses. Typical vertical barn plank siding has been reinterpreted into a chevron 'plumage', a nod to the brand's iconic wild turkey mascot. The dark exterior stain also offsets a maintenance issue peculiar to bourbon producing regions: it minimizes the need to clean off a non-toxic black fungus, which feeds on evaporating bourbon distillates, that gradually darkens building exteriors.

Old site plan

① Distillery complex
② New visitor center
③ Kentucky River

01 / Southeast view

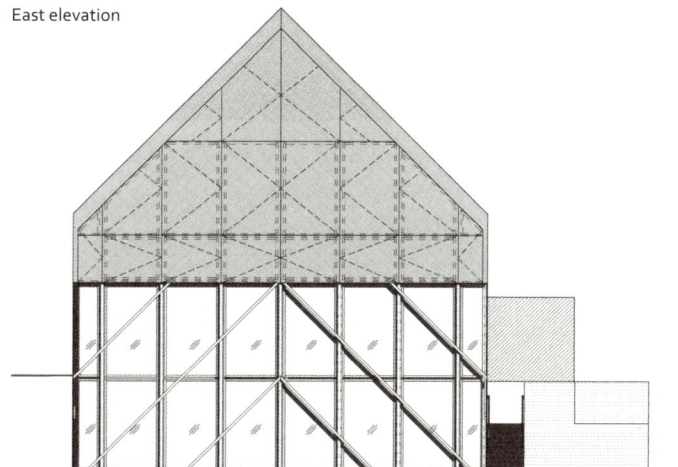

East elevation

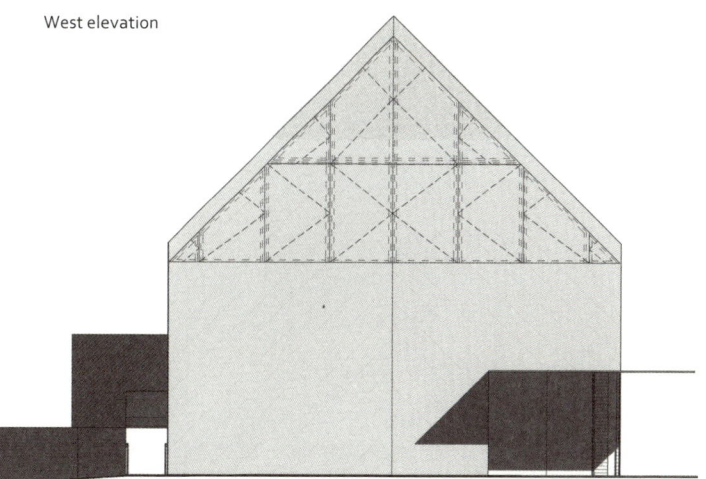

West elevation

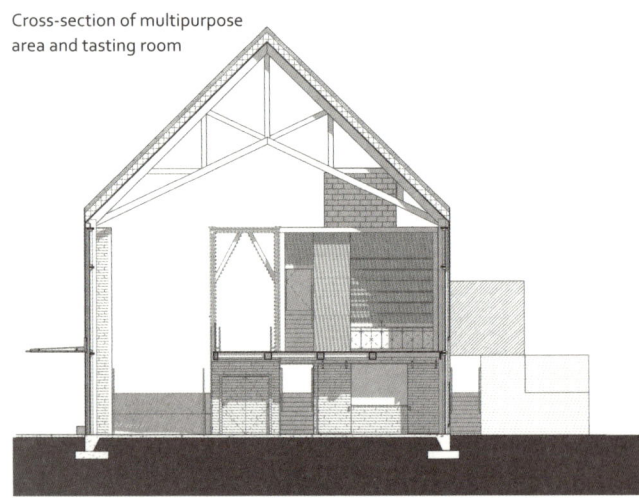
Cross-section of multipurpose area and tasting room

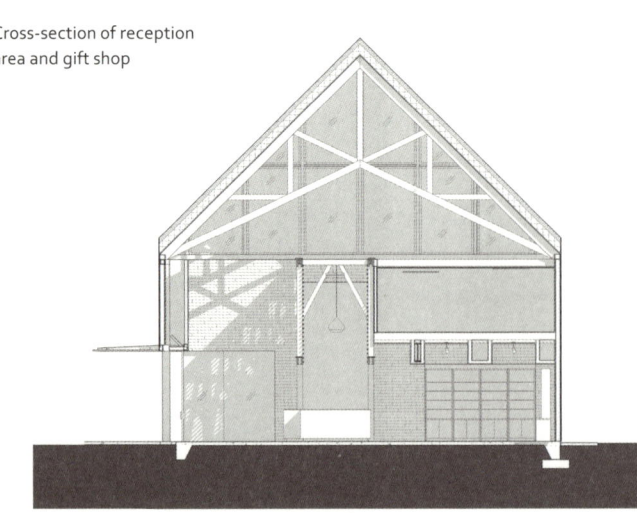
Cross-section of reception area and gift shop

02 / Northwest view with Kentucky River beyond
03 / West view of entry canopy
04 / East view

05 / Detail view of eastern glazing
06 / Detail view of entry canopy with distillery buildings beyond

Cross-section of exhibit ramp

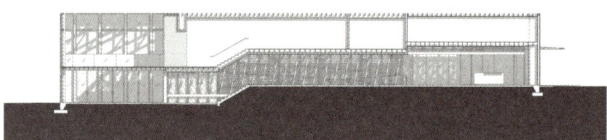
Cross-section of service hallway facing south

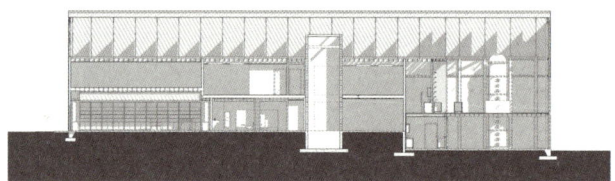
Cross-section of service and administration areas

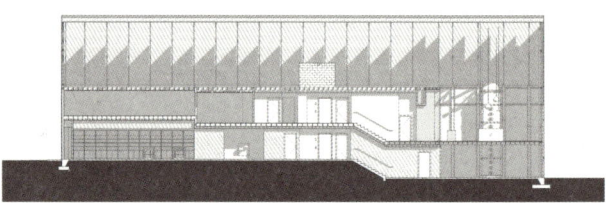
Cross-section of service hallway facing north

Tasting area floor plan

1. Maintainence area
2. Office
3. Conference room
4. Restroom
5. Elevator
6. Storage room
7. Upper catering area
8. Tasting room

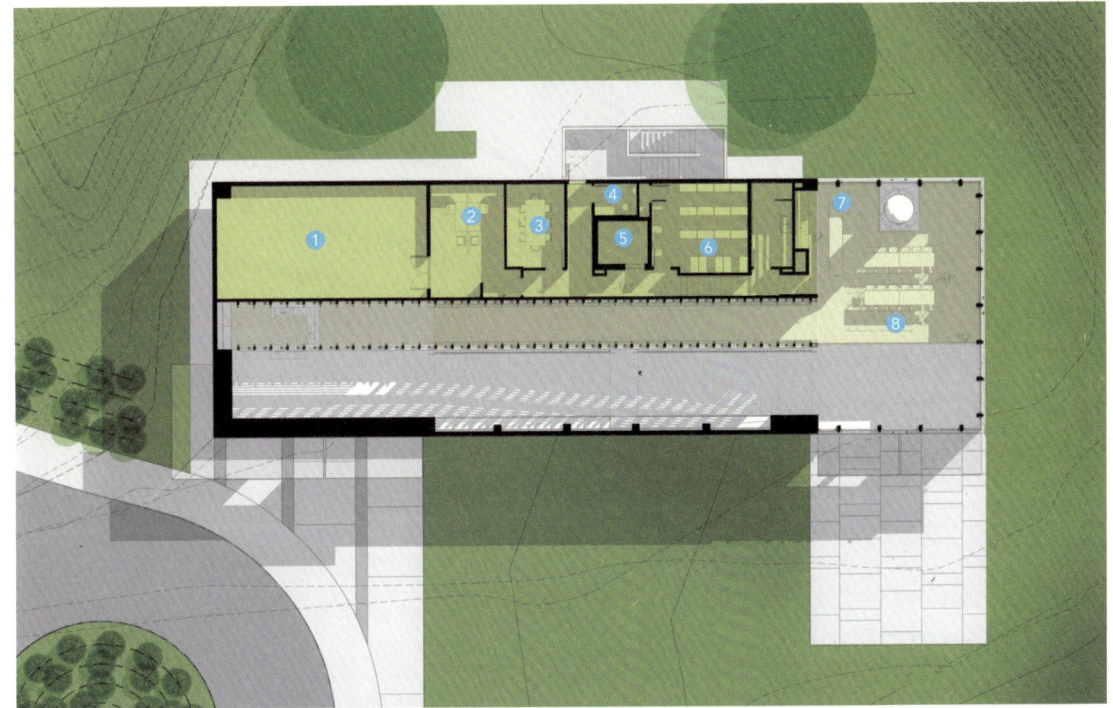

Ground floor plan

1. Gift shop
2. Restroom
3. Elevator
4. Storage room
5. Lower catering area
6. Hallway
7. Tasting room ramp
8. Multi-function area
9. Reception area
10. Exhibit area
11. Entry plaza
12. Meadows
13. Outdoor event terrace

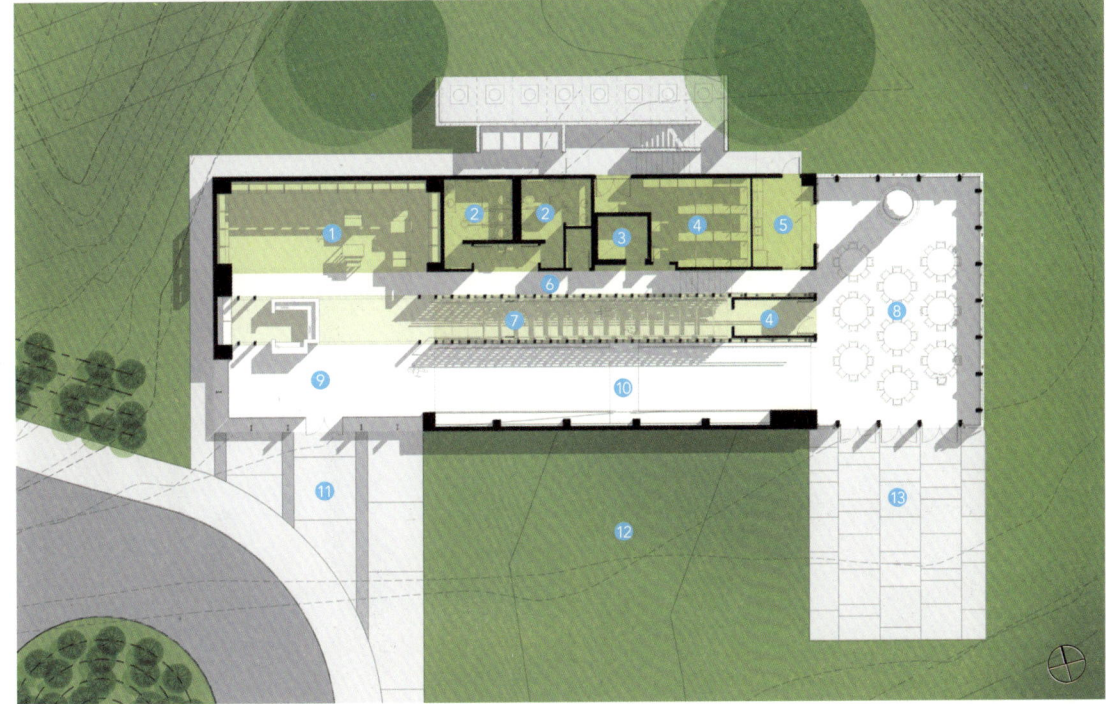

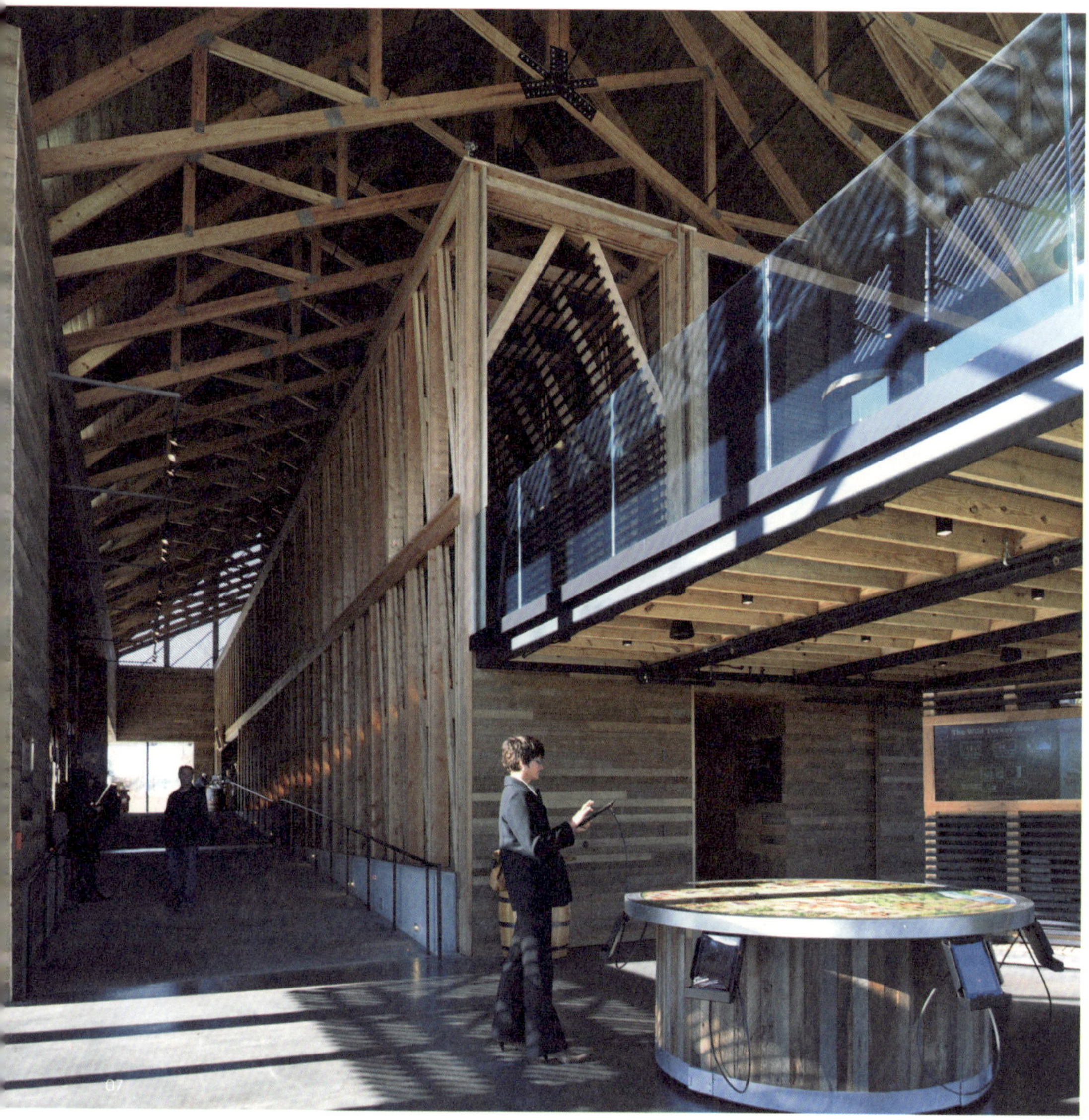

07

08

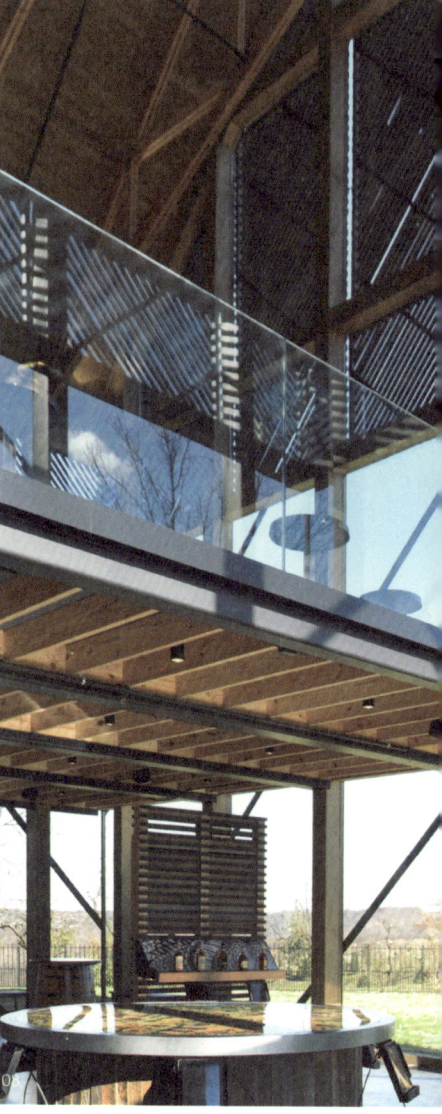

07 / Ramp leading to tasting area
08 / Multi-functional space with tasting area above
09 / Side view of passage to tasting area
10 / Side view of ramp to reception area
11 / Gift shop
12 / Tasting area with vintage copper still

11

12

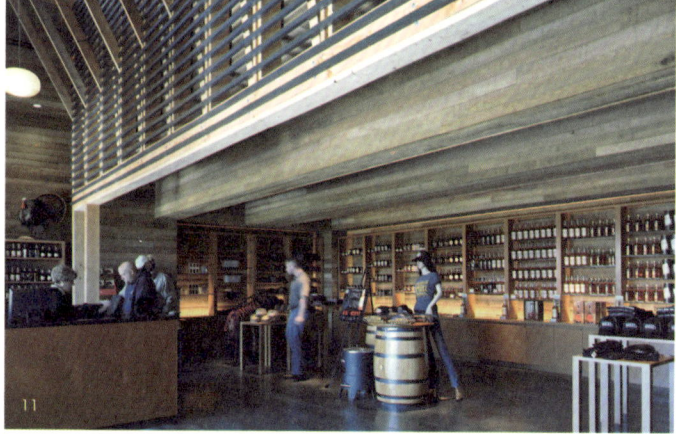

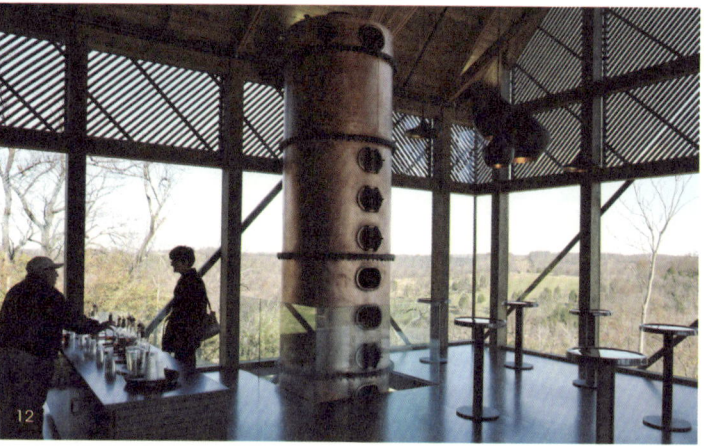

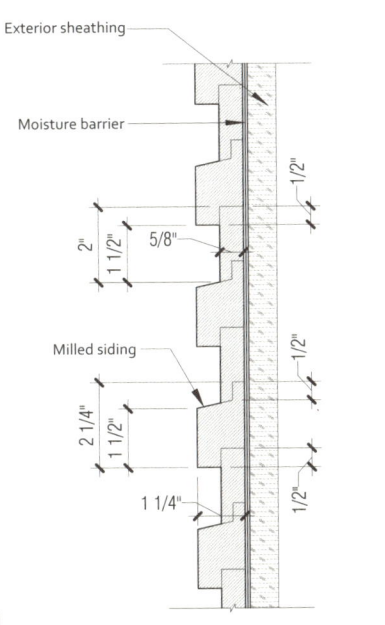

Siding detail

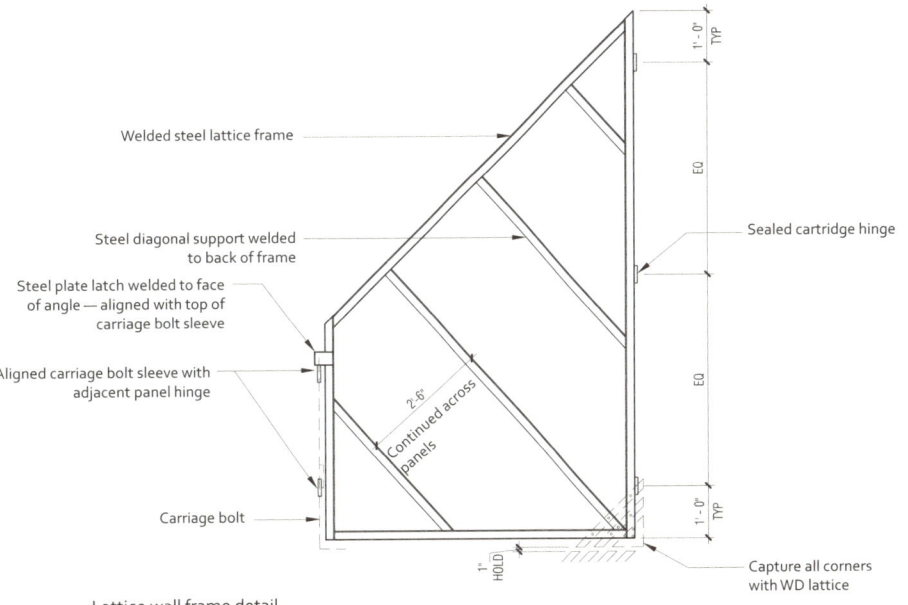

Lattice wall frame detail

Visitor Center for Architectural Miniatures Park

Location / Shekvetili, Georgia
Area / 2799 square feet (260 square meters)
Completion / 2016
Architect / Laboratory of Architecture #3
Photography / Nakanimamasakhlisi

The newly-completed architectural miniatures park opened its doors in August 2016 at the Black Sea coastal resort Shekvetili. This small Georgian village has already enjoyed the grand opening of a nearby 10,000-seat concert arena, a five-star hotel, and an amusement park.

The developing coastal region will be able to host thousands of tourists and offer them sandy beaches, seaside eucalyptus forests, and unique leisure infrastructure. Among the tourist sites available, one can visit a theme park called 'Georgia in Miniatures.' The park is full of architectural monuments at 1:25 scale, gathered from all around Georgia. The park aims to display rich architectural heritage of the country.

The 10-year old Georgian architectural company, Laboratory of architecture #3, developed the park layout and a visitor center building, which is located at the entrance and serves as a kind of introduction to the whole area. It is important to mention that the building is built out of 98-feet (30-meter) unused concrete cylindrical drum from an abandoned sewage cleaning facility.

The visitor goes through a poetic space, flanked on one side by a 197 feet (60 meter) long curved, black bamboo fence and a ribbed fiber concrete pavilion on the other. Bamboo is a very native material in local vernacular architecture as it is very cheap and easy to find throughout the region. However, painting bamboo black is the first experimental attempt of this kind within the area. The use of radical coloring continues in the yellow educational space of the outdoor amphitheater and in the blue staircase heading to the rooftop terrace.

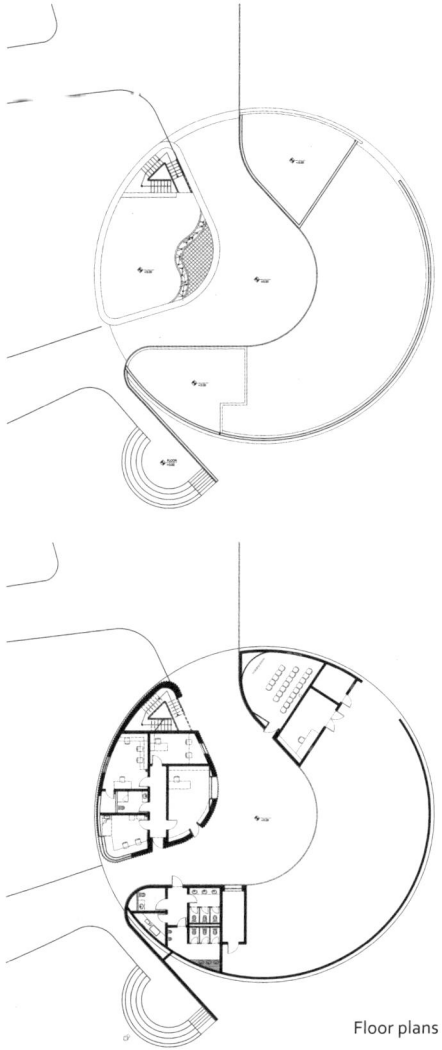

Floor plans

01 / View from entrance

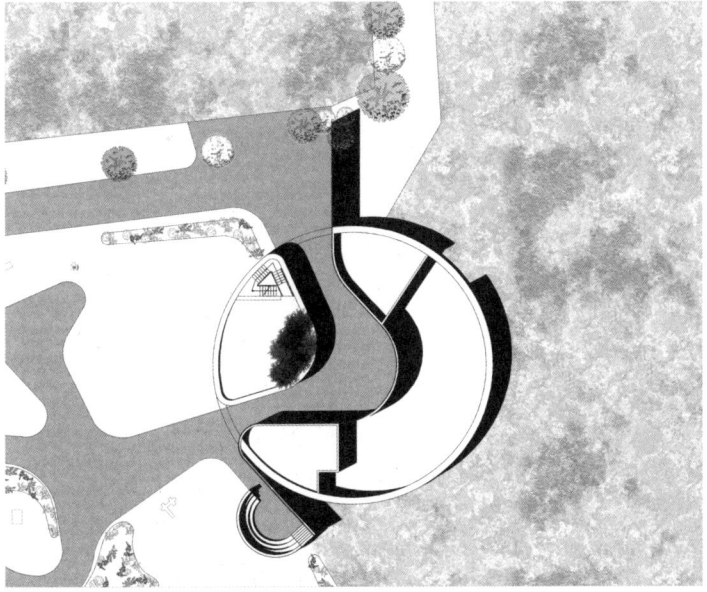
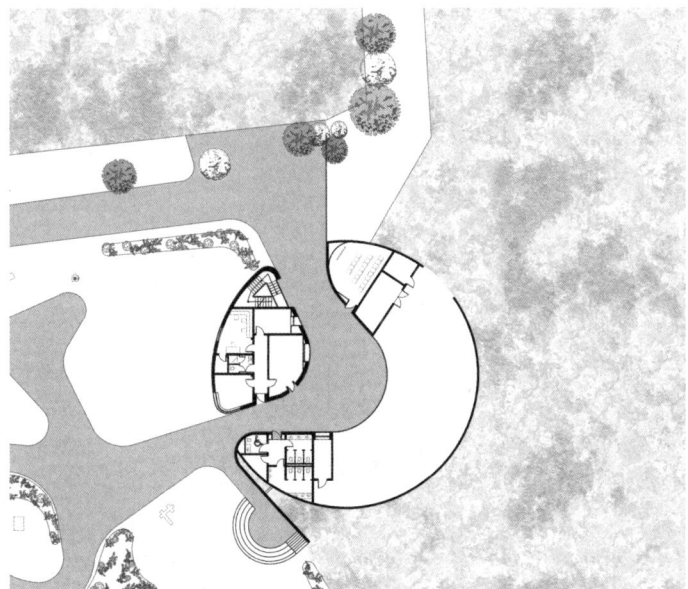

Site plans

02 / Entrance
03-04 / Black bamboo fence
05 / Ribbed concrete pavilion

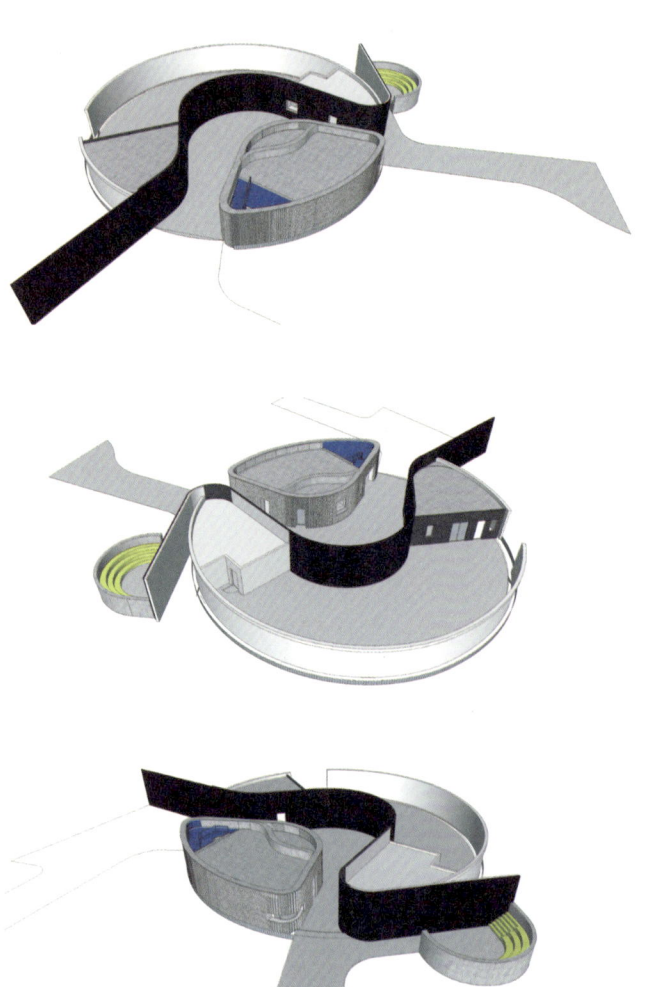

Perspective drawings

Function areas

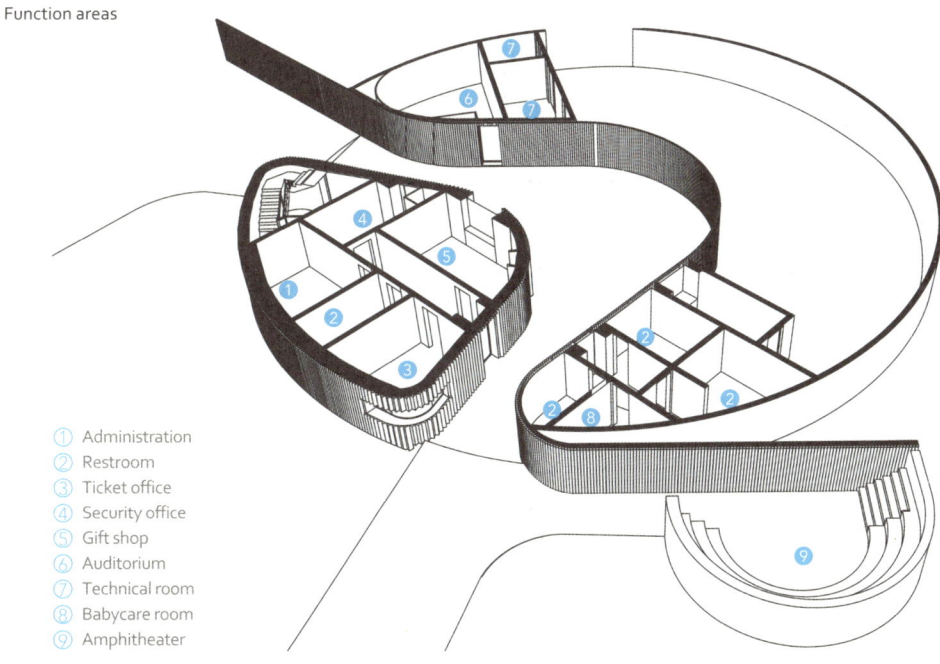

① Administration
② Restroom
③ Ticket office
④ Security office
⑤ Gift shop
⑥ Auditorium
⑦ Technical room
⑧ Babycare room
⑨ Amphitheater

06 / Entrance details
07-08 / Details of pavilion
09-10 / Details of stairs
11-12 / Details of ribbed concrete

Fazer Visitor Center and Meeting Center

Location / Vantaa, Finland
Area / 55,219 square feet (5130 square meters)
Completion / 2016
Architect / K2S Architects Ltd.
Photography / Mika Huisman
Client / Oy KARL FAZER Ab

The bakery, confectionary and food products company Fazer is one of the best-known Finnish brands in the country, boasting a strong heritage. In essence, the new visitor center transforms the existing candy factory area in to a tourist destination.

The new visitor center is a pavilion, which has become the architectural signature for the area. The pavilion is the first object one sees while approaching Fazer village. The front entrance is transformed through landscaping. The large yet necessary parking areas are planted with cherry trees. The visitor is guided to the main entrance through a garden of different grains. The raw materials of Fazer products are strongly present.

A wooden cantilevered ceiling projects a strong identity to the visitor center. In the main entrance, the visitor encounters the café and the factory shop. A green room housing cocoa plants, sugar cane, and vanilla presents another experience of the raw materials in chocolate making. The unstructured plan offers a platform for future experimentation of different concepts and product launches.

The exhibitions present both chocolate making's heritage and future directions. Events such as chocolate making or cooking courses can be attended. All public spaces in the visitor center are located on ground level, which allows easy access and flexibility of all spaces.

The new Meeting Center serves as an entrance to the existing Headquarters and also links the Visitor Center to the existing office spaces. This allows easy indoor access from the Meeting Center both towards the Visitor Center and the existing offices and factories. This results in synergy and effective usage of space.

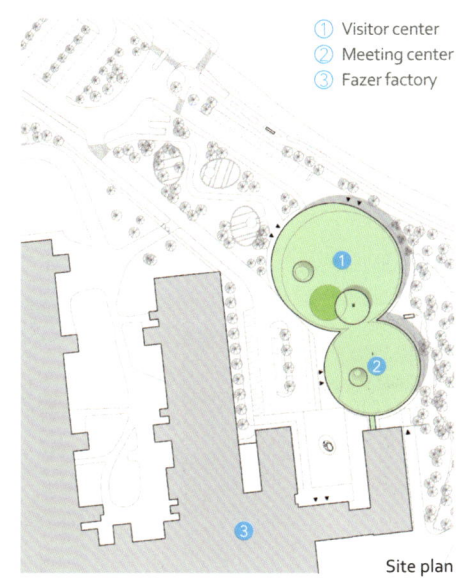

① Visitor center
② Meeting center
③ Fazer factory

Site plan

01 / Aerial view

Visitor center — Meeting center — Factory

West elevation

Visitor center — Factory

North elevation

Second-floor plan

First-floor plan

① Visitor center entrance
② Meeting center entrance
③ Fazer café
④ Fazer store
⑤ Exhibition space
⑥ Multipurpose space
⑦ Green room
⑧ Cabinet
⑨ Meeting room
⑩ Kitchen
⑪ Information center
⑫ Restroom
⑬ Office
⑭ Terrace
⑮ Skylight
⑯ Storage room
⑰ Technical space
⑱ Parking hall
⑲ Existing building

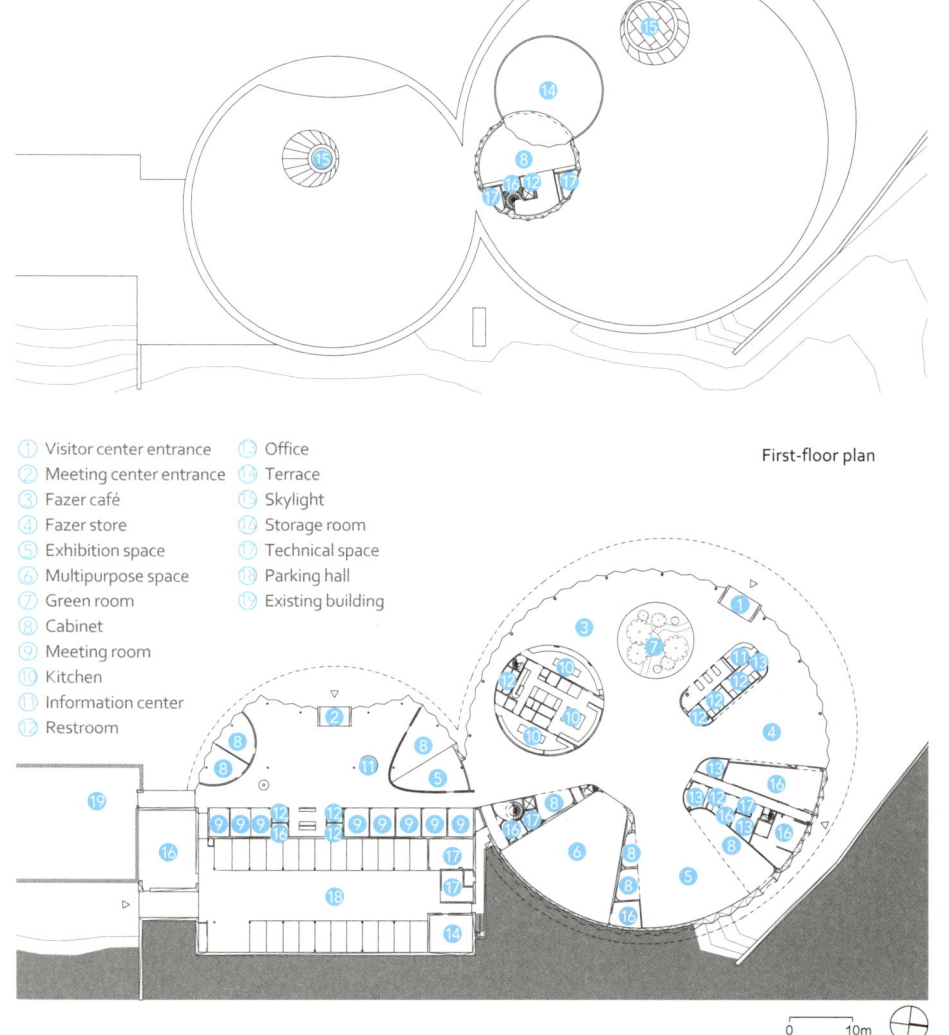

02 / Glass façade
03-04 / Entrance to meeting center
05 / Fazer store

05

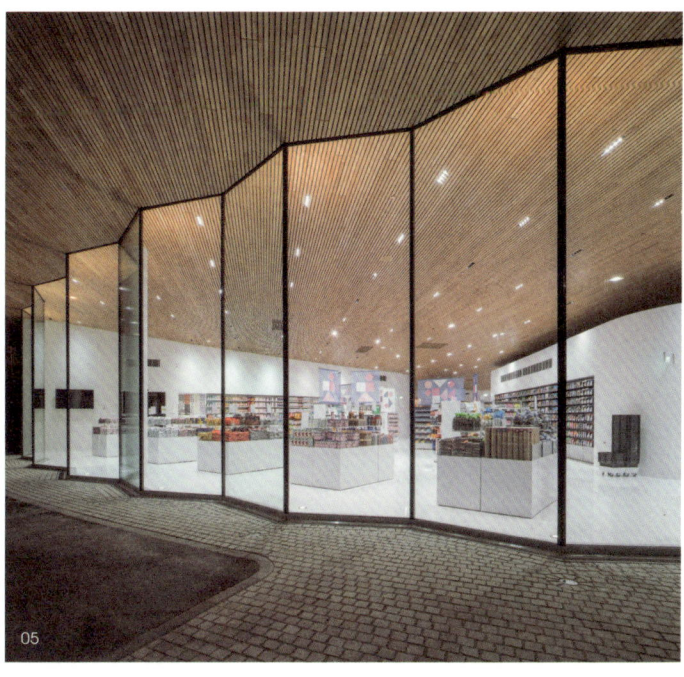

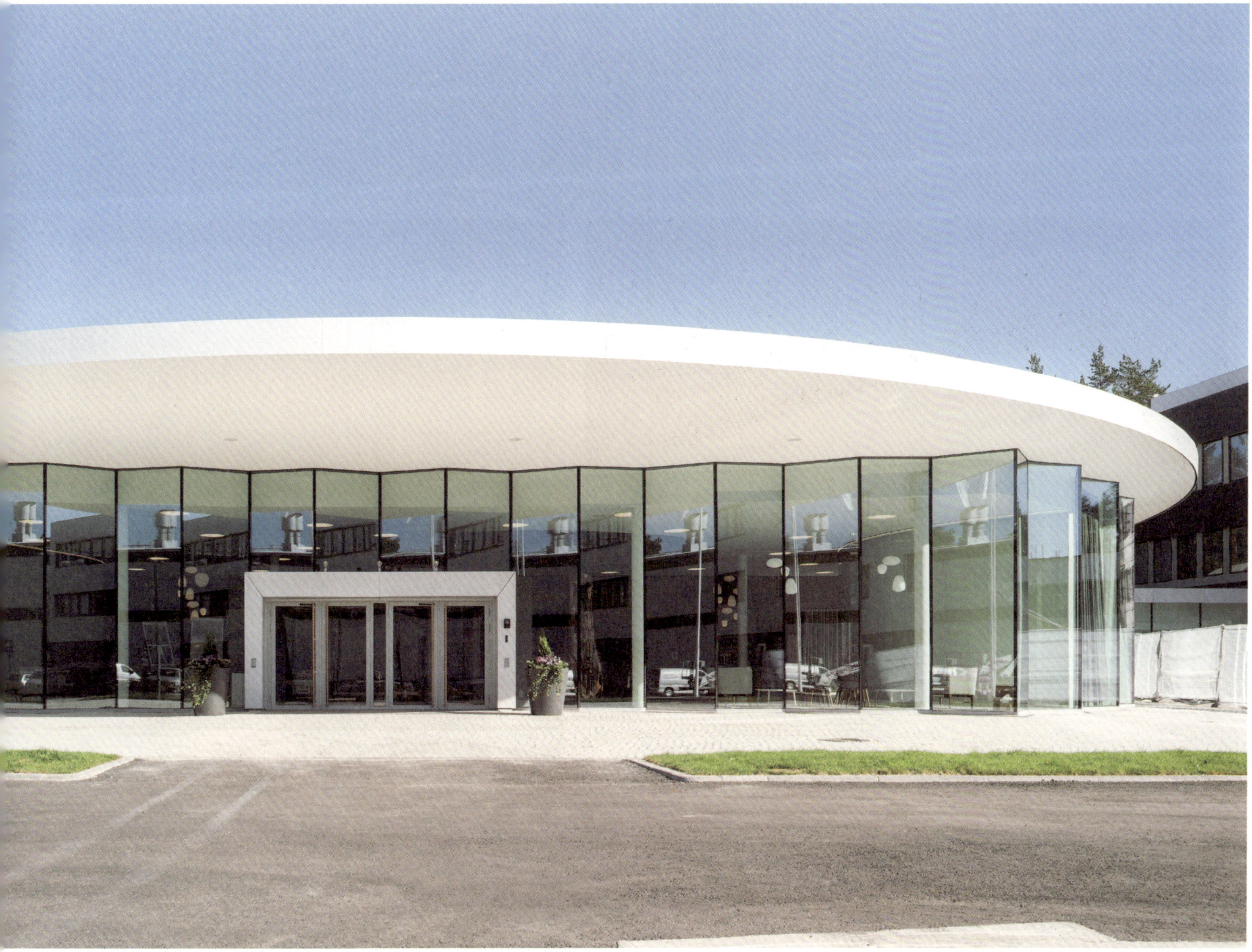

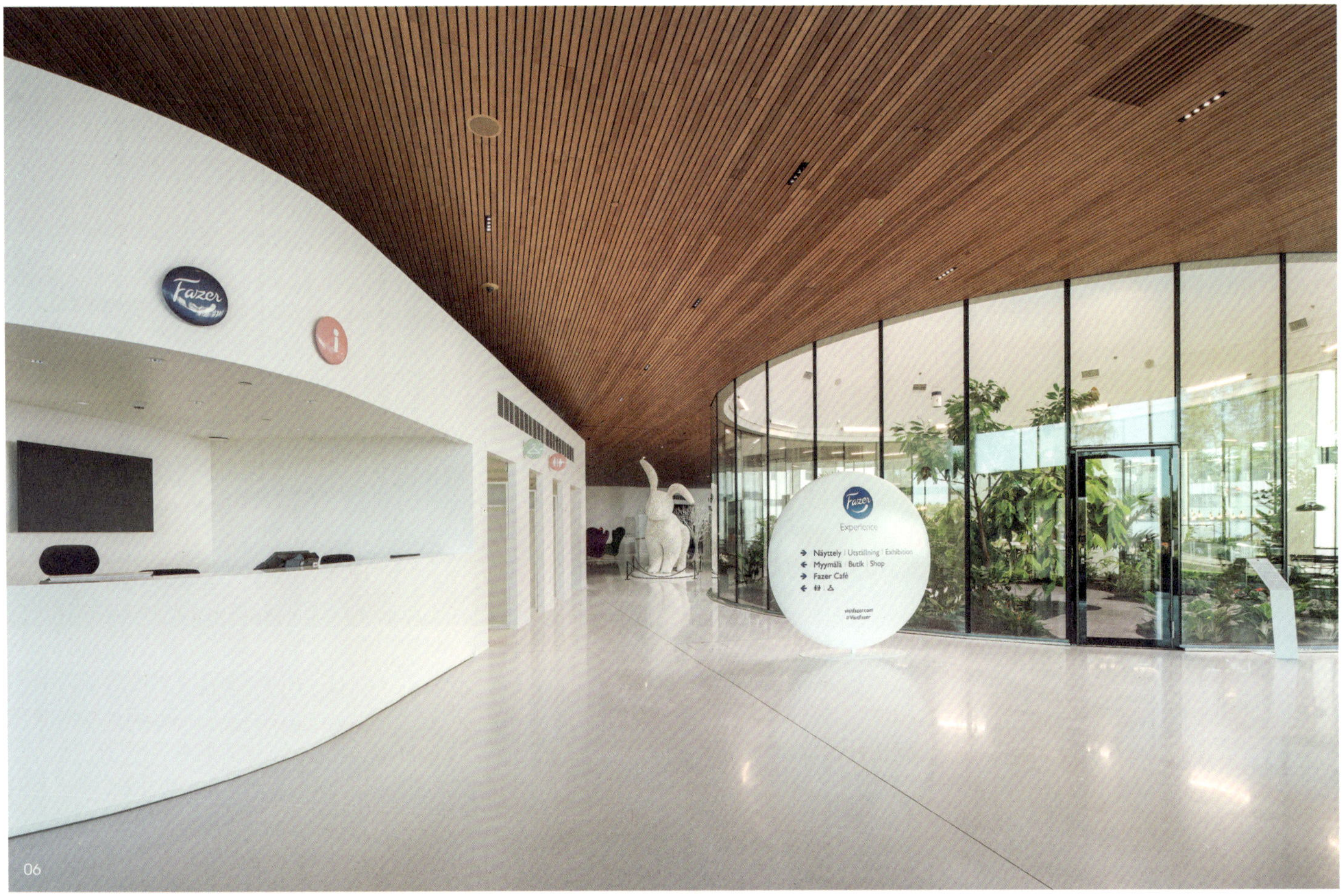

06

07

08

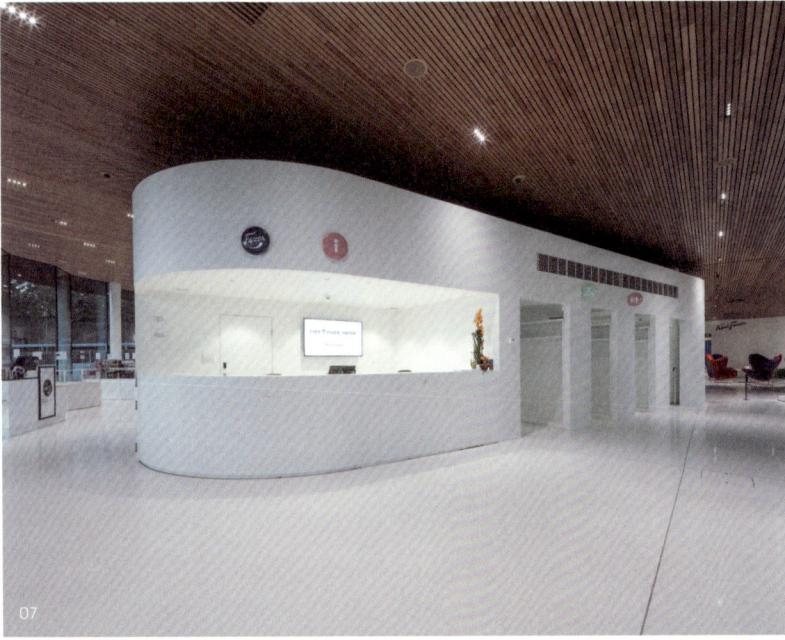

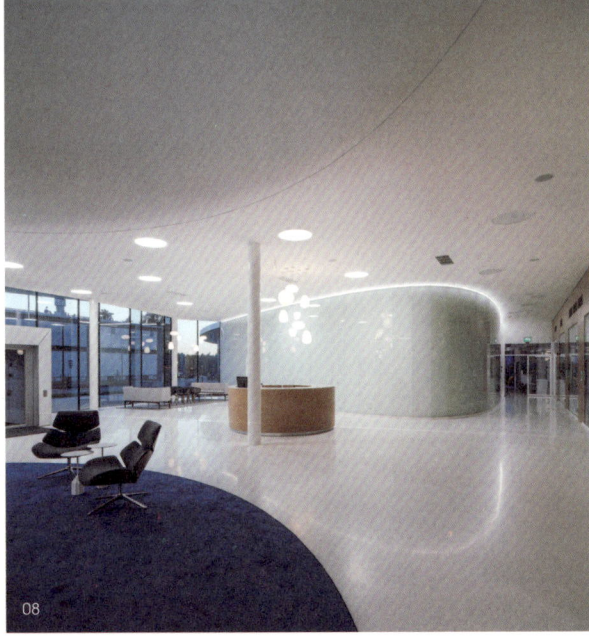

06-07 / Entrance to visitor center
08 / Lobby of meeting center
09 / Greenhouse with cocoa trees
10 / Fazer café

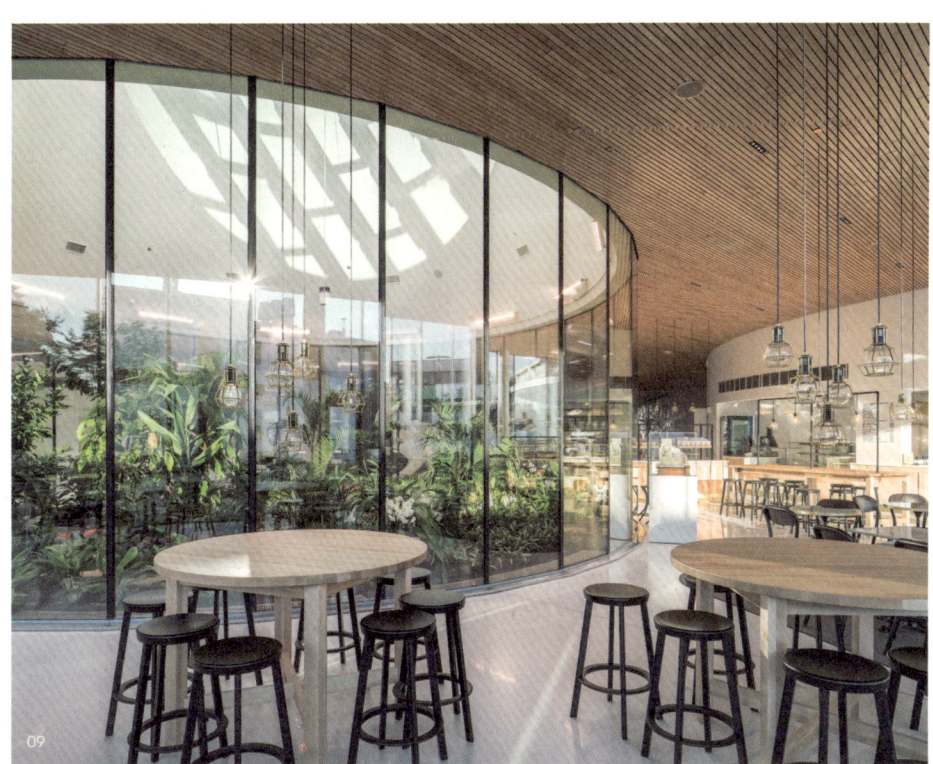

Red Rock Canyon Visitor Center

Location / Las Vegas, Nevada, USA
Area / 8600 square feet (799 square meters)
Completion / 2010
Architect / Line and Space, LLC
Photography / Robert Reck
Client / United States Department of the Interior Bureau of Land Management
Budget / $17 million (including exhibits)

Within the Mojave Desert, the 200,000-acre (80,937 hectare) Red Rock Canyon National Conservation Area stands out as a place of wonder. The new visitor center serves as the gateway to the Conservation Area and includes a visitor arrival space, classroom with outdoor patio, gift shop, 300-seat amphitheater, shaded outdoor gathering areas, and 38,500 square feet (3577 square meters) of exterior exhibit space.

The visitor center's architecture emphasizes environmental conservation, is responsive to climate and environment, and demonstrates appropriate desert design. The goal is that visitors will go away with a new understanding of resource conservation, buildings that respond appropriately to their environment, and energy conserving practices, products, and ideas that they can use in their personal lives.

The single idea with the greatest impact on demonstrating resource conservation is locating the majority of exhibits and circulation in sheltered outdoor pavilions. Of the 24,000 square feet (2230 square meters) of programmed space, only 8,600 square feet (799 square meters) is interior air-conditioned space. This innovative strategy eliminates 64 percent of air-conditioned interior spaces well as the resources and materials to construct and maintain it. It also presents the unique experience for the visitor, of being submerged in the landscape, with interpretation to guide and encourage the exploration of the surrounding Conservation Area.

The outdoor pavilions use passive solar energy strategies, such as orientation and calculated roof overhangs to provide shade in the summer and warming sun in the winter. East and west exposures are minimized by masonry wing walls that also block the cold winter winds from the west. Low-energy strategies, such as evaporative cooling and fans, engage during the hottest months of the year.

Thousands of people move to Las Vegas each year. It is a city of excess where many have diverse backgrounds, experiences, and knowledge, but few understand what it is like to live in the desert. The Mojave Desert is a delicate place where extreme heat and little rain exaggerate the time it takes the land to recover from human disturbance. Educating this growing population on sustainable living in the desert is our priority.

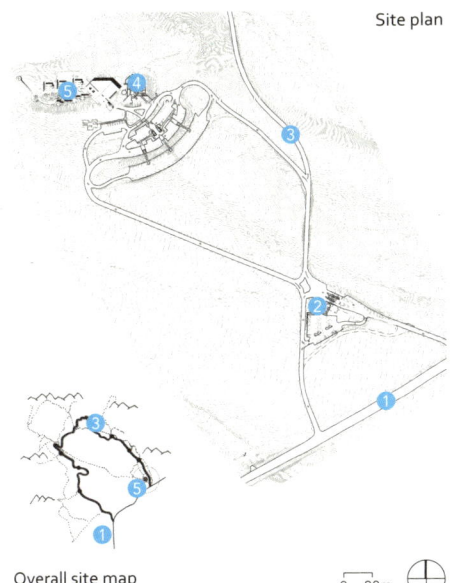

Site plan

Overall site map

① Highway 159
② Contact station
③ 13-mile (21-kilometer) loop road
④ Reuse of existing structure for administrative offices
⑤ New visitor center

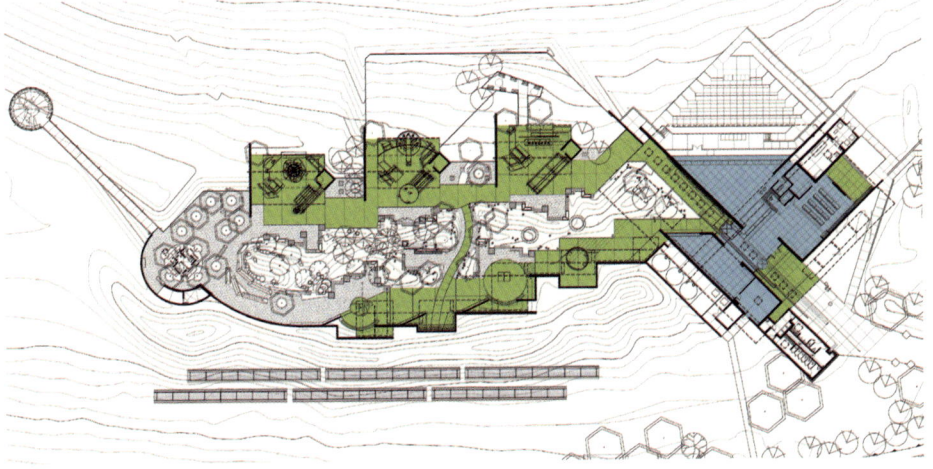

Space allocation

01 / Steel and concrete masonry blending in with natural surroundings

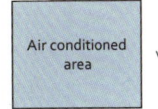

Air conditioned area vs. Exterior, tempered microclimates area

These diagrams illustrate how the exhibit and circulation spaces, originally programmed as air conditioned interior spaces, were designed as outdoor microclimates that utilize solar orientation, evaporative cooling and energy-efficient fans to provide year-round comfort. The result is a 64% reduction of conditioned interior space.

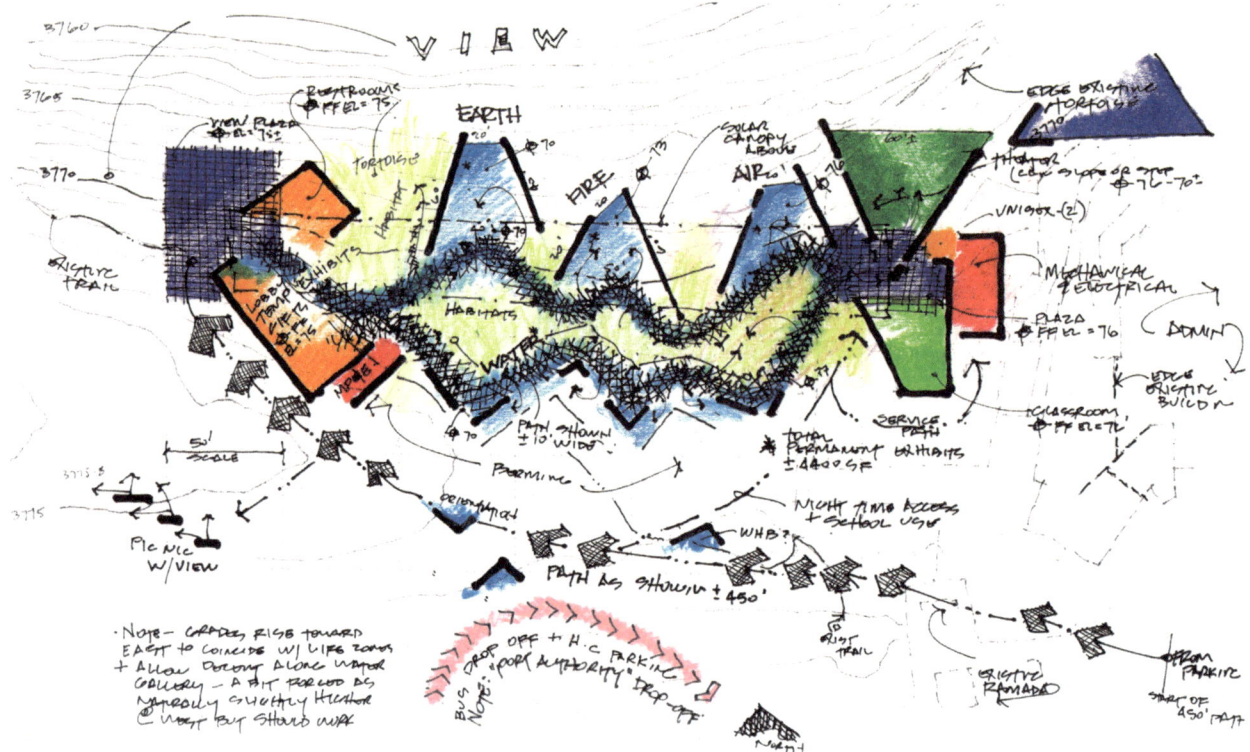

Concept sketch: 'Thread of Life'

The visitor center provides an experience that promotes community interaction and instills in individuals a sense of personal responsibility for their land's wellbeing. The entry plaza, outdoor amphitheater and exhibits all bring people together around a common environmental interest. The ecological design elements of the facility are visibly expressed and most offer tactile interaction aimed to educate visitors on the importance of resource conservation. The focus is on giving visitors new insight into simple strategies that can be implemented in their own community to reduce dependence on non-renewable resources.

Existing parking areas have been utilized. No new parking capacity has been added to the site. Carpool, bus tour, and alternative fuel vehicle parking space has been made available for groups coming from nearby Las Vegas and bike racks are provided for the many visitors who ride to the site from surrounding communities.

02 / Solar collection wall used for conditioning interior space
03 / Elevated platfrom providing 360° view of surrounding Red Rock Canyon Conservation Area
04 / Minimal visual impact of new visitor center on landscape

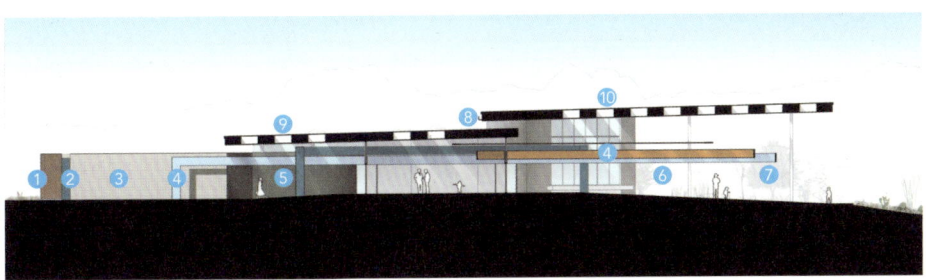

① Transpired solar collector
② Drip fountain
③ Exposed split-face concrete masonry
④ Graphic interpretive bands for wayfinding
⑤ Transition space/Entry
⑥ Shaded outdoor gathering space
⑦ Exterior exhibits and natural habitats
⑧ Gutter
⑨ Skylights (daylight transition space)
⑩ Skylights (shaded gathering space)

Section A

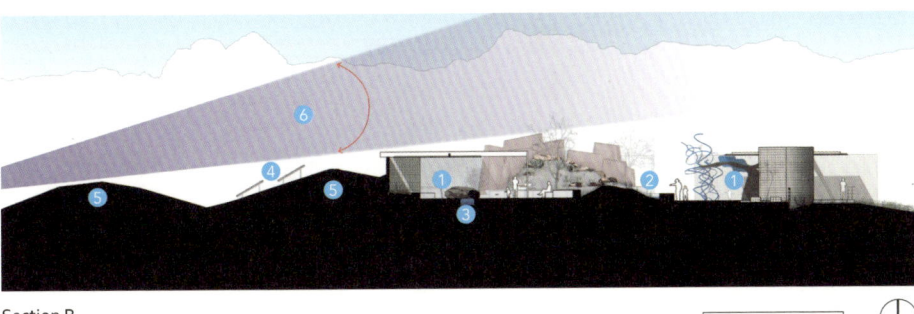

① Exhibits housed in microclimates
② Natural habitats
③ Desert spring exhibit
④ Exposed split-face concrete masonry
⑤ 60 kW photovoltaic array
⑥ Earth berms to reduce visual impact of site

Section B

0 — 32m

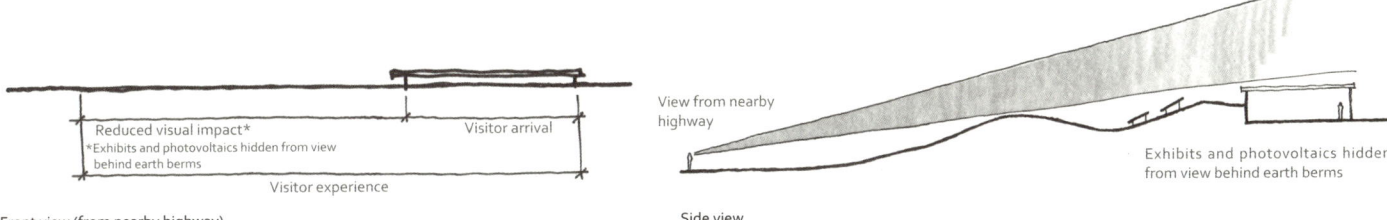

Front view (from nearby highway)

Side view

View diagrams

1. Entry plaza
2. Transition space/Entry
3. Temporary exhibits
4. Classroom with patio
5. Information desk
6. Gift shop
7. Arrival area
8. Panorama window
9. Outdoor amphitheater
10. Shaded gathering space
11. Earth pavilion
12. Tortoise habitat
13. Fire pavilion
14. Air pavilion
15. Four elements exhibit
16. 360° view deck
17. Cliff wall exhibit
18. Water walk
19. Natural habitats
20. Desert spring exhibit
21. Canyon creek exhibit
22. Desert ecosystem exhibit
23. Water harvesting storage
24. Earth berms
25. 55 kW photovoltaic array
26. Transpired solar collector
27. Picnic area
a. Outdoor exhibits area
b. Visitor arrival building

Site plan 0 40m

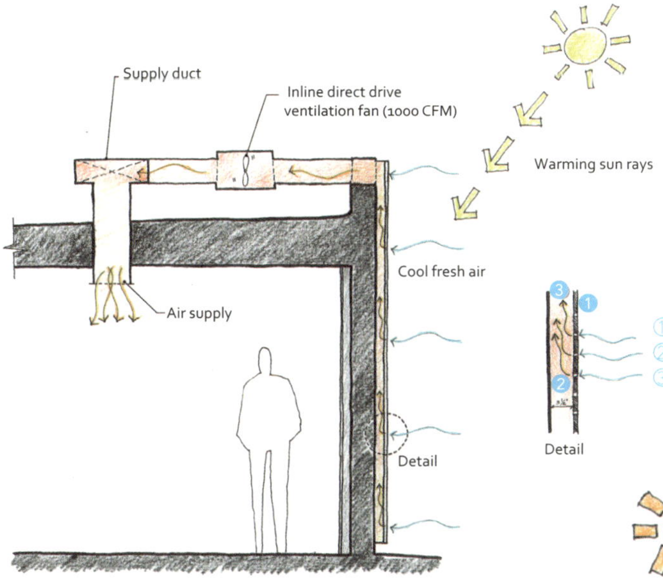
Supply duct
Inline direct drive ventilation fan (1000 CFM)
Warming sun rays
Cool fresh air
Air supply
Detail
3
1
2

Detail

① Perforated metal panels of solar wall heated by sun
② Ventilation fan creating negative air pressure to draw fresh air into system
③ As air is drawn through the perforations in the metal panels, it is heated and rises to the top of the wall, where it is distributed throughout the building interior

Diagrams of transpired solar wall

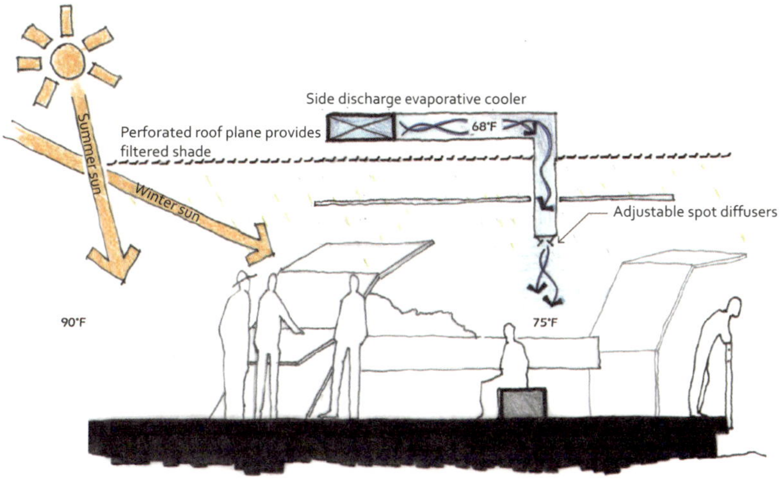
Side discharge evaporative cooler
68°F
Perforated roof plane provides filtered shade
Adjustable spot diffusers
Summer sun
Winter sun
90°F
75°F

Diagrams of tempered microclimate

05 / Large roof with skylights to provide thermal and visual transition zones
06 / Exhibit space utilizing wing walls that block summer sun and cold winter wind

06

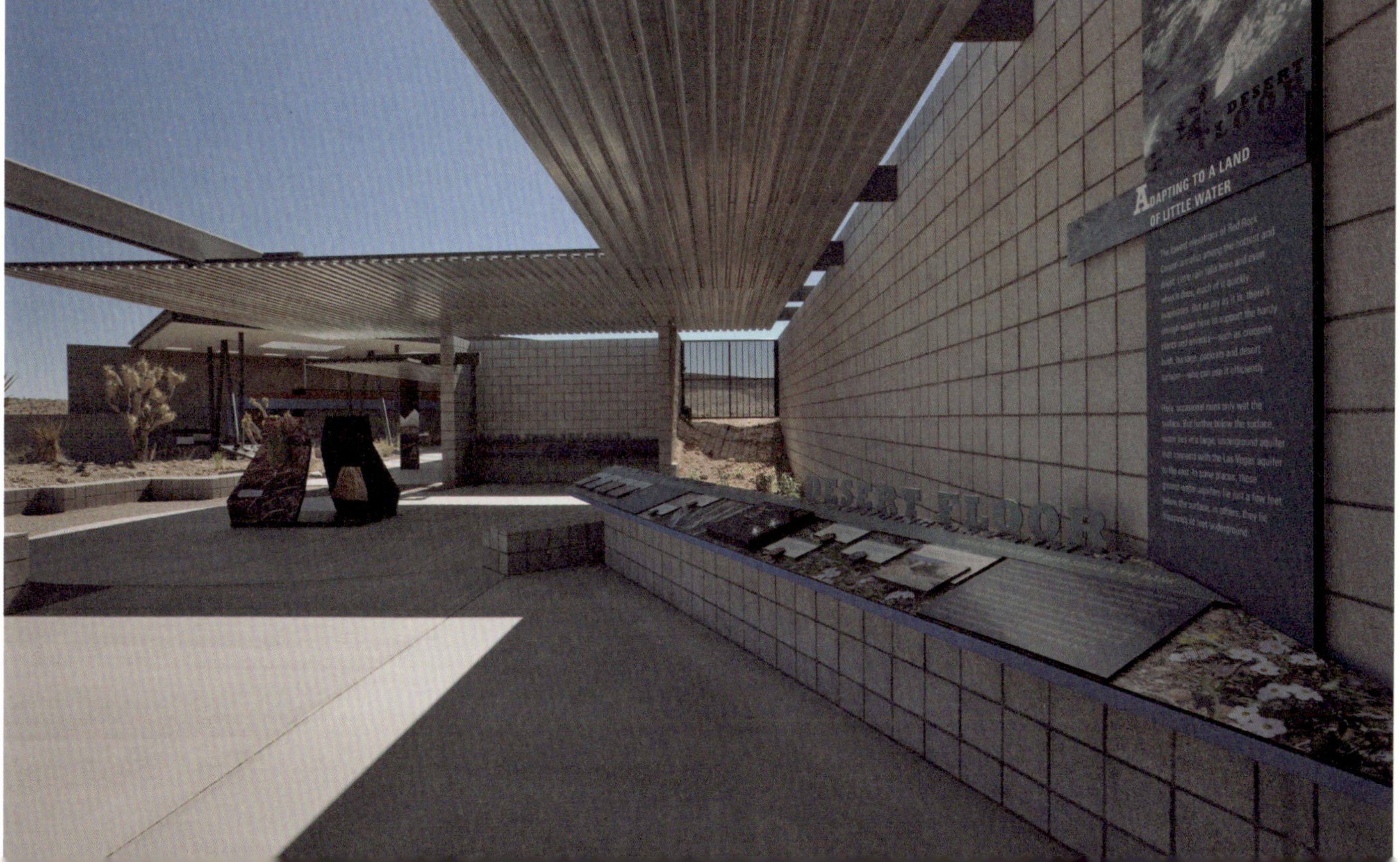
DESERT FLOOR
ADAPTING TO A LAND OF LITTLE WATER
DESERT FLOOR

94

07 / Fire and water pavilions
08 / Air pavilion

Water harvesting diagram

① Roof
② Rainfall and snowmelt
③ Gutter
④ Rainwater storage
⑤ Distribution to exhibit interpretation
⑥ Distribution to native drought-tolerant vegetation

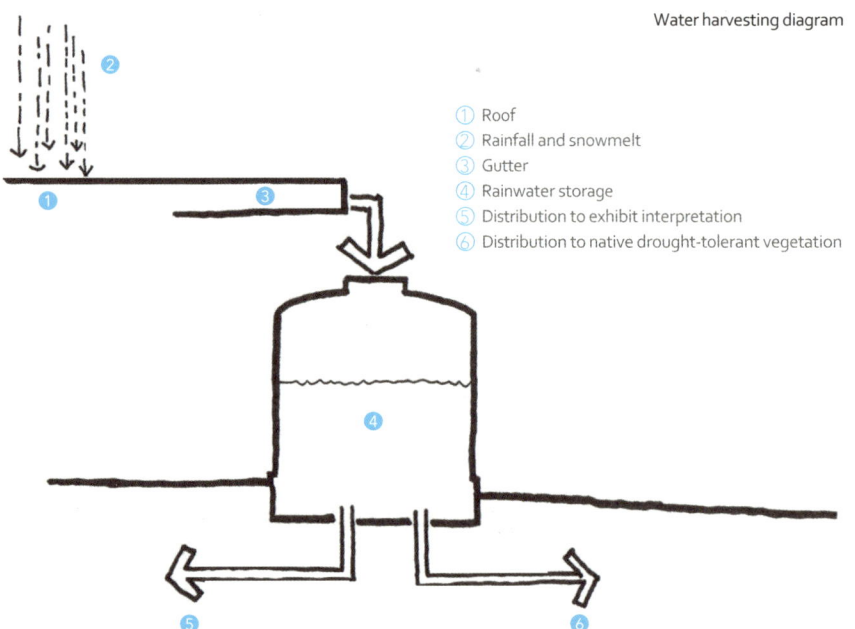

① Cold water is drawn into the solar collectors' evacuated glass tubes
② As the sun's solar energy heats the water, it begins to rise to the top of the tubes
③ The heated water at the top of the tubes is directed to a storage tank where it can supply hot water to buildings and help preheat water for the mechinary

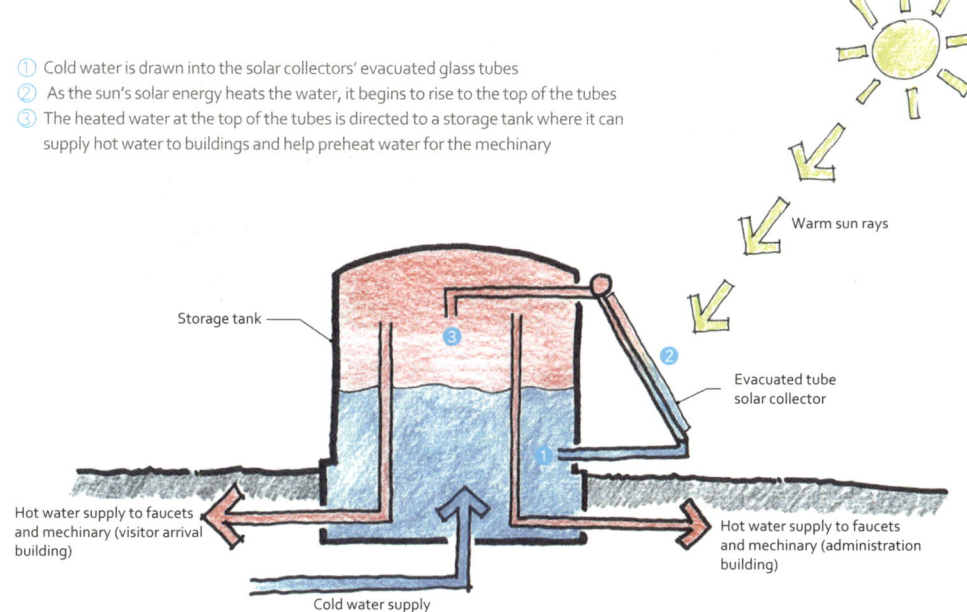

Diagram of solar water heating system

09 / Natural habitats around project form basis for educational exhibits
10 / 80-foot-long (24.4-meter-long) window providing dramatic connection to outdoors

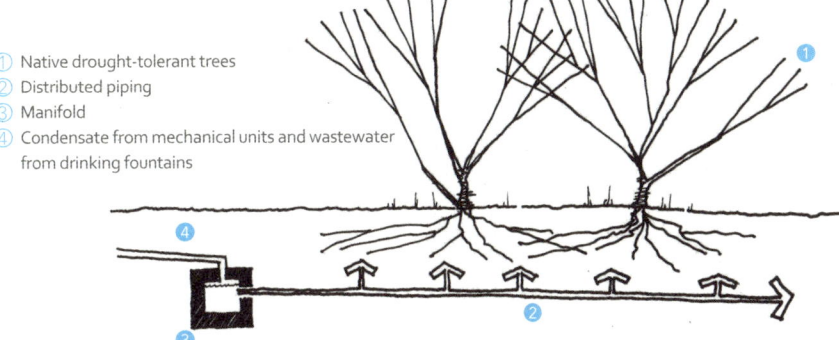

① Fountains use harvested rainwater
② Native drought-tolerant vegetation to reduce runoff
③ Bioswales collect and clean rainwater

Cross-section of natural habitats

① Native drought-tolerant trees
② Distributed piping
③ Manifold
④ Condensate from mechanical units and wastewater from drinking fountains

① Runoff from hardscape surfaces
② French drain
③ Distributed perforated piping
④ Native drought-tolerant vegetation

Water harvesting (direct irrigation)

Naples Botanical Garden Visitor Center

Location / Florida, USA
Area / 14,000 square feet (1301 square meters)
Completion / 2014
Architect / Lake|Flato Architects
Photography / Lara Swimmer

The Naples Botanical Garden Visitor Center sits delicately upon a world-class, 160-acre (65 hectare) botanical garden. The vision for the gardens sought to preserve 160-acre (65 hectare) natural resources from conversion to urban development space. The visitor center continues a legacy of preservation by partnering with the local ecosystem in an environmentally responsible way. Wooded pavilions crafted from local and durable sinker cypress entwined throughout lush gardens and plant collections to create an immersive and engaging experience for visitors and researchers as well as an enticing venue for events.

As visitors enter through an intimate walkway that meanders through plant life, buildings are scaled as a backdrop to the larger landscape and the program is broken down into a series of smaller buildings so visitors will be continually engaged by the restored natural habitats. The visitor center has 14,000 square feet (1301 square meters) of interior space for ticketing, retail, exhibits, and café/dining, with 16,000 square feet (1486 square meters) of exterior areas. Exterior circulation features trellised gathering spaces with the center immersed in restored natural habitats and 'Gardens with Latitude'—lush vegetation from seven tropical regions weaving throughout the park as a demonstration of habitat diversity.

The garden's spine, a corridor of aquatic plants known as the River of Grass, pays reverence to the Everglades—South Florida's most dominant landscape feature—while filtering storm water at the heart of the garden. Walkways thoughtfully terminate onto pavilions that overhang and float in lush fields of flora. Providing strong contextual place to the garden, a wood-paneled prow above the cultivated greenery gives visitors views of Everglade palms below and distant glimpses of saw grass wetlands beyond.

01 / View of entrance
02 / Pathway

① Children's garden
② Brazilian garden
③ Caribbean garden
④ Asian garden
⑤ River of grass
⑥ Healing garden
⑦ Florida garden

Site plan

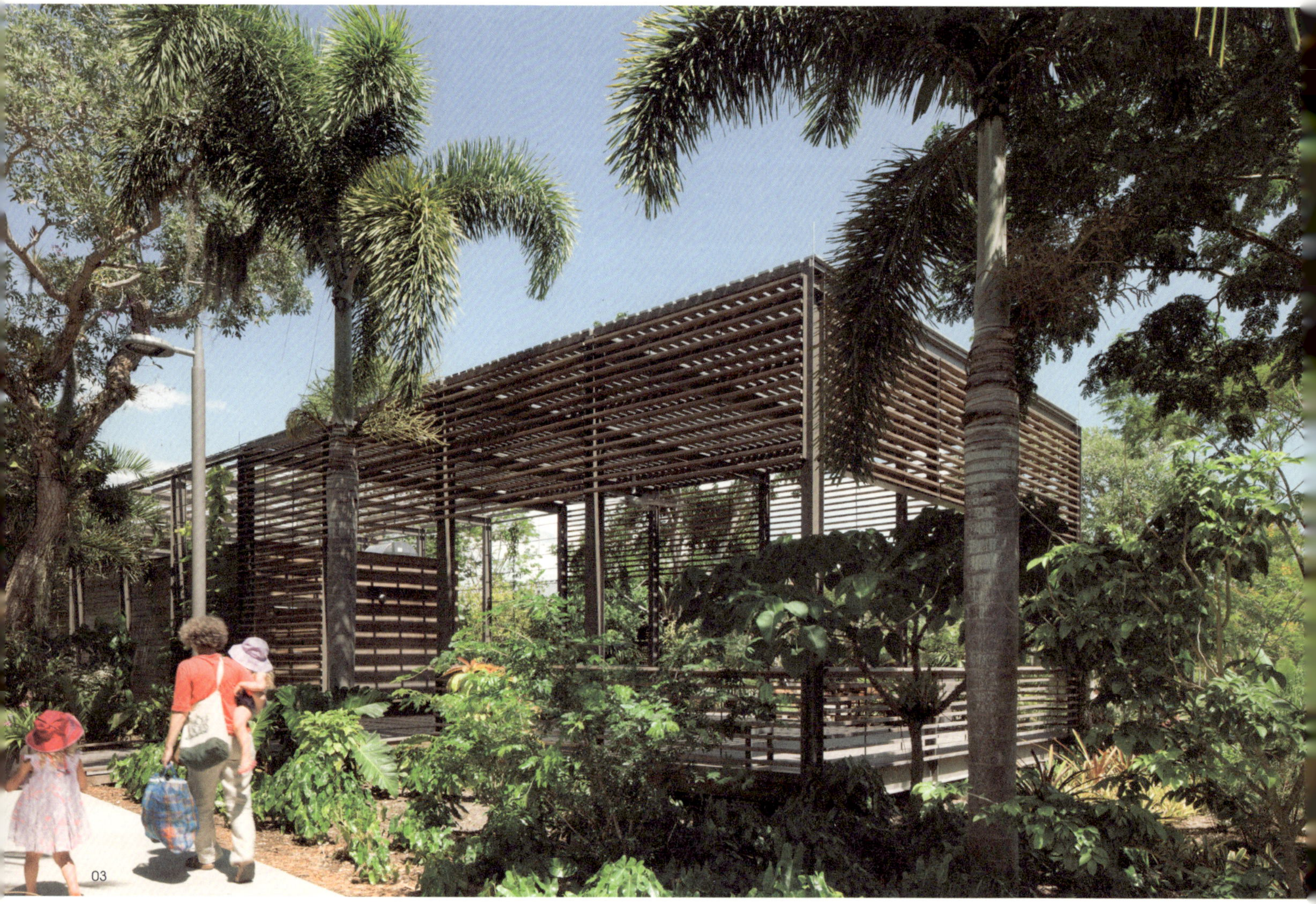

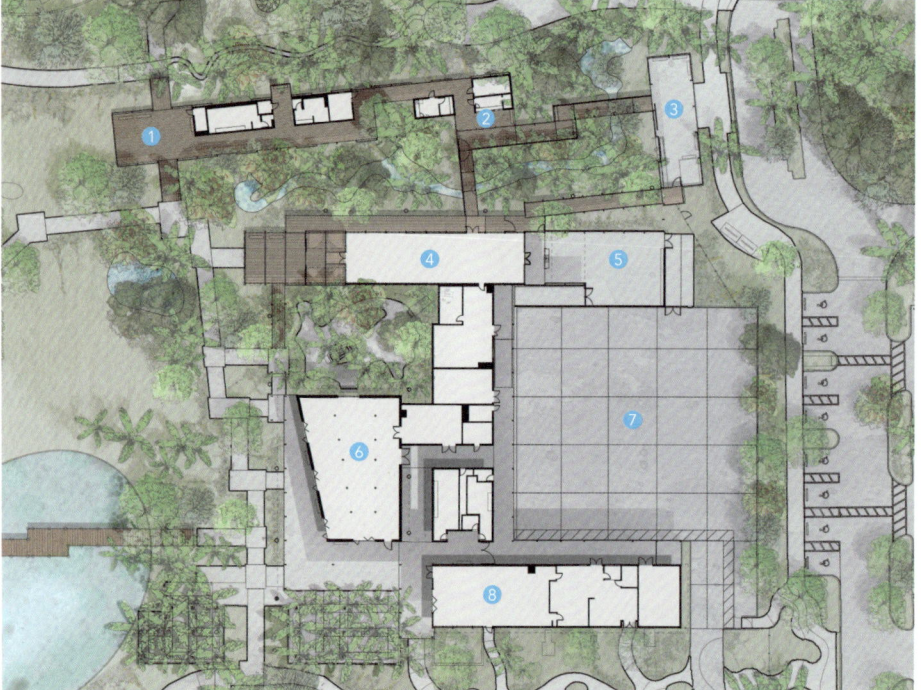

03

1. Pier
2. Ticketing room
3. Entry
4. Retail shop
5. Plant shop
6. Auditorium
7. Service room
8. Café

Plan

03 / Vegetation around entrance
04 / Corridor of aquatic plants
05 / Walkway
06 / Wooded pavilion

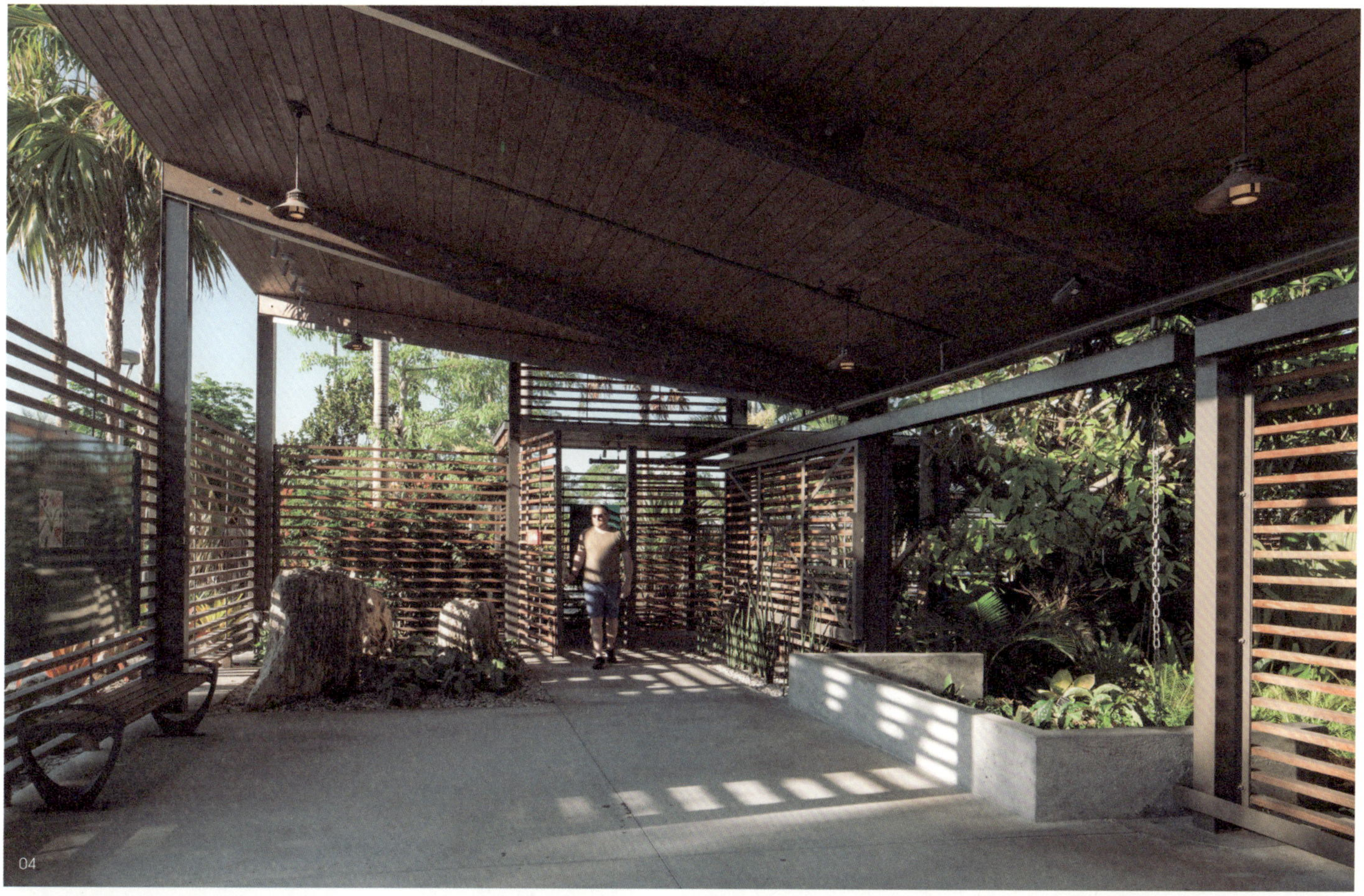

04

05

06

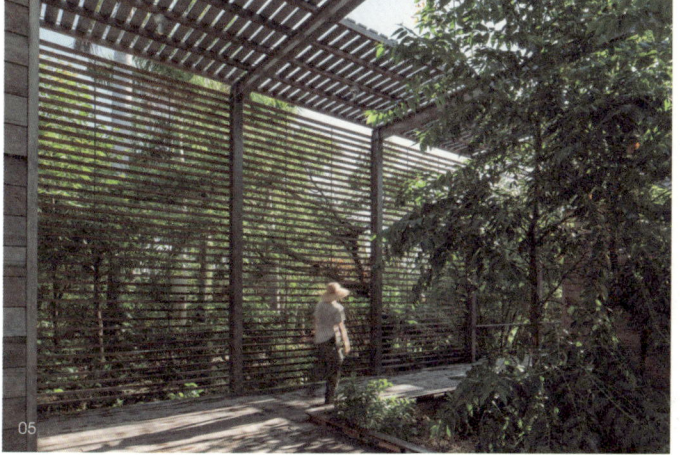

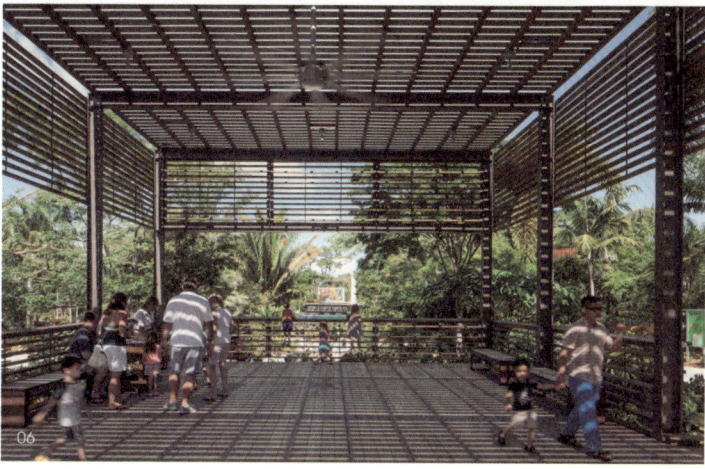

07

08

07 / Retail and exhibit area
08 / Café and dining
09-10 / Corridor of aquatic plants

Villers Abbey Visitor Center

Location / Villers-la-Ville, Belgium
Area / 4521 square feet (420 square meters)
Completion / 2016
Architect / Binario Architects
Landscape / PIGEON OCHEJ PAYSAGE
Scenography / L'Escaut Architectures SCRL
Photography / François Lichtlé
Budget / €3,277,180 Excl. VAT

The Villers-La-ville abbey is the largest ruins in Europe, covering 89 acres (36 hectares). The site is divided by the N275 national road, destroying the site's original logic and unity. Architecture, through a combination of landscaping and scenography, tries to reunite the full Cistercian composition plan. The project creates a sequence from the parking to the ruins, preparing the visitors.

A newly designed path links the visitor center to all areas of the site. The ground floor of the mill has a shop and reception area, while the first floor features a large model of the abbey and a media room. The different spaces are connected by CorTen steel walkways emerging in the mill and reaching the hill across the new footbridge. Outside, the route features a floor panels with dates recording the history of the abbey until the path reaches the garden. There, a footbridge crosses over the national road and finally leads down into the ruins.

A range of new materials was chosen in order to strengthen the unity between the architecture, landscape and scenography on display at the site. The materials create a strong visual link while enhancing the historic heritage. We used CorTen steel, exposed aggregate concrete, board-formed concrete, earth-formed concrete and

01 / South façade of former mill and view on main entrance of visitor center
02 / View of ruins from garden's pharmacy

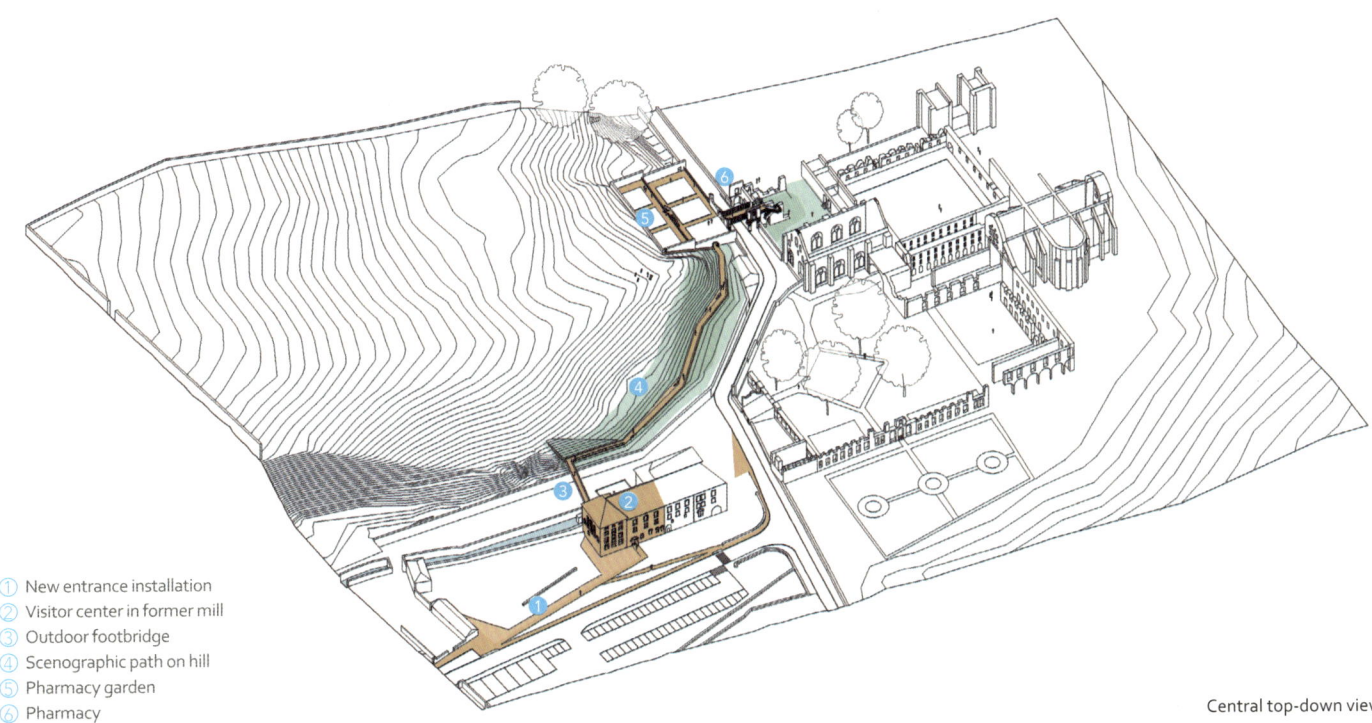

① New entrance installation
② Visitor center in former mill
③ Outdoor footbridge
④ Scenographic path on hill
⑤ Pharmacy garden
⑥ Pharmacy

Central top-down view

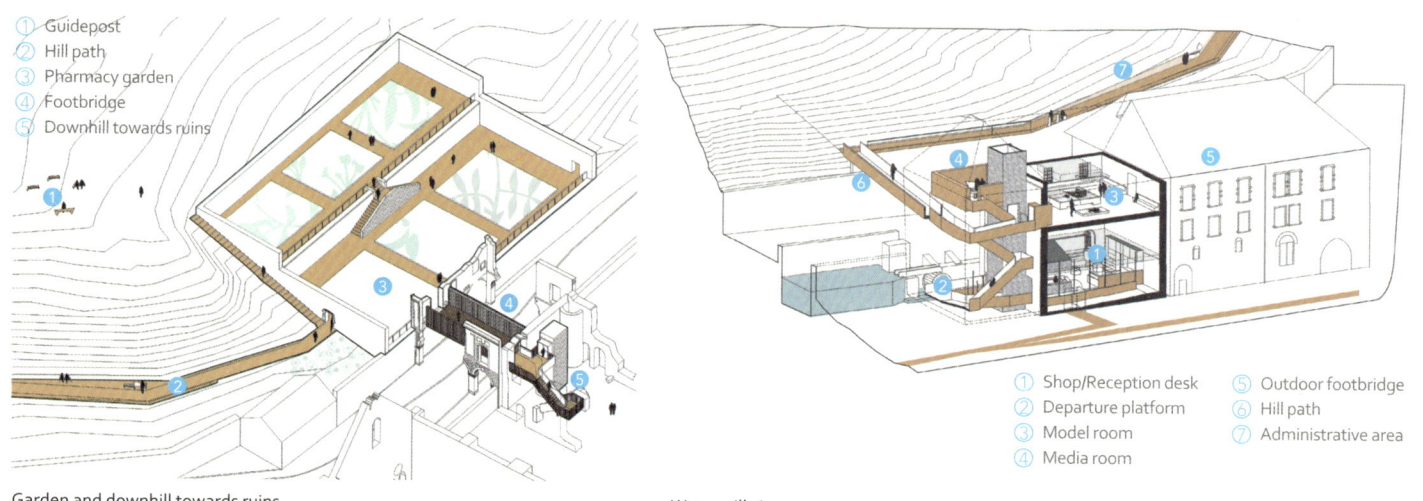

Garden and downhill towards ruins

① Guidepost
② Hill path
③ Pharmacy garden
④ Footbridge
⑤ Downhill towards ruins

Watermill view

① Shop/Reception desk
② Departure platform
③ Model room
④ Media room
⑤ Outdoor footbridge
⑥ Hill path
⑦ Administrative area

solid wood (for the indoor and outdoor footbridges). Inside the watermill, the new bay windows are covered with an anodized aluminum screen filter and reflect light.

Various additions build upon the existing site. The watermill now has a new entryway, a reception desk, a shop, a discovery path, a media room, and a room for models. The outdoor renovations extended discovery path, added new viewing areas and orientation maps, restored the former garden, and built new footbridge over the national road towards the ruins. A new water wheel has been installed to supply electricity. The Villers Abbey Visitor Center is a large-scale remodeling of the largest abbey ruins in Europe.

03 / Panoramic view of ruins from new pathway new hill path
04 / Panoramic view of orientation table map
05 / New footbridge linking former mill and hill
06 / View of new hill path

07-08 / Staircase and external elevator going to ruins
09 / New footbridge over national road dividing the Cistercian site
10 / View of footbridge linking watermill and hill

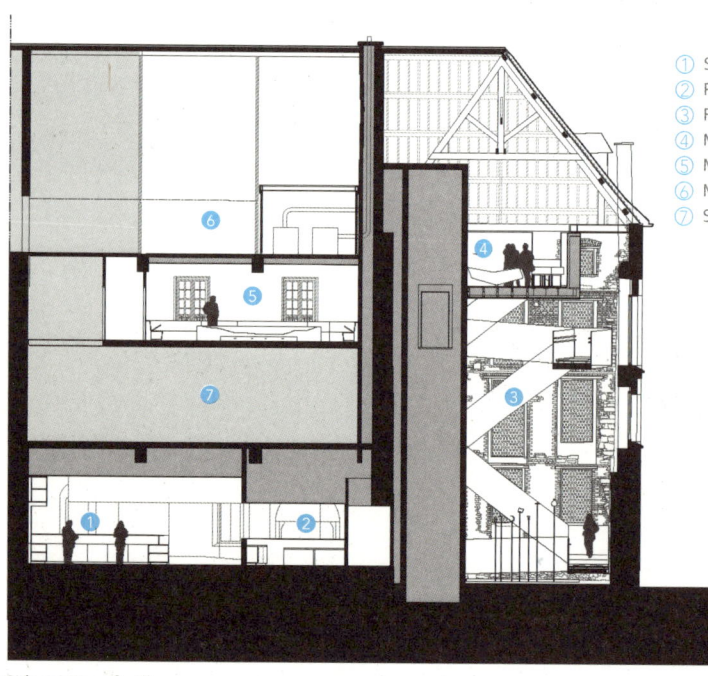

① Shop
② Reception desk
③ Footbridge leading outside
④ Media room
⑤ Model room
⑥ Maintainence room
⑦ Shared multifunctional room

Side section of mill 1

Side section of mill 2

① Departure platform
② Footbridge leading to outside
③ Media room
④ Outdoor footbridge
⑤ Hill path
⑥ Electrical supply

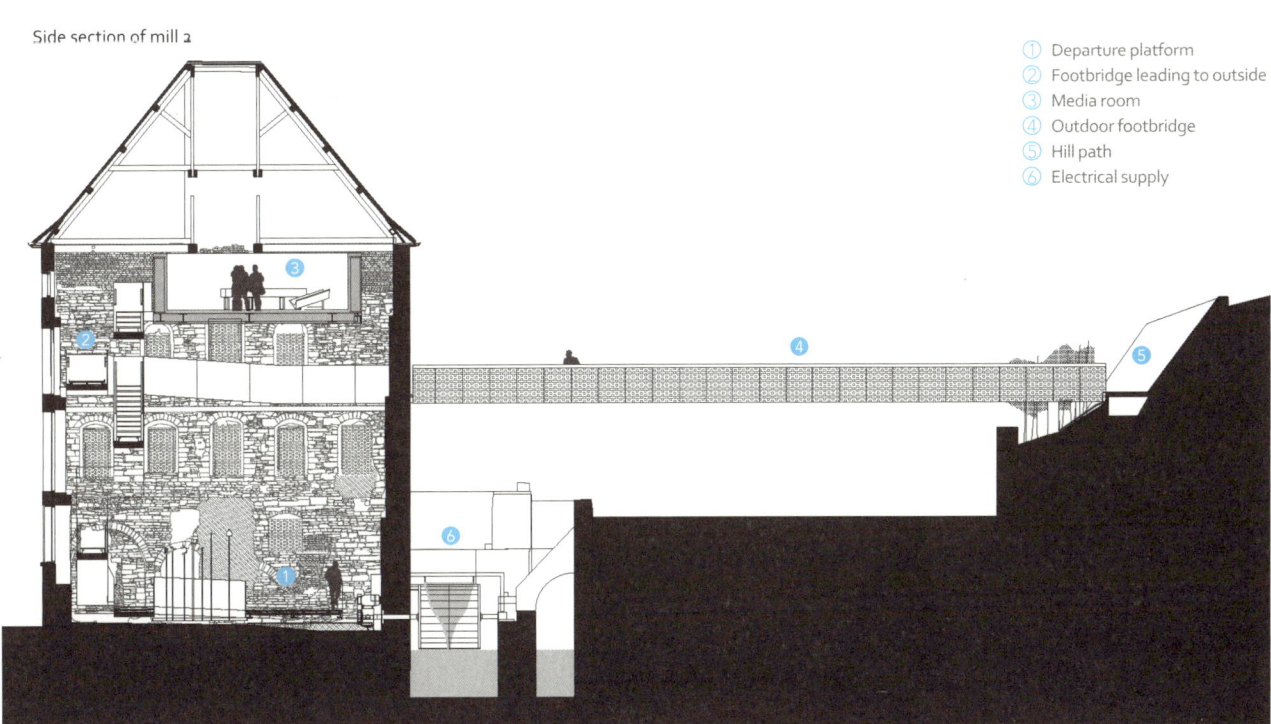

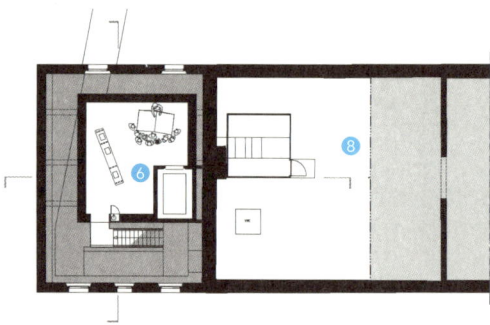

Third-floor plan

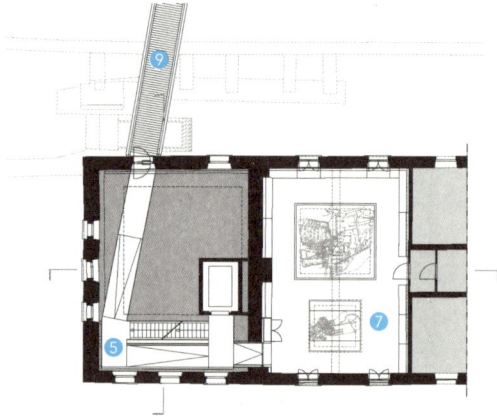

Second-floor plan

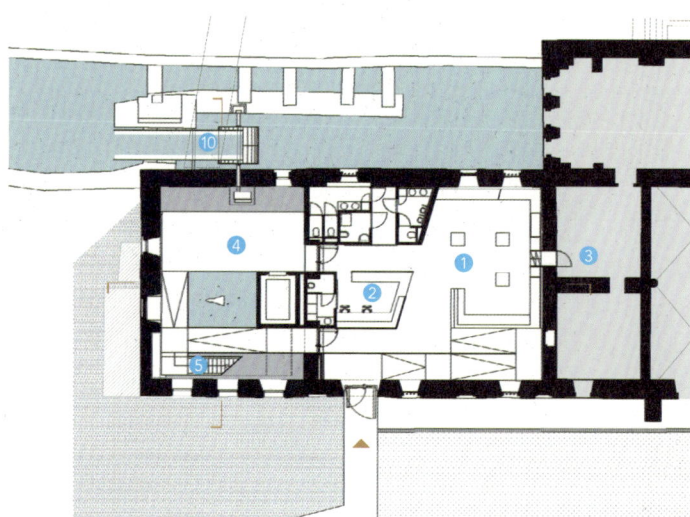

First-floor plan

① Shop
② Reception desk
③ Connection with restaurant
④ Departure platform
⑤ Footbridge leading outside
⑥ Media room
⑦ Model room
⑧ Maintainence room
⑨ Outdoor footbridge
⑩ Electrical supply

11 / Model room in former mill
12 / Attic media room
13 / Shop entrance

14

15

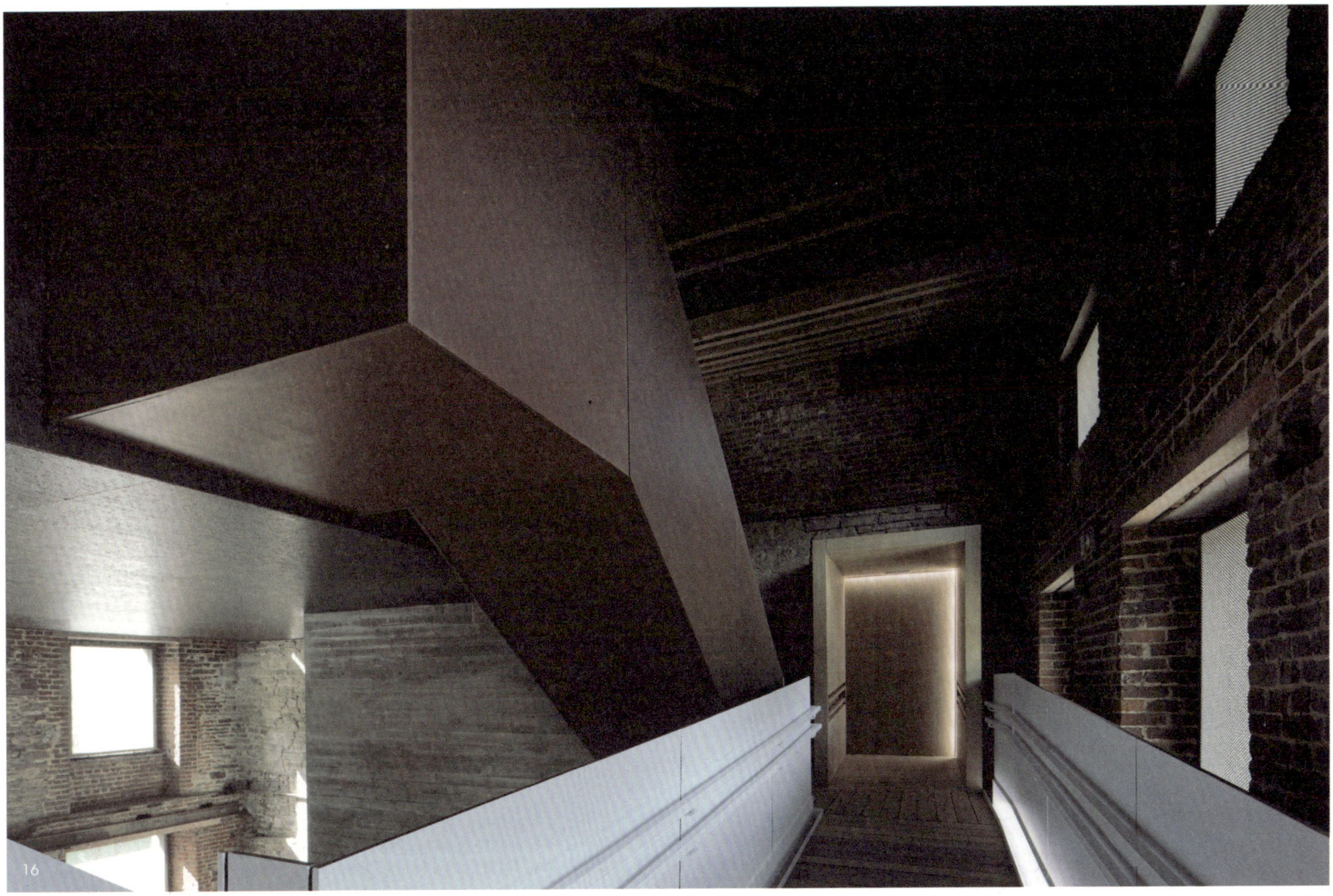

16

17

18

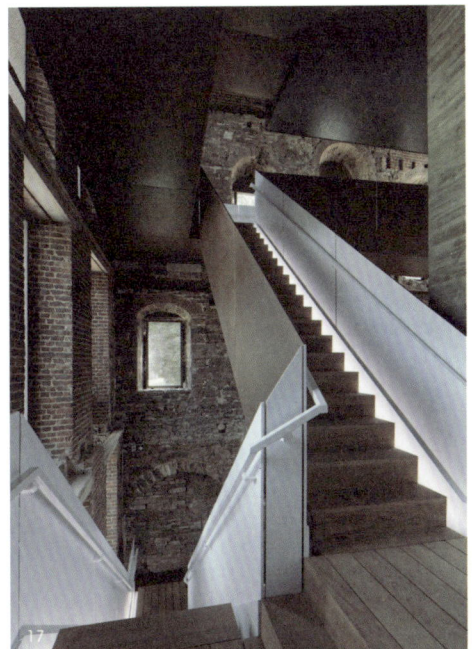

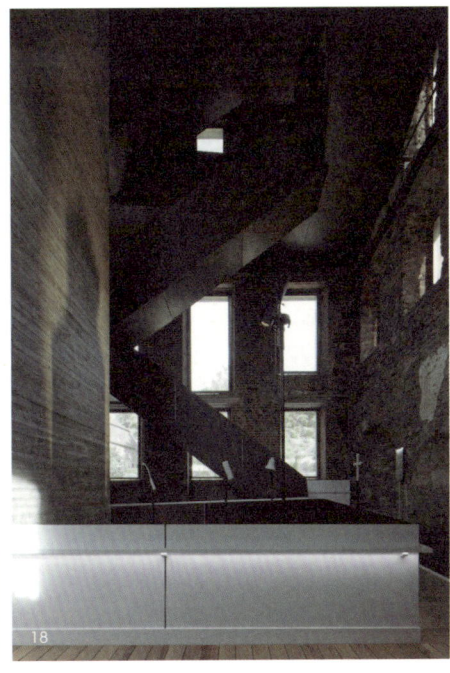

14 / Shop
15 / Information desk
16-18 / Staircase in former watermill

Coedy Brenin Visitor Center

Location / Snowdonia National Park, Wales
Area / 4306 square feet (400 square meters)
Completion / 2013
Architect / Architype
Photography / Leigh Simpson
Client / Forestry Commission Wales
Budget / £1.2 million

In the South Snowdonia National Park, the new building is linked to the current visitor center by an overhead bridge and has been built using a revolutionary construction technique, Brettstapel, which could open up an exciting new market for Welsh timber.

The building, which was completed in June 2013, has been made entirely from homegrown timber and sets high standards in energy efficiency by using high levels of insulation, excellent air tightness and natural light. The 4306 square feet (400 square meters) extension includes a new bike shop and the public can hire facility on the ground floor, with a multi-functional conference room and café area and much needed 24-hour access public restrooms on the first floor.

The concept behind the building's design was derived from feedback from the consultations, the design aspirations and as a response to the site and the location of the building. The elements—the new building and the proposal's extension of the entrance—were designed to integrate with and be located next to the existing building whilst being distinct from it. Both have an elegant and simple form and take inspiration from the forest and landscape. The new building sits separately from the existing building. Its two-story form is partially dug into the ground and follows the direction of the hillside's contours. Its form is simple and emerges out of the landscape. To the north, the building is closed up and sheltered while, to the south, it opens up to make the most of the far-reaching views and natural daylight.

Side section

01 / Main entrance
02 / Information area

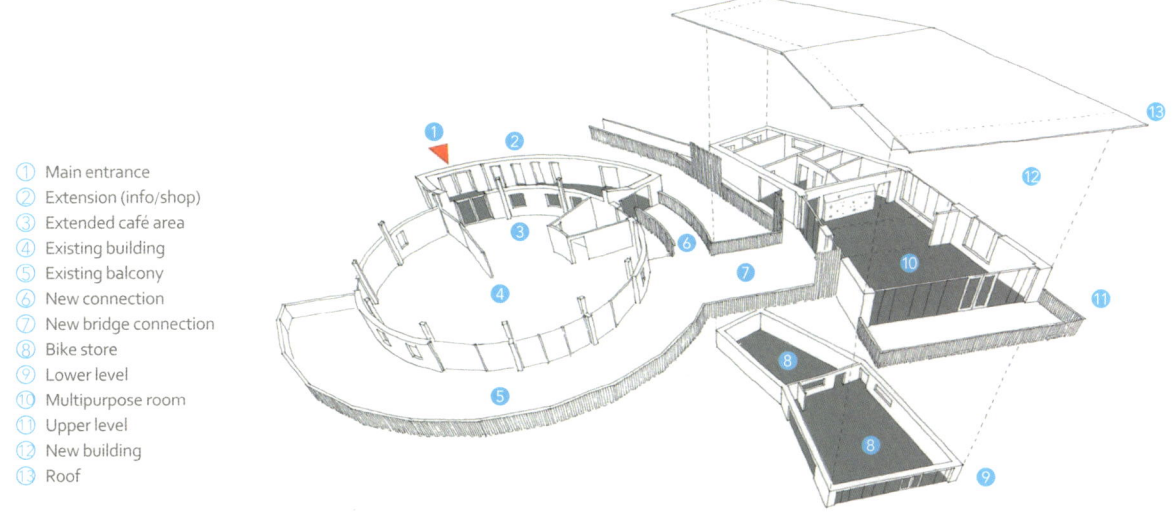

① Main entrance
② Extension (info/shop)
③ Extended café area
④ Existing building
⑤ Existing balcony
⑥ New connection
⑦ New bridge connection
⑧ Bike store
⑨ Lower level
⑩ Multipurpose room
⑪ Upper level
⑫ New building
⑬ Roof

Building sketch

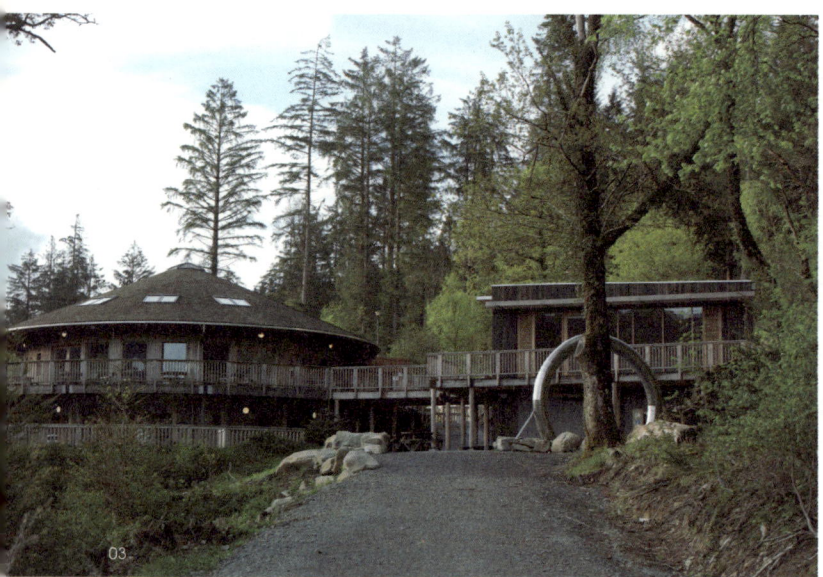

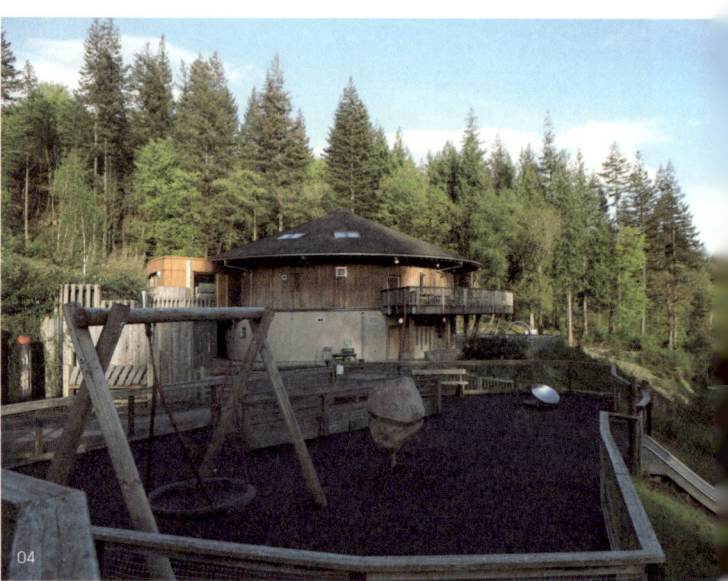

03

04

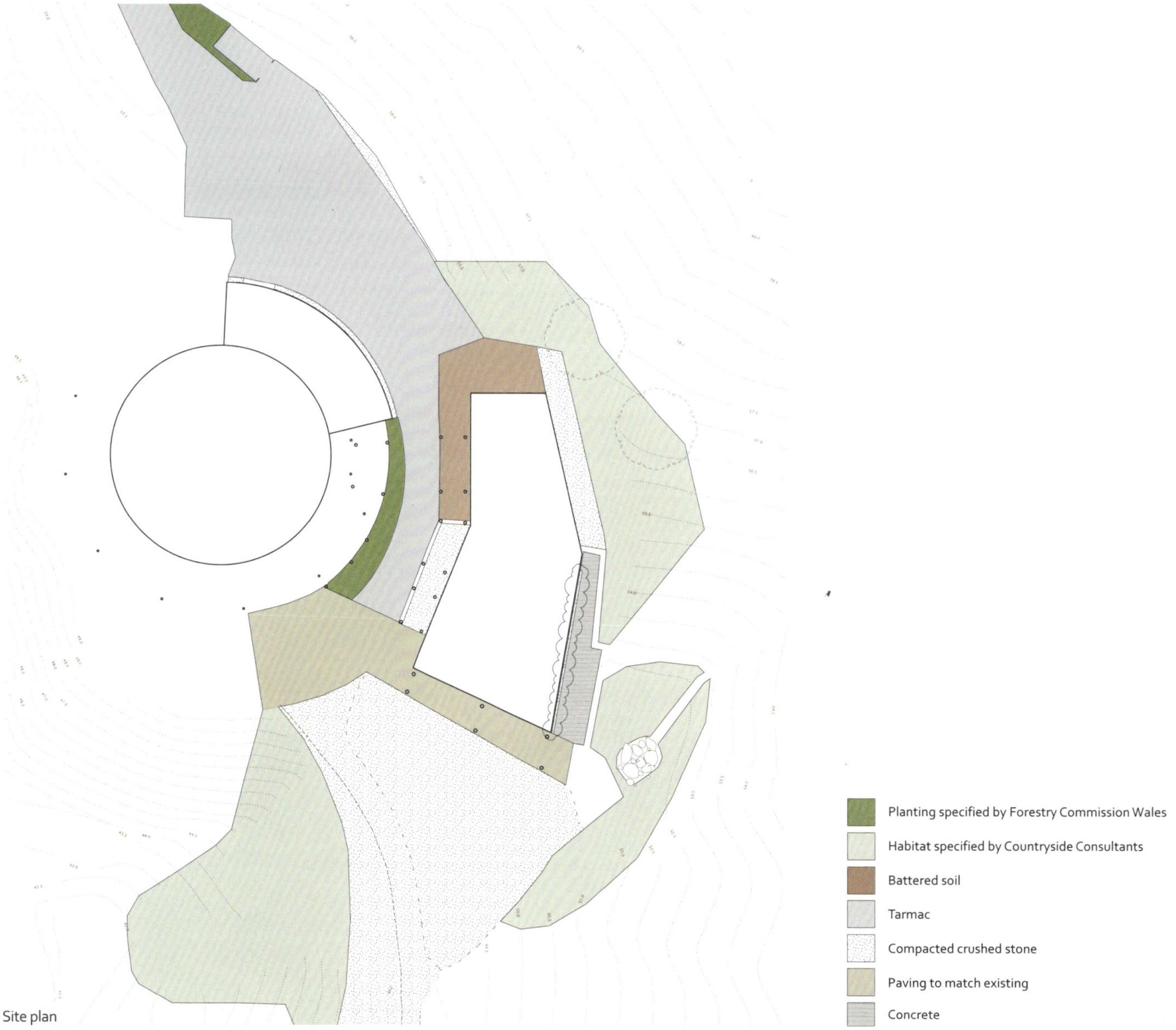
Planting specified by Forestry Commission Wales
Habitat specified by Countryside Consultants
Battered soil
Tarmac
Compacted crushed stone
Paving to match existing
Concrete

Site plan

03 / Extended café area
04 / Existing balcony
05 / New connection
06 / Bike store

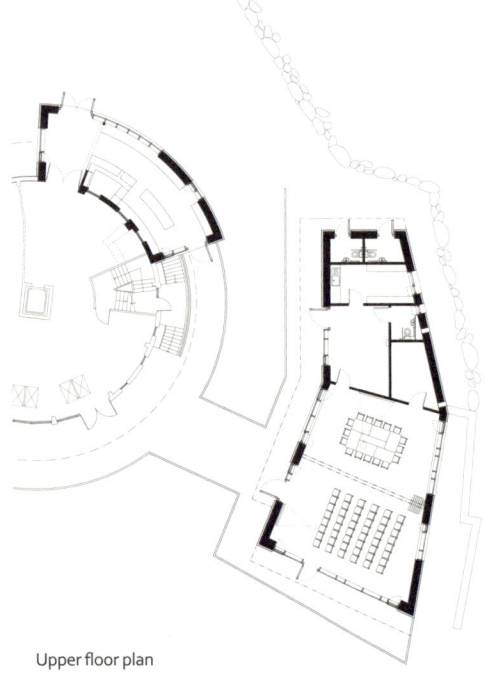

Upper floor plan

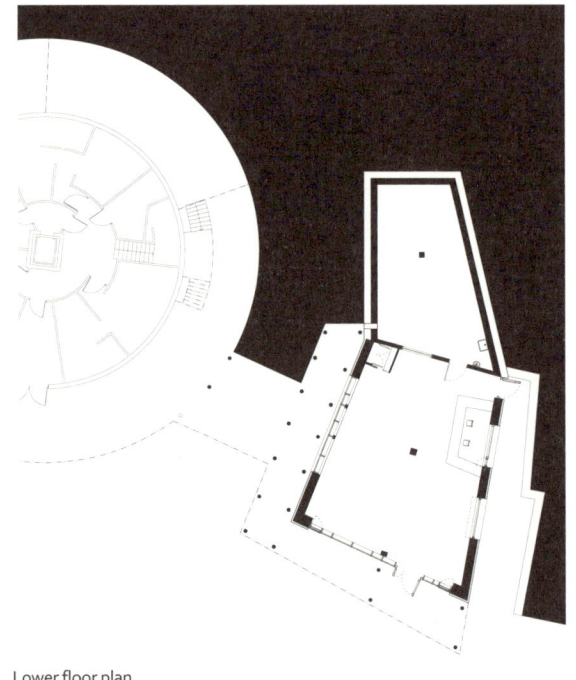

Lower floor plan

07 / Multipurpose room
08 / Roof
09 / Upper floor
10 / Lower floor

08

09

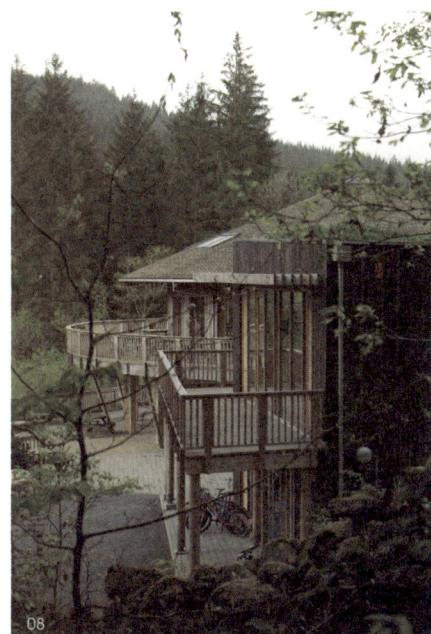

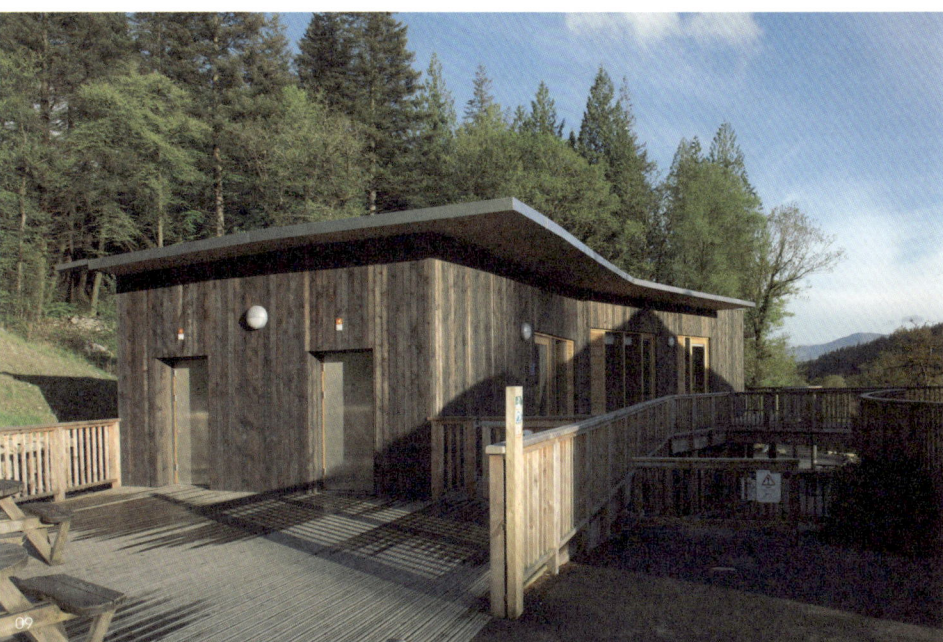

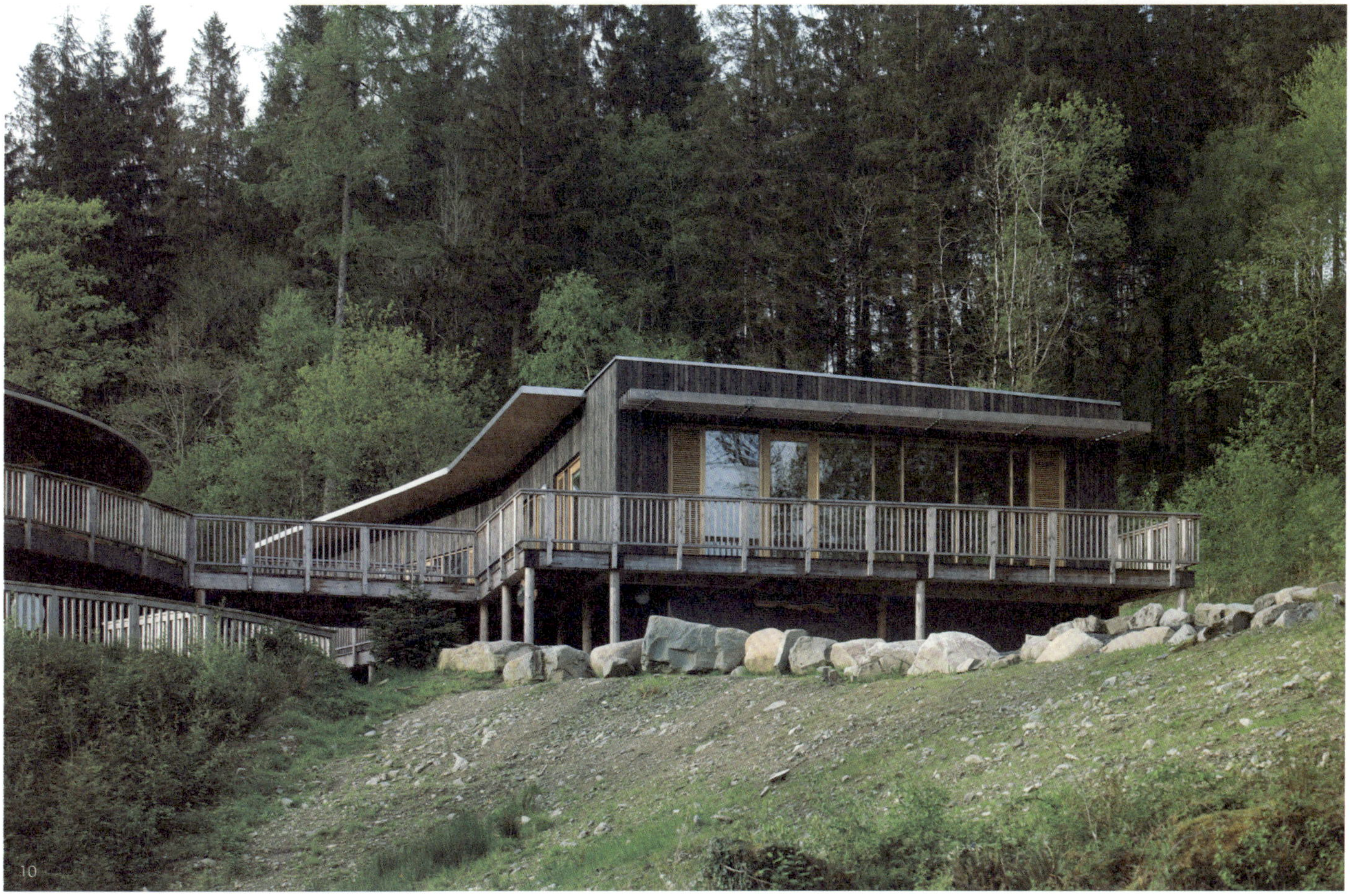

10

11 / Exhibit area
12 / Gathering area
13 / Interior details
14-15 / Room entrance

12

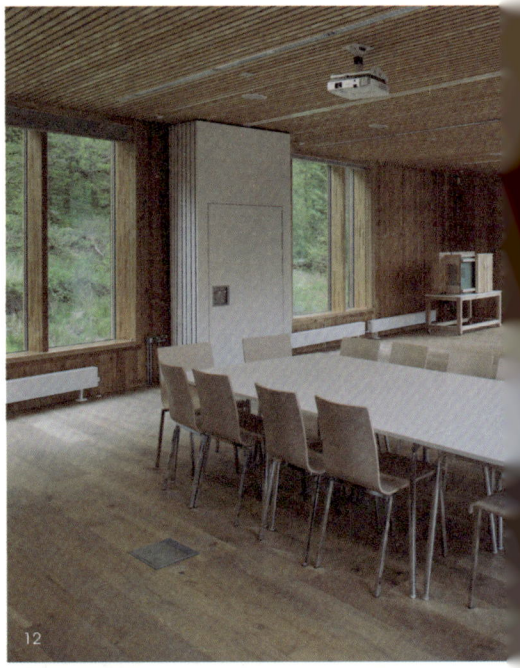

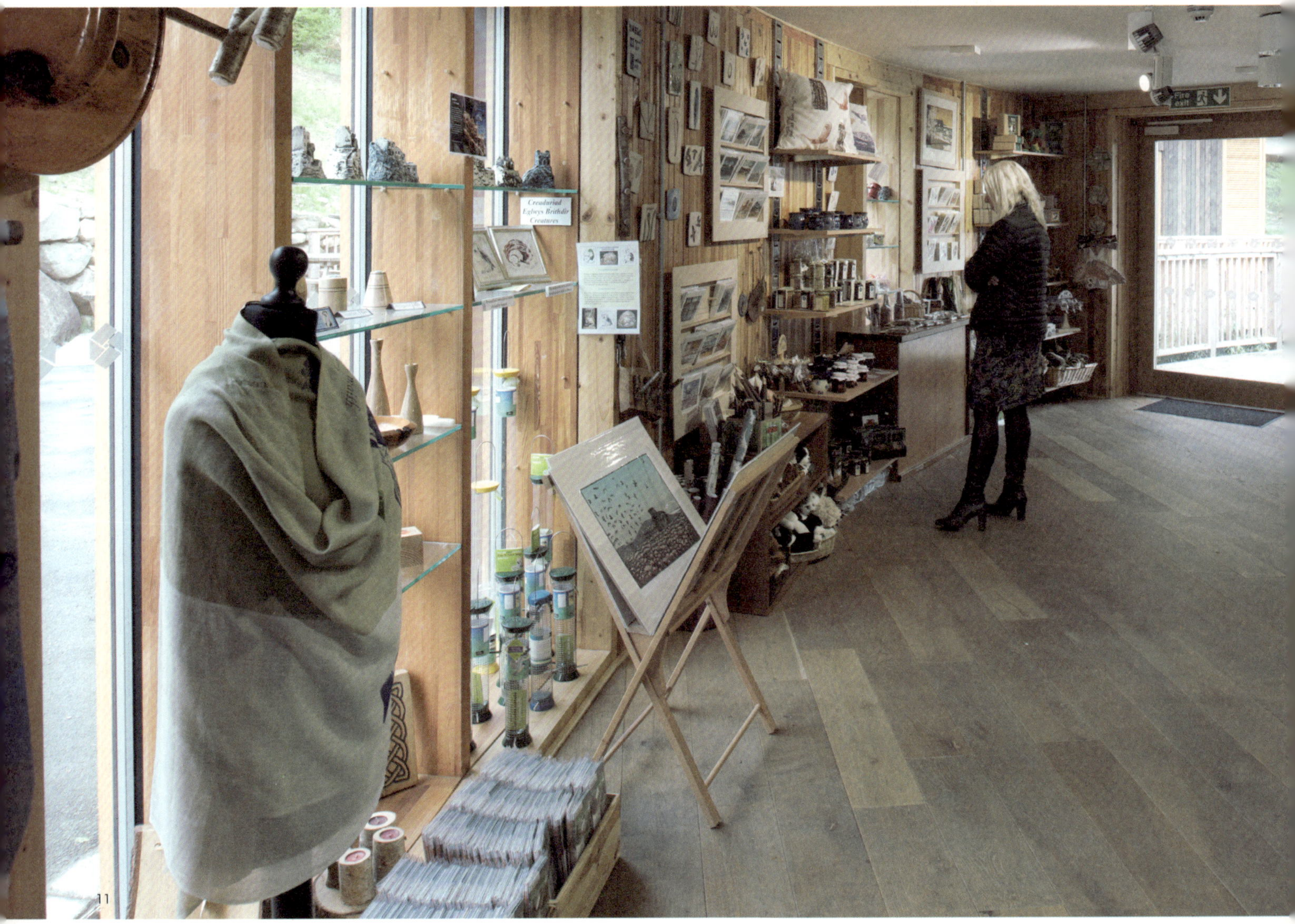

11

Cabañeros National Park Visitors Center

Location / Horcajo de los Montes, Ciudad Real, Spain
Area / 49,912 square feet (4637 square meters)
Architect / Álvaro Planchuelo
Photography / Ricardo Santonja, Alberto Cubas

The Cabañeros National Park Visitors Center is a public architectural project whose main objective is to promote eco-tourism through information, exhibitions, research and careful protection of this natural space's main values. One of the main features of this center is that the architecture and the interactive museum, from the beginning, were designed simultaneously by the same team, so that their content complements each other and shows the unique biodiversity that exists in Cabañeros. The content is conveyed in a rigorously scientific manner yet also in a engaging way at the same time. The center supports the National Park, offering a gateway to knowledge and enjoyment for visitors.

The main idea in implementing the different sections of the center was display the landscape, from the access road to the Sierra del Gavilán on the horizon, gradually immersing visitors in nature. The structural and construction design elements used were inspired by nature itself.

The sections in the foreground represent the most 'human' or artificial environment and thus, primarily use load-bearing walls with white reinforced concrete, interpreting the typology of the traditionally built environment, building a series of white structures linked by courtyards (patio-corral) to form a succession of full and empty spaces. The hall, the library, and the cafeteria together form the entrance courtyard façade of the main building. Here the concrete walls are crowned with perimeter windows that make the slab of the sloping roof to 'float,' suggesting the shape of a bird of prey, a shape derived from the isolated groups of inclined columns, which are inspired by the small woods of evergreen oaks that are scattered in grasslands of the Park.

On the third level, the walls protrude from the half-buried space and display an exhibition, which is covered with local stone, resembling a crag over the mountains. The roof is flat and landscaped with native plants. During construction, special attention was taken not to damage the nearby vegetation. That way, the evergreen oaks close to the structure contribute to hiding the architectural disturbance, blending it into the landscape.

The last plane is covered by olive groves, scrub bushes, and the imposing Sierra del Gavilan in the background, now in the National Park, with pairs of black vultures and other birds of prey a frequent site flying over the building.

The design gives priority to the protecting the building from excessive sunlight to avoid air conditioning usage during hot months, which is a common element of increased consumption. The passive design through architectural measures, such as volumetric fractionation, orientation of buildings, subterranean land use as thermal

01 / Aerial view

① Local road
② Visitor center
③ Reservoir

Site plan

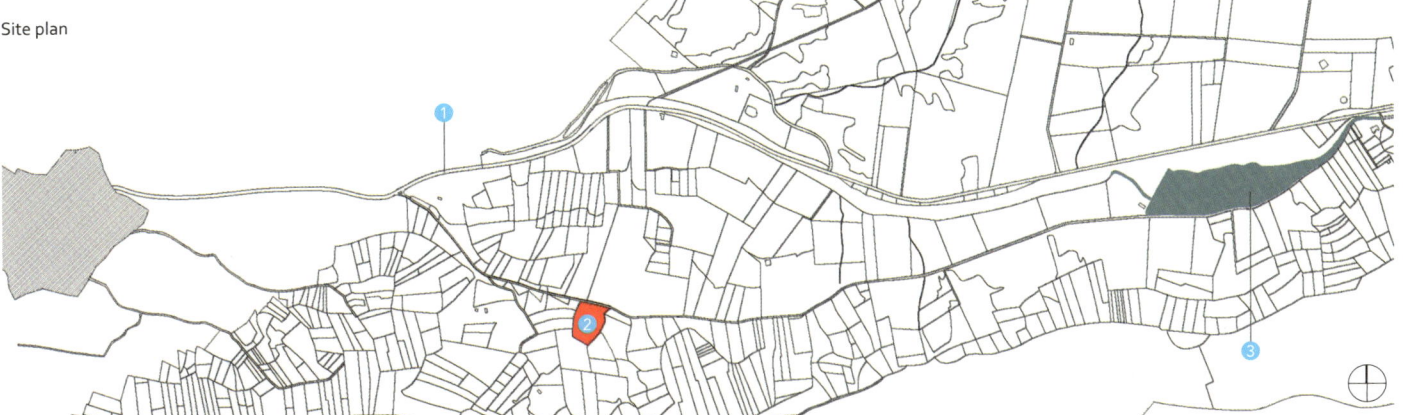

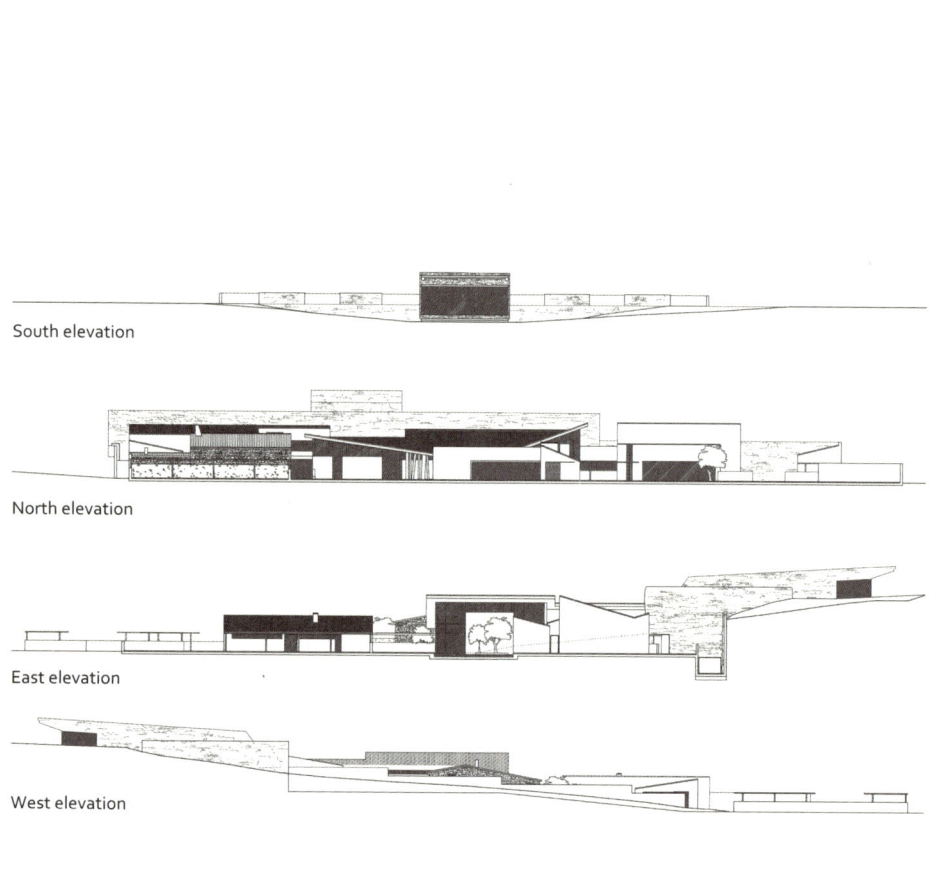

South elevation

North elevation

East elevation

West elevation

insulation, the incorporation of natural light within the exhibition space, along with the use of electric heat pumps are the measures contributing to achieving high energy efficiency without emitting polluting gases into the atmosphere.

Park biodiversity is shown in a direct way, without author interpretations, rigorously using scientific knowledge, ethology (animal behavior), and biogeography (species distribution in the territory). The center takes advantage of digital photo reproduction, representing all the wildlife park in photomontages at real-life scale, forming scenes of Cabañeros wildlife at different times (e.g. seasons, equinoxes and solstices), all illuminated with natural light overhead. These scenes inform the visitor the when, where, and why of major events within nature occurring in the park, allowing visitors to better observe them out in nature itself.

The permanent exhibition ends in the main building and shows the most significant aspects of the park. Biogeographic aspects include the distribution of species of wildlife and vegetation in over the course of the year, as shown in the 'Hall of Seasons.' In addition, the center includes geology and fossils in the Main Hall. Showcasing the different aspects of the landscape includes interpretation of landscape evolution, as shown in the 'Biorama Room,' which makes use of an audiovisual multi-screen to explain the outside landscape's composition. Ethnographical aspects include traditional production systems of the evergreen oak and the cork oak, as shown in the 'Quintería,' which uses audiovisual and interactive methods.

02 / Panorama
03 / Main access
04 / Secondary access

05

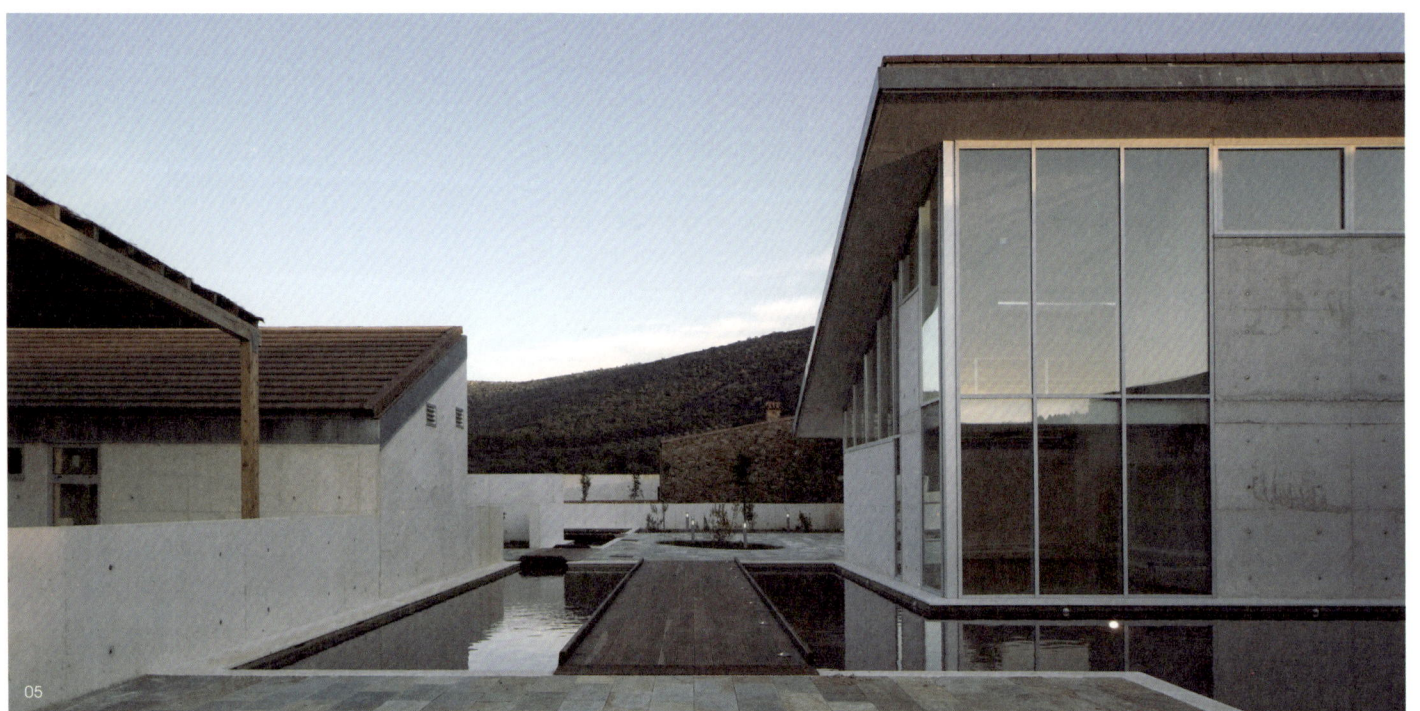

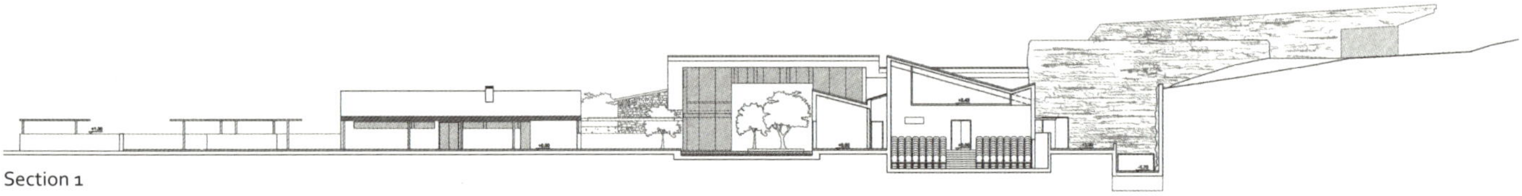
Section 1

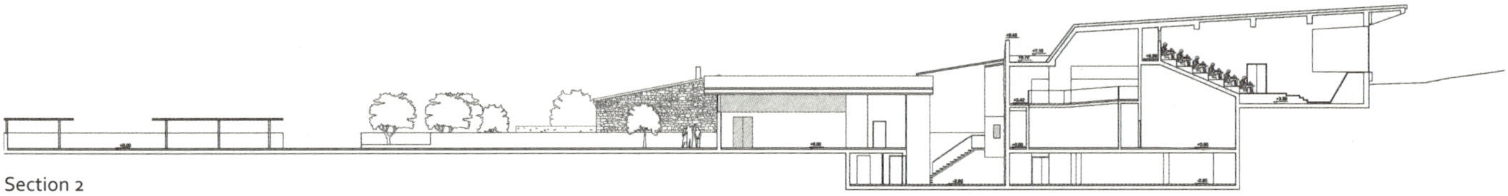
Section 2

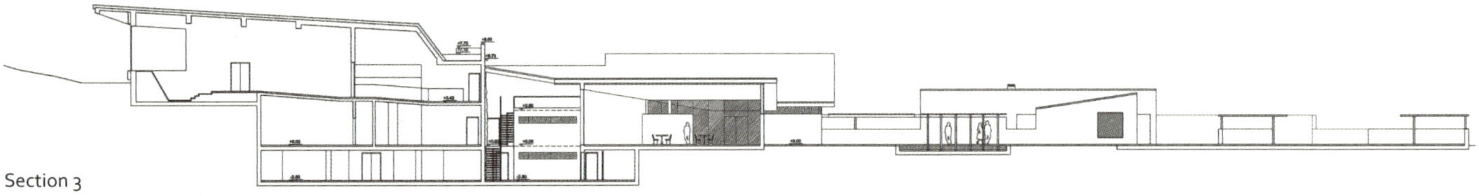
Section 3

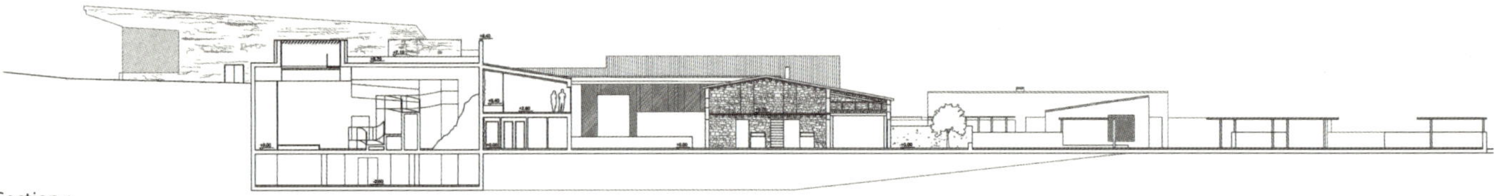
Section 4

05 / Guard station and library
06 / Connecting yard
07 / Biorama room

08 / Shop
09 / Library
10 / Basement access

Third-floor plan

Roof floor plan

09

08

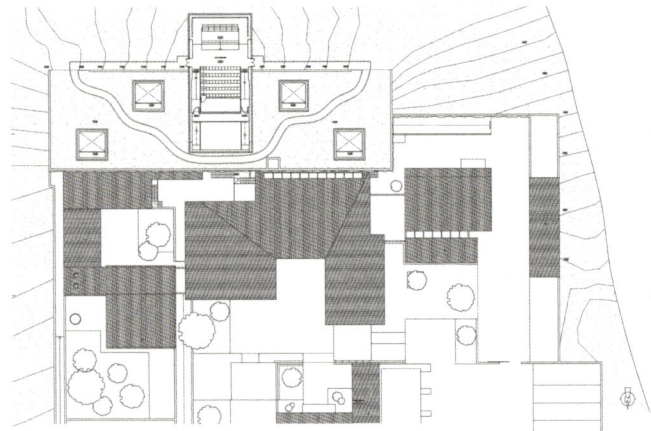

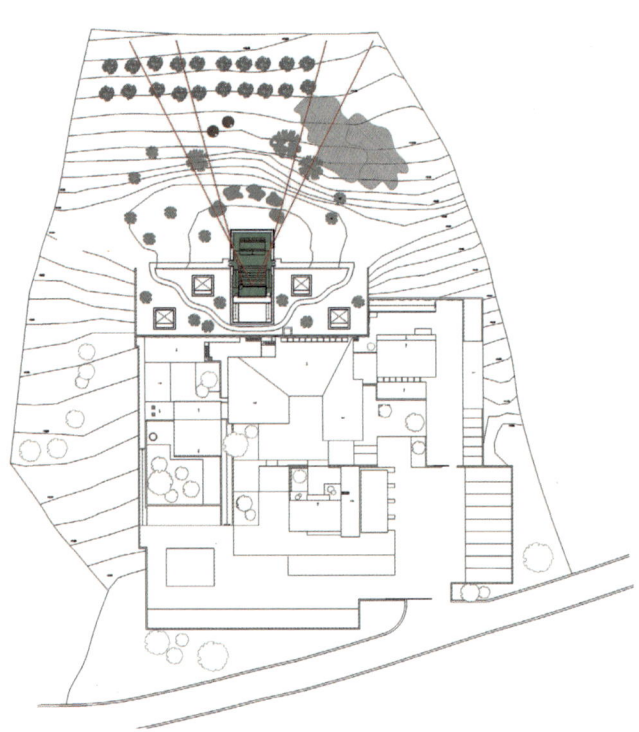

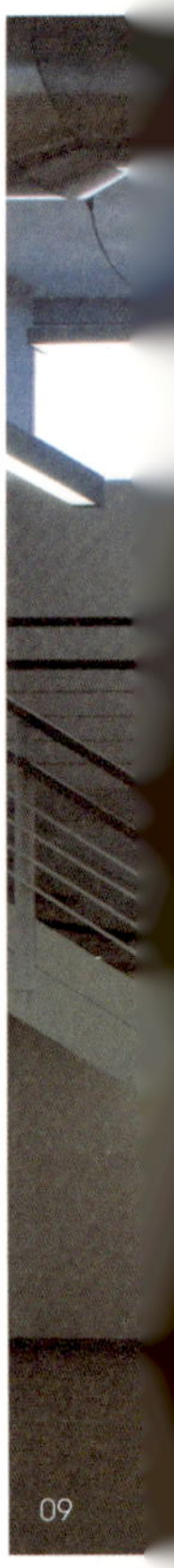

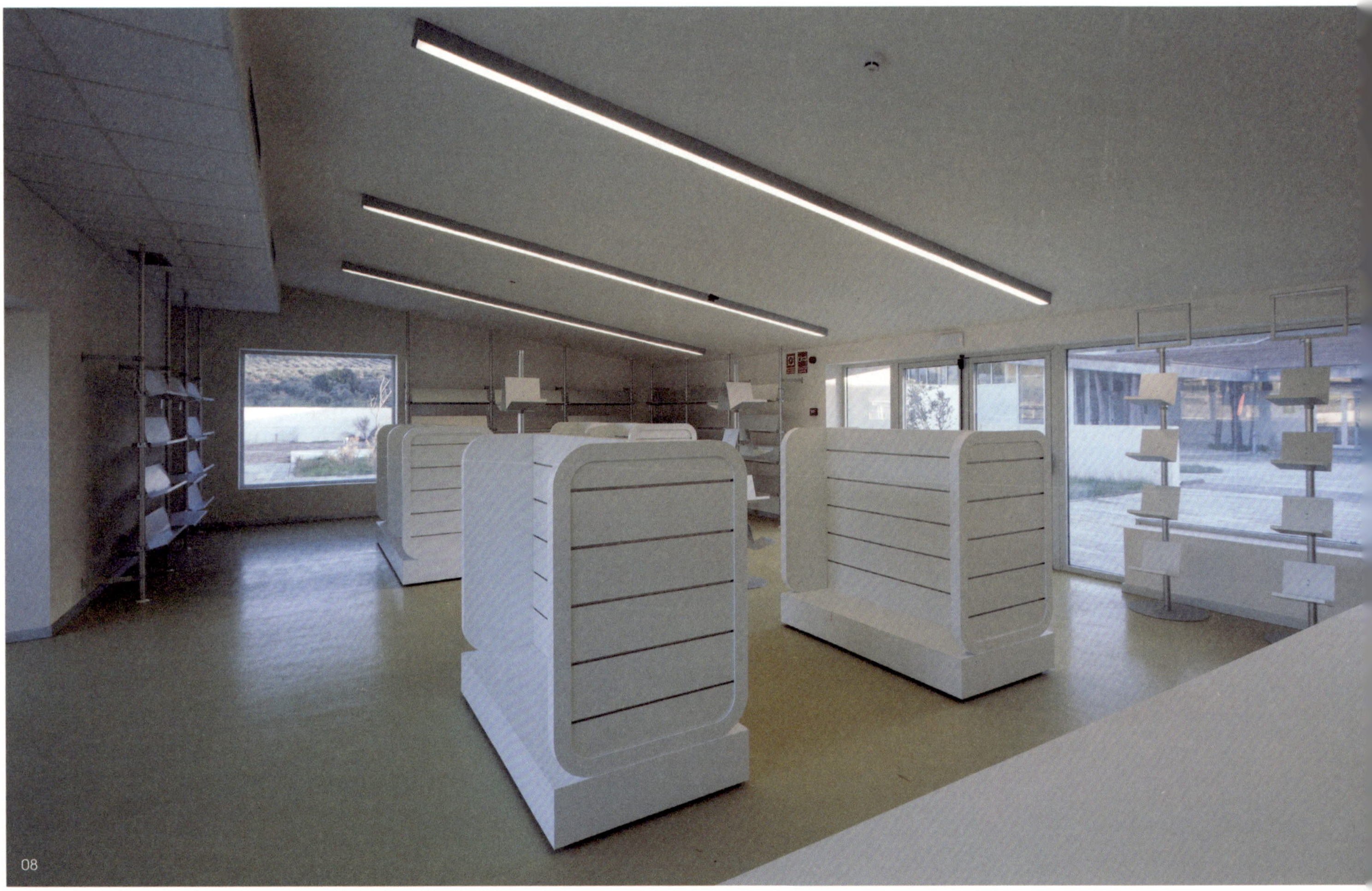

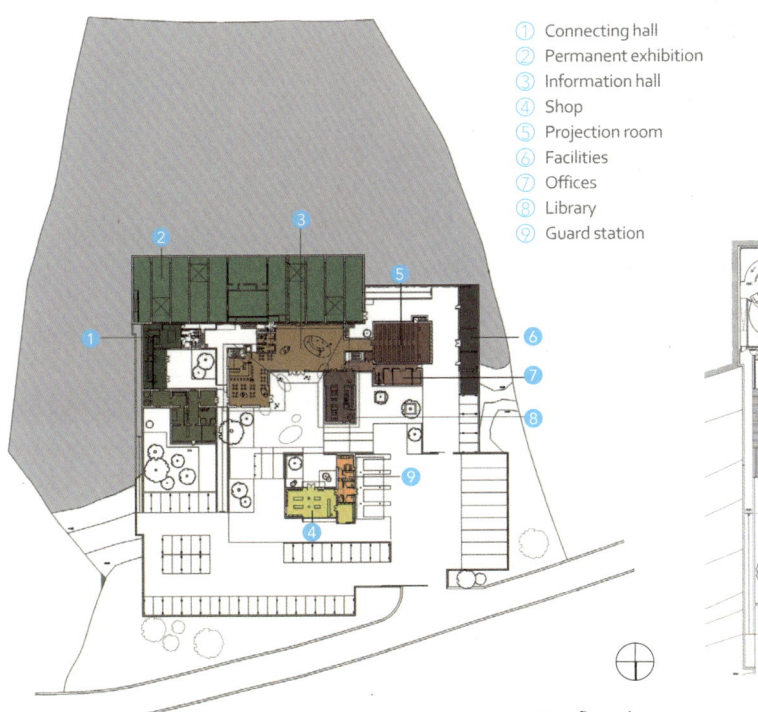

① Connecting hall
② Permanent exhibition
③ Information hall
④ Shop
⑤ Projection room
⑥ Facilities
⑦ Offices
⑧ Library
⑨ Guard station

First-floor plan

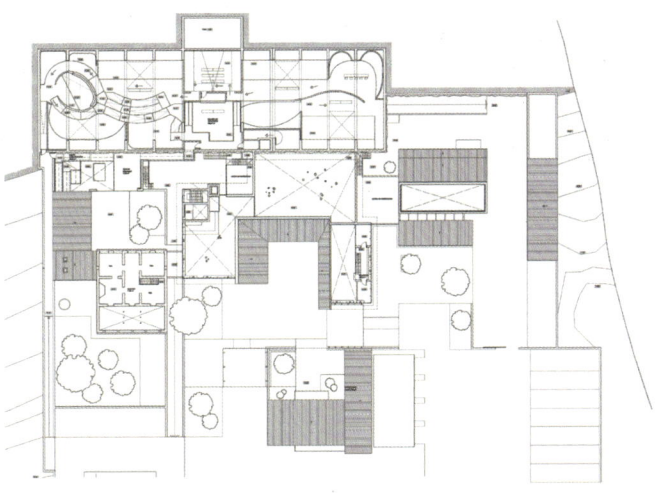

Second-floor plan

11 / Information hall
12 / Projection room
13 / Café

Visitor Center of Mont-Tremblant National Park

Location / Mont-Tremblant National Park, Canada
Area / 6458 square feet (600 square meters)
Completion / 2014
Architect / Smith Vigeant Architectes
Photography / Stéphane Brugger
Client / SÉPAQ
Budget / CAD $ 2.7 million

Located in the Mont-Tremblant National Park in Québec Canada, the Discovery Center offers a stunning view of Lake Monroe and its surrounding hills and mountains. The building consists of three distinct sections: an amphitheater, a discovery zone, and service facilities, all grouped into two main buildings connected by a large canopy. A continuous ribbon of rustic wood folds is used to create walls, floors and ceilings, defining the shape and organization for the structures.

The architects' main intention was to connect the project with the surrounding landscape. A continuous glass façade offers views toward the lake and gives visitors the sensation of being a part of nature while the wooden path between the main structures alternatively provides visitors with a physical connection to the lake. This relationship with nature was carried through into the amphitheater whose screen walls allow viewers to lookout and feel as if they are sitting in the forest. Additionally, a reflective surface on the west façade was incorporated to project the surrounding landscape onto the building itself.

Given its pristine location in the heart of nature, the use of wood as the primary material allowed for the harmonious insertion of the building into the unspoiled setting. A wide variety of wood species were used on both the exterior and interior, thus reinterpreting the site's richness in textures and colors, while providing the building with durability and resistance. Among the varieties were: hemlock for the ribbon and the amphitheater, white pine for the wood ceiling, American elm for the furniture, Canadian east cedar for the exterior cladding and western red cedar for the curtain wall.

The Discovery Center was designed around the site's natural and climatic features and in respect to bio-climatic principles. The development of the project was founded on the assiduous integration of the building into the site as well as its sensitivity to the surrounding area.

Translated from French, the architects believe that 'the illuminated spaces, both interior and exterior, offer an interesting play of volumes. The unique building form awakes the senses and invites it to be discovered. The use of abundant and diverse wood types creates the warm and welcoming interior spaces.'

01 / Outside patio and lake access

Volumes

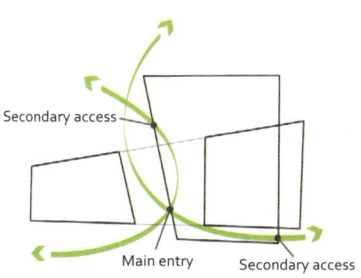
Access

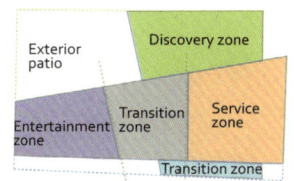
Interconnected zones

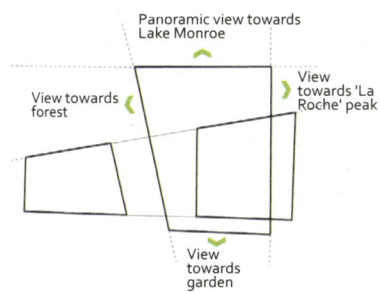
Visual connections with surrounding landscape

Site plan

1. Scenic view
2. Main road
3. Visitor parking
4. Bike path
5. Passage
6. Lake Monroe
7. Preservation zone for aquatic vegetation
8. Center access
9. Mineral garden
10. Beach
11. Recreational dock
12. Visual connection to discovery center

02 / Mirror reflecting nature
03 / Entrance

Southeast elevation

Northeast elevation

Southwest elevation

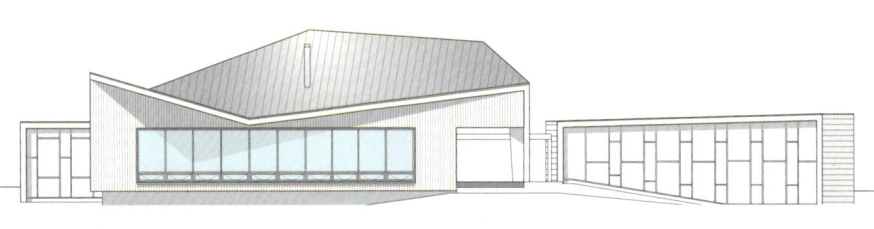
Northwest elevation

0   5m

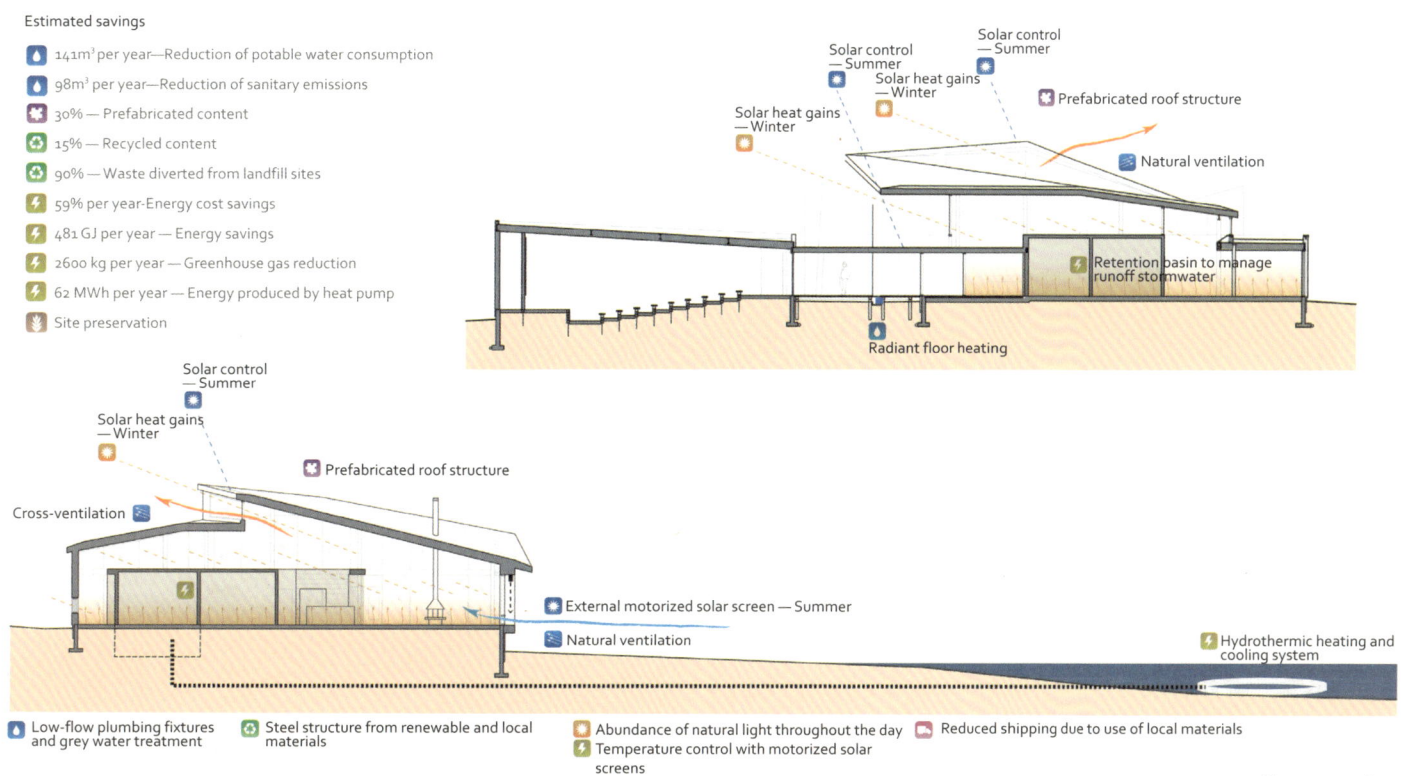

Estimated savings

- 141m³ per year—Reduction of potable water consumption
- 98m³ per year—Reduction of sanitary emissions
- 30% — Prefabricated content
- 15% — Recycled content
- 90% — Waste diverted from landfill sites
- 59% per year-Energy cost savings
- 481 GJ per year — Energy savings
- 2600 kg per year — Greenhouse gas reduction
- 62 MWh per year — Energy produced by heat pump
- Site preservation

Low-flow plumbing fixtures and grey water treatment • Steel structure from renewable and local materials • Abundance of natural light throughout the day • Temperature control with motorized solar screens • Reduced shipping due to use of local materials • Site preservation

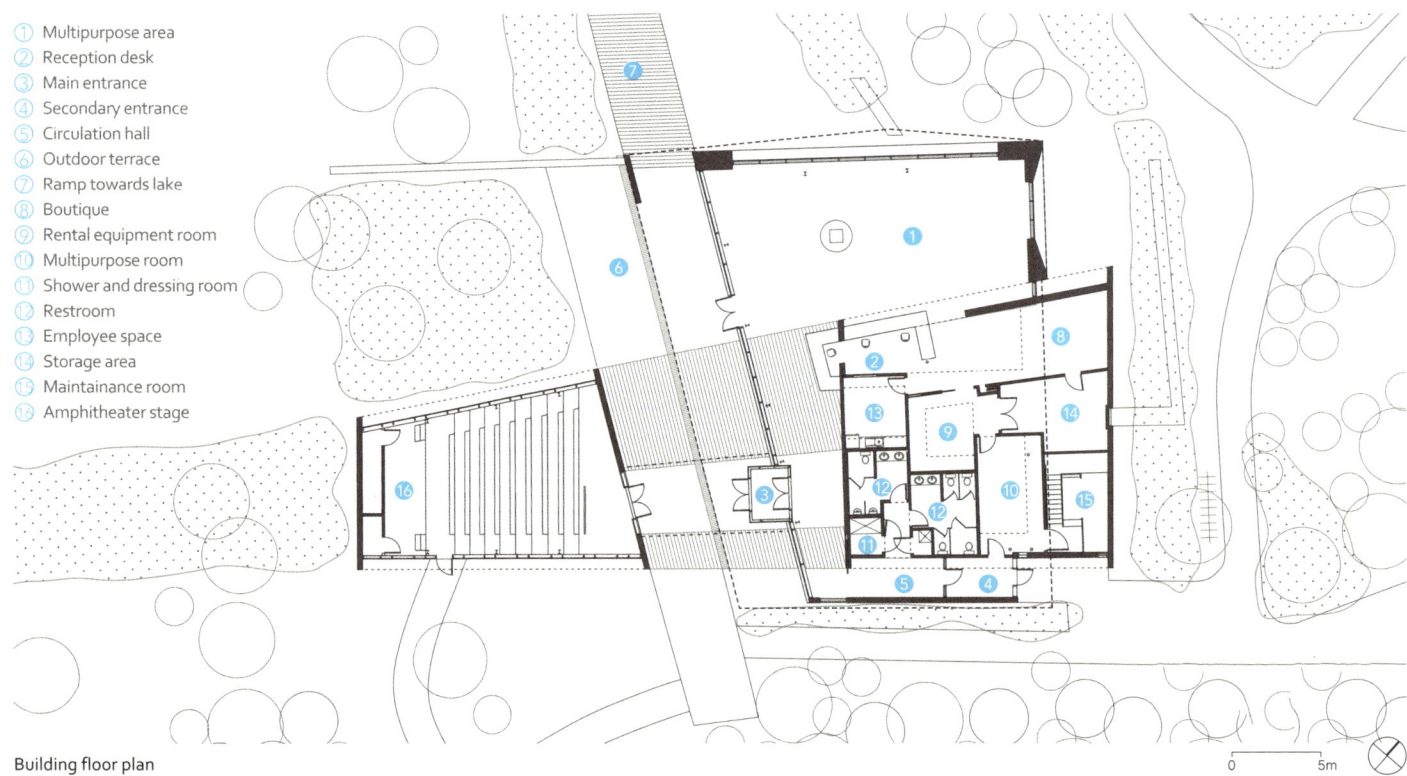

1. Multipurpose area
2. Reception desk
3. Main entrance
4. Secondary entrance
5. Circulation hall
6. Outdoor terrace
7. Ramp towards lake
8. Boutique
9. Rental equipment room
10. Multipurpose room
11. Shower and dressing room
12. Restroom
13. Employee space
14. Storage area
15. Maintainance room
16. Amphitheater stage

Building floor plan

04 / Terrace
05 / Information center
06 / Circulation

07 / Front view of amphitheater
08 / Side view of amphitheater
09 / Circulation area

2 Scenic Overlook Design

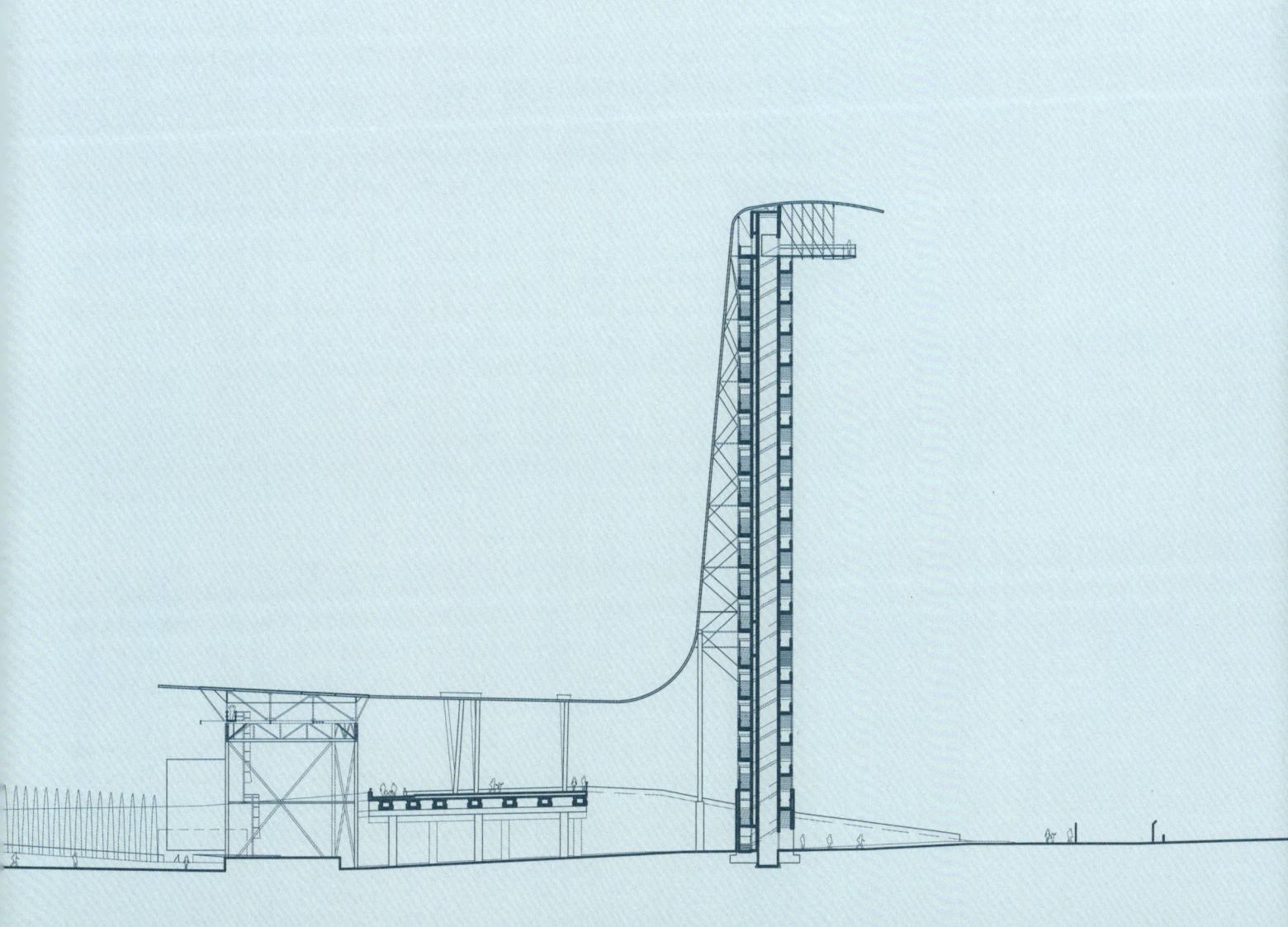

Introduction

Overlook has become a popular infrastructure in modern tourism. Due to its selected site, breathtaking appearance, and excellent scenery provision, visitors tend to take itself as kind of scenery. Thus more and more planners are attaching great importance to the design of overlooks in a scenic site.

An overlook is a high place where people can gather to view scenery (often with binoculars), and to take photos. Scenic overlooks are typically created alongside mountain roads, often as a simple turnout where motorists can pull over onto pavement, gravel, or grass on the right-of-way. Many are larger, with parking areas, while some (typically on larger highways) are off the road completely. We can also find many creative, fabulous, and striking scenic overlook designs, as the projects included in this book. In this chapter, we'll discuss the basic design strategies of scenic overlooks.

Scenic Overlook Design Guidelines

Viewing is the primary activity at overlooks; however, they often serve as rest stops. People are attracted to overlooks with wide panoramas, which can provide excellent opportunities for interpreting geology, cultural features, historical events, wildlife, or topics that address a broad landscape view. The extent of development depends on its location and its context within the byway. Improvements that enhance the visitor's experience at overlooks can include viewing decks, benches, telescopes, shelters, and interpretive artifacts. In areas where overlooks attract large numbers of visitors, consider amenities such as kiosks, restrooms, and picnic tables.

The criteria for selecting new overlooks should include sites that highlight resources identified in the interpretive plan. Consider areas where people already congregate, as these often indicate points of interest and good viewing opportunities. Sites must have enough physical area to support the proposed facility and to safely access the byway.

The physical layout of the overlook should allow adequate room for the expected number of visitors to enjoy the view. Often an overlook is accessed by a short trail from the parking area. Safety features such as fences or walls may be necessary along the trail and at the overlook to protect visitors or natural resources. The design of the overlook and the trails should be fully accessible and complement the byway's thematic design guidelines.

Approach signs and site identification signs that are clearly visible are essential in helping visitors find their way. The approach to the overlook should offer safe and easy access from the byway. Adequate parking should be provided for standard and oversize vehicles.

Some overlooks are merely areas to pull out of the travel lane for safely viewing the scenery and are generally referred to as pullouts or turnouts. These areas contain no interpretation or other amenities. Consider siting a turnout where people are already stopping or at a safer location nearby that offers the same view. Since pullouts are highly visible while traveling a byway, it is important to design them to enhance rather than detract from the scenic character. Consider the size and shape so that it does not draw attention to itself, but still provides safety.

As a very specific type of tourist infrastructure, there are no specific design guidelines for scenic overlooks. Considering the most common spot for a scenic overlook is roadside, a wealth of resources is available to refer to for information, such as Scenic Byways: A Design Guide for Roadside Improvements, Continental Divide National Scenic Trail Trailhead Design Guidelines, and Guidelines for Visual Resource Management,

Landscaping, and Hardscaping.

This chapter provides guidelines to help successfully plan and locate a scenic overlook. Safety, attractiveness and the logical arrangement of functional spaces are important factors to consider when creating a site plan.

A thorough site analysis is vital to ensure the designer has the information needed to develop a sensitive site plan that respects natural and cultural resources, responds to needs of each partner and landowner, and provides a quality visitor experience.

The Influencing Factors

This section summarizes how each of these factors may influence the development of a project.

Overall Context

This step includes consideration of the surrounding and natural environments. For example, the famous American National Scenic Trail, Continental Divide Trail, whose overlooks located in Glacier National Park, has greatvariety within its ecological context. It falls within two broad ecological/cultural regions, the Southwest and the Rocky Mountains. These two provinces, although different in certain respects, are mainly characterized by:

- Sparse rainfall
- Low humidity
- Abundant and intense sunlight
- Numerous rock outcrops
- Long dramatic views
- Wide open landscapes
- Limited protection from wind and sun

This section summarizes how each of these factors may influence the development of a project.

Ecosystems

The cultural environment along a specific site is often a clear expression of the unique cultures that settled in the area and their response to the landscape. The surrounding culture andthe materials at hand often influenced landscape design in these areas.

Cultural influences are expressed through many factors, such as the dwellings, farms, ranches, mines and railroad sites. Early inhabitants took advantage of their surroundings by using local materials for construction, landscaping and siting structures to capture winter sun, protecting against summer heat, directing cooling summer breezes to building interiors and capturing water for irrigation.

For example, in the Rocky Mountain region, settlers took advantage of natural materials with boulders, stone and wood dominating the design of walls, steps, seats, shelters and walks. Once the railroads came to the Rockies, cast-iron and prefabricated materials were mixed with the native materials. In the Southwestern region, the Native American design aesthetic is layered with the influences from the Spanish–Mexican cultures. Landscape features are built of adobe (straw and clay), stone and tile with minimal use of wood.

All of these landscape expressions are specifically derived from the climate, geography, vegetation and scarcity of water.

Minimizing Site Disturbance

The natural character of the site should be retained to the greatest extent possible when developing the site plan. Sites that are disturbed should be restored and carefully integrated into the surrounding natural environment. One must consider all the natural resource elements (e.g., slopes, drainage, vegetation, water table/hydrology, geology, soils, wildlife) when determining the program and arranging uses on the site to minimize disturbance while providing needed facilities. Options for minimizing site disturbance include:

- Preserve/Protect: Preserve natural features and resources where possible (e.g., drainages, vegetation, wetlands, slopes, rocky outcrops).

- Retain/Enhance: This strategy is generally applied to significant archeological and historic features.

- Reuse/Restore: Use disturbed areas before constructing in undisturbed areas. Restore unsightly areas.

- Minimal Disturbance: Avoid locating facilities in areas with steep slopes, high water tables, natural drainage corridors, significant tree stands, or key wildlife corridors/habitats.

- Adapt Grading: Avoid creating steep grades, excessively cutting or filling slopes, creating sharp slope cuts, destroying vegetation, disturbing wildlife corridors and habitats, and concentrating water flows.

Sustainable Organization and Appearance

Thoughtful site planning will result in a scenic overlook that is enjoyable to use, attractive, educational and sustainable. The site plan should reflect the special setting, patterns, and conditions of each particular area. Individual elements should use building and landscape materials, and engineering methods that reflect the local area to create a high-quality lasting appearance. This will result in facilities of scenic overlook that fit their environments, are truly beautiful, and provide a positive 'sense of place.'

Overall principles for site planning/design are:

- Gentle: Integrate and protect natural qualities of the site, gently place facilities away from sensitive resources, and use local features, materials and native landscaping.

- Modest: Keep the plan subservient to the landscape. The natural landscape should always dominate the scene.

- Context: Establish a landscape architectural style that fits into the ecosystem and cultural context at each particular scenic overlook.

- Nature as mentor: Notice how seasonal rituals/change, sun, wind, temperature, slope, soils and moisture affect on-site processes and stability.

- Permanence: Use high quality, long-lasting local materials to give a sense of permanence and connect to geological processes of change.

- People and ecosystem: Take in account visitor needs and habits to benefit the site rather than thinking about them as a detriment to long-term stability. At the same time, ensure the impact of visitor use on the local area is accounted for when thinking about individual site elements.

- Sustainability: Sustainability: Recognize and enhance ecological systems at the site, such as water flow, wildlife habitat corridors and cover.
- Perceptions: Use design elements that both fit and help shape visitors perception of the scenic area.
- Maintenance: Design site for low maintenance, but obtain maintenance commitment from agency managers.

Specific Site Plan Considerations:
- Obscure: Locate facilities at hill side edges, among trees and rocks or behind landforms rather than out in the open.
- Protect: Preserve natural corridors for site buffers, visual amenities and habitat.
- Blend-in: Provide natural-appearing grading and site-drainage.
- Sustain: Use drainage patterns to support vegetation and improve the site's aesthetics.
- Water Processes: Allow adequate space for water recharge/cleansing/infiltration.
- Views: Enhance and protect significant view corridors related to the site.
- Wildlife: Allow existing wildlife movement through site.

A Quality Visitor Experience

It is a common sense that visitors will have different expectations and desires. Some will be travelers who merely want to take a break before traveling on, while others will want to use the scenic overlook as a start or finish for their experience; some visitors may spend from five minutes to an hour at the site, while others will stay overnight or weeks at a time. All users will want to have comforts, be protected from adjacent roadways, and understand the layout of the facility.

Often there are uses at larger sites that have nothing to do with the site itself and take away from the visitor experience. These include concession facilities, maintenance areas and public utility access. These other uses will need to be accommodated, while also protecting the visitor's experience.

- Visitor needs: Consider visitor movement patterns from before the visitor reaches the site to the time that person leaves.
- Visitor use sequence: Create alogical arrangement of facilities. Carefully consider the order in which visitors should experience facilities.
- Transition: Arrange usage of facilities in a way to help visitors transition from a roadway experience to a more primitive and natural experience.
- Appropriateness: When locating facilities, make sure visitors will feel comfortable while engaged in each experience (e.g., reading interpretive materials, waiting for a friend or crossing a road).
- Compatibility: Place compatible usages together and separate or screen incompatible usages. For example, information kiosks should be located at the entry while storage

facilities should be located out of a user's sight.

- Attractiveness: Screen unsightly facilities, such as maintenance areas.

- Information: Provide interpretive sign exhibits to orient and educate scenery visitors about the landscaping area and its environment.

- Existing facilities: Reorganize existing assorted sitesand their facilities so they work as part of the overall plan.

- View from scenic overlook: Provide a positive impression of the site for the user arriving from the trail. Help them gently move from a primitive environment to a more developed area.

- Safety: Ensure facilities are sited in safe areas in relation to dangerous elements such as traffic, rock fall zones and steep edges or cliffs.

- Accessibility: Provide for users with special needs by adhering to local accessibility guidelines for buildings and facilities standards throughout the design.

- Provides attractive views and establishes a positive visitor experience at the entry and exit: Place parking in a convenient area without distracting from the visual quality of the trail entry experience or other site uses. Sensitive screening is likely to be needed.

Circulation

Roadways, parking and pathways must be carefully site-planned and designed to minimize noise, erosion and habitat degradation.

The movement and accommodation of many types of vehicles and users must be considered early in the scenic overlook development process. Planning and design for these uses should provide safe, direct and comfortable access and circulation while ensuring that the motorized uses do not dominate and overwhelm trail users and other visitors.

As an overlook project, the circulation design may provide valuable references for designers:

Entry/Exit Roads

- Regulations: To design roads off national or provincial highways, use local highway standards. Some overlooks may need costly acceleration/deceleration lanes.

- Unobstructed views: Recognize site lines, distances and distractions when locating the access road. Make sure you can clearly see in all directions.

- Multiple access points: Realize that sometimes circulation works better with more than one entry and exit.

- Information: Ensure that directional signs communicate necessary information in advance of reaching the overlook.

- Trail users: Create safe access to the overlook. Users (i.e. hikers, equestrians, cyclists) may be using the highway to access the overlook. In these cases, they should enter the site at the vehicle access point.

- Site markers: Reserve space for overlook sign, and native landscaping at entry points.

- Appearance: Create a quality first impression by preserving, establishing or enhancing natural areas at site entries.
- Trail transition: Create an attractive entry for the overlook site. The natural environment and native landscaping should dominate the trail user's experience when entering the overlook.

Roadway System
- Preserve: Design roads to save existing landscape features (e.g., rocks, trees, vegetation clusters).
- Vehicle types: Accommodate all traffic uses anticipated (i.e. cars, trucks with trailers, 18 wheel trucks, RVs, buses, hikers, horses and bicyclists).
- Safety: Minimize conflicts between different uses: separate trucks, buses and RV circulation from auto traffic.
- Large vehicles: Provide pull-over lanes for large vehicles so they do not have to back up.
- Information: Provide way-finding signs at key circulation points.
- Connectivity: Create easily legible circulation flow that connects compatible areas.
- Landscaping: Landscape road edges with native plants, rocks and logs as a natural way to prevent vehicles from driving off road.
- Upkeep: Ensure maintenance vehicles can access parking and service areas (e.g., restrooms, trash receptacles, septic systems).

Parking Systems
- Disturbance: Locate parking to minimize environmental impacts.
    - Use existing disturbed areas.
    - Select well-drained, gently sloping areas with few trees.
- Visual impacts: Reduce the visual intrusion of parking.
    - Screen parking from the road and the overlook.
    - Integrate parking into the landscape by using natural sloping edges, local boulders, mounds and/or vegetation.
    - Place large vehicle parking in areas that do not overwhelm the visual appearance of the overlook.
- Scale: Reduce the scale of parking lots, while maintaining function.
    - Produce multiple parking areas.
    - Landscape with native materials.
    - Preserve trees, rocky outcrops and other natural features in the parking lot.
    - Screen with local natural landscape materials.
    - Accurately determine parking/user demand; do not base on infrequent peak events.
    - Include informal overflow areas, when possible.
- Compatibility: Separate large vehicle parking away from automobile/motorcycle

parking.

- Circulation safety: Provide pull-through parking for oversized vehicles and equestrian loading.
- Separation: Provide separate parking areas or designate parking locations for different uses (e.g., restaurant parking vs. overlook parking).

Pedestrian Circulation System

There are two types of pedestrian circulation systems at the overlook: the road system that passes through the overlook and the pedestrian system that links overlook facilities.

Decide if a pathway system is needed. Small-scale overlooks, with limited facilities, may not need a pathway system.

- How many people are being planned for?
- What activities will they be doing?

Circulation for Large-scale Overlooks

- Configuration: Identify facilities to be connected, and provide minimum number of paths.
- Efficiency: Position paths to provide the shortest distance between facilities. This will minimize 'social' or unwanted paths.
- Adjacent uses: Avoid cases where paths would disturb resources or users (e.g., picnic sites, rest areas).
- Minimize disturbance to the site: locate pathways away from wetlands, steep slopes or densely vegetated areas; avoid rocky outcrops, and mature tree stands.
- Blend-in: Integrate pathways into the natural environment by using materials present in the local environment.
- Accessibility: Connect all overlook facilities with an accessible route.

Grading

Grading at the scenic overlook should blend topography into the surrounding landscape, prevent erosion, and provide an opportunity for water to soak into the ground.

- Match topography: Place site elements to adapt to natural topography to minimize disturbance from grading.
- Preserve terrain: Retain, where possible, natural site landform and drainage patterns; this will minimize site disturbance and damage to surrounding vegetation.
- Drainage: Sensitively control runoff.
    - Create small check dams with natural appearance inside drainages.
    - Create natural appearing retention and siltation basins with slow drainage releases. Utilize these basins for pollution management for parking lot runoff.
- Drainage ways: Design drainage ways, to appear as natural depressions in the landscape that allow for water infiltration and absorption.

Landscaping

Planting appropriately is essential to creating a sustainable scenic overlook. Planting provides both buffer and habitat for wildlife, shelters users from sun and wind, slows runoff, prevents erosion, and cleans runoff from parking lots and roads. Planting also is used in design to provide edges, textures and screens, pedestrian circulation cues, links to surrounding views, and spatial definition.

Public Services

Large scenic overlook may include toilet facilities. Optional facilities might include drinking water, lighting and phone service. One should carefully consider if these additional facilities are appropriate. The placement and maintenance of these facilities in remote and environmentally challenging places can be difficult and invasive to the natural character of the site. In addition, they could attract visitors not interested in the scenery, but who view the site as a 'rest area.'

- Shared facilities: If the site has toilet facilities managed by another entity, attempt to arrange for visitors to use that facility.
- Viable: Determine if toilet facilities are needed based on past use, and whether they can be maintained.
- Position: Place toilet facilities to fit with the character of the site.
- Operations: Make toilet facilities accessible to maintenance vehicles.

Concessionaire Facilities

Certain site furnishings and services, while not provided by the managing agency as part of the scenic overlook, may be desired by adjacent concession operators. When placing these items, concessionaires should meet the following requirements.

- Bicycle racks: If bicycle racks are provided, locate to minimize pedestrian/bicycle conflicts.
- Water: If drinking water is provided, place the dispenser(fountain or spout) along an accessible route
    - Location should avoid drawing additional traffic into the overlook parking lot.
    - Comply with local requirements for providing safe drinking water.
- Phones: If phones are provided, place them along an accessible route near urban elements, such as the parking lot or any restaurant/shop facilities.

Site Furnishings and Amenities

Modest furnishings to accommodate basic needs of visitors should complement the simplicity of the project's purpose and the focus on sustainability of design. Large scenic overlooks will use furnishings and other additions throughout the site to provide a comfortable environment for users, yet fit into the natural environment. Furthermore, waste receptacles, parking/road edges and fencing will encourage the larger number of users at these sites to not litter or damage surrounding areas.

Medium-sized and small overlooks will have minimal site furnishings, but will still use parking/road edges and fencing to keep users out of sensitive areas and adjacent privately owned land.

Material used in construction is an important aesthetic factor, and each specific site may have its own featured material. For instance, sedimentary, igneous and metamorphic rocks are all present along the Continental Divide National Scenic Trail of the United States.

- Focus on materials best adapted to harsh weather conditions.
- Minimize use of prefabricated items, as much as possible.
- Provide seating areas to allow visitors to relax and take in the overlook and its surroundings.
- Consider using fences as one method to contain traffic flow and grazing animals in open areas. Keep fences to a minimum, as they can distract from the surrounding environment.
    - Consider fencing when needed to keep vehicles from entering open or sensitive areas.
    - Think about fencing services that need protection from visitors.
    - Fence cattle from the overlook in areas that are subject to grazing.
    - Consider wildlife movement through the site for fence location.
    - Provide waste disposal places to discourage visitors from leaving trash elsewhere on the site. Prevent wind from blowing trash out of the bin by providing a semi-open top or closed top.
- Provide waste disposal places to discourage visitors from leaving trash elsewhere on the site. Prevent wind from blowing trash out of the bin by providing a semi-open top or closed top.

Supplemental Facilities/Built Structures

The natural and cultural context that guides site planning and designed elements should inform the design of built structures. Buildings should be resource-efficient, constructed of long lasting and easy to maintain materials, and fit harmoniously into their context.

Steep, rugged topography with large vegetation forms and harsh winters should have large-scaled building forms with a vertical emphasis. Warmer areas with subtle topography, finer-scaled vegetation and intense sunshine should have moderate-scaled structures with horizontal emphasis. The ideal choice is to use building materials indigenous to the site, and augment only with materials that contribute to an ecologically sound design.

Building Rehabilitation and Restoration

In altering existing built elements, seek opportunities to employ principles previously described to integrate the existing structure and site elements into the natural context. Specific opportunities may include the following:

- Material/Color: At a minimum, employ new exterior materials and colors that fit with the scale, texture and color of surrounding vegetation and geology.

- Building/Ground intersection: Improve integration of building with its site by adding a 'base' to the bottom portion of the wall. Extend any special treatment into the ground plane surrounding the structure. This may be achieved by a change of material, or elevation.

- Openings: Where appropriate locate openings that help to scale the structure to its site, as well as to take advantage of solar access for day lighting and heating.

- Signage: Where possible, relocate and/or revise signage to integrate with the scale and character of both existing and new structures.

- Roof: With this highly-visual building element, it is important to seek opportunities to adjust its profile, pitch, overhang, and material. Choose such aspects that echo characteristics of the surrounding context.

References

Built Environment Image Guide, USDA Forest Service, 2001

Dorward, Sherry, *Design for Mountain Communities: A Landscape and Architectural Guide,* New York: Van Nostrand Reinhold, 1990

Guiding Principles of Sustainable Design, US National Park Service, 1994

Landscape Aesthetics: A Handbook for Scenery Management, USDA Forest Service, 1995

Lyle, John Tillman Lyle, *Regenerative Design for Sustainable Development,* New York: John Wiley & Sons, Inc., 1996

Partnership Guide, USDA Forest Service, 1999

ROS Primer and Field Guide, USDA Forest Service, 1990

The Continental Divide National Scenic Trail Comprehensive Plan, USDA Forest Service, 2002

Aurland Lookout

Location / Aurland, Norway
Completion / 2005
Architect / Saunders Arkitektur, Wilhelmsen Arkitektur
Photography / Todd Saunders, Bent René Synnevåg, Nils Vik
Client / The Norwegian Highways Department

Only a three-hour drive from Bergen, Norway's second largest city, the site sits above Aurland, a small town in Sogn og Fjordane, one of the larger fjords on the West Coast of Norway, attracting people from all over the world. The architects designed their competition entry while keeping in mind the uniqueness of the place in their overall vision.

Nature first and architecture second was the guiding principal in designing this project. It was immediately obvious that in such beautiful surroundings one must make the least possible encroachment on the existing landscape and terrain. The landscape is so fantastic that it is difficult to improve the place, but at the same time very easy to destroy the atmosphere by inserting too many elements into the site. Even though designers chose an expressive form, the concept itself is minimalistic, in an attempt to conserve and complement the existing nature.

Today, many people stop at this site to enjoy the phenomenal views over the fjords. At times, the areas get filled with cars and tour buses. One of the first things the designers decided to do was to form a small parking area for 2 buses and 10 cars further up the road to help keep the place pure and not to disturb the lookout. The construction is a bridge suspended in the air that one can go out onto. The structure is 13.1-foot-wide (4-meter-wide), 98-foot-long (30-meter-long), and 29.5-foot-high (9-meter-high) out at the very end.

To make visiting the site even more dramatic, it was important to develop the experience of leaving the mountainside. The designers wanted people to feel as if they were emerging out of the air. The construction creates a distinct horizon: a bridge in the open area of this large fjord. It is imperative that the landscape and the vegetation not altered, but are protected so that one can come out from the landscape and experience it from a new standpoint.

The architects have managed to preserve all of the large pine trees on the site. This allows them to create an interaction between the structure and nature. People can walk up into the sky through the treetops, helping to dramatize the experience of nature and the larger landscape area.

01 / Lookout around pine trees

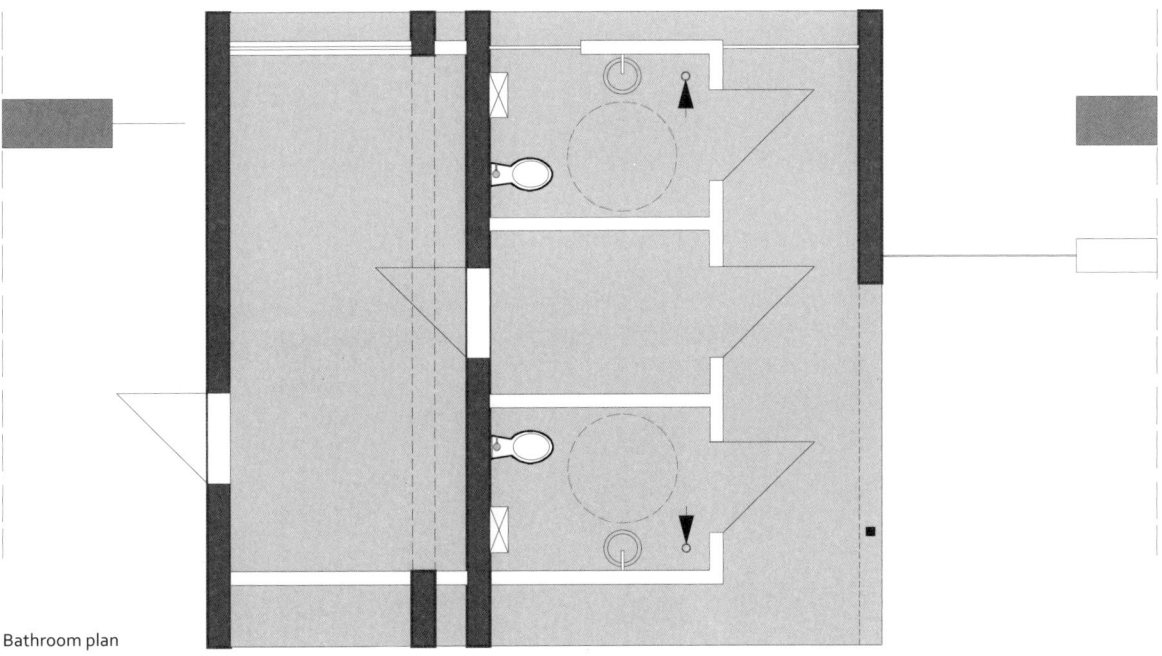

Bathroom plan

To make the situation even more dramatic, it was important to create the experience of leaving the mountainside. Designers wanted people to come out in the air. The construction creates a distinct horizon: a bridge in the open room of this large fjord. It is imperative that the landscape and the vegetation not altered, but are protected so that one can come out from the landscape and experience it from new standpoint.

The architects have managed to behold all of the large pine trees on the site. This allows them to create an interaction between the structure and nature. People can walk out into the air through the treetops, helping dramatise the experience of nature and the larger landscape room.

Elevation A

Elevation B

02 / Tourists gathered on deck
03 / Side view of lookout
04 / Close-up of lookout

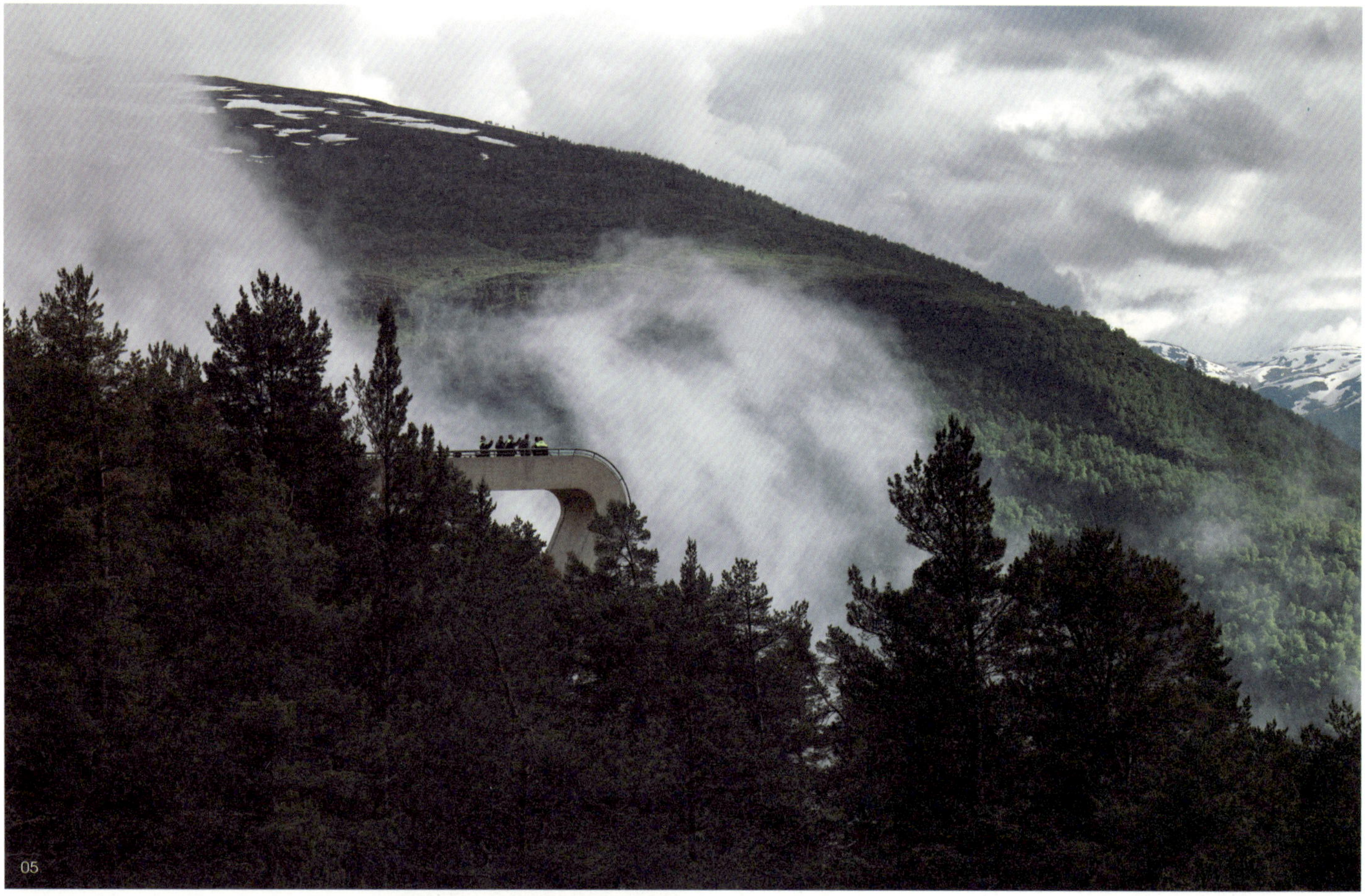

05

06

07

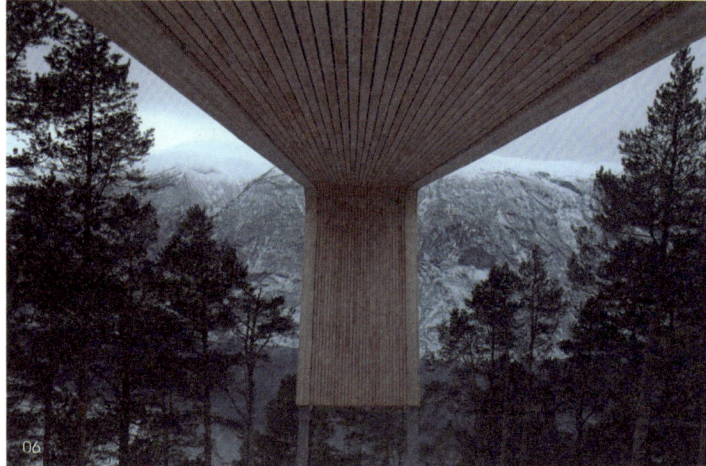

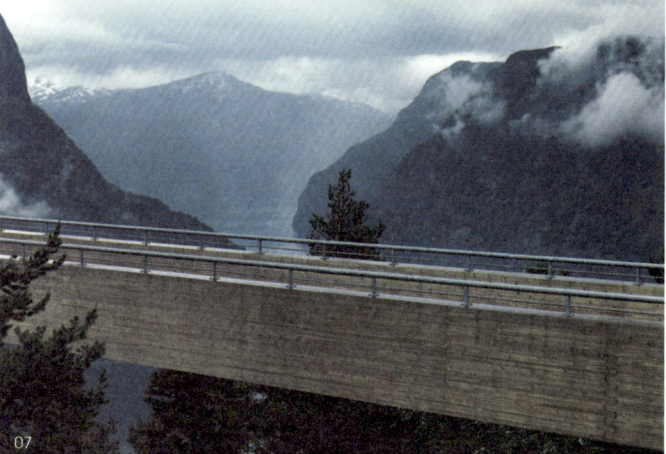

05 / Panoramic view of lookout
06 / Bottom of lookout
07 / Side of lookout
08-10 / Tourists on lookout at various angles

Section A

Section B

Austin Observation Tower

Location / Austin, Texas
Area / 30,492 square feet (2833 square meters)
Completion / 2005
Architect / Miró Rivera Architects
Photography / Paul Finkel | Piston Design, Keith Rizzo | Circuit of the Americas, Michael Hsu | Miró Rivera Architects, Ted Parker Jr. | Circuit of the Americas, Steve Colburn
Client / Circuit of the Americas

Capturing the energy of Formula 1 racing in its iconic form, the 251foot-tall observation Tower provides a dramatic focal point for the Circuit of the Americas and a new landmark for central Texas. Conceived as a visual finale to the central Grand Plaza, the tower also serves as a memorable backdrop to the Austin360 Amphitheater concert venue at its base. The structure's unique design anchors visitors' experience of the motorsports and entertainment complex and fosters a sense of place that is essential to the new circuit's identity.

The construction of the Austin Observation Tower represents the successful integration of material efficiency with thoughtful structural design and elegant aesthetics. The Tower's primary structure consists of a continuously-welded double-helix stair wrapped in a filigree-like diagrid. Each stair run serves as a helical diaphragm that transfers loads to a layered perimeter of vertical and diagonal HSS tubes. These small, distributed members contribute the necessary overall strength by number rather than individual brawn, enhancing the feeling of lightness and verticality that the tower embodies. Together, the stair stringers/diaphragm, diagonal HSS layer and vertical HSS layer form a fully-braced tube.

Like Formula 1 racecars, the form of the tower is directly influenced by its performance. Inspired by the image of red streaks of glowing light that tail lights leave behind in the dark, a roof of red steel tubes fans out over the amphitheater stage, converging at the base of the Tower to form a 'veil' that sweeps up and over the central elevator core. The tubes not only have a strong visual impact, but also contribute to the structural stability of the Tower by acting as an outrigger column for lateral load resistance via a series of struts and rods that tie back to the primary structure.

Seemingly suspended from the red pipe steel canopy is a 900-square-foot (84-square-meter) viewing deck that offers a sweeping panorama of the entire track, downtown Austin, and the nearby Hill Country from an elevation of 230 feet (70 meters). A portion of the floor is structural laminated glass, allowing more daring

01 / Full view of tower

① Main stage
② Ticket building #1
③ Observation tower
④ Austin360 amphitheater
⑤ Grand Plaza
⑥ Ticket building #2
⑦ T11 Pedestrian Bridge
⑧ T3 pedestrian bridge

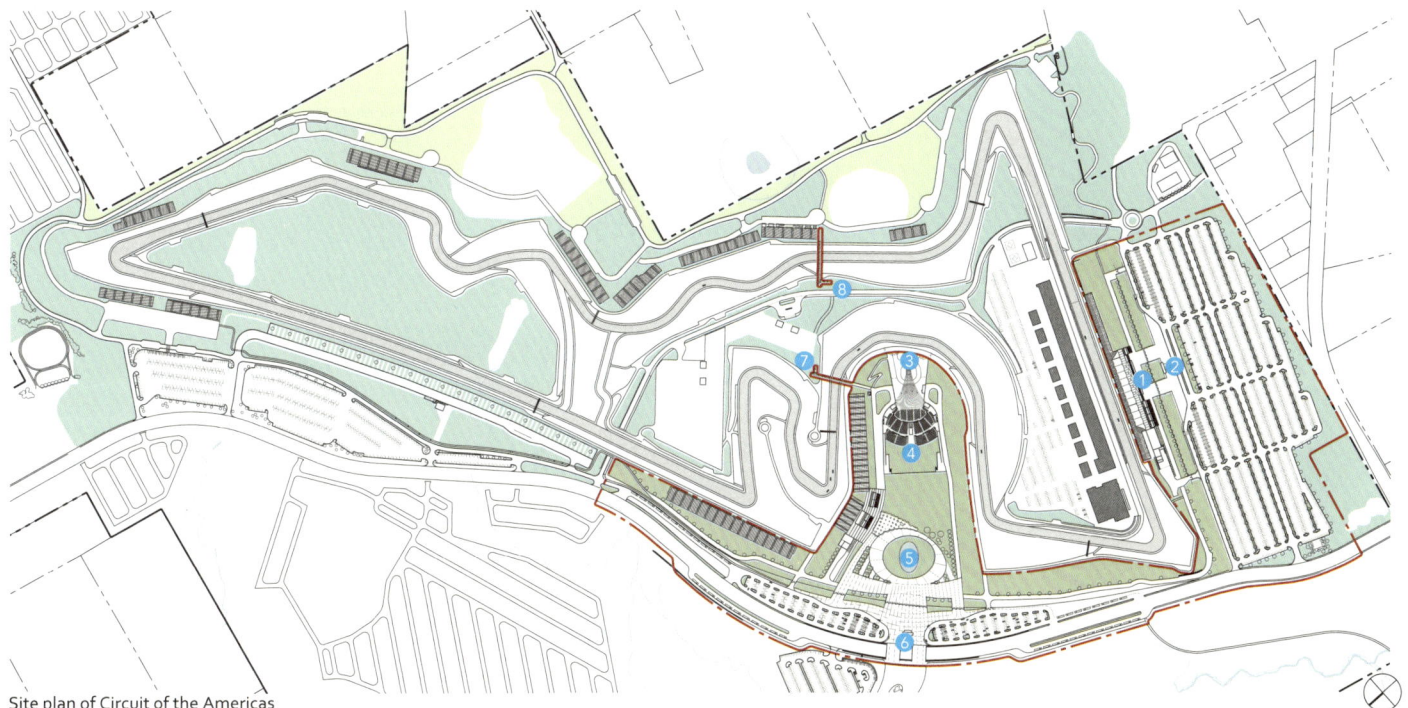

Site plan of Circuit of the Americas

visitors to look straight down to the ground below their feet. To reach the viewing deck, visitors can either ride a high-speed elevator or climb up 428 steps to their destination. At night, the stairs are illuminated by LED lights capable of producing an unlimited number of color combinations.

In both its design and construction, the Austin Observation Tower embodies the sense of precision, lightness and sleek dynamism associated with racing. Evoking the notion of split-second speed, the landmark structure reflects the spirit of the Circuit of the Americas and serves to establish the emerging identity of the complex as a world-class recreation and entertainment destination.

Site plan of Grand Plaza

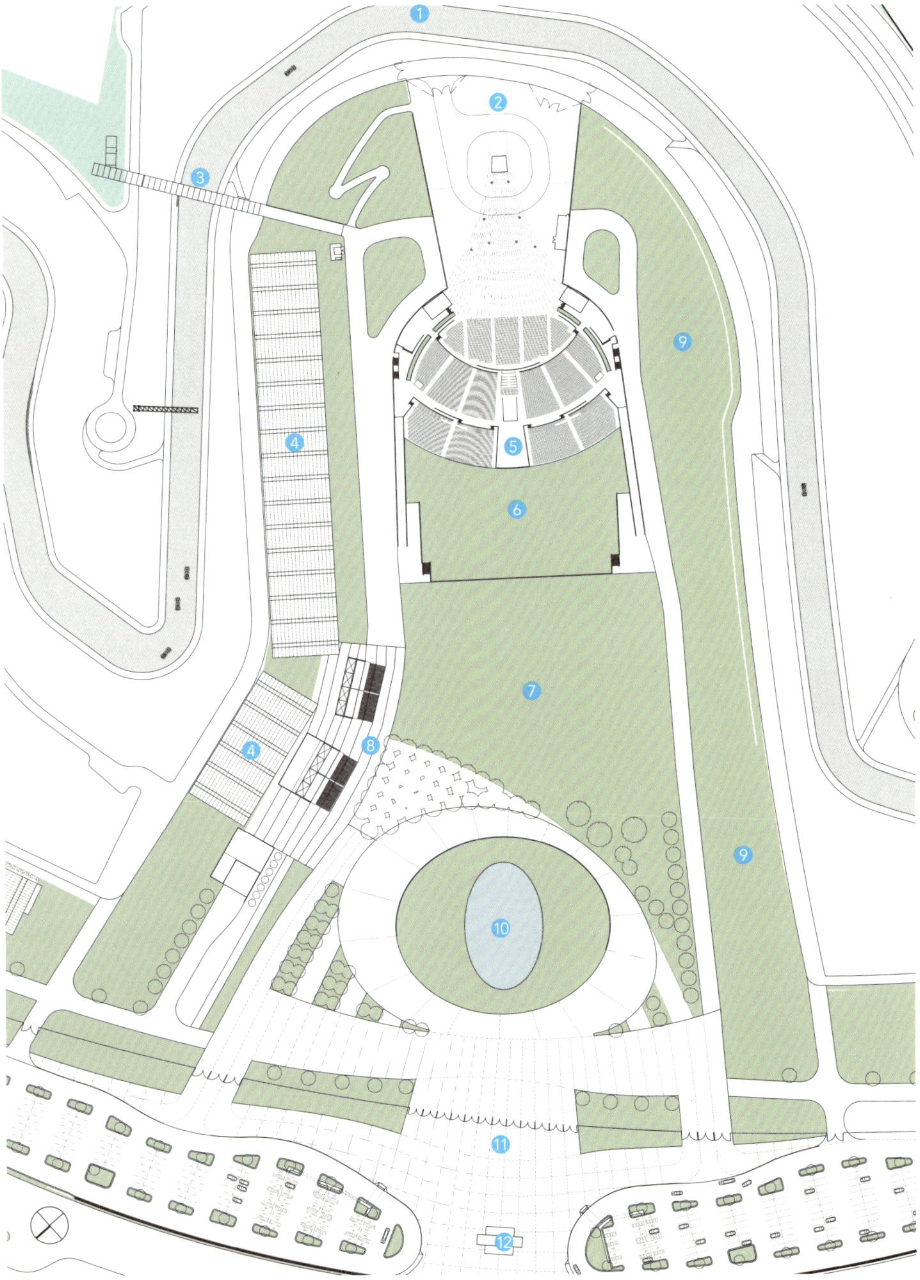

02 / View of race track from tower

① Track
② Observation tower
③ Pedestrian bridge
④ Stands
⑤ Austin360 amphitheater
⑥ Lawn seating
⑦ Great lawn
⑧ Concessions
⑨ Berm seating
⑩ Reflecting pool
⑪ Entry gates
⑫ Ticket building

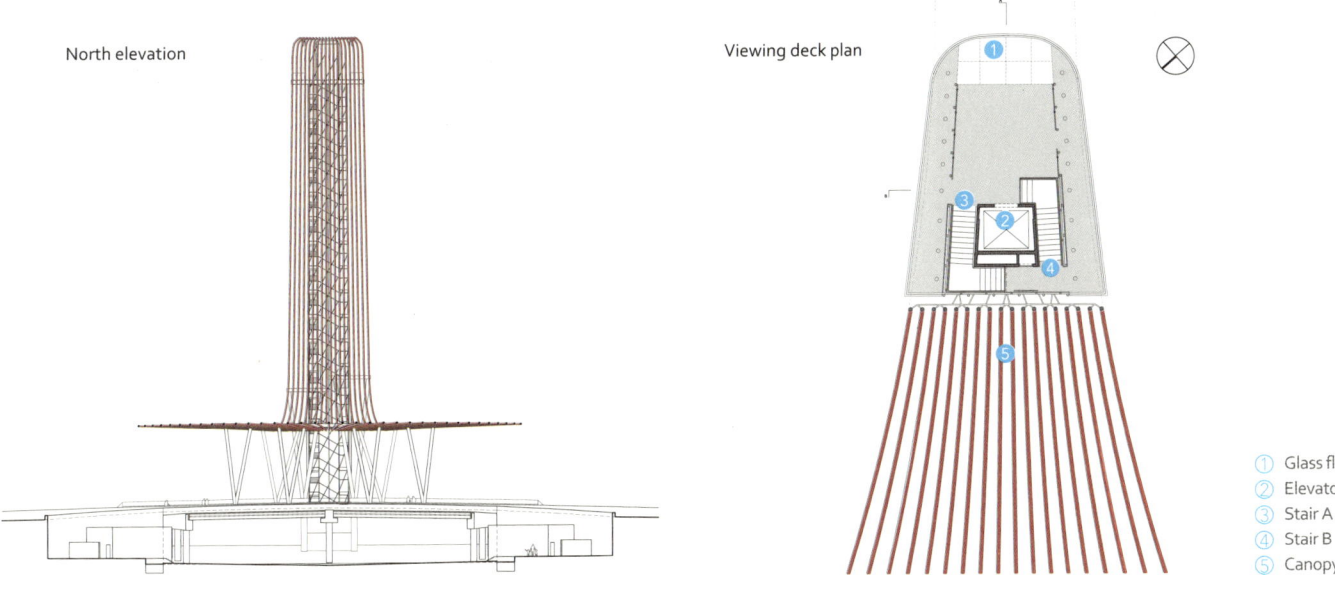

North elevation

Viewing deck plan

① Glass floor
② Elevator/Core
③ Stair A
④ Stair B
⑤ Canopy

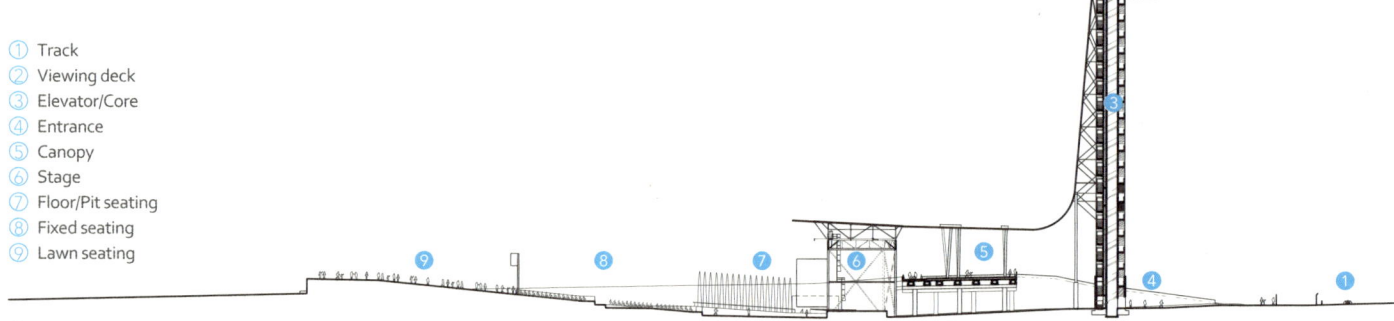

① Track
② Viewing deck
③ Elevator/Core
④ Entrance
⑤ Canopy
⑥ Stage
⑦ Floor/Pit seating
⑧ Fixed seating
⑨ Lawn seating

Section A

03 / Tower during the day
04 / Spiral staircase
05 / Red steel frame
06 / Viewing deck

04

05

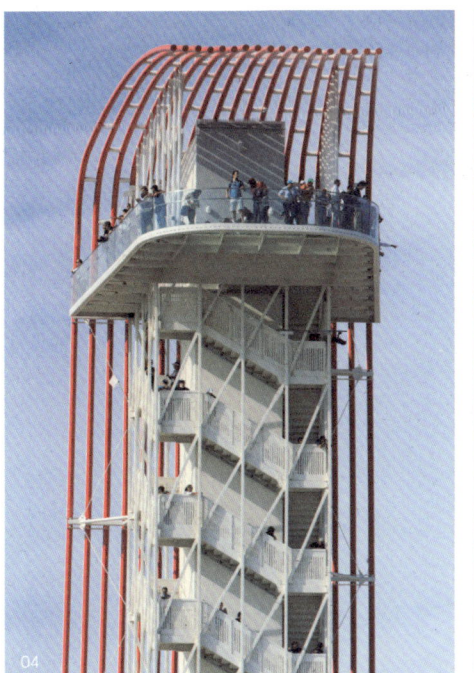

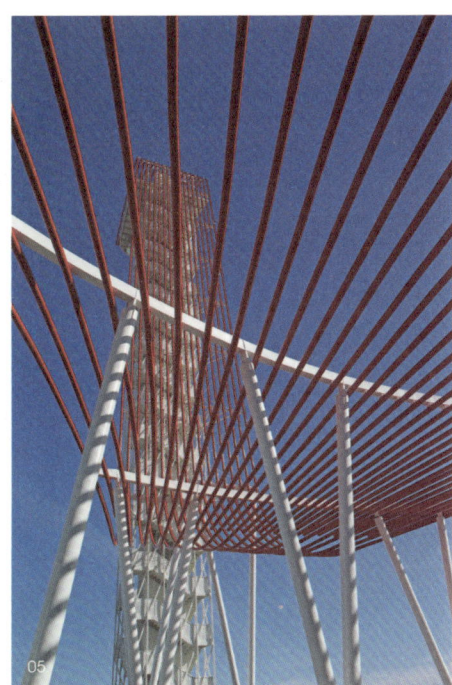

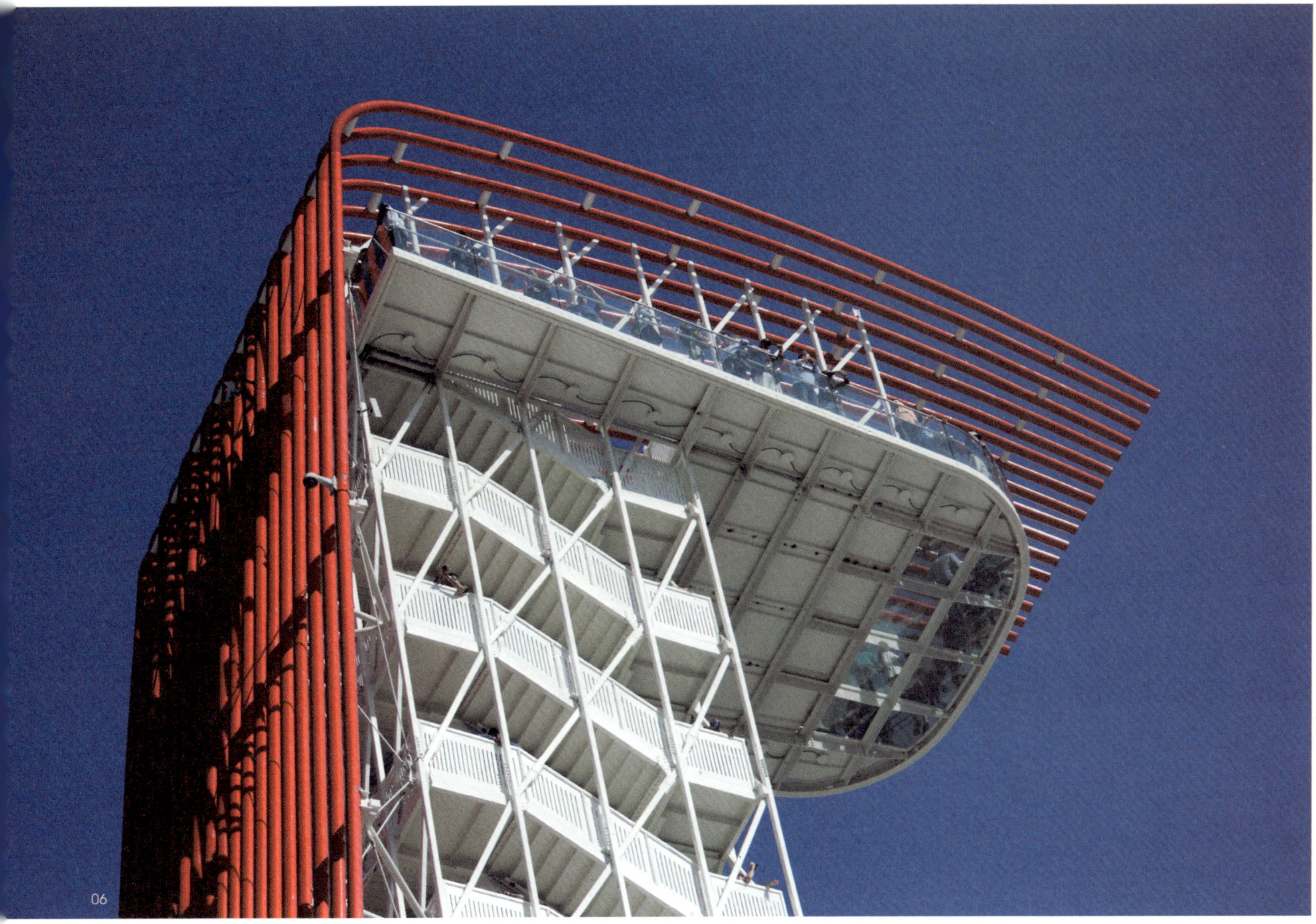
06

07-09 / Tower at night

① Beacon light
② Metal flashing with drip edge
③ Metal ladder with extending safety post
④ Light fixture
⑤ Speaker
⑥ Elevator relief mechanism
⑦ Roofing
⑧ Insulation
⑨ Steel deck
⑩ Elevator mounting structure
⑪ Elevator cab
⑫ Steel tube
⑬ Steel canopy tube
⑭ Steel column and bracing
⑮ Steel brace and rod
⑯ Cane guard
⑰ Steel plate
⑱ Steel beams
⑲ Laminated glass guardrail
⑳ Concrete wall
㉑ Steel handrail
㉒ Metal stairs
㉓ Concrete foundation
㉔ Steel column
㉕ Drainage
㉖ Asphalt

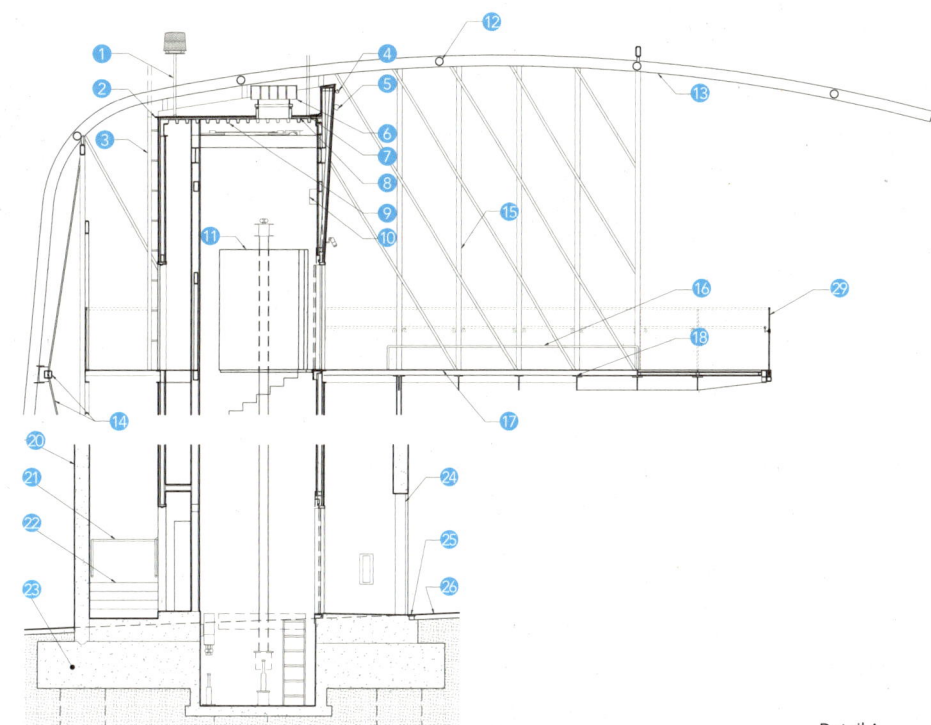

Detail A

① Speaker
② Sidewall
③ Handrail
④ Steel stairs
⑤ Steel tubes
⑥ Laminated glass guardrail

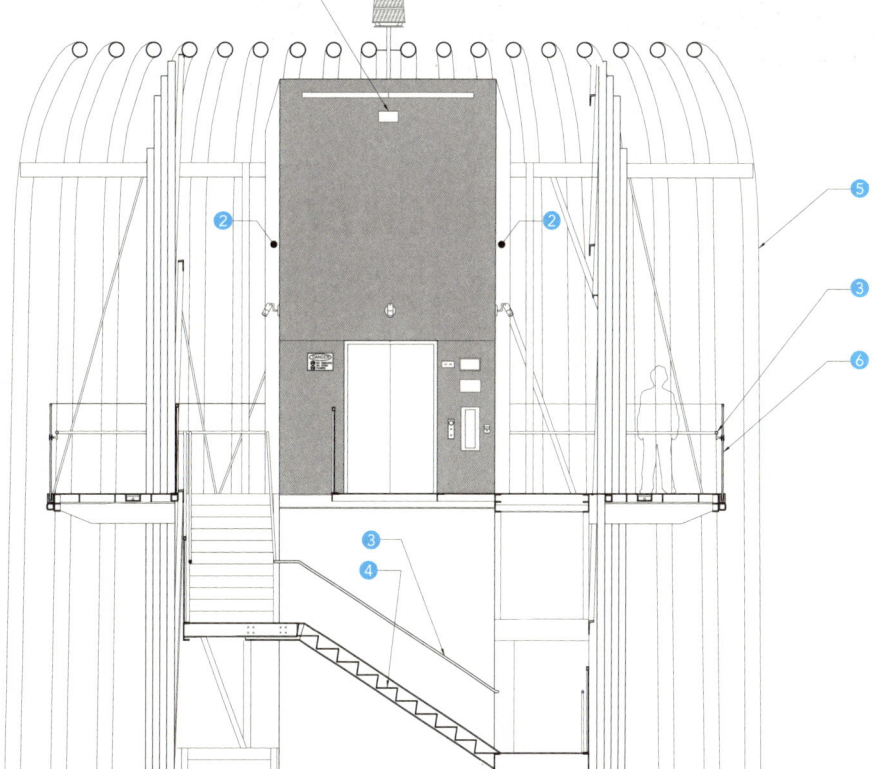

Detail B

Viewing Platform Trautmansdorff

Location / Meran Bolzano, Italy
Completion / 2005
Architect / Matteo Thun + Partners
Photography / The Gardens of Trautmansdorff
Client / The Gardens of Trautmansdorff

01 / Viewing deck in shape of binoculars

The spectacular viewing platform, which is about 90 percent transparent, is based upon an idea from South Tyrolean architect and designer Matteo Thun. Viewing Platform Trautmansdorff is a steel structure suspended on a central pillar, about 82 feet (25 meters) above rocky precipice. Visitors 'float' above the gardens, ascending towards the heavens by the staircase. Formed in the shape of binoculars, the platform affords breathtaking view of the Adige Valley, the Merano Valley Basin and the surrounding mountains.

In the most beautiful botanic garden in Italy, a panoramic platform for a sensation of flying, 'Scala Bellavista' is conceived as a suspended promontory among the hills in the Gardens of Trauttmansdorff Castle, offering a view on Merano and the surrounding mountainous landscape. The steel grid floor creates awareness and a sense of floating: 82 feet (25 meters) above the rocks underneath, 656 feet (200 meters) over the bottom of Adige Valley. The northern village of Hafling is precisely positioned on the extension, towards the south of Ultental, with a view to the Presena-Adamello Glacier.

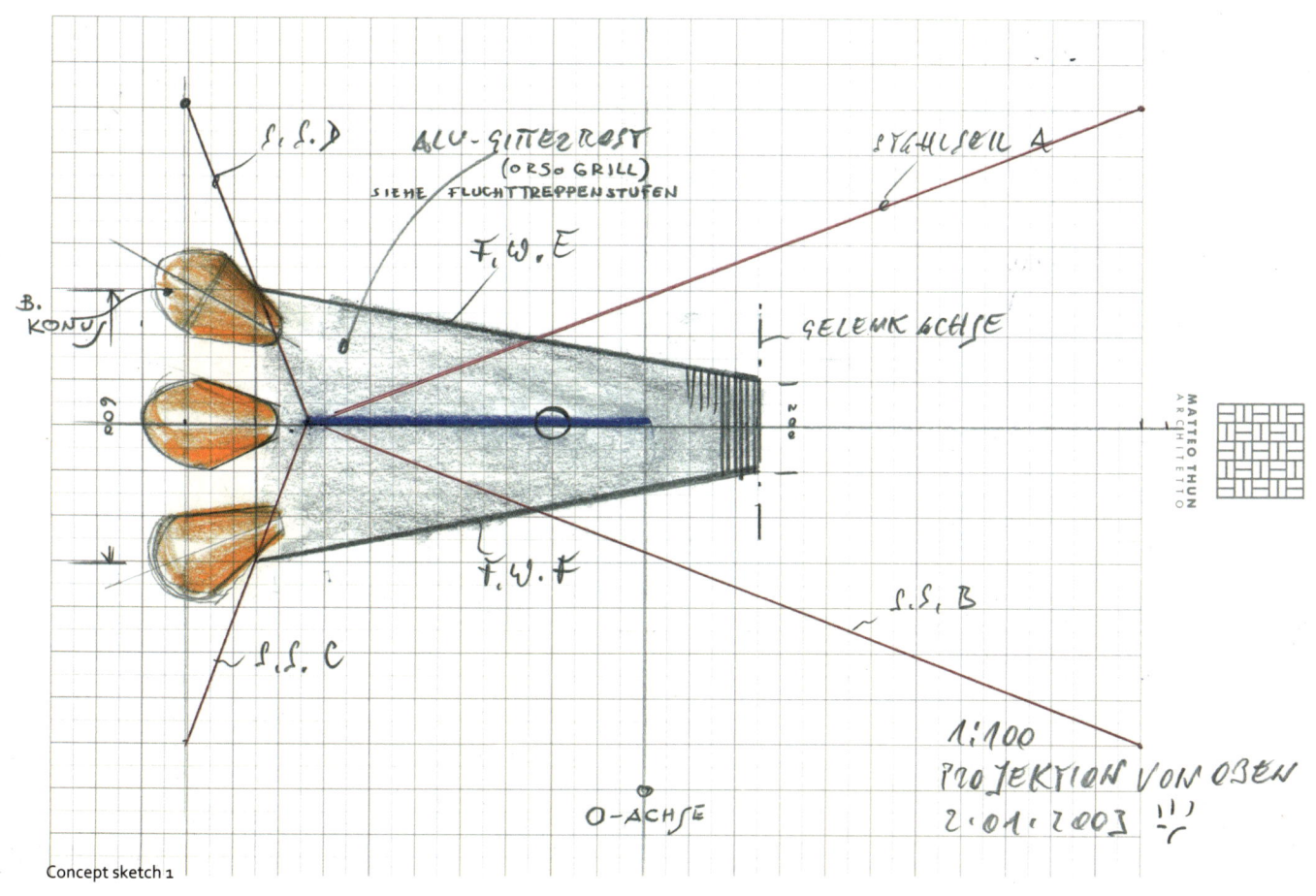

Concept sketch 1

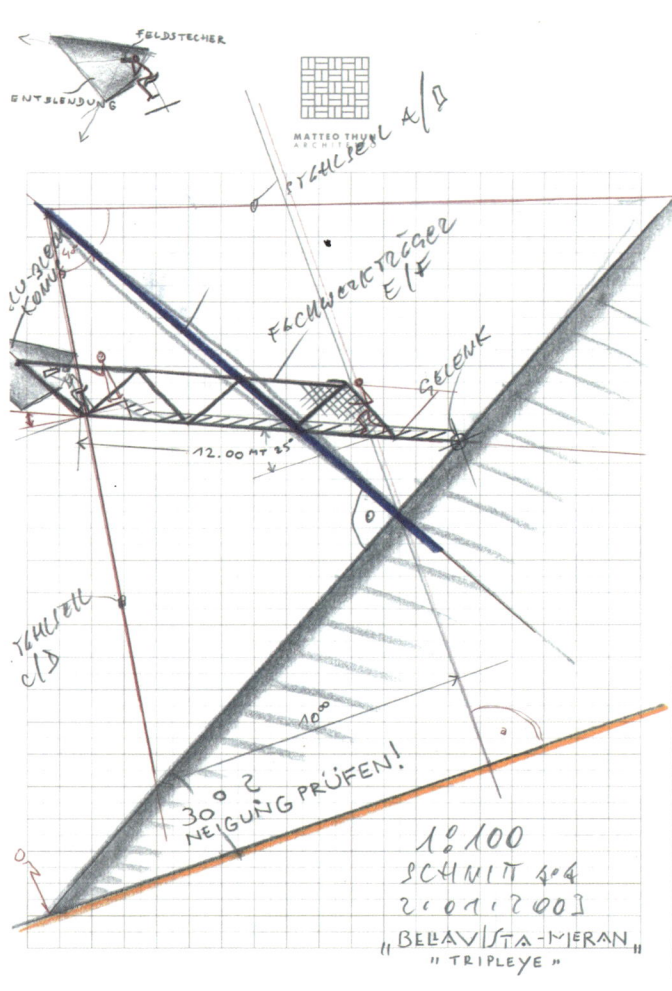

Concept sketch 2

02 / View of Trautmansdorff Garden
03 / Steel structure suspended on a central pillar
04-05 / Viewing deck above rocky precipice
06 / Close-up of lookout

Mountain Peak Platform on Top of Tyrol

Location / Tirol, Austria
Completion / 2009
Architect / LAAC Architects
Photography / LAAC Architects
Client / Wintersport Tirol AG & Co, Stubaier Bergbahnen KG, CEO Reinhard Klier

This panorama platform was commissioned by the management of one of the five glacier ski arenas in Austria. Like most of its competitors, the management is intent upon retaining a high level of attractiveness for its ski region. One hour's drive from Innsbruck, the Stubai Glacier offers a large variety of mountain climbs and hikes. The aim of the newly erected platform is therefore mainly the revival of seasonal and summer tourism. During the winter season, the platform can still beaccessed, if weather conditions permitting.

The mountain station Schaufeljoch at 10,433 feet (3180 meters) above sea level is reached via the mountain station. The path to the mountain peak platform starts from the funicular. One climbs up a number of steps to the ridge leading to the Great Isidor. After another 229–foot (70-meter) walkthrough natural landscape, one arrives at the platform.

The Great Isidor is centrally positioned in the Stubai Glacier and divides the Stubai Glacier into a western and an eastern half. Only by creating access doesa panorama view become feasible, enabling the onlooker to grasp the dimensions of the landscape. The breath-taking 360-degree panorama stretches from the Zillertal and Stubai Alps to the Dolomites and Chalk Alps. The platform invites the visitor to take a rest and to enjoy the peace and beauty of the mountains.

The clients wanted to create a spiritual place in which even stressed mountaineers can find peace and recuperate while letting their thoughts wander and enjoying the seemingly endless expanse of the mountain world.

As unusual as the panorama from the platform might seem, so crucial is the question concerning the solution to the invasion of nature or natural space. The platform is intended to represent a reaction and also form part of this natural environment. Thus, the design goal was more the design of a situation in space rather than a building.

By setting in scene and exaggerating the existing topography, the landscape generates shaped architecture, in other words, an artificial landscape. The architecture expresses both a dynamic and static aspect and forms part of its transformation: an obstruction interacting with the landscape, each reflecting and influencing the other.

01-04 / Viewing deck covered in snow

05 / Platform made from weather-resistant steel
06 / Side view of viewing deck

Due to its high iron content the rock has a red hue. It is clearly textured and serrated, which gives it a unique character. The choice of materials emphasizes a contrast to the zinc covered steel structures of the surrounding ski region. The platform is a steel construction made from weather-resistant steel. The construction principle of the girder grate is an unstructured grid. The twisted, excrescent swords of CorTen sheet steel form box-section beams with a triangular cross-section. Reinforcement strips support the standing girders to the rear of the foundations.

Between the 1.64 feet (0.5 meters) tall supports, there is the floor grating. The arched railing is monolithic. The handrail and bench are made of larch wood and the filling consists of a stainless steel net.

The load is transferred to the foundations and to the upslope rock anchors. The platform lies in the high alpine permafrost area. This requires the foundations to be braced by 49-foot-long (15-meter-long) rock anchors in the load area and a steel-reinforced concrete foundations on which the structure rests.

The sandblasted steel swords of weather-resistant steel extend 29.5 feet (9 meters) beyond the rock edge. All in all 19 tons of CorTen steel, 645 square feet (60 square meters) of grating and 164 feet (50 meters) of wood banister larch with stainless steel net were used. The structure was erected exclusively by helicopter. Therefore, the adaptation of the elements of the structure to fit the load limits of the helicopter, the positioning onto the mounting surfaces, and accuracy of fit were essential aspects of the structural design.

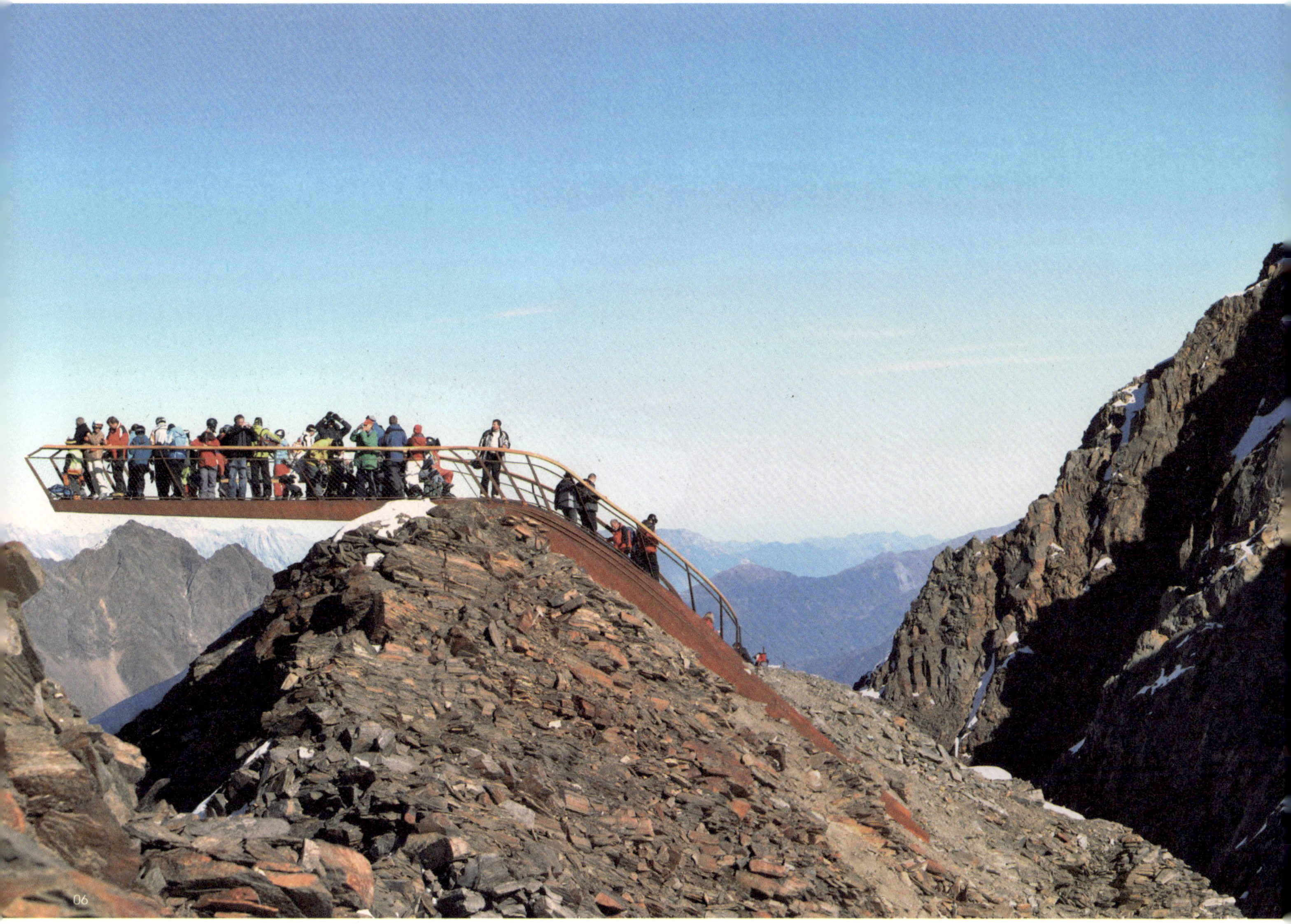

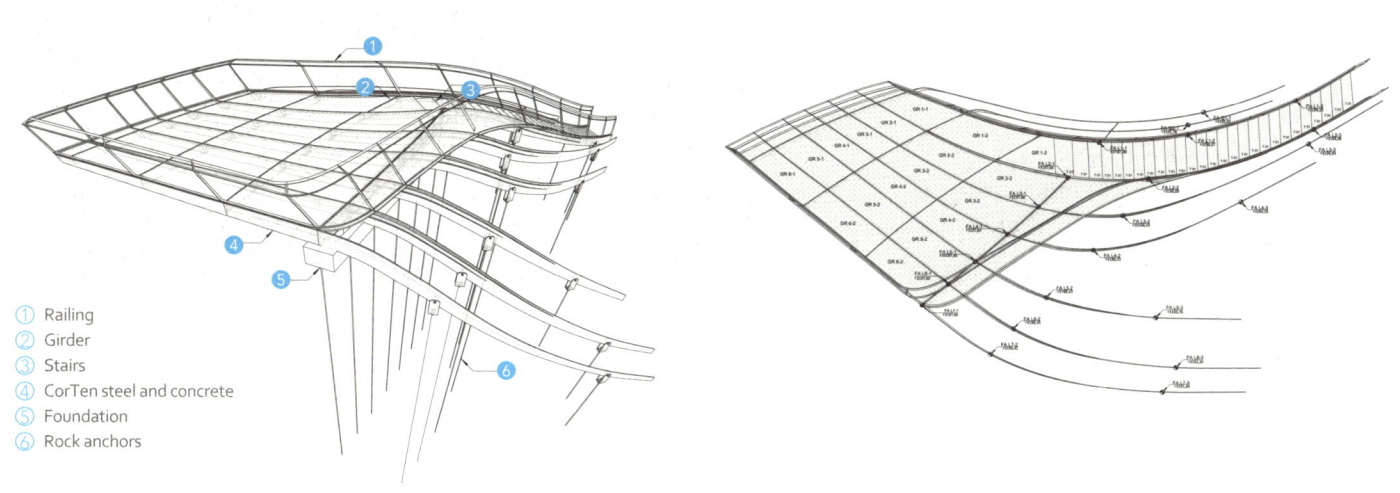

06

1
2
3
4
5
6
① Railing
② Girder
③ Stairs
④ CorTen steel and concrete
⑤ Foundation
⑥ Rock anchors

Perspective

Steel structure

① CorTen railing support
② Stainless steel grid
③ Girder
④ Railing
⑤ Girder grades
⑥ Bent grating

① Mounting plate
② CorTen steel
③ Shear connector
④ Mounting surfaces
⑤ Bolts

① Concrete foundation
② Rock anchors 14m
③ Anchor console
④ Rock anchors 4m

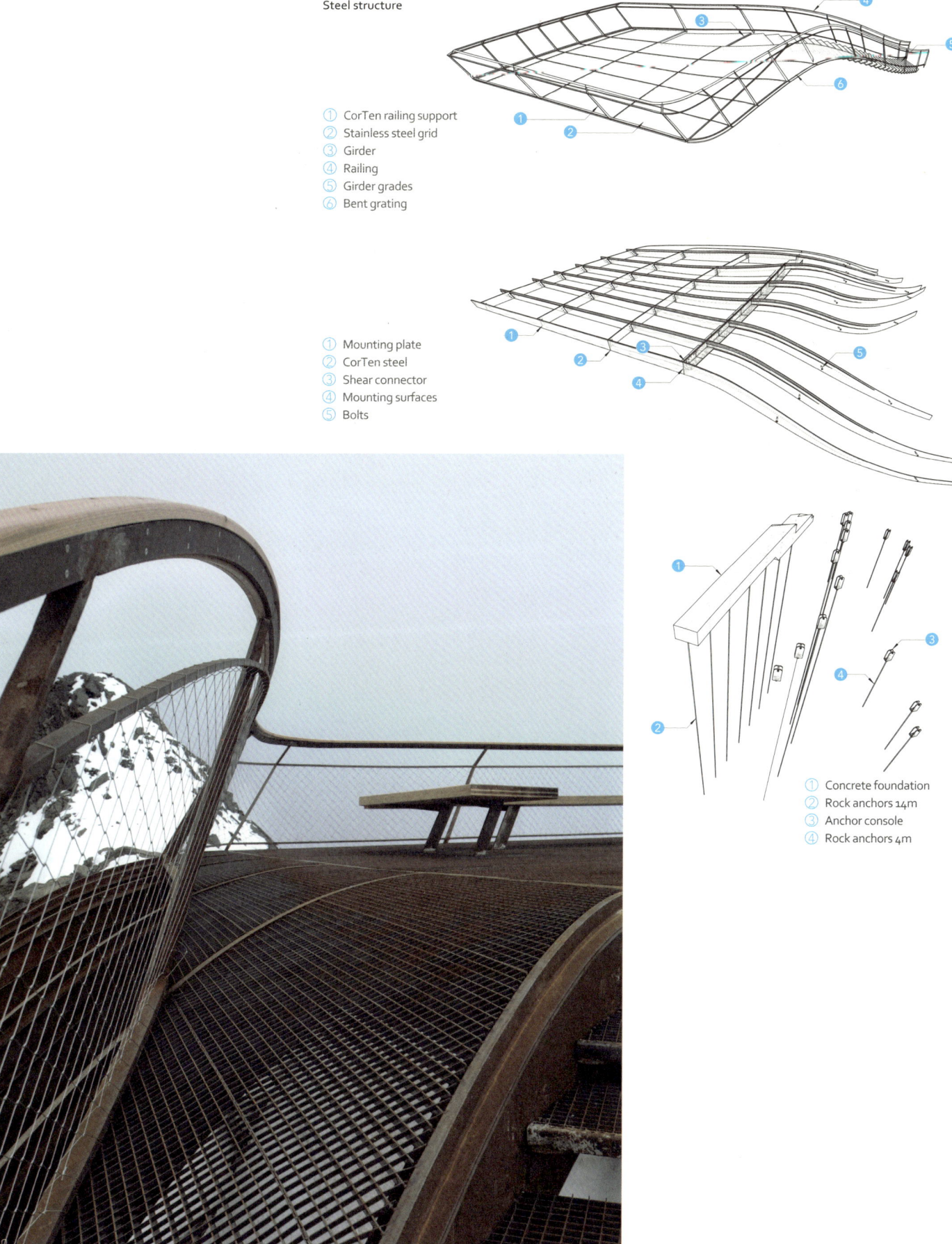

07-10 / Stainless steel grid

Quilotoa Crater Overlook

Location / Zumbahua, Ecuador
Area / 6630 square feet (616 square meters)
Completion / 2013
Architect / Jorge Javier Andrade Benitez
Photography / Lorena Darquea, Pablo Puente, Javier Mera, Daniel Moreno Flores, Cynthia Macias Leiva, Santiago del Hierro

The project is located in the top edge of the crater of an active volcano that has a lake inside of it, Because of its geographical peculiarities, the Quilotoa Crater, together with its lake, has become a tourist site of growing popularity in Ecuador.

Located in the Andes, this elevation is 557,742 feet (170,000 meters) south of Quito. Its altitude is 13,038 feet (3974 meters) above sea level, and the diameter of the crater is approximately 9843 feet (3000 meters). Due to the minerals present in its water, the lake in the crater has a distinctive turquoise color, the main characteristic of this site. The ecosystem of this area is an Andean páramo, meaning the surrounding vegetation includes low grasses, shrubs and small trees. All these elements add to create a landscape of restrained beauty.

The Ecuadorian Tourism Ministry responded to a community initiative by providing complementary infrastructure to the tourist facilities: an overlook at the top edge of the crater and a footpath to connect it with the main area of the tourist complex. The Ministry aimed to support the community's venture by helping locals increase their income through involving them in tourist services.

The effect that this project delivers revolves around creating opportunities for the visitor to see the landscape in different ways at every point in the crater. The user experience is enriched through the creation of a platform extending from the edge of the crater over the cliff face, giving the visitor the opportunity to 'fly' over the landscape, producing a vertigo-like sensation. At the same time, a space for passive viewing is created, where the user is protected from the elements and can have a moment of contemplation and introspection.

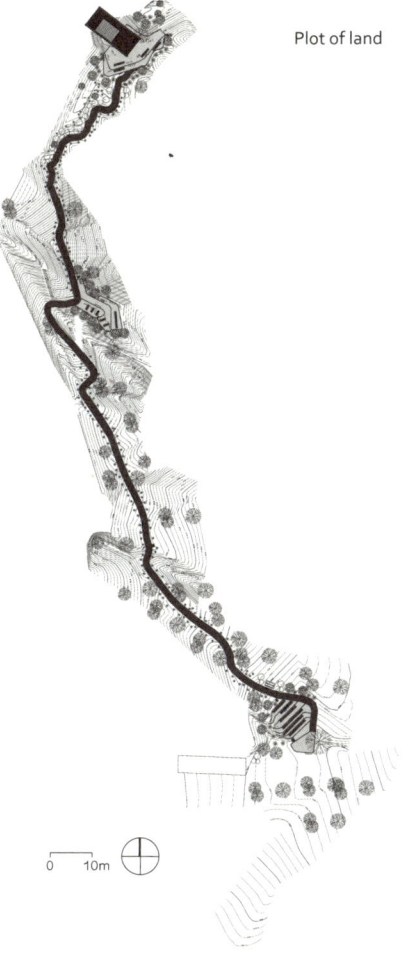

Plot of land

01 / Overlook allowing visitor to view crater from different angles
02 / Upper platform sheltering visitors
03 / Panoramic view of crater from overlook

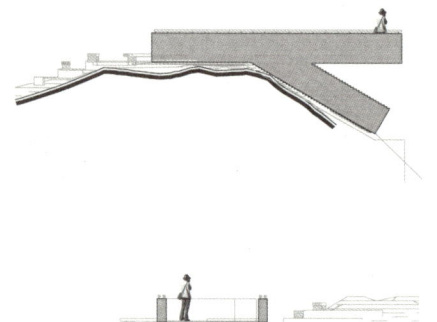

Sectional view 0   5m

The attempt to provide these opposite but complementary experiences for the user results in the creation of a structure comprising of an upper platform that extends further beyond the border of the crater and, directly underneath, bleachers that follow the natural slope where users have the opportunity to rest and enjoy the natural landscape. These simple but clear, architectonic gestures give the visitor the opportunity to have a different experience than what could be found in the rest of the crater.

The discrete but magnificent beauty of the landscape demands the architectonic response to be austere, in an attempt to merge itself with the surrounding landscape. A simple form and the uniform use of materials give the construction the same aesthetic qualities as the site. The structure is composed of an internal steel truss system and the skin is built with wood, which locates the construction within the chromatic palette and texture of the landscape. The broader features in the project are designed to safely allow a clear view of the surroundings. Therefore, glass is the only material used in the open ends of the overlook.

The footpath that connects to the overlook is built with stone edges and filled with gravel, looking to mark a defined route and to create a walkable surface without altering the natural qualities of the landscape. Every gesture in the construction attempts to avoid modifying the current harmony present in the site. For this reason, the entire structure is designed to be easily dismantled and removed if in the future the overlook is no longer needed.

Since the creation of this overlook, there has been a noticeable increase in the tourist activity in the community. Additionally, locals have engaged in the upkeep of the installation and are committed to keep it in good condition. This could be considered a successful case where the contributions of the state, the community and the designers have reached the expected outcome.

04 / Wood and glass finish for overlook
05 / Overhead view of volcano
06 / Upper platform of overlook
07 / Stairs to overlook

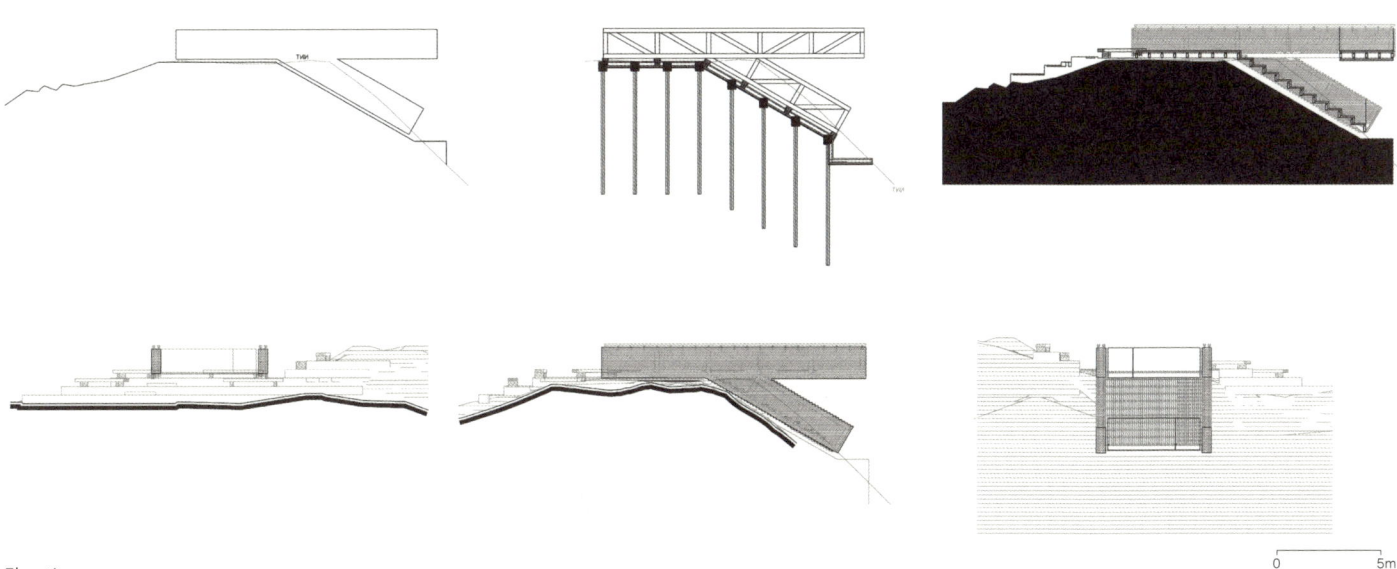

Elevations

0 5m

Structure analysis

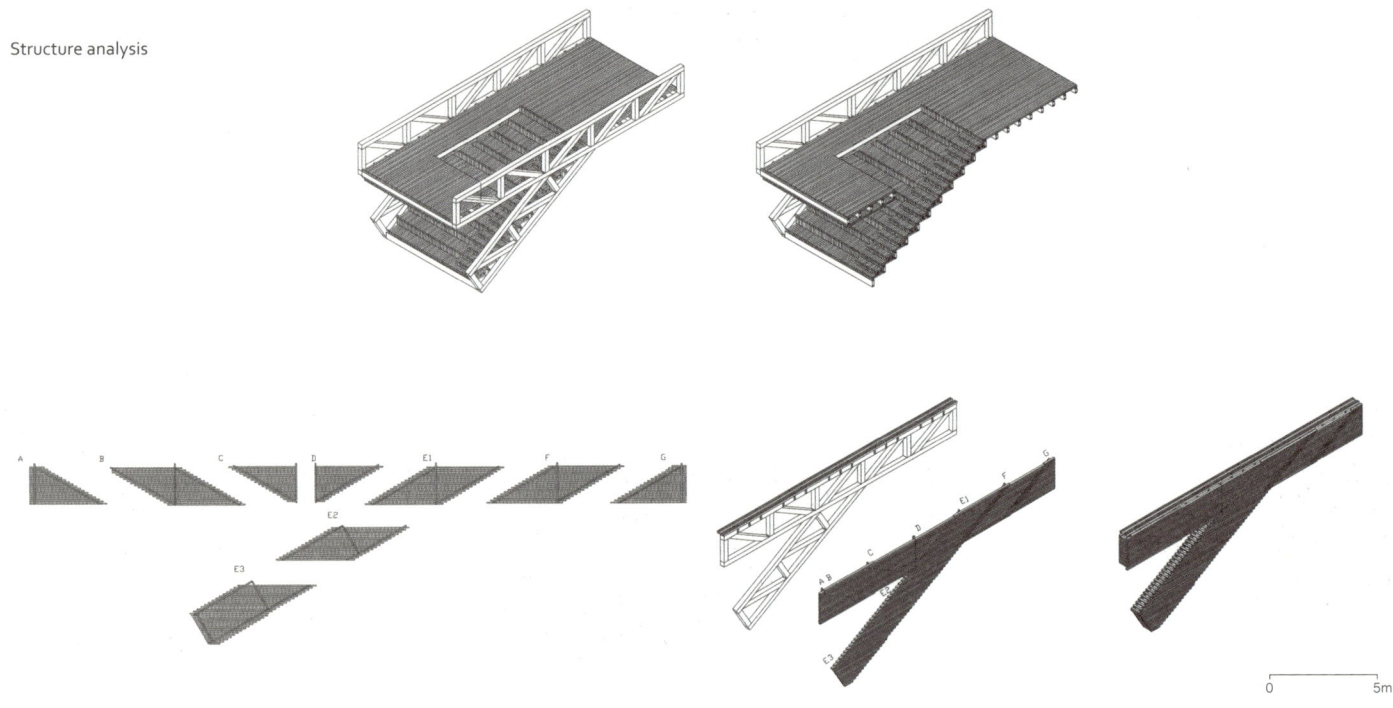

08 / Panoramic view of crater
09 / View of lower platform from upper
10 / Footpath connecting overlook with road
11 / Benches arranged footpath for visitors
12 / Small sign greeting visitors at start of footpath

Viewpoint from Palm Grove

Location / Daya Vieja, Spain
Area / 2960 square feet (275 square meters)
Completion / 2014
Architect / Joaquín Alvado Bañón
Photography / David Frutos
Client / Diputacion of Alicante

The decision to design a structure to retrofit the tree was taken after the collapse of one of its trunks during an episode of strong winds. This palm tree is in Daya Vieja, a small town located in the southeast of Spain in the province of Alicante. The tree belongs to the Phoenix Dactylifer variety and is more than 210 years old with a height of 67 feet (20 meters) and a perimeter of about 62 feet (19 meters); it is located in the main square of the town.

The first requirements that were imposed on the project were that it should neither harm the tree nor acquire a greater prominence than it. The project was designed to highlight and to protect the tree, yet it also had a specific use. The project was adjusted step by step from the initial conception to the final version, considering many different options. The three-dimensional steel frame structure was finally chosen as the one that would best comply with the prerequisites both in service and during its construction.

The final proposal was based on the external geometry of the Guggenheim Museum in New York. The structure consists of a helical steel truss beam that completes three ascending laps enveloping half the height of the trunks, embracing the tree completely. At the top, there is a steel ring where each trunk of this palm is anchored through cables at several points. These cables reduce significantly the force that winds generate on the base of the trunks. This reduces the risk of breakage and excessive deformation of each trunk during episodes of strong winds.

The design also intended to visually connect the town center with the surrounding fields to show visitors the relationship between the town and its surroundings as well as the change of the landscape with the coming of the different seasons. A lookout landmark, with a spiraling promenade that culminates in a narrow overpass jutting out over a major town thoroughfare, was created. The result of this special structure is the 'Variation Guggenheim 3,' or 'Viewpoint from the Palm Grove,' a 3D steel-frame spiraling walkway. Despite the fact that this construction certainly used more materials and took up more space than a simple retrofitting system, the designed structure allows visitors walking close to the tree, to enjoy an especially pleasant experience, and has created a valuable architectural icon as well. In addition to the

01 / Full view of structure
02 / Side view

Site plan

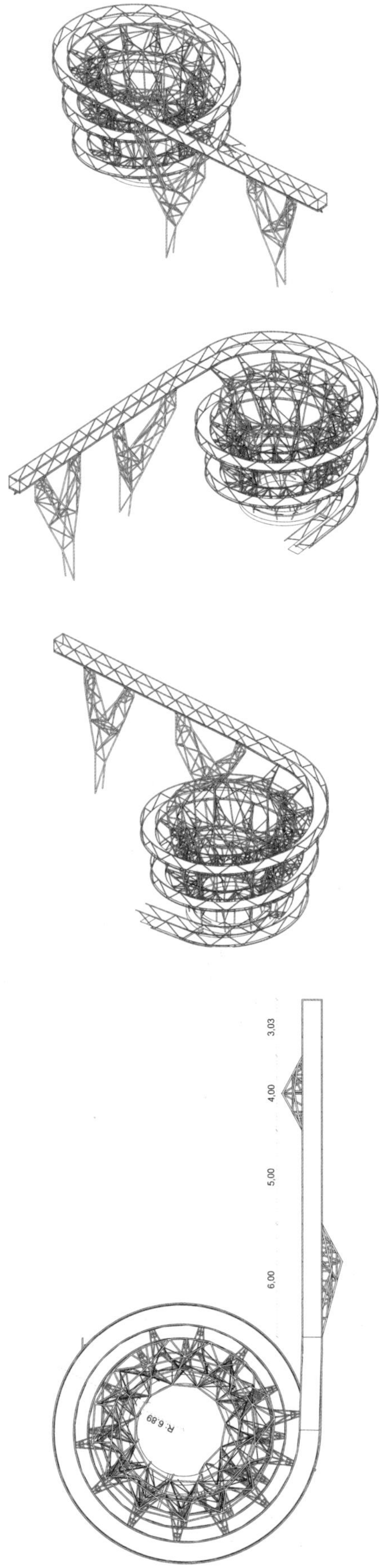

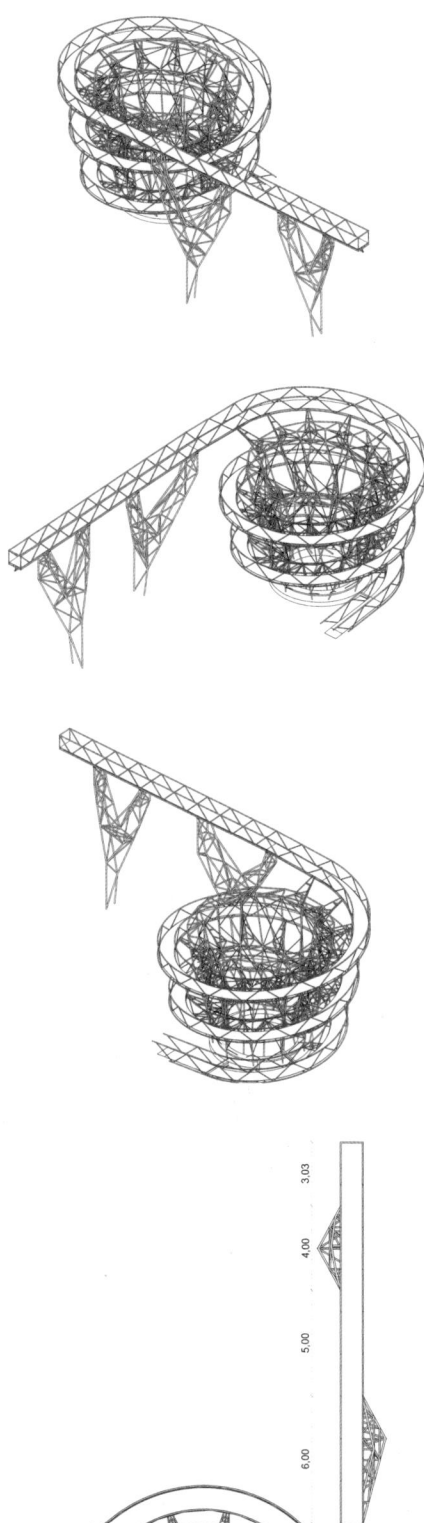

Concept sketches

alluring views and the fun pedestrian walk, the idea of making the tree a focal point and, conversely, to extol it, is an example of the sustainable thinking that infiltrates much of today's architecture.

The tower resembles a roller coaster made for pedestrians. This roller coaster offers, instead of speed, awesome 360-degreeviews of Daya Vieja and unique points of view of the palm tree, while protecting it from collapse. Thus the Mirador de la Palmera serves both as a spiraling walkway/lookout tower and a brace for the unique palm tree that it embraces.

In 2014, this structure was finalist for the Architecture Awards presented by the Diputación de Alicante for the best construction projects in 2010-2014. The steel spatial walkway and lookout now connects the town center of Daya Vieja with the surroundings, the fields and the landscape. The idea was to achieve two goals at the same time: a structural solution for the monumental six-headed tree and an audacious footbridge to provide a view of the surrounding territory. The design plan was to construct a 3D, light steel frame structure to protect the palm tree while at the same time projecting a unique structure to promote the image of this small southeastern Spanish village. The 'Variation Guggenheim 3' is a new facility for the citizens to appreciate both the natural and artificial beauty of Daya Vieja.

03 / View from bottom
04 / Overhead view
05 / View from walkway

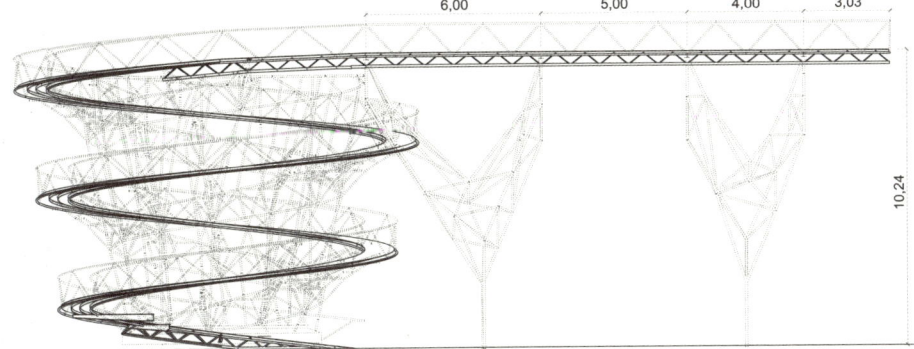

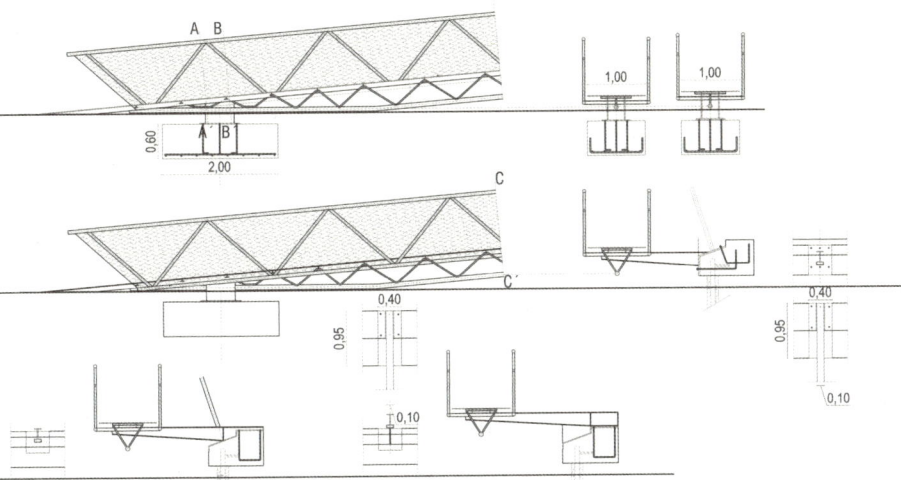

Structural details of walkway

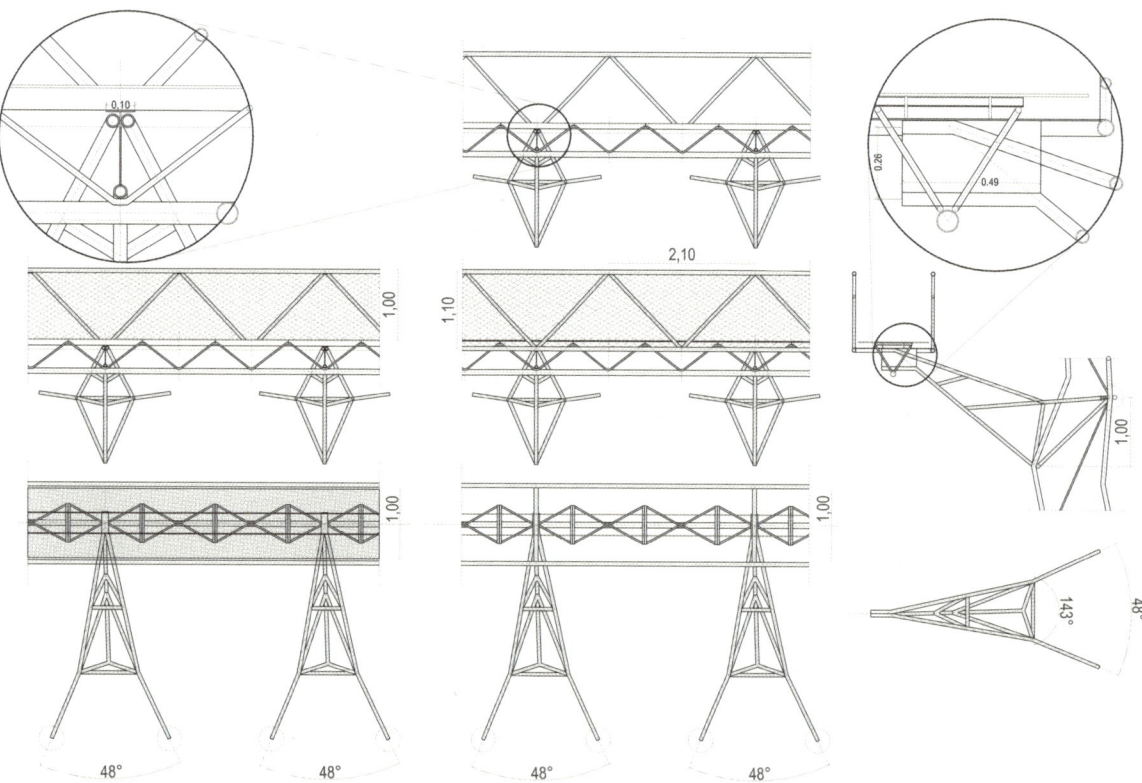

Structural system to support walkway

06 / View of walkway
07-08 / Structural view
09 / Platform view

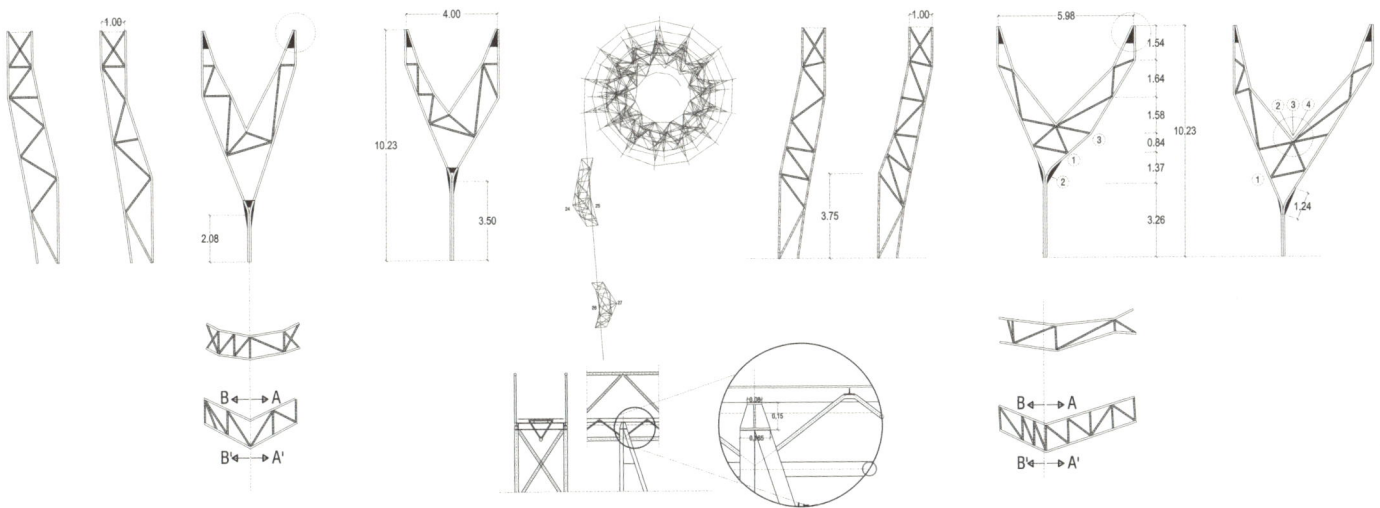

Structural details of tree-shaped pillars

The Pyramid Viewpoint

Location / Inveruglas, Scotland
Completion / 2015
Architect / BTE Architecture
Photography / Andrew Lee, Ross Campbell, Mick McGurk
Client / Scottish Government

The site is located on a peninsula overlooking the United Kingdom's largest stretch of inland water, Loch Lomond. From the car park with adjoining jetty, a system of pathways lead onto the peninsula and continue along its exposed edges formed by big rocks, or through the site sheltered by trees and bushes. The rocks locate the site high above the water's edge and a series of steps and easily accessible ramps lead the visitor through the sloped interior of the site. The pathways interlink, creating a parlor with rendezvous points adding emphasis to these junctions. The topography of the site allows the surrounding landscape to be experienced as a panorama, with the site itself visible from afar, as a rock amongst water.

The viewpoint takes the shape of a triangular platform and is positioned at the end of a long curved path stretching from the car park to the highest point of the peninsula. It is first seen as a narrow vertical stack amongst the tree trunks surrounding the path. Only a glimpse towards the loch is visible through a long tunnel that marks the entrance situation of the viewpoint. The single-story tunnel, which is as narrow as the path, leads from one vertex of the triangle to its base with views over the loch disguising the scale of the project. Only after having passed through this entrance and then looking back into the triangle, the viewpoint manifests itself as a steep rising platform that is accessed by steps going up and around the perimeter of the form.

01 / Triangular platform
02 / Area around platform
03 / Aerial view

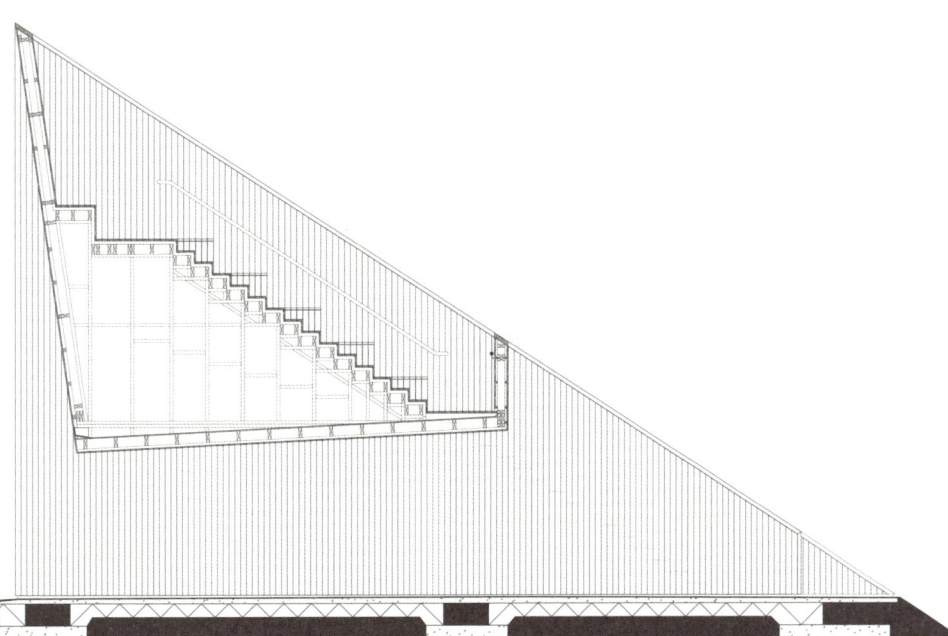

Detail setion

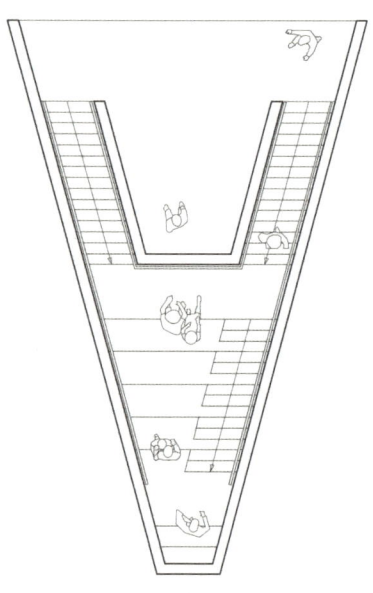

Second-floor plan

Benches, interspersed between the steps, create the central core. As the structure rises, the more exposed the benches become, mimicking the seating arrangements of an arena.

Externally, the viewpoint creates a distinctive point of attraction. With a strong visual impact, it embraces the vast drama of the landscape, which wants to be experienced in such an exposed location. The inviting gesture of the beacon attracts visitors from a distance to explore an alternative view, a pause in their journey on this scenic seat. The sculptural character of the project is strengthened through the use of one singular material. Both walls and the horizontal steps and benches are finished with a vertical timber rain screen. Its bold appearance contrasts and complements the various greens within its natural surroundings and the usable interior of the structure invites the visitor to have a seat on a warm material that wants to be touched.

04 / Scenary around platform
05 / View of lake from platform

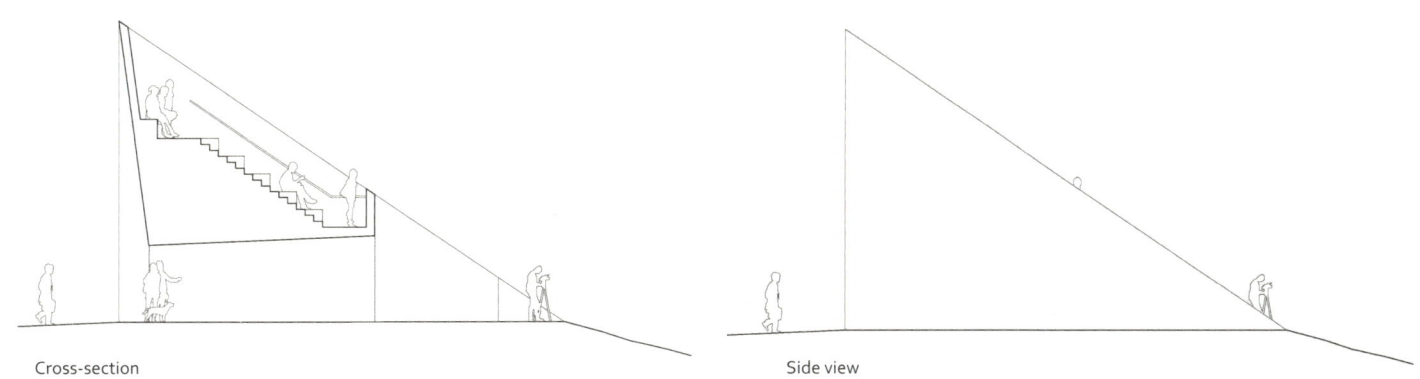

Cross-section

Side view

06 / Footpath to viewing deck
07-09 / Hallway leading to viewing deck

Entrance elevation

First-floor plan

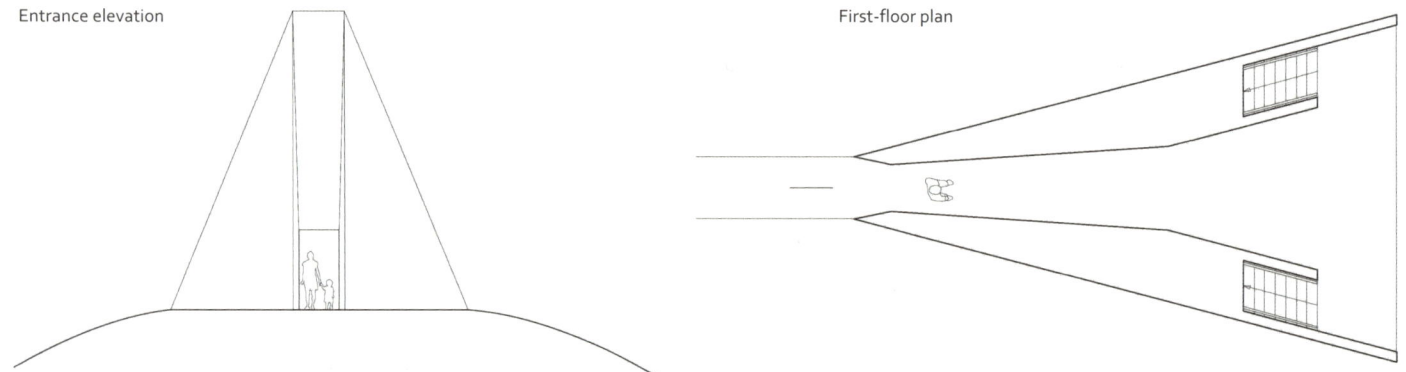

Löyly

Location / Helsinki, Finland
Area / 32,582 square feet (3027 square meters)
Completion / 2016
Architect / Avanto Architects Ltd.
Photography / kuvio.com, Archmospheres.com, Mikko Ryhänen|Joanna Laajisto Creative Studio
Client / Antero Vartia and Jasper Pääkkönen, Kidvekkeli Oy

The project started as an initiative from the city of Helsinki. The site is unique. Being less than 6561 feet (2000 meters) away from the city center, it is very central, but at the same time the landscape, is like in an outer archipelago. The plot is situated in a future coastal park that will be part of a broader 'Helsinki park,' connecting the capital city to the sea. The building was designed to be slim and elongated so as not to cut the narrow park strip. The volume is kept as low as possible so that it doesn't block views from the future residential blocks. Instead of building a conventional building, the sauna was developed to bean easy-going, faceted construction that is more part of the park than a conventional building. When the wooden building turns gray, it resembles a rock on the shoreline.

The architectural idea is simple: a rectangular black box containing warm spaces, covered with a free-form wooden 'cloak.' Instead of being mere decoration, the sculptural structure made of heat-treated pine has several functions.

First, it provides people with visual privacy. However, the cloak doesn't obstruct the sea view while inside it, rather the cloak functions like venetian blinds, preventing those outside from looking in. There are sheltered spaces outside between the warm mass and cloak to cool down in between sauna bathing. The cloak forms intimate terraces between the slopes, serving as a place to sit. The structure protects the building from the harsh coastal climate. It shades the interior spaces with big glass surfaces, helping to reduce the use of energy to cool the building.

Moreover, the stepped cloak also forms stairs to climb on to the roof and look out from the terraces on top of the building. The construction forms a big outdoor auditorium for the future marine sports activities in the sea. There are around 4000 planks that were precisely cut to individual forms by a computer-controlled machine. The big wooden terrace is partly on top of the sea and you can hear the sound of the waves under your feet.

The building consists of two parts: public saunas and a restaurant. The saunas and public spaces open up to the sea, with interesting views to city center and even to the open sea. The atmosphere is calm and the spaces dimly lit. Different areas are

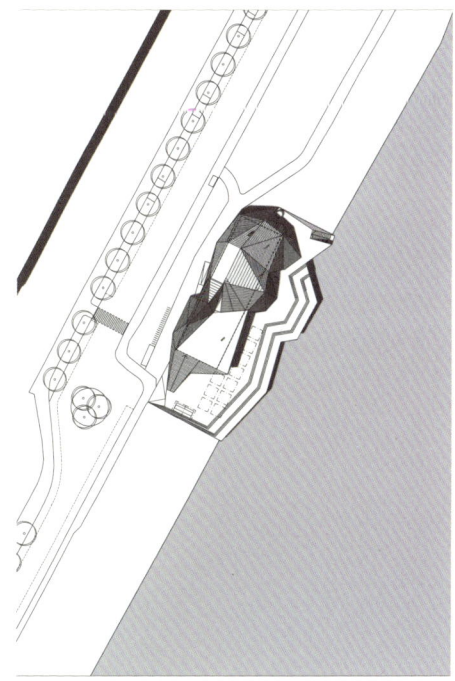

Site plan

01 / Overhead view of building

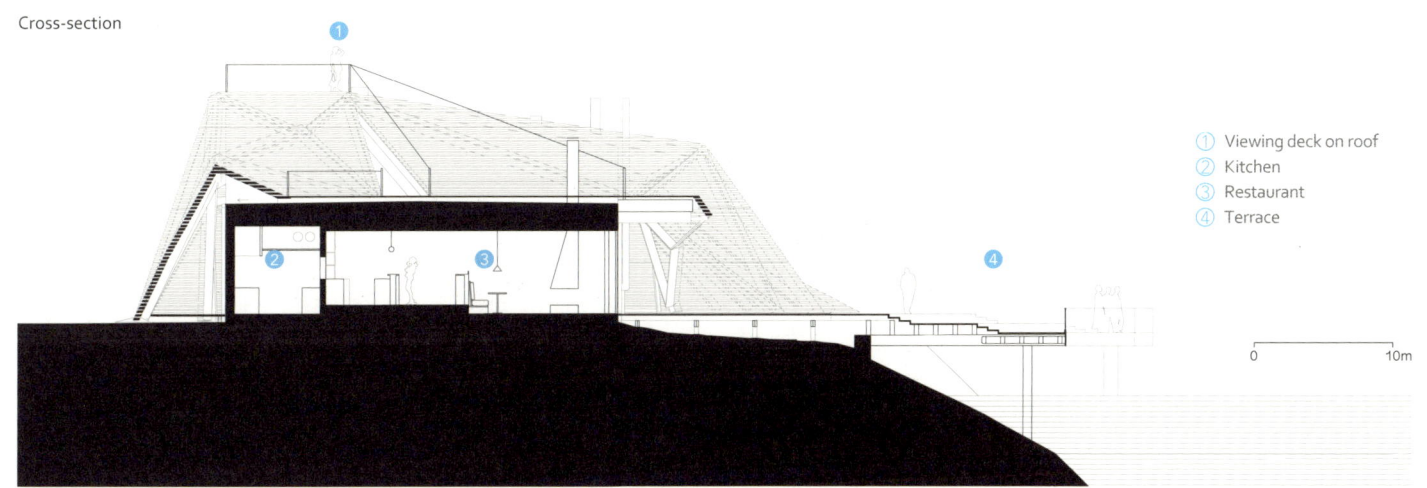

Cross-section

① Viewing deck on roof
② Kitchen
③ Restaurant
④ Terrace

02 / Cloak-like mass allowing people to climb to terrace on top
03 / Stairs leading to roof deck
04 / Terrace facing sea
05 / West façade of building
06 / Side view of building

conceived as spaces within a space. Interesting views open between closed spaces as you move from one area to the next.

The interior design of the restaurant and the sauna lounge create an atmospheric restaurant, which complements the strong architecture of the building. The approach could be called soft minimalism. The challenge was to create intimate seating areas in a large hall-like space with two walls of windows. People often feel most comfortable sitting their backs against the wall. The solution was to build a raised platform for the bar area that divides the space into two different areas. A wooden half wall anchors the long custom-designed sofas, which have a great view of the sea.

The main materials used in the interiors are black concrete, light Scandinavian birch wood, blackened steel and wool. All materials are durable and long lasting. The wood used is pressed, glued and slightly heat-treated birch, a new sustainable Finnish innovation made of left-over materials from the plywood industry that normally is burned to produce energy. This is how waste is turned into a beautiful recycled material. Its manufacturing process produces a beautiful cool color tone and heavy durability.

In addition to the long sofas, the designer used the glued laminated birch on the walls, tabletops, the long bar counter, and even in the unisex toilet sink. The upholstered chairs, which add softness to the space, are by Italian manufacturer Torre. All fabrics are soft natural wool made by Kvadrat. The bar stools are by Gubi and the wooden chairs in the sauna lounge are by Finnish Nikari. The string lights designed by Micheal Anastassiades create a subtle rhythm to the space without blocking views of the Baltic Sea.

Löyly has become one of the key tourist attractions in Helsinki and it is included in all the new city guidebooks. It is a place where foreign visitors have a possibility to experience the three different types of saunas together with local residents. Bathing in the heat of the sauna and swimming even in winter when the sea is frozen is memorable experience for tourists. The project is an example of a new active urban culture where abandoned areas are activated and people take active use of public areas.

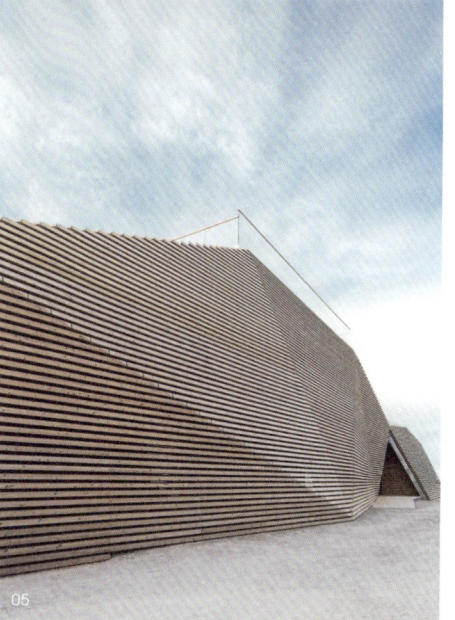

07 / View of terrace by sea
08 / Interior view
09 / Wood slating acting as privacy blinds for sauna
10 / Sauna stove

First-floor plan

1. Kitchen service
2. Kitchen
3. Sales desk
4. Restaurant
5. Fireplace
6. Campfire
7. Terrace
8. Lobby
9. Restroom
10. Elevator
11. Wood storage
12. Locker room
13. Smoke sauna
14. Sauna lobby
15. Lounge area
16. Unisex restroom
17. Sauna
18. Fireplace lounge
19. Cold water pool
20. Hot tub

The Infinite Bridge

Location / Aarhus, Denmark
Area / 32,291 square feet (3000 square meters)
Completion / 2017
Architect / Gjøde & Partnere Arkitekter
Photography / Aarhus|Billeder, DANISH TM, Peter Hastrup Jensen, Gjøde & Partnere Arkitekter
Client / Aarhus Municipality

The Infinite Bridge is a sculpture by Danish architect studio Gjøde & Povlsgaard Arkitekter built and exhibited in connection with the international biennale, Sculpture by the Sea 2015, which takes place in the scenic coastal landscape surrounding the city of Aarhus.

The designers have created a sculpture that is all about experiencing the surroundings and becoming aware of the relation between the city and the magnificent landscape of the bay. Walking on the bridge tourists experience the changing landscape as an endless panoramic composition and, at the same time, tourists enter a space of social interaction with other people experiencing the same panorama.

The Infinite Bridge has a diameter of 197 feet (60 meters) and is positioned half on the beach and half in the sea. It consists of 60 identical wooden elements placed on steel pillars housed about 6.6 feet (2 meters) into the sea floor. The deck of the bridge rises between 3.3 feet (1 meter) and 6.6 feet (2 meters) above the water surface depending on the tide. The curvature of the bridge follows the contours of the landscape as it sits at the mouth of a small river valley extending into the forest from the beach.

In addition to unfolding the seaside panorama, The Infinite Bridge establishes a connection between the present and the history of the specific site, as it reconnects the beach to a long forgotten scenic spot at sea.

The bridge touches the landing dock of another pier located at the site where people used to arrive in steamboats from the city to relax and enjoy themselves. The historic Varna Pavilion that sits on the hillside above the beach was a popular destination in the scenic landscape with its terraces, restaurant and dancehall. Situated on the edge of the forest facing the sea, the pavilion was meant to be experienced from the landing dock of the pier that no longer exists. The Infinite Bridge reestablishes this historic connection and offers a new perspective on the relation between the city and the surrounding landscape.

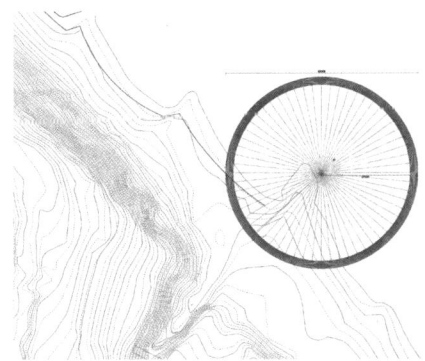

Site plan

01 / Aerial view of bridge
02-06 / Models

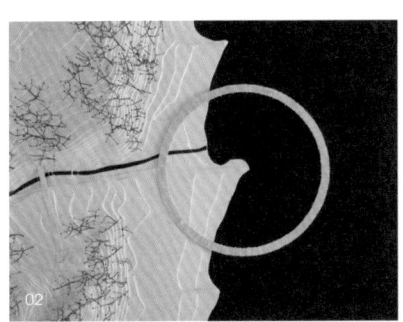

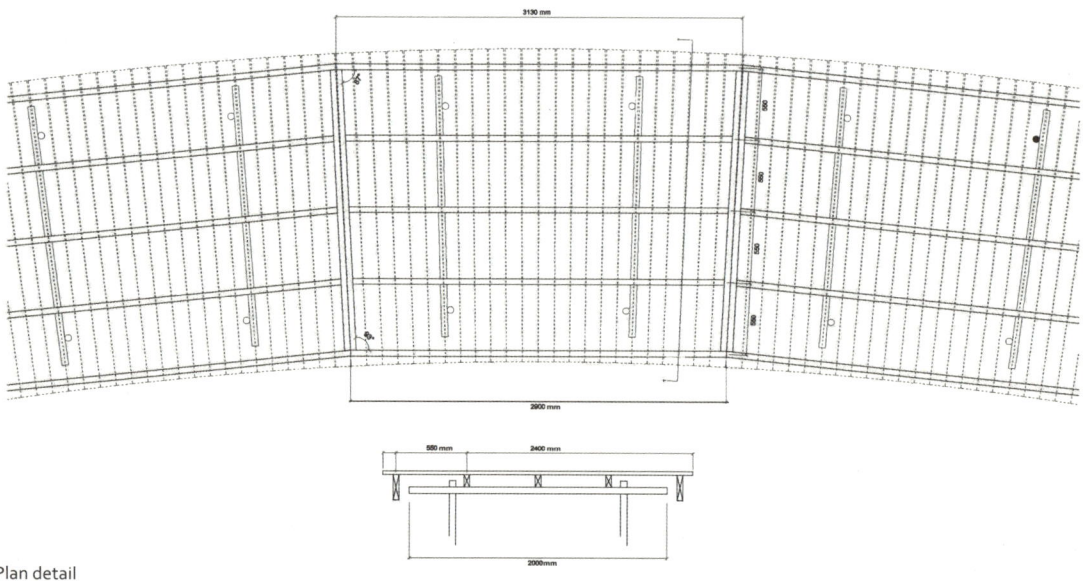

Plan detail

07 / Full view of bridge
08 / View of bridge from sea
09 / View of bridge from beach

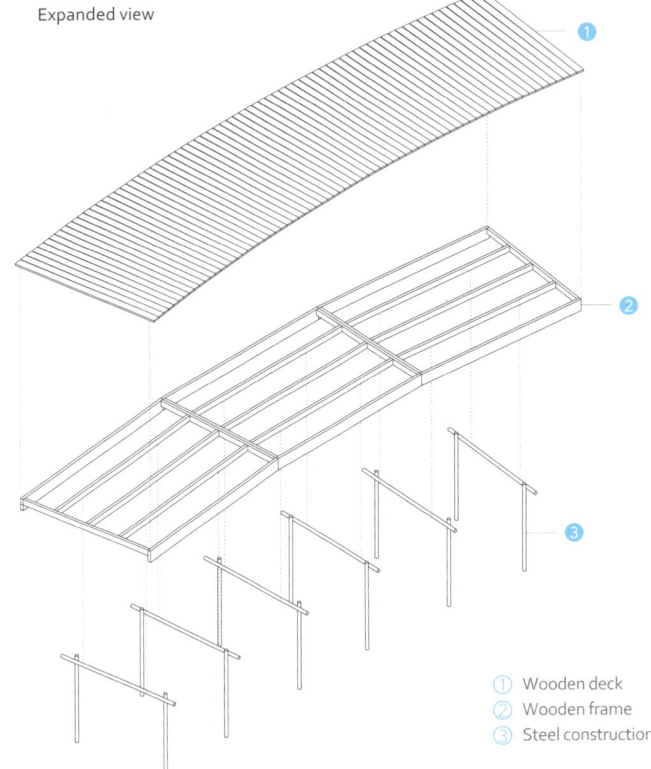

Expanded view

① Wooden deck
② Wooden frame
③ Steel construction

Sky Walk

Location / Dolní Morava City, Czech Republic Country
Completion / 2015
Architect / Fránek architects, Taros Nova
Photography / BoysPlayNice
Client / Dolní Morava

Sky Walk is located very close to the cottage Slaměnka, at the top station of the chair lift Sněžník at an altitude of 3661 feet (1116 meters) above sea level. Its height is 180 feet (55 meters) and the summit can be easily reached along a wooden path with strollers and wheelchairs. More adventurous visitors can use unique 331-foot-long (101-meter-long) stainless steel slide with windows.

Visitors can enjoy the beautiful views of the entire Králický Sněžník massif alongside the scenic Morava river valley and the main ridge of Jeseníky and Krkonoše mountains in the distance.

For the architects, constructing the Sky Walk was a unique experience. Indeed, it very much was a test of courage and a path of self-knowledge for them. Up to this point, the architects had overcome various challenges, but during the construction of Sky Tower, they had found themselves in a situation they never encountered before: constructing a building 3887 feet (1185 meters) above sea level in difficult terrain where all of the materials and equipment had to be transported. other major obstacle the architects had to face was volatile weather. Down in the valley, the sun shines so intensely that you could walk around in just at-shirt, but up top is terribly cold with strong gusts of wind, making the construction work even more difficult. Velice důležitá byla také součinnost zainteresovaných lidí, kteří museli, prokázat velkou dávku diplomacie při takto složité stavbě. The coordination of everyone involved was very important and people had to show a great deal of diplomacy where the complexity of the construction was concerned.

Thanks to all their hard work, this completely different kind of construction gave the architects a unique experience in multiple ways. The architects say that they definitely don't regret their decision because the time spent on this project enriched them from both a technical as well as from a personal point of view.

It is rare to use timber on a construction of this magnitude, which also creates a new kind of experience where people better realize how small they are in the bosom of nature. It offers an endless amount of views, situations, and moments where an indiscernible human being enters the depth and emerges on the outskirts of this natural structure.

01 / View of tower in winter

Cross-section

02 / Entrance pavilion
03-04 / Detail footbridge
05 / View of tower in winter

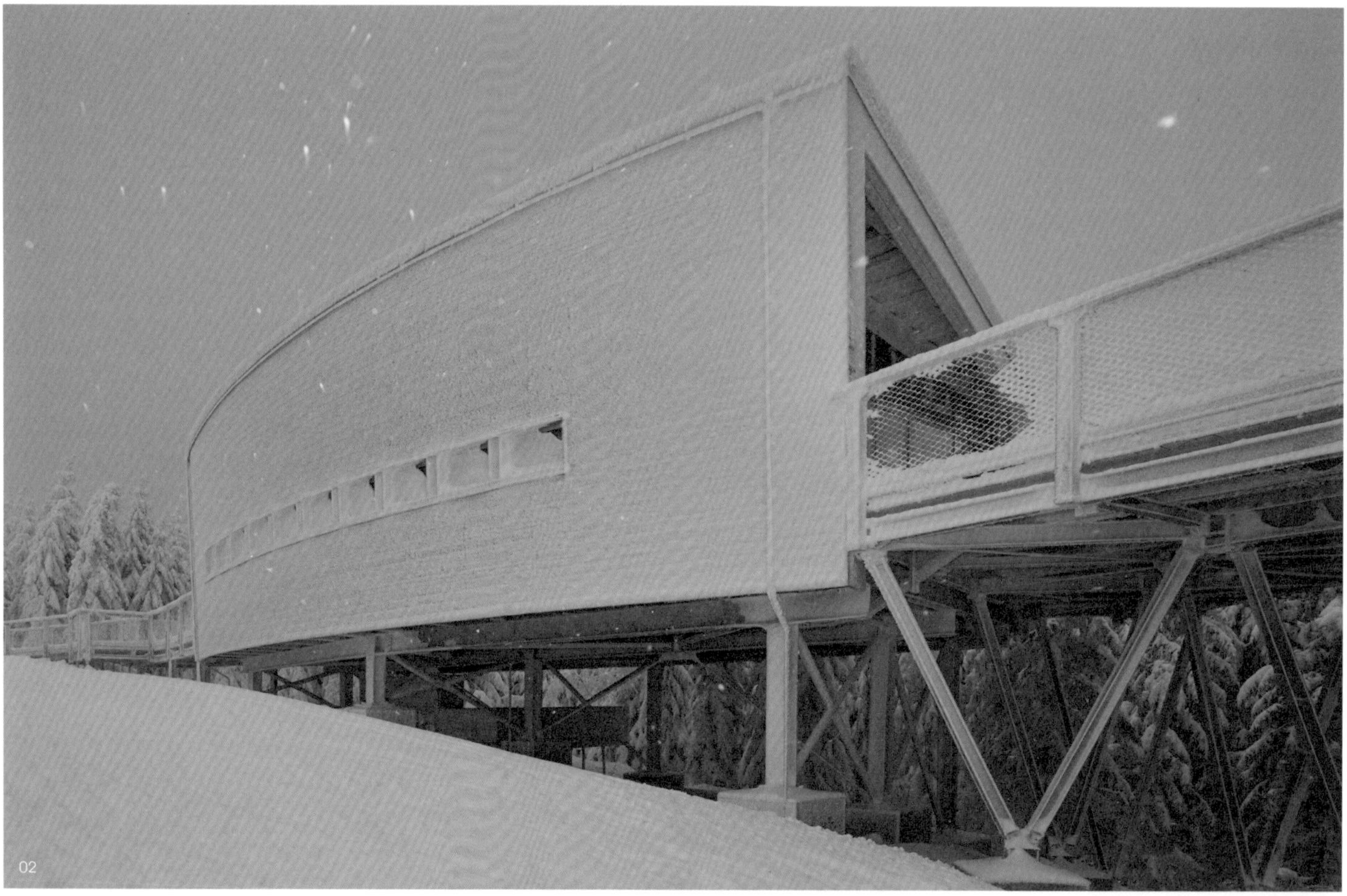

02

03

04

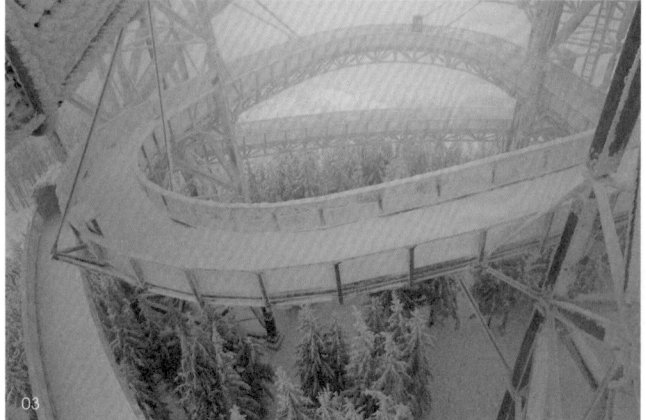

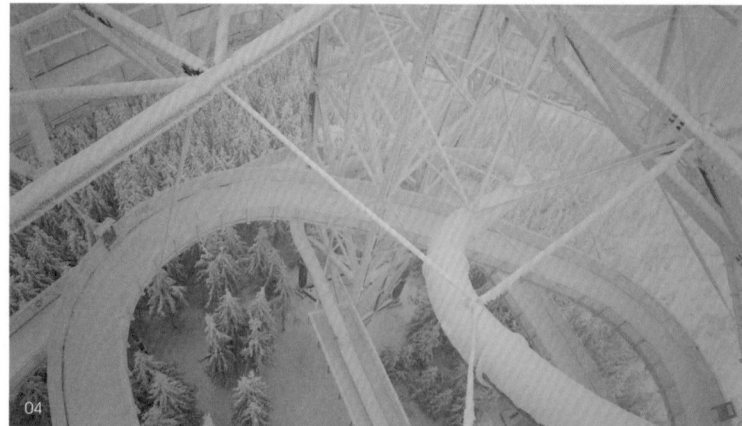

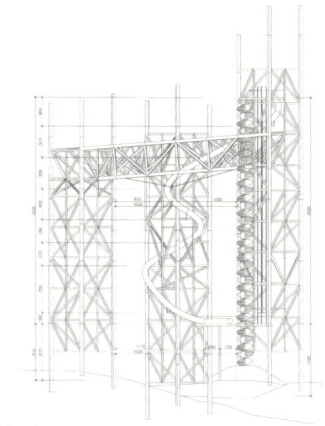

Side view 1

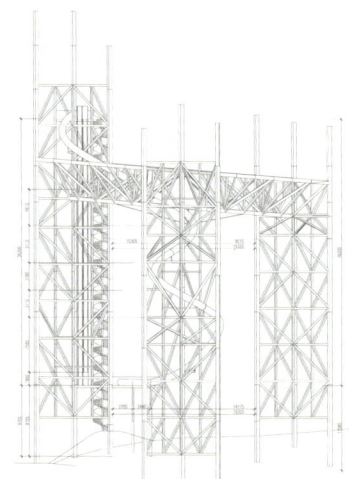

Side view 2

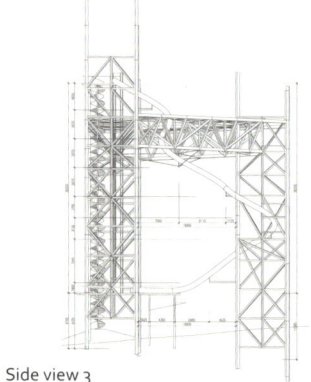

Side view 3

Perspective

06 / View of tower in daytime
07 / View from a distance

The World Championship Ski Jump

Location / Oslo, Norway
Area / 344,445 square feet (32000 square meters)
Completion / 2011
Architect / JDS ARCHITECTS
Photography / Marco Boella
Client / Oslo Kommune, Idrettsetaten

Holmenkollen Ski Jump is the world's most visited sports facility. Nevertheless, as a ski jump, it is one of the smallest hills in the World Cup tournament. The project has become a beacon for the city and a new showcase for the sport of ski jumping.

Rather than having a series of dispersed pavilions on site, the design unifies the various amenities into one holistic diagram. The judging booths, the commentators, the trainers, the royal family, the VIPs, the wind screens, the lobby, the entrance to the arena and the arena itself, the lounge for the skiers, the souvenir shop, the access to the existing museum, and the public viewing square at the very top—everything is contained within the jump area. The resulting solution's simplicity improves the experience of the spectators and brings clear focus to the skiers jumping.

The ski jump is clad with a mesh of stainless steel and rises 190 feet (58 meters) in the air. Its 226 feet (69 meters) cantilever makes it the longest of its kind. On the first day of jumping tests, the record of the longest jump made at Holmenkollen was broken.

Atop the ski jump is a platform where visitors can take in some of the most breathtaking views of Oslo, the fjord, and the region beyond. It is a new form of public space, using an unlikely architectural form as its host, affording the same spectacular vantage point for everyone who comes to Holmenkollen.

Site layout

Site plan

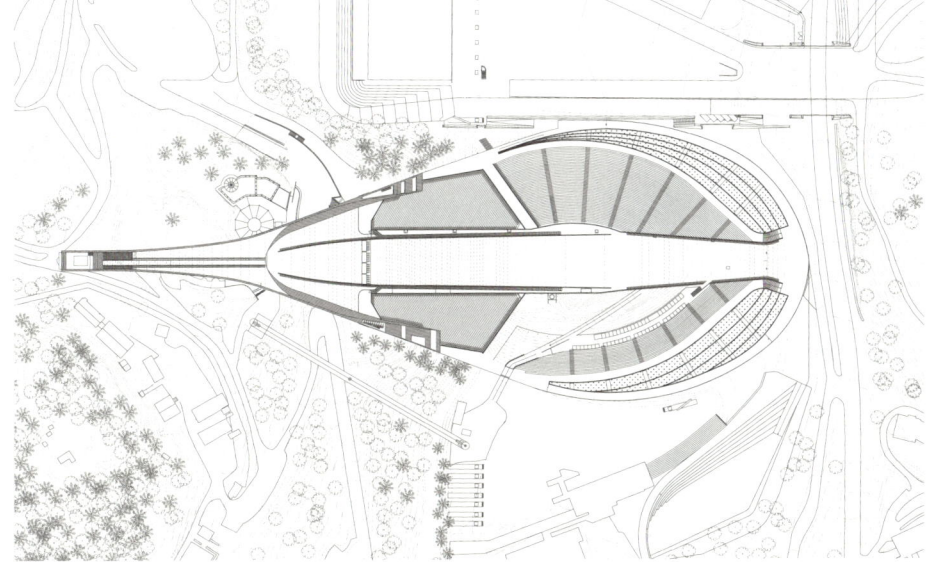

01-02 / Full view

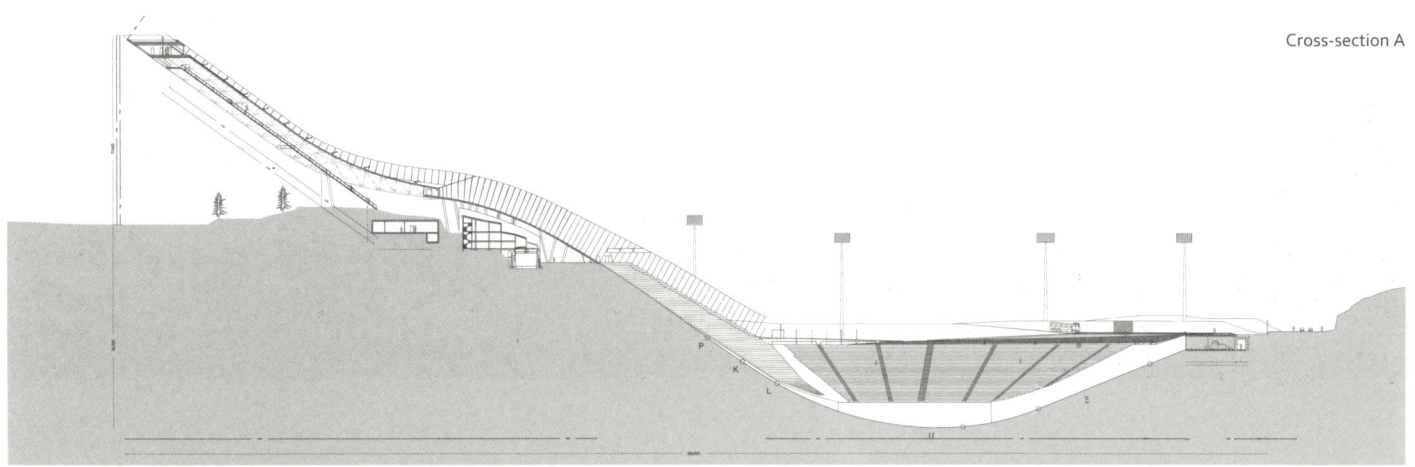

Cross-section A

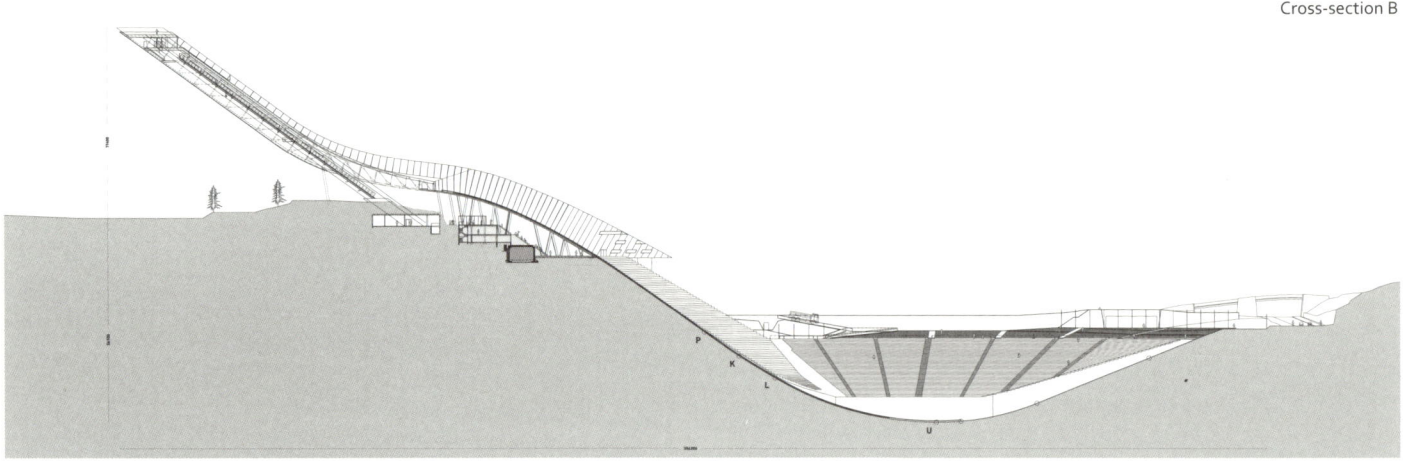

Cross-section B

03 / Ski jump clad with stainless steel
04 / Bottom view
05 / View of jump
06 / Top view
07 / Platfrom for watching games

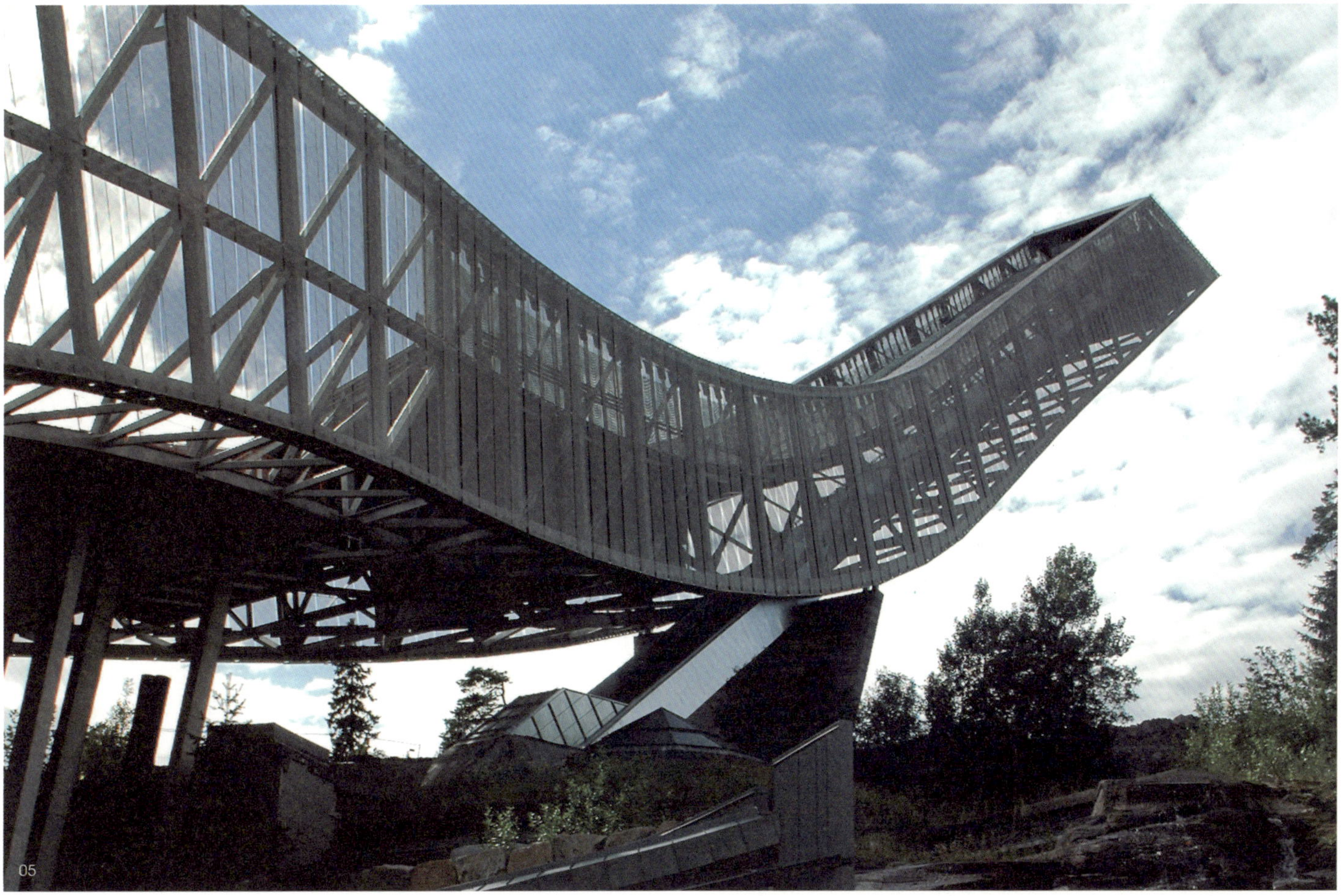
05

06

07

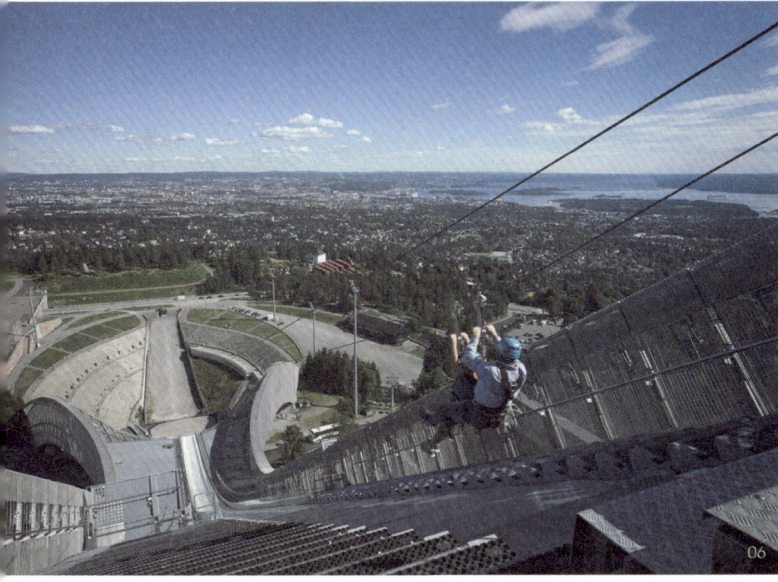

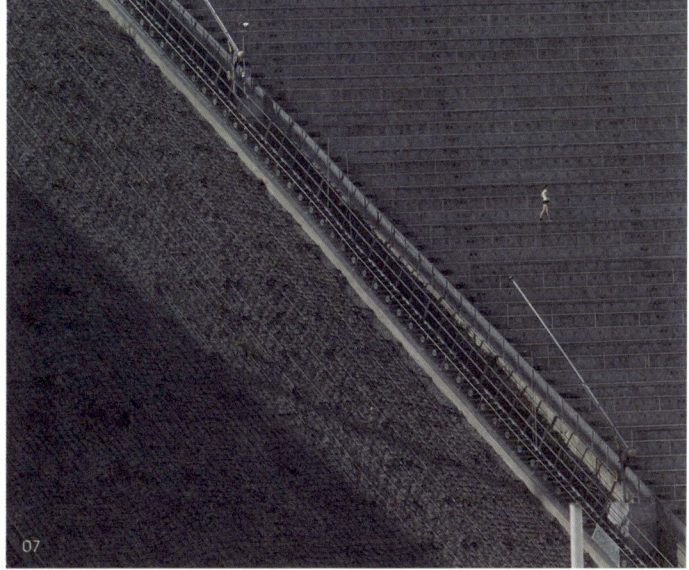

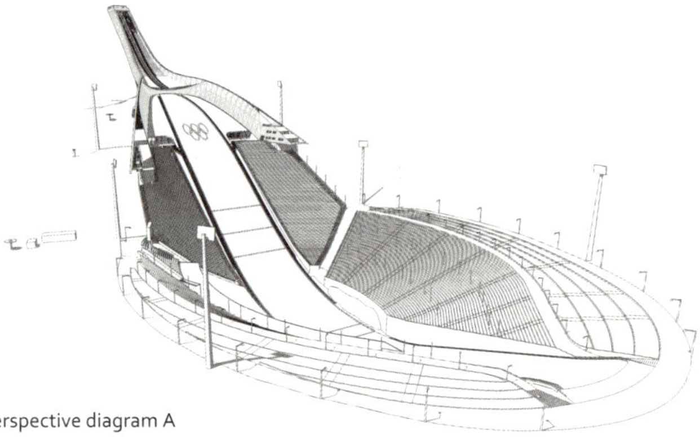

Perspective diagram A

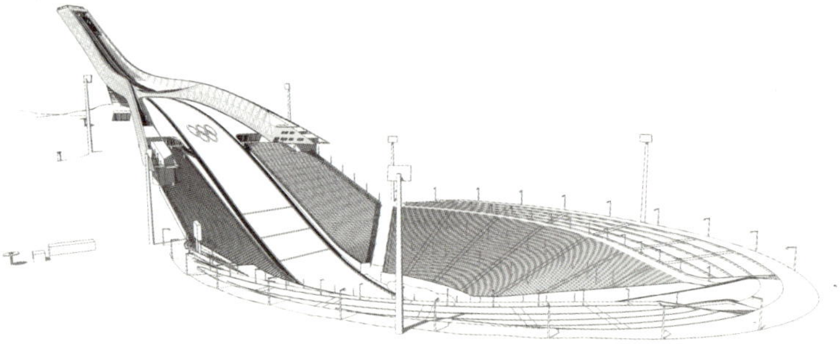

Perspective diagram C

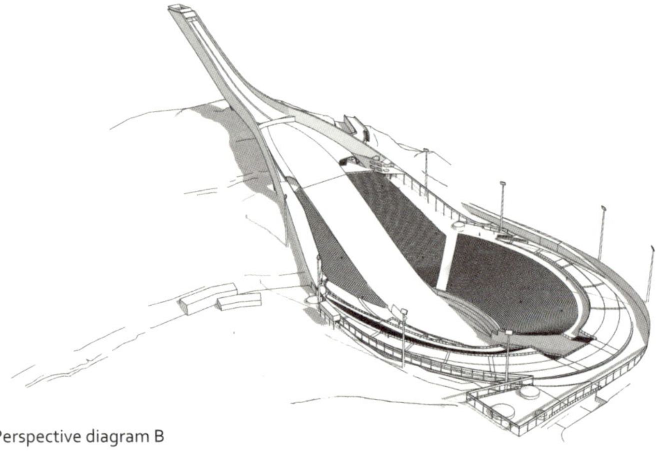

Perspective diagram B

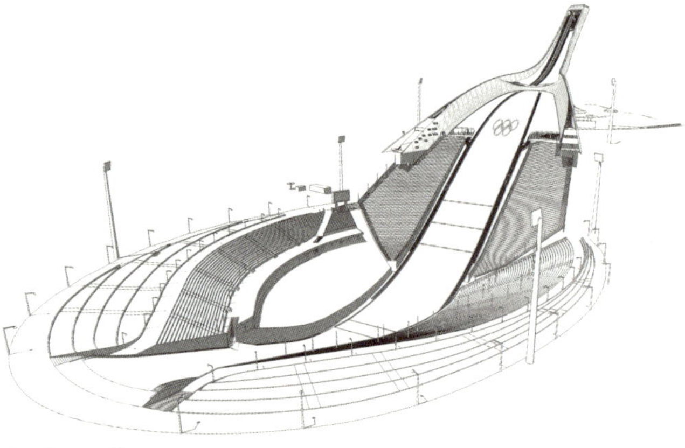

Perspective diagram D

08-09 / View of ski jump in winter
10 / Ski jump

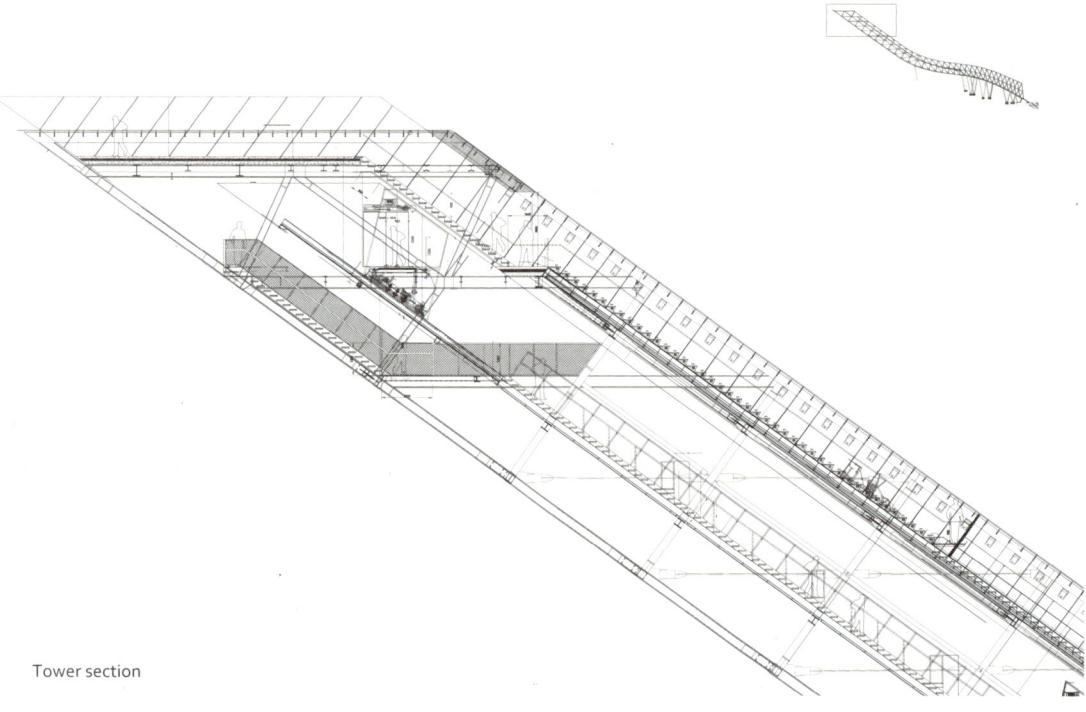

Tower section

11 / Side view during winter
12 / Interior view
13, **15** / View from top of ski jump
14 / Stainless steel supports

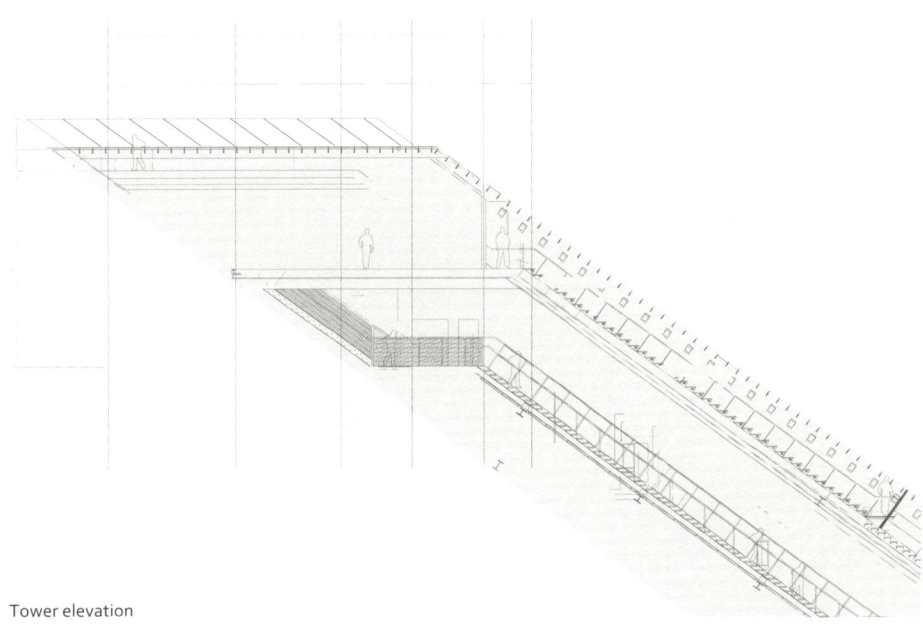

Tower elevation

3 Campsite Facilities Design

Introduction

Pan Youcai

With growing level of living and increasing families with private cars, self-driving travel becomes a hot choice today and campsites play an increasingly important role in self-driving tourism.

From the layout of campsites around the world, we can see Europe and Asia are the earliest and most mature regions in developing them, while Asian-Pacific region and Japan enjoy a good growth of them. In these developed countries, campsite travel has become a common travel consumption habit and a major way of leisure.

Campsites, as tourism infrastructure, have remarkable participatory and interactive characteristics. As traveling by car becoming a first choice to the majority, campsites play an integral role in future tourism service. Greatly different from traditional parking areas, hotels, inns and restaurants, campsites in reality are transitional products from sightseeing tourism to holiday tourism. They are equipped with comprehensive supporting facilities, which include accommodation, catering, business and leisure sports and others.

As to construction standards of campsites, there are International Campsite Establishment Standards of World Camp Association (FICC) and relative campsite standards formulated by developed countries, including USA, France, Britain, Japan and Swiss, in which campsites prevail. At present, China has introduced the System of Star Rating for campsite construction, in which National Tourism Administration and General Administration of Sport of China jointly participate in the check and approval of campsites and classify them into three levels: Five-star, Four-star and Three-star.

Generally, campsites consist of basic camp sites (including camp sites, RV camp sites and self-driving camp sites), feature accommodation, leisure and logistic supporting facilities. They are usually built in locations with good transportation and beautiful scenic views. There are several basic principle to follow in the construction of them: easy transportation, safety and security, complete supporting facilities, beautiful environment and rich experiences. A qualified campsite shall have the above elements.

For the construction of campsite, the planning and design of basic camp sites don't have much variability and focus on the convenience and comfort in using camp sites. Camp sites, other than meeting needs of camping activities of visitors, shall be adequately equipped with necessary supporting facilities, such as water, electricity, bathroom accessories and wireless network, and consider the design of humanized details. Campsites shall be reasonably planned and divided based on the site's topography and natural scenic views, givinga full consideration to the safety, experience, interaction and privacy of tourists and highlighting its fun, privacy and experience. It is proposed that the planning and layout of campsites shall be with a theme and featured grouping characteristic and can meet different experiential demands of various visitors.

The feature accommodation of campsites is a key, which represents individualism, experience and comfort. Common feature accommodations include cabin hotels, tree house hotels, tent hotels, container hotels, cave hotels, bunker hotels, starry sky hotels and bubble hotels. Feature accommodation could meet needs of many tourism novelty-seekers and is remarkable efficient in attracting visitors and branding and marketing. According to their own natural resources and regional cultures, campsites can explore experience, fun and comfort in its design, creates it own feature accommodation form and form unique campsite features.

Leisure and entertainment supporting facilities are topmost important in the planning of campsites. Diversified and comprehensive supporting facilities and rich entertainment activities form the attraction of campsites. In China's self-driving travel population, both families with children and the aged as well as the young who yearn for nature and love outdoor activities take a big proportion. Other than general catering, feature business and leisure and entertainment supporting facilities, campsites could build a feature core attraction system and secure a sustainable development by providing supporting facilities for business conferences, outdoor sports, children activities and fitness and health.

With increasing private cars, an obvious huge self-driving tourism market and increased national economic income and spiritual culture, the majority of families and young people increasingly tend to choose some newly-developing feature tourism products that are highly interactive, with distinct features and are close to nature. The huge potential of consumption in China constantly attracts support of national policy and diverse substantial capitals. However, campsites in China are still a new tourism product that meet leisure and fashion needs of modern people. Nowadays, there are not many built campsites and they are not well known by many people. Major problems the campsite industry face are to construct a batch of standard, large-scale and high quality campsites, popularize and spread relative information for visitors, guide and promote them to form stable consumption habit, create a good brand for campsites in tourism industry and make campsite a daily travel product for people.

Campsite Facilities Design Guidelines

For many people, campgrounds provide a unique opportunity to live temporarily as part of one of the many natural environments protected in regional parks. The value of this experience for many visitors, especially children, lies in its simplicity and educational worth. The quality of the camping experience relies on the naturalness of the park landscape, of which the park facilities form a part.

Campground roads and campsites are relatively small elements. They can be accommodated in a variety of park landscapes and not detract from the landscape character.

Unlike day-use areas, campground use is limited by the availability of space and facilities. This factor controls stress on the park environment. So in this chapter, readers will find campsite functional spaces and facilities design guidelines. These guidelines are prepared by U.S. Bureau of Reclamation, which are intended for the references of the designers.

Campground Layout

Each campground layout design should be reviewed onsite to ensure that grade transitions can be accomplished smoothly and without costly post-construction remedial efforts. When siting the roads in a campground, full consideration should be given to aesthetic factors, smooth traffic flows, and site topography as well as cut and fill balances. It is important that proposed field changes be approved by the appropriate designers. In all cases, picnic grounds and campsites should be sited with the emphasis on safety, program goals, and eliminating user conflicts.

Comfort stations should be sited so that trampling and erosion impacts, as well as intrusions on other campsites, are minimized. Reasonable effort should be made to provide vegetative screening at those campsites nearest the comfort station to maximize privacy and minimize disturbance from the activities at the comfort station. Placement of vault comfort stations should be downwind from the prevailing winds for odor management at campsite or other campground activities. Accessible parking spaces and outdoor recreation access routes shall be provided at each comfort station.

Lighting within a campground should be low intensity and provide illumination only where necessary for safety. Light fixtures should aim the light at the ground rather than into the night sky. Lighting at comfort stations should illuminate the external sidewalks and nearby ground surfaces. Choose lighting sources that use the least electricity, such as light-emitting diodes.

Each campground should have a permanent display that contains a site map or plan that effectively communicates site layout, accessible features, regulations, and items of interest and their relative locations. The map must meet accessibility requirements, including providing tactile and/or Grade II Braille characters for persons with sight impairments and using symbols, pictographs, pictograms, color, and hierarchical language for effective communications with persons who have cognitive impairments. All facilities within the campground, such as comfort stations, parking lots, and accessible campsites, as well as places of interest, shall be linked by an outdoor recreation access route. Portions of an outdoor recreation access route can follow the circulation road so long as that is the pathway taken by others.

Campgrounds shall meet or exceed the minimum accessible scoping requirement. Accessible sites shall be dispersed throughout the campground and offered in several preferred types, including recreational vehicle (pull-through, back-in), tent, walk-in, boat-in, group, etc. If the minimum scoping requirement has not yet been met, then apply the scoping requirement where campsites are altered or added until the minimum requirements are met. Contact an accessibility specialist for more information, including applicable exceptions.

Campground Utilities and Trash

Utilities and trash receptacles in campgrounds may be provided in various combinations and locations. The operable parts of all utilities and trash receptacles within accessible campsites shall be within a 15-inch (38-centimeter) to 48-inch (122-centimeter) reach range. Operable parts for water hydrants and water utility hookups must be between 28 inches and 36 inches above the finish ground surface. The clear spaceat and around the utilities and trash receptacles shall have a firm and stable surface. (A stable surface remains unchanged by applied force so that when the force is removed, the surface returns to its original condition. A firm surface resists deformation by indentation.) If the surface is concrete, asphalt, or boards, the clear ground space slope shall be no more than 2.08 percent in any direction throughout the entire surface area. If the surface is other than concrete, asphalt, or boards, then the clear ground space slope is allowed to increase up to 3.33 percent in any direction if needed for drainage (but not for other reasons).

Electricity

When electricity is provided to a campsite, it should be provided in a covered and grounded electrical box that is mounted to a post or in a manufactured assembly that includes a ground fault interrupter. The post should be located on the driver's side of the parking spur at a point 0 feet to15 feet (0 meters to 4.6 meters) from the rear of the spur. In addition, the accessible site shall have a minimum 30-inch (76-centimeter) by 60-inch (152-centimeter) accessible clear space adjacent to, and centered on, the post. Locate the space so that the hook-ups are at the rear center of the space. The long side of the clear space should adjoin or overlap an accessible parking space or pull-up space for recreational vehicles. The post, as well as other manufactured electrical boxes, should be protected by a steel guard post located 18inches (46 centimeters) to 24 inches (61 centimeters) away on the side nearest the road. Bollards or other barriers shall not obstruct the clear space required in front of the hook-ups. Guard posts should be 4 inches (10 centimeters) to 5 inches (12.7 centimeters) in diameter and filled with concrete. Warning tape should be placed in the trench above the electric lines. Electrical facilities at each campsite should be sized to comply with local electrical code.

Water

Water provided should be from a water hydrant or water spigot and, in some cases, includes a splash basin. All water sources should include a backflow preventer. In instances where both a drinking fountain and a water hydrant or water spigot are provided at the same site, both features should share the same splash basin and underground supply lines, if feasible. When water alone is to be provided to a campsite, the splash basin should be located no closer than 5 feet (1.5 meters) from the road in the vicinity of the general living area of the site.

When water and electricity are both to be provided at a campsite, the hydrant or spigot should be located on the driver's side of the parking spur at a point 15 feet (4.6 meters) from the rear of the spur. Guard posts should be installed as described above. The water line and electrical line should be installed in the same trench when appropriate, according to codes, and there is to be a warning tape just above the electrical line.

Accessible Water Hydrants and Spigots

Hydrants and spigots, other than water utility hookups (included below), that are located along a campground outdoor recreation access route or at an accessible campsite, shall have a 48-inch (122-centimeter) by 72-inch (183-centimeter) minimum accessible clear space centered on the water hydrant, with the long side of the space adjoining or overlapping an outdoor recreation access route or another clear ground space. Locate the space so that the water spout is 11 inches (28 centimeters) minimum and 12 inches (30.5 centimeters) maximum from the rear center of the long side of the space. The spout shall be located between 28 inches (71 centimeters) and 36 inches (91 centimeters) above the ground surface. The splash basin must have a level accessible surface. If a grate is used, the openings in the grate shall not allow the passage of a 0.5-inch-diameter (1.3-centimeter-diameter) sphere or dowel rod and the openings shall be placed perpendicular to the dominant direction of travel. If the surface is concrete, asphalt, or boards, the clear ground space slope shall be no more than 2.08 percent in any direction throughout the entire surface area. If the surface is other than concrete, asphalt, or boards, then the clear ground space slope is allowed to increase up to 3.33 percent in any direction if needed for drainage (but not for other reasons). In all cases, the clear space shall be firm and stable.

Accessible Water Utility Hookups

The water utility hook-up shall have a 30-inch (76-centimeter) by 60-inch (152-centimeter) minimum accessible clear space adjacent to, and centered on, the post. Locate the space so that the hook-up is at the rear center of the space. The long side of the clear space must adjoin or overlap an accessible parking space or pull-up space for recreational vehicles. Bollards or other barriers shall not obstruct the clear space required in front of the hook-up. If the water hydrant has a water spout, it shall be located between 28 inches (71 centimeters) and 36 inches (91 centimeters) above the ground surface. If the surface is concrete, asphalt, or boards, the clear ground space slope should be no more than 2.08 percent in any direction throughout the entire surface area. If the surface is other than concrete, asphalt, or boards, then the clear ground space slope is allowed to increase up to 3.33 percent in any direction if needed for drainage (but not for other reasons). In all cases, the clear space shall be firm and stable.

Sewer Hookups

When water and sewer hookups are located at the same spur, the two hookups should be separated by at least 8 feet to 10 feet (2.4 meters to 3 meters). In addition, the accessible site shall have a minimum 30-inch (76-centimeter) by 60-inch (152-centimeter) accessible clear space adjacent to, and centered on, the post. Locate the space so that the hook-ups are at the rear center of the space. The long side of the clear space must adjoin or overlap an accessible parking space or pull-up space for recreational vehicles. Bollards or other barriers shall not obstruct the clear space required in front of the hook-ups.

Trash

Trash receptacles within accessible campsites shall meet the standards. If more than one is provided within the campsite, then 20 percent, but not less than two, trash receptacles shall be accessible and located on an outdoor recreation access route. When trash receptacles are located in public use or common use areas that serve the accessible camping sites, 20 percent of the receptacles shall be accessible, and be located on, or adjacent to, an outdoor recreation access route. The accessible receptacles shall have a minimum clear space of 36 inches (91 centimeters) by 48 inches (122 centimeters) positioned for forward approach to the receptacle opening, or 30 inches(76-centimeter) by 60-inch (152-centimeter) positioned for a parallel approach to the receptacle opening. The surface of the clear space shall be firm and stable.

Campsite Parking Spurs

Two preferred types of campsite parking spurs are back-in and pull through. Single-wide parking spurs should be 14 feet (4.3 meters) wide, and double-wide spurs should be at least 24 feet (7.3 meters) wide. Parking spurs should be constructed of compacted road base, asphalt, or concrete. The minimum parking spur length should belong enough to accommodate a trailer plus a towing vehicle such as a car or truck.

Back-In Parking

Back-in spurs may be located on either side of a one-way road, but preferably on the left side for driver's side visibility. Back-in spurs may vary in length to accommodate site features. The preferred spur to road angle for back-in is 30 degrees to40 degrees, as measured from the road. Back-in spur angles should not exceed 60 degrees.

Pull-Through Parking

Pull-through campsites should be located only on the right side of the road so the living space is away from any road traffic. These pull-through spaces should be a minimum of 100 feet (30 meters)long.

Accessible Campsite Parking

RV parking spaces at accessible campsites shall be 20 feet (6 meters)wide minimum; except where there are two adjacent parking spaces, then one space is permitted to be 16 feet (5 meters) wide minimum. Additional parking spaces at an accessible site for any kind of vehicle other than recreation vehicles shall be a minimum of 16 feet (5 meters) wide, except where there are two adjacent parking spaces, then one parking space is permitted to be8 feet (2.4 meters) wide minimum. If the surface is concrete, asphalt, or boards, the clear ground space slope shall be no more than2.08 percent in any direction throughout the entire surface area. If the surface is other than concrete, asphalt or boards, then the clear ground space slope is allowed to increase up to3.33 percent in any direction if needed for drainage (but not for other reasons). In all cases, the clear space shall be firm and stable throughout the entire surface area. (A stable surface remains unchanged by applied force so that when the force is removed, the surface returns to its original condition. A firm surface resists deformation by indentation.) Parking spaces shall have a minimum vertical clearance of 98 inches (249 centimeters).

Note: If this is a first come first served campground, then it is recommended to post a sign at each accessible space(s) to identify them.

Campsite Layout and Components

The living area of each campsite should be located to the right or rear of the parking spur. This location is preferred because the doors of recreational vehicles are on the right side (passenger side of the vehicle) when facing the direction of traffic flow. Each campsite should include a picnic table, fire ring, and/or pedestal grill. Highly developed facilities in hot, shadeless areas that service a large number of visitors may feature shade shelters for campsites. It is recommended that at least one-half of the campsites accommodate a tent space, either included within the designated overall living area or separate, but associated with the site's larger living area. The designer should strive to create privacy and a buffer zone between adjacent spaces. It is preferred, but not required, that site components in non-accessible campsites comply with accessibility standards. This is because the site will then be usable by more people than it would otherwise be.

Picnic Tables

The table should be of heavy-duty construction. The recommended minimum length is 8 feet (2.4 meters) and shall meet accessibility scoping requirements and standards. It is recommended that a variety of wheelchair-seating locations be provided (e.g. end, center, or side access) and that the edges of the bench seats be painted on either side of the wheelchair-seating location to alert persons with visual impairments that no bench seat is present in the space. Picnic tables shall provide one wheelchair space for each24 linear feet (7.3 linear meters) of usable table surface perimeter.

Fire Ring

Placement of tent pads and location of bushes, brush, and trees should be considered when siting fire ring location to reduce potential fire hazards. The fire ring should also bedown wind from the table during the prevailing evening winds to avoid fire hazards and to minimize smoke in the living area. In all cases, the ground surface under the fire ring and for2 inches (5 centimeters) beyond the edge of the fire ring should be of compacted road base or gravel, but never non-fireproof concrete, due to the danger of extremely hot concrete exploding.

Pedestal Grill

The grill should be located at the edge of the living area and downwind from the table. It is recommended that the cooking surface of the pedestal grill be large enough for a camp stove to be set upon it and be stable. The grill should be installed so that the cooking surface is not more than 34 inches (86 centimeters) above the living area surface.

Accessible Campsites

All accessible campsite components shall comply with accessibility standards and be connected to other accessible campground and common use features by an outdoor recreation access route. The different types of campsites offered (recreational vehicle, tent only, walk-in, boat-in, etc.) must be scoped separately and the minimum number of each type provided. Placement of the accessible campsites shall be provided within desirable locations and not always near or next to the comfort station or vault toilet. If more than one accessible site is provided they shall be dispersed throughout the campground depending upon the type of experience offered. Plans for, and construction of, all accessible campsites should be reviewed by an accessibility specialist to ensure compliance.

The number of accessible campsites to be provided depends on the number of campsites within the sites and shall be scoped as shown on the table listed below:

An accessible campsite shall include an accessible table that has a minimum 36-inch-wide clear pathway around all usable sides (measured from the back edge of the bench seats), and meets knee and toe clearance requirements. The table should be fixed to the ground so it cannot be moved into a noncompliant position. Each table should have a wheelchair space that is 30 inches (76 centimeters) by48 inches (122 centimeters) minimum and positioned for a forward approach. It is recommended that a variety of wheelchair-seating locations be provided (e.g. end, center, or side access). Picnic tables

Table / Camping units

Total number of camping unites provided in camping facility	Minimum number of accessible camping unites required
1	1
2 to 25	2
26 to 50	3
51 to 75	4
76 to 100	5
101 to 150	7
151 to 200	8
201 and over	8, plus 2 percent of the number over 200

shall provide one wheelchair space for each 24 linear feet (7.3 linear meters) of usage table surface perimeter.

If a center-cut or side-cut table is used, it is recommended that a warning be painted on the ground or around the edges of the cut surface with color that contrasts sharply with the surrounding concrete to alert persons with visual impairments that there is no bench seating in this location.

Accessible campsites will provide the same features as other sites within the campground (tent pad, pedestal grill, fire pit, etc.). If there is a tent pad or tent platform, it shall be surrounded on all usable sides by a 48-inch x 48-inch (122-centimeter x 122-centimeter) clear ground space. If a pedestal grill or fire ring is provided, there shall be a 48-inch by48-inch (122-centimeter) minimum clear maneuvering space around all usable sides of the grill or fire ring. The clear ground space must be centered on the fire ring or grill. The fire-building surface shall be 9 inches (23 centimeters) minimum high. The cooking surface shall be between15 inches (38 centimeters) and 34 inches (86 centimeters) high. If there is a raised edge around the fire ring (e.g. the fire ring is surrounded by a concrete barrier), then the depth of the edge or barrier must not be more than 10 inches (25 centimeters).

All features within the campsite shall be accessible and connected by an outdoor recreation access route. All features shall have clear maneuvering space that complies with the standards. The surface throughout the living area and the clear maneuvering spaces shall be firm and stable. (A stable surface remains unchanged by applied force so that when the force is removed, the surface returns to its original condition. A firm surface resists deformation by indentation.) If the surface is concrete, asphalt, or boards, the clear ground space slope shall be no more than 2.08 percent in any direction throughout the entire surface area. If the surface is other than concrete, asphalt, or boards, then the clear ground space slope is allowed to increase to 3.33 percent in any direction if needed for drainage (but not for other reasons).

References

Recreation Facilities Design Guidelines, U.S. Department of the Interior, Bureau of Reclamation, 2013

International Self-driving and RV Campground at Ranwu Lake

Location / Ranwu Town Ranwu Lake Scenic Spot, Tibet, China
Area / 502,330 square feet (46,668 square meters)
Completion / 2016-2017
Architect / Xiaoyin Architectural Design Office
Photography / Arch-exist
Client / Tibet Xiangteng Tourism Development Co., Ltd

The campground is a stop for self-driving travelers to enjoy beautiful views of Ranwu Lake. It covers an area of 2153 square feet (200 square meters), gently sloping from the North at an altitude of 12,831 feet (3911 meters) to the South at an altitude of 12,726 feet (3879 meters) with a maximum height difference of 46 feet (14 meters).

The design concept is to turn 'waste' into wealth with minimum intervention into the site, maximum environmental protection, multiple eco-environmental projection measures and consideration to local preference, thus creating a sustainable developing self-driving and RV campground which coexists with nature and site and create convenience for both visitors and business operations.

The construction of the campground is planned in two phases. Phase 1 has a building area of 25,833 square feet (2400 square meters), consisting of a comprehensive service center, 9 high-end resort hotels, a lounge bar, a recreation tea room, a Tibet special products exhibition and sales center, a barbecue buffet, a medical center, star bath facilities, camp tents, parking lots for 176 cars 5 tour buses and 7 RVs.

The buildings in the campground are all piled-structures and accurate calculations have been done based on variation in water level as well as viewing sightline and angle. From South to North, the topography gradually rises and the buildings, from the lakeside bar, are given a ground level of 12,795 feet (3900 meters), 12,812 feet (3905 meters) and 12,833 feet (3912 meters). The designers, taking advantage of the difference in height of the original topography and adjusting the height of open floors, make sure that buildings are increasing gradually in height from lakeside to No. 318 National Road and don't block each other. They, through adjustment of open floor height, lift the whole main building 6 meters to 8 meters higher than No. 318 national road and set up a viewing light tower about 66 feet (20 meters) high near the entrance facing the national road so as to offer safety, expression and maximum use of landscape resources.

The main building mainly uses white and red, which are favored and revered by Tibetans. With white cement fiberboards, red weather resisting steel plates, super-thick transparent glass, dark gray steel, local wood and local pebbles and

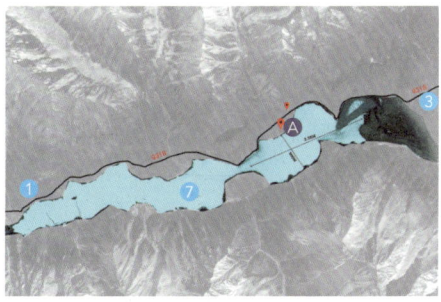

① Bomi　　　　　　　　　　　Topography
② Boxoila Ling
③ Baxoi
④ Kangri Garpo Snow Mountain
⑤ Azar Gongla Glacier
⑥ Zayu
⑦ Restaurant
Ⓐ Ranwu Lake

01 / Southeast view of snow-covered landscape

① 318 National Highway
② Entrance/Exit
③ Lighthouse
④ Vehicle maintenance/Car wash
⑤ Parking lots
⑥ Service center
⑦ Plaza
⑧ Hotel
⑨ Bridge
⑩ Tent campsite
⑪ Bar/Sky viewing platform
⑫ BBQ/Activity area
⑬ Water trestle
⑭ Floodway

Site plan

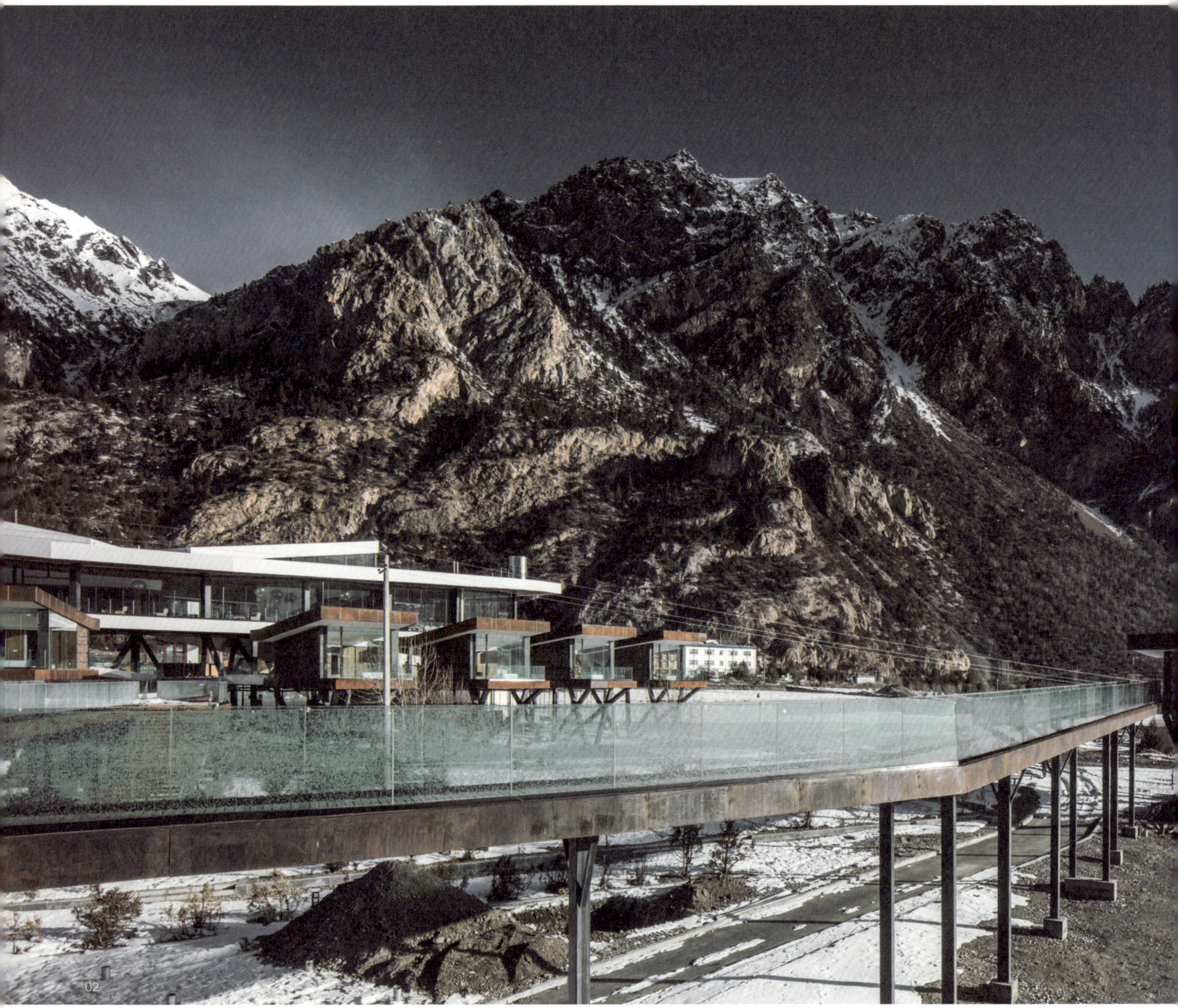

02

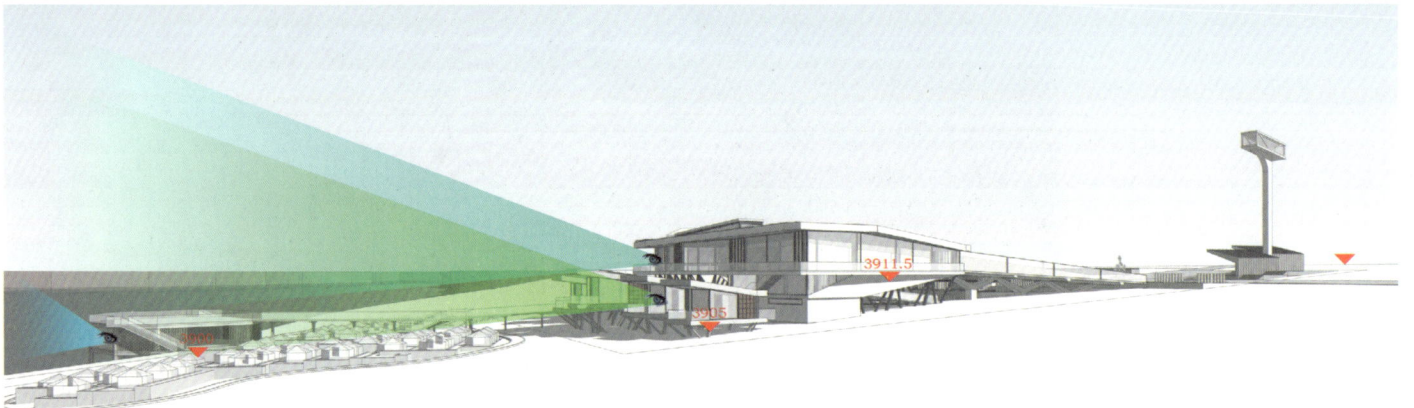

Side diagram of building

02, 05 / Sky bridge
03 / Viewing terrace in service center
04 / North side of 318 National Highway

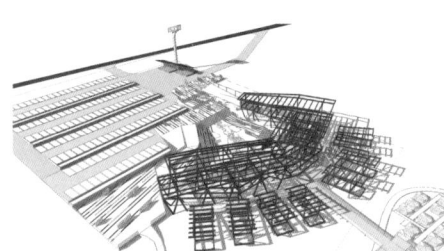

Sketch of steel structure

06 / Snow-covered main entrance
07 / East view of site
08 / Site before construction

other materials, the structure creates a unique, natural, warm and unusual spatial environment. With horizontal and vertical variations of form, the building finally connects with the ground by gentle ramps. The appearance of the main building follows the rolling of topography, like a eagle with wide open wings resting at the lakeside.

The first floor of the main building contains functional spaces such as tourist service information center, management center and other service facilities that are in high demand in the area. Designers put medical aid and star bath facilitates/ Tibet medicine cultural exhibition hall and equipment management room with lower requirements for landscape in the 8m high open floor under the main structure to offer safe, comfort and quality auxiliary service facilities for visitors.

The landscape in the campground is relatively wild, interesting, rough and native in a whole. Big areas paved with local gravels are seen everywhere and vertical spatial scenic spots rebuilt from discarded timber sleepers are scattered among them. Besides the parking area, efforts are put to control the areas with hardened surface and re-culture vegetation that can adapt to local environment so as to return greenness to this barren land.

For the purpose of reducing its affect on local and neighboring environment as much as possible and protect the natural environment of Ranwu Lake Scenic Spot in a better way, the designers give consideration to the difficulties of material transportation in the local area as well as the influences of climate to construction. They design the whole building and structure into an assembled steel structural architecture with reinforced steel concrete only for the foundation.

① 24-hour convenience store
② Café
③ Self-service terminal
④ Hotel information desk
⑤ Tourism advisory
⑥ Women's shower
⑦ Men's shower
⑧ Medical room
⑨ Men's restroom
⑩ Women's restroom

① Cashier
② Souvenir showroom
③ 24-hour convenience store
④ Waiting area
⑤ Medical room
⑥ Women's restroom

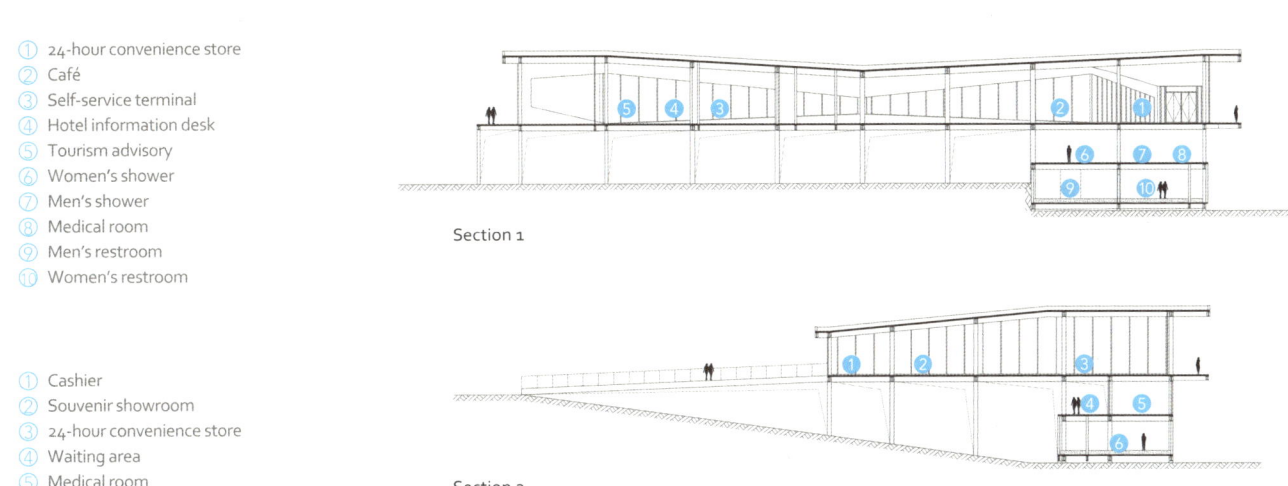

Section 1

Section 2

The domestic wastewater is gathered and disposed in biodegradable septic tanks and then transported to the sewage disposal plant in Basu County for disposal. The septic tanks with steel plates for outermost encasing and bottom boards are casted by reinforced concrete. With enhanced inside and outside waterproof treatment, they allow no filtration of domestic sewage. Kitchen sewage are discharged and cleaned on daily basis and collected into the septic tanks and then transported to the sewage disposal plant in Basu County for centralized disposal. Kitchens are also equipped with nation certified oil fume tertiary purification system and release no oil fume. The comprehensive service center guarantees supply of hot water and heat energy through decorative electric radiators and solar power. The hotel guest rooms use decorative Tibet electric pit furnaces and electric radiators to supply heat energy. All campground water heaters are air-source heat pump oners which can maximally reduce the whole energy consumption in the campground.

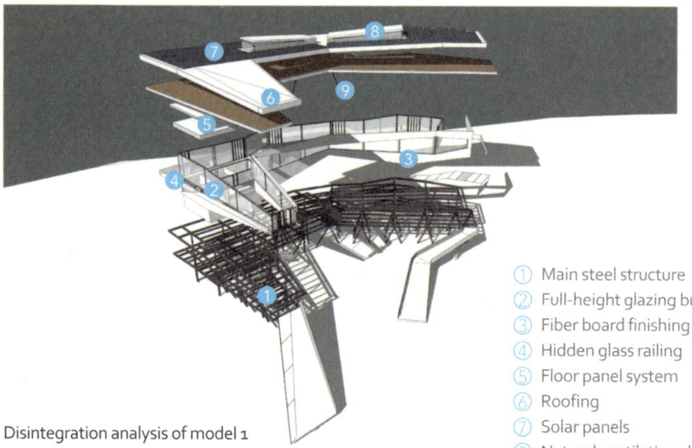

Disintegration analysis of model 1

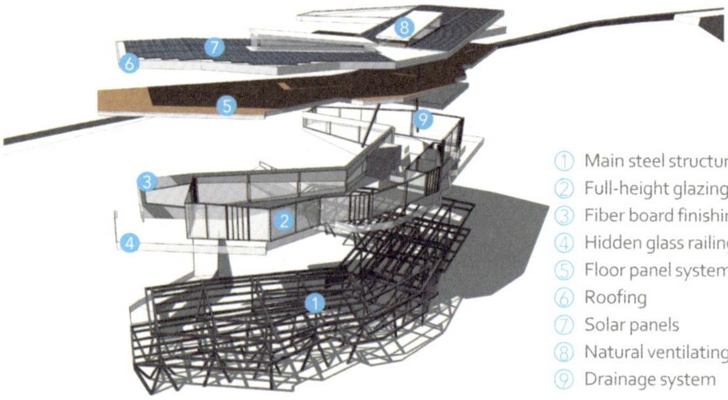

① Main steel structure
② Full-height glazing building envelope
③ Fiber board finishing
④ Hidden glass railing
⑤ Floor panel system
⑥ Roofing
⑦ Solar panels
⑧ Natural ventilating skylights
⑨ Drainage system

Disintegration analysis of model 2

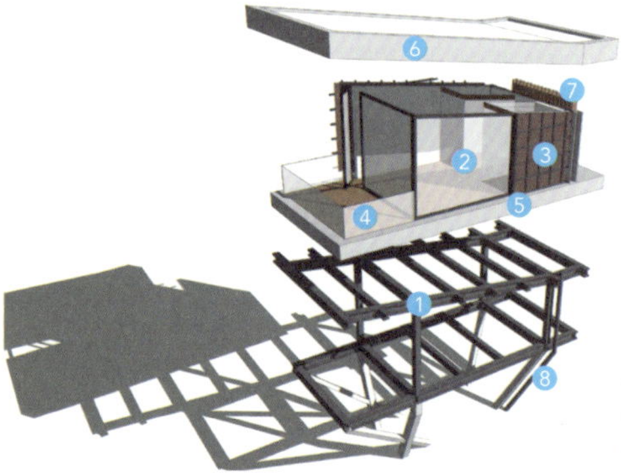

① Main steel structure
② Full-height glazing building envelope
③ Fiber board finishing
④ Hidden glass railing
⑤ Floor panel system
⑥ Roofing
⑦ Solar panels
⑧ Natural ventilating skylights
⑨ Drainage system

Disintegration analysis of model 3

① Main steel structure
② Full-height glazing building envelope
③ Pebble wall
④ Hidden glass railing
⑤ Floor panel system
⑥ Roofing
⑦ Wooden grill
⑧ Drainage system

Disintegration analysis of model 4

① Main steel structure
② Full-height glazing building envelope
③ Screw steel mesh for pebble wall
④ Steel mesh for pebble wall
⑤ Pebbles for pebble wall
⑥ Interior wall
⑦ Hidden glass railing
⑧ Floor panel system
⑨ Roofing
⑩ Wooden grill

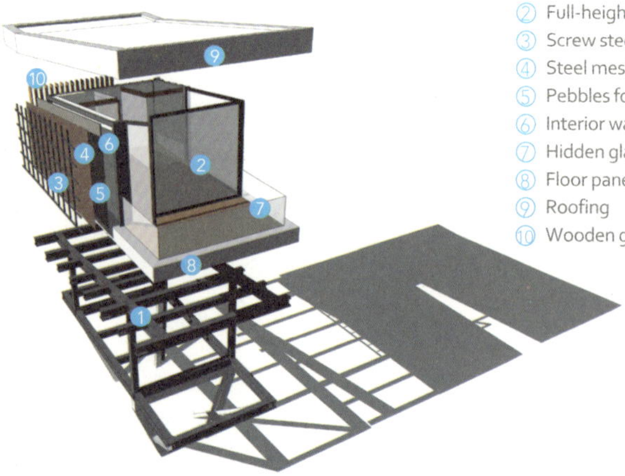

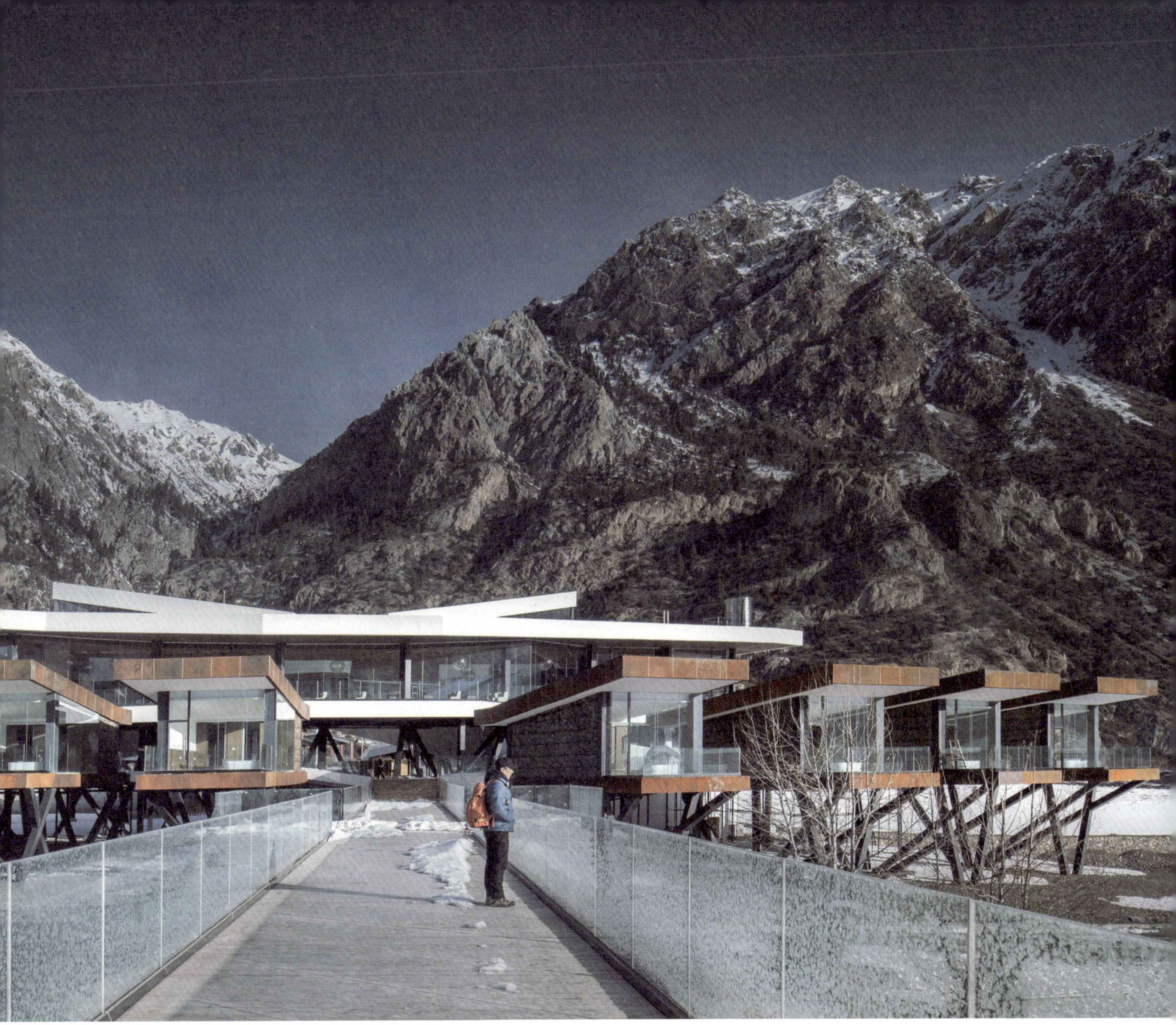

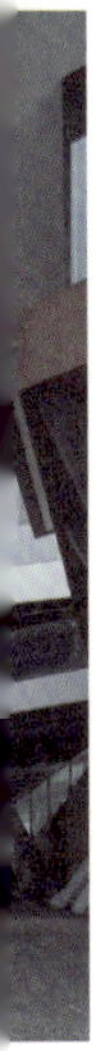

09 / South view of building
10 / Hotel
11 / Open corridor at service center

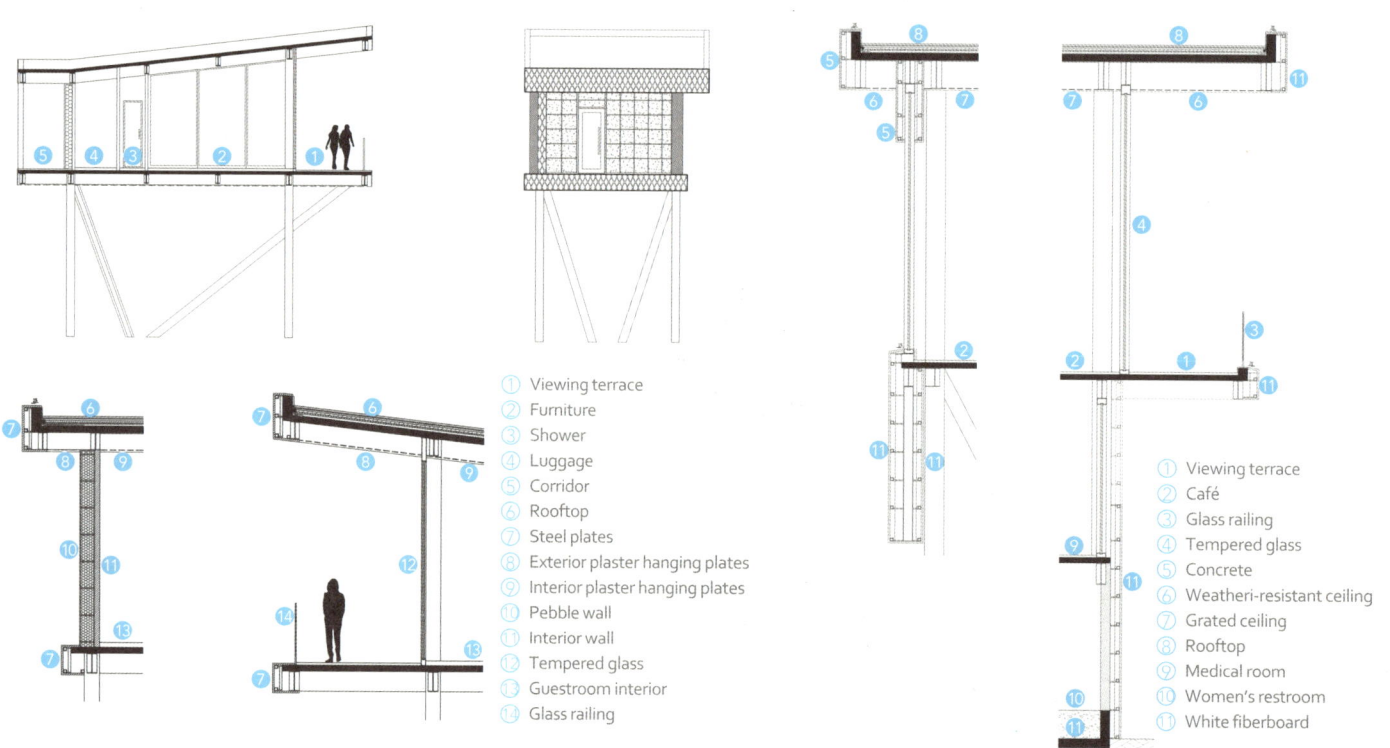

① Viewing terrace
② Furniture
③ Shower
④ Luggage
⑤ Corridor
⑥ Rooftop
⑦ Steel plates
⑧ Exterior plaster hanging plates
⑨ Interior plaster hanging plates
⑩ Pebble wall
⑪ Interior wall
⑫ Tempered glass
⑬ Guestroom interior
⑭ Glass railing

Details of hotel

① Viewing terrace
② Café
③ Glass railing
④ Tempered glass
⑤ Concrete
⑥ Weatheri-resistant ceiling
⑦ Grated ceiling
⑧ Rooftop
⑨ Medical room
⑩ Women's restroom
⑪ White fiberboard

Details of service center

12 / Corridor of hotel
13 / Corridor to viewing platform
14 / Viewing terrace of hotel suite
15 / View of campsite at dawn

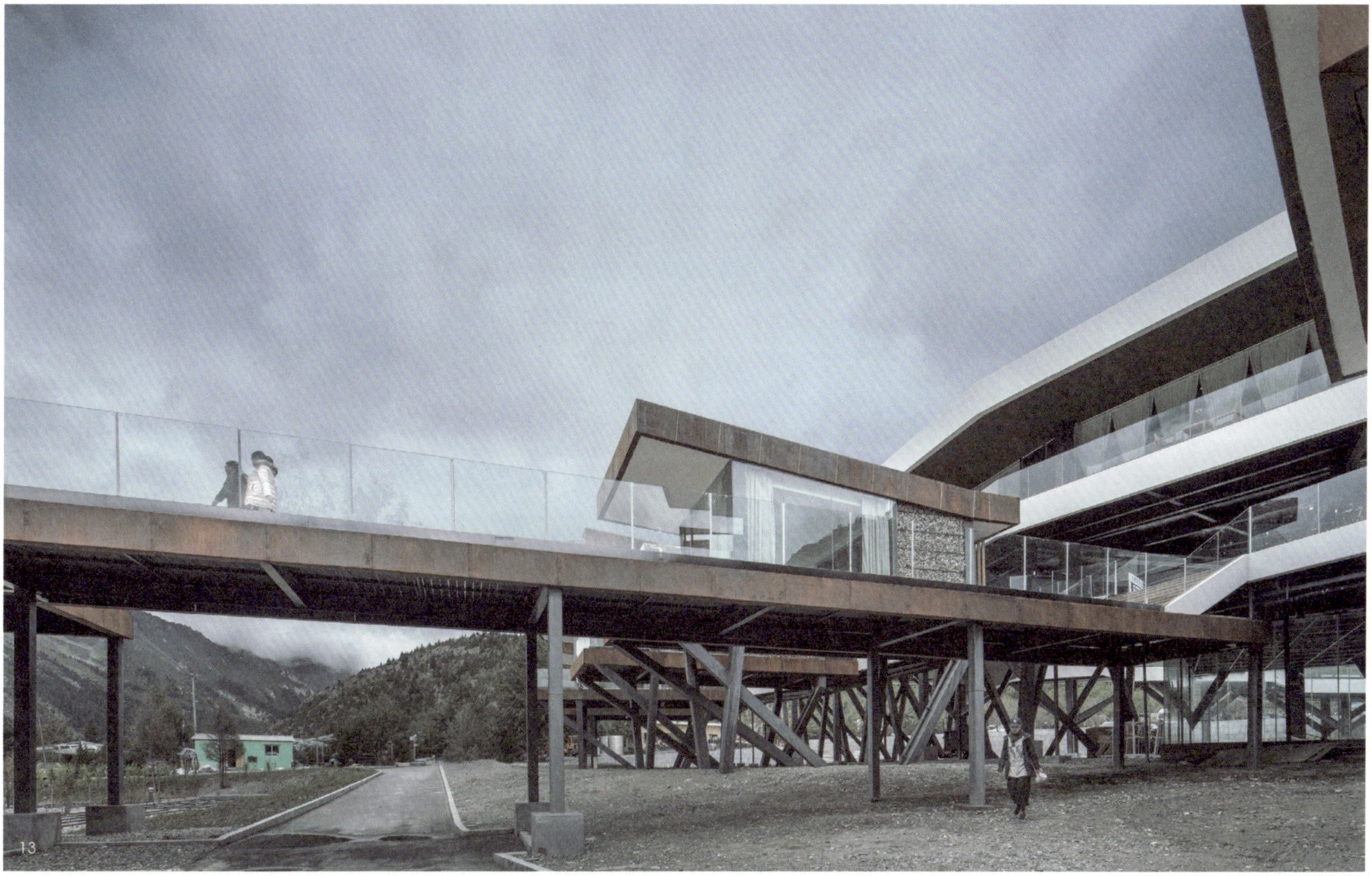

13

14

15

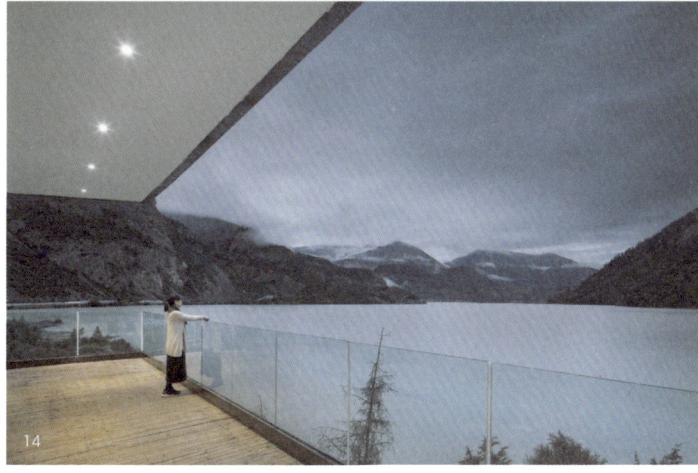

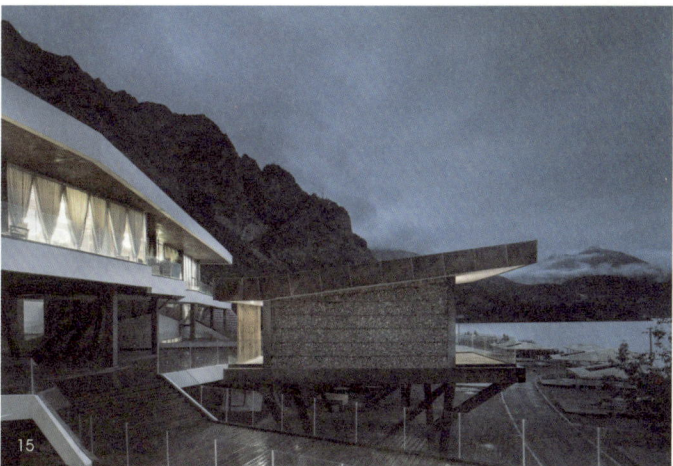

Service center first-floor plan

① Cashier
② Souvenir showroom
③ Corridor
④ 24-hour convenience store
⑤ Café
⑥ Self-service terminal
⑦ Rest area
⑧ Tourism advisory
⑨ Hotel information desk
⑩ Luggage room
⑪ Reception area
⑫ Machine room
⑬ Storage
⑭ Console
⑮ Bar counter
⑯ Viewing terrace

① Corridor
② Security monitor
③ Duty room/Lounge
④ Women's shower
⑤ Men's shower
⑥ Waiting area
⑦ Medical room/Emergency medical station

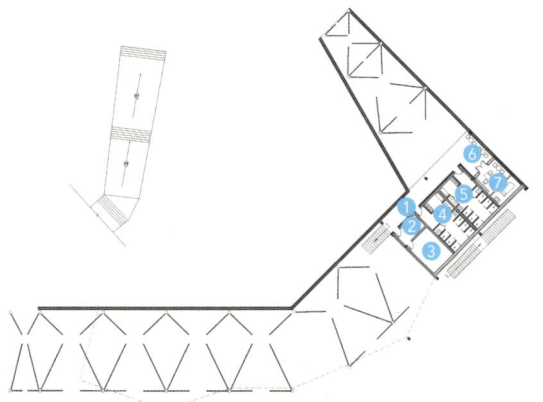

Service center underground first-floor plan

① Corridor
② Men's restroom
③ Accessible restroom
④ Women's restroom
⑤ Tool room

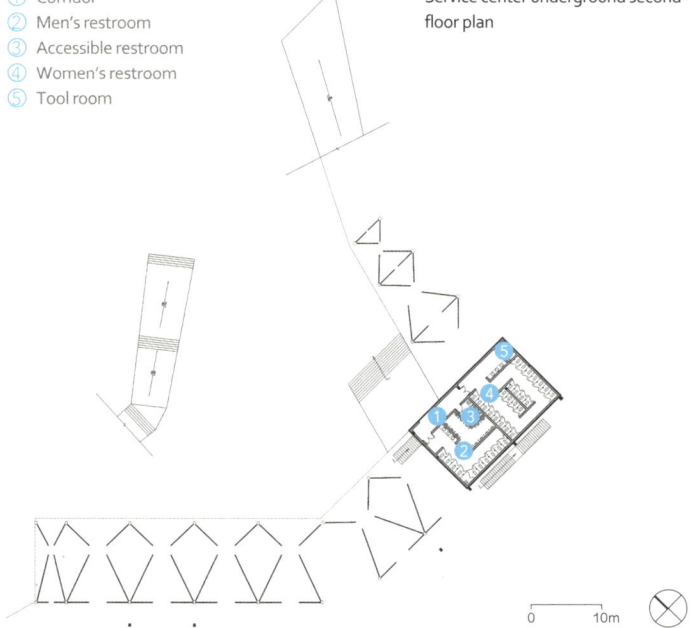

Service center underground second-floor plan

0 10m

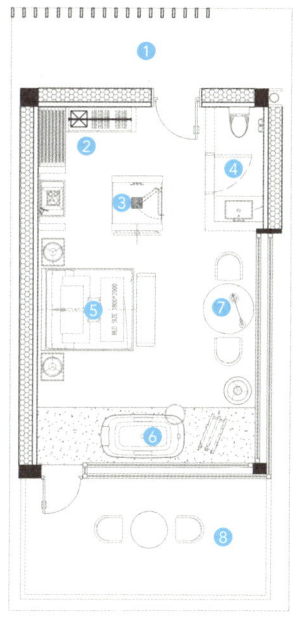

① Corridor
② Luggage area
③ Shower
④ Toilet
⑤ Bed
⑥ Bathtub
⑦ Furniture
⑧ Viewing terrace

Hotel plan

16, 17 / Café in service center
18 / Guest room in hotel

Xinduqiao RV Campground along No.318 National Road

Location / Sichuan, China
Area / 753,474 square feet (70,000 square meters)
Completion / 2015
Architect / Chengdu Hengji Decorative Engineering Co., Ltd.
Photography / Hai Zi, Ma Liang, Ai Jun

Xinduqiao RV campground is located at Waze village Xinduqiao township Kangding County Ganzi region Sichuan. It covers an area of 753,474 square feet (70,000 square meters) and can allow 300 cars and 15 small, medium and big motor homes. It has 100 tent campsites, 3 entertaining cabins with 21 beds, a motel with 29 four-star guest rooms and 57 beds, 16 hostel rooms with 40 different beds and a dining room with 220 seats. It can entertain 500-600 people.

The RV campground is sited at the self-driving golden tour ring of West Sichuan, 23miles from Kangding airport, 400 miles (644 kilometers) from Daocheng Yading, 152 miles (245 kilometers) from Danba Beauty Valley and 45 miles (72 meters) from Tagong Grassland. Thus, it has extremely convenient transportation and is the first RV campground in China that features West Sichuan photography culture.

Xinduqiao RV campground has a comprehensive service zone, a RV camping zone, a tent camping zone, recreational activities experience zone and other zones. Motels in it have a standard not lower than 3-star hotels. Each cabin is about 646 square meters (60 square meters), like a standard hotel room. Hostels are provided specially for the backpackers with separate male and female public baths and public toilets and wide beds for a number of people.

The hightlighted areas are RV and tent campsites which, as standardized demonstrative campsites, are supplied with water and electricity and special garbage disposal service. One one hand, the campground work staff are responsible for collecting garbage and on the other hand, it has fixed sewage pipes connected to RVs. The tent camping site can allow 100 tents and barbecue facilities are available for rent for cooking.

In addition, Xinduqiao is a fascinating heaven for photographers and a poetic and picturesque land of idyllic beauty located at South of No. 318 national road and north fork on the road. Magic light, wide grassland, winding creek, golden cypress and poplar trees, rolling hills, concealed stockaded villages and quiet flocks and herds that are grazing, the plain scenery of West Sichuan are blossoming beautifully. Xinduqiao, also named Dongeluo, is a township, not a scenic spot. It is at an altitude about 3300m without any outstanding iconic landscape, but it has an over 10 miles (16 kilometers) segment called 'Corridor of Photographers.' In the photography corridor of the campground, visitors can directly look far into the Gongga snow mountain, the most beautiful view in the mortal world. They could also enjoy snow mountains and Haizi (lakes) against blue sky and white clouds and be lost in wild, endless and fanciful thoughts.

Rendering of campsite

01 / Aerial view

Foundation drawing of campsite

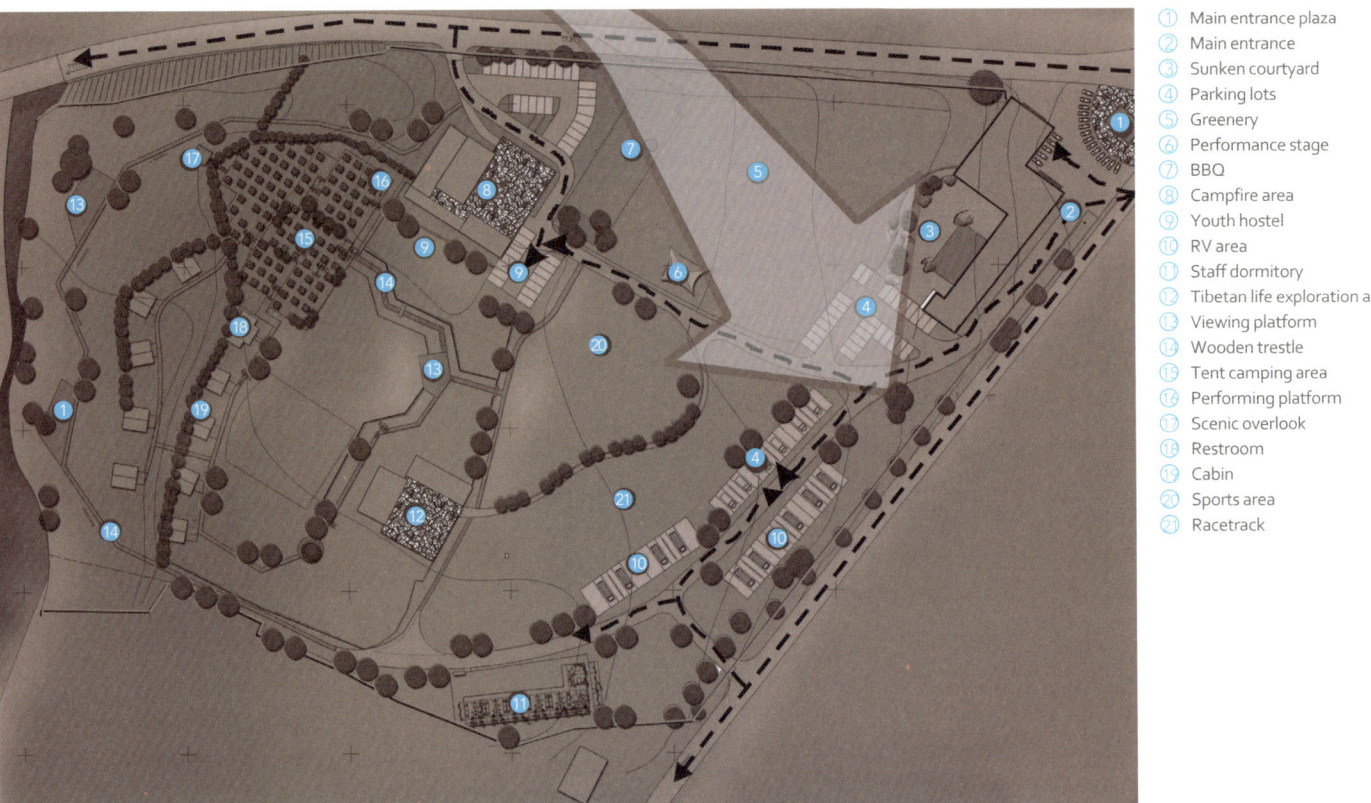

Campsite plan

① Main entrance plaza
② Main entrance
③ Sunken courtyard
④ Parking lots
⑤ Greenery
⑥ Performance stage
⑦ BBQ
⑧ Campfire area
⑨ Youth hostel
⑩ RV area
⑪ Staff dormitory
⑫ Tibetan life exploration area
⑬ Viewing platform
⑭ Wooden trestle
⑮ Tent camping area
⑯ Performing platform
⑰ Scenic overlook
⑱ Restroom
⑲ Cabin
⑳ Sports area
㉑ Racetrack

02 / Main entrance
03 / Restaurant
04 / Convenience store
05 / Rest area

03

04

05

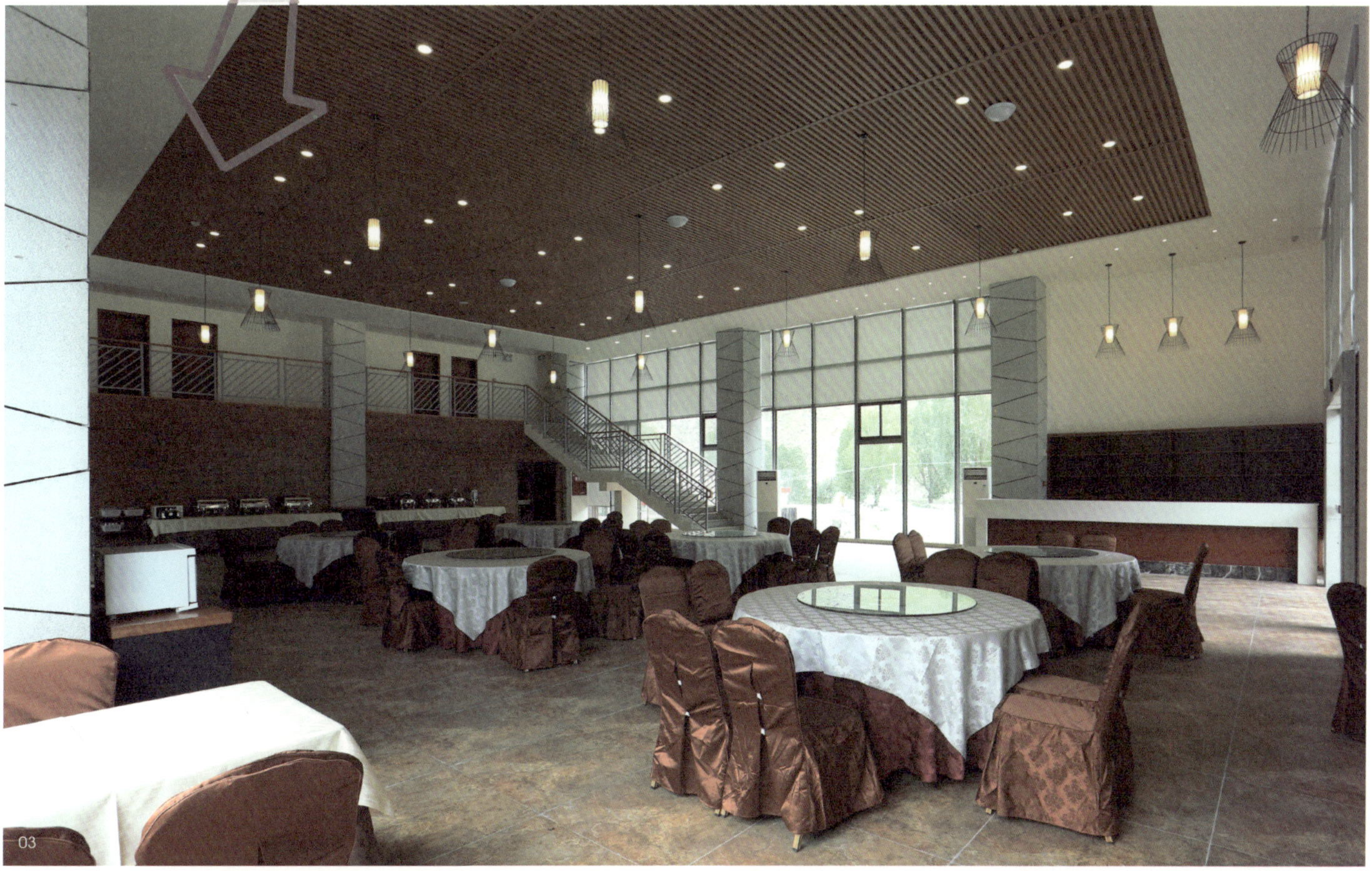

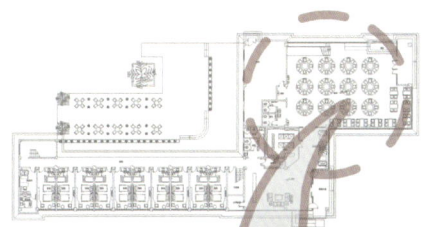

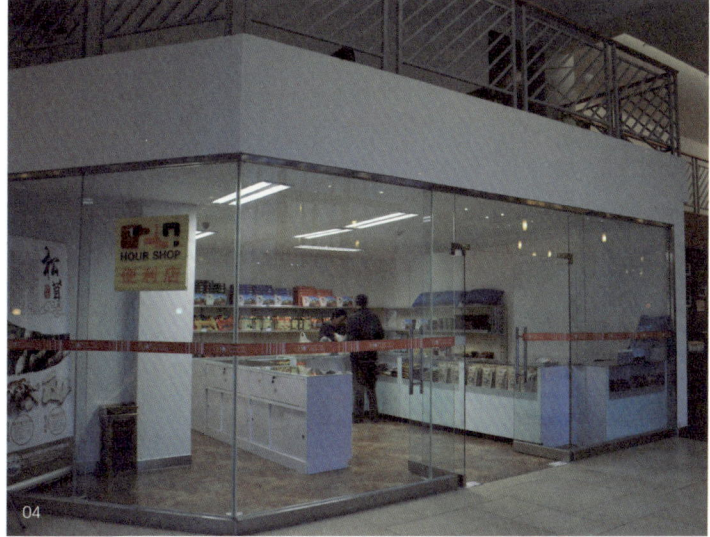

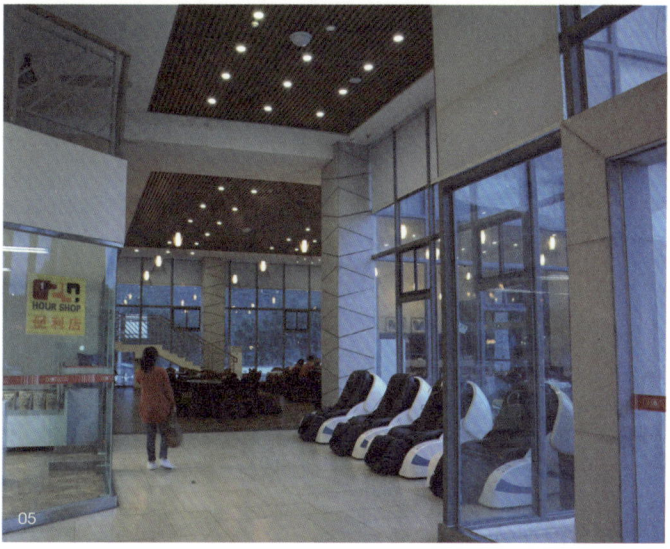

06-08 / Exterior of youth hostel
09 / Restroom in youth hostel

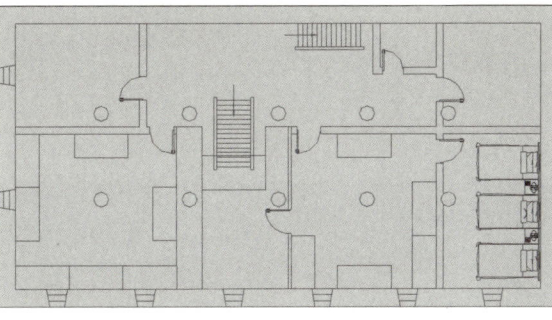
Second-floor plan of youth hostel

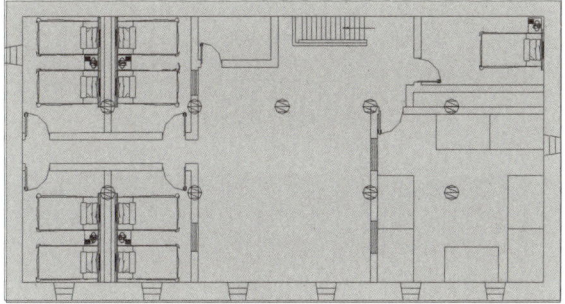
Third- floor plan of youth hostel

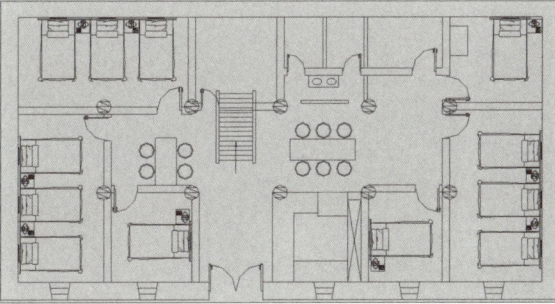
First-floor plan of youth hostel

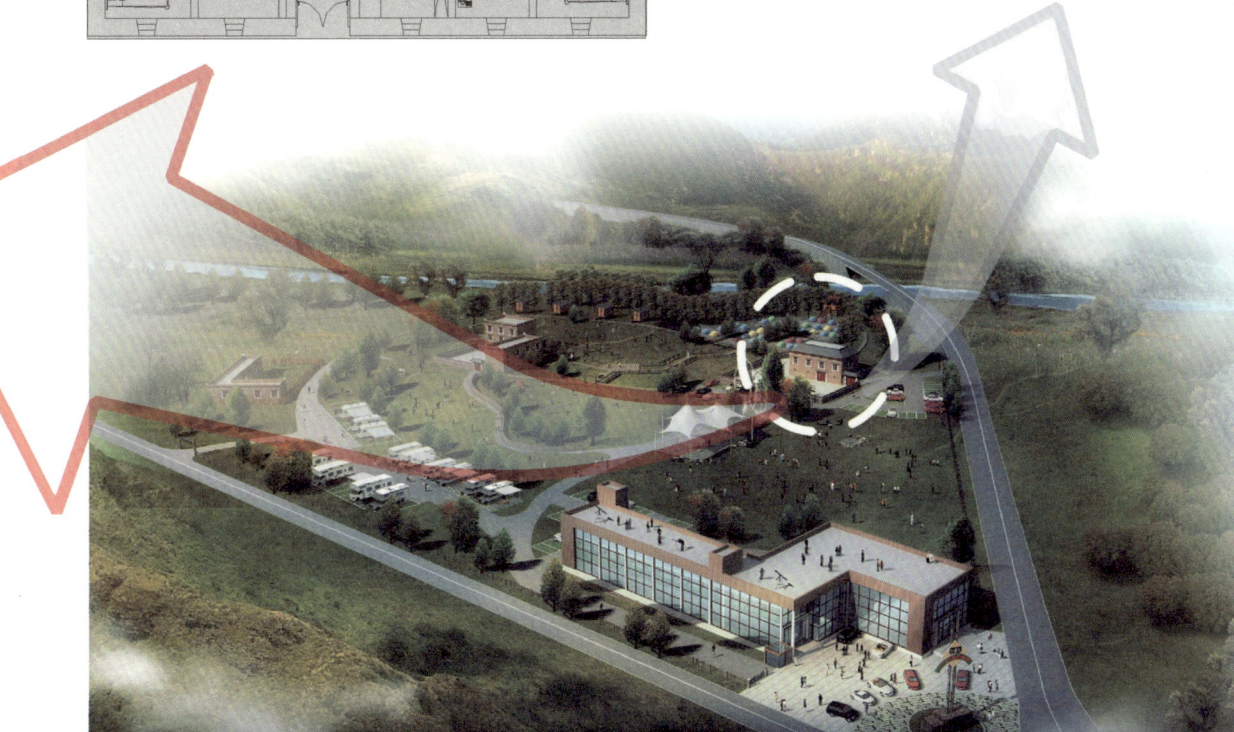

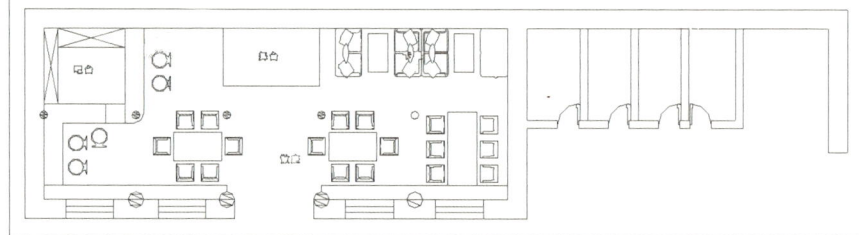

Site plan of youth hostel

Floor plan of Tibetan-style bar

Rendering of BBQ area

10 / Tibetan-style bar
11-12 / Interior of Tibetan-style bar
13 / Performance stage

Rendering of racetrack

Rendering of site

14-15 / Wooden villa
16 / Wooden villa suite
17 / Wooden villa standard room

Rendering of camping area

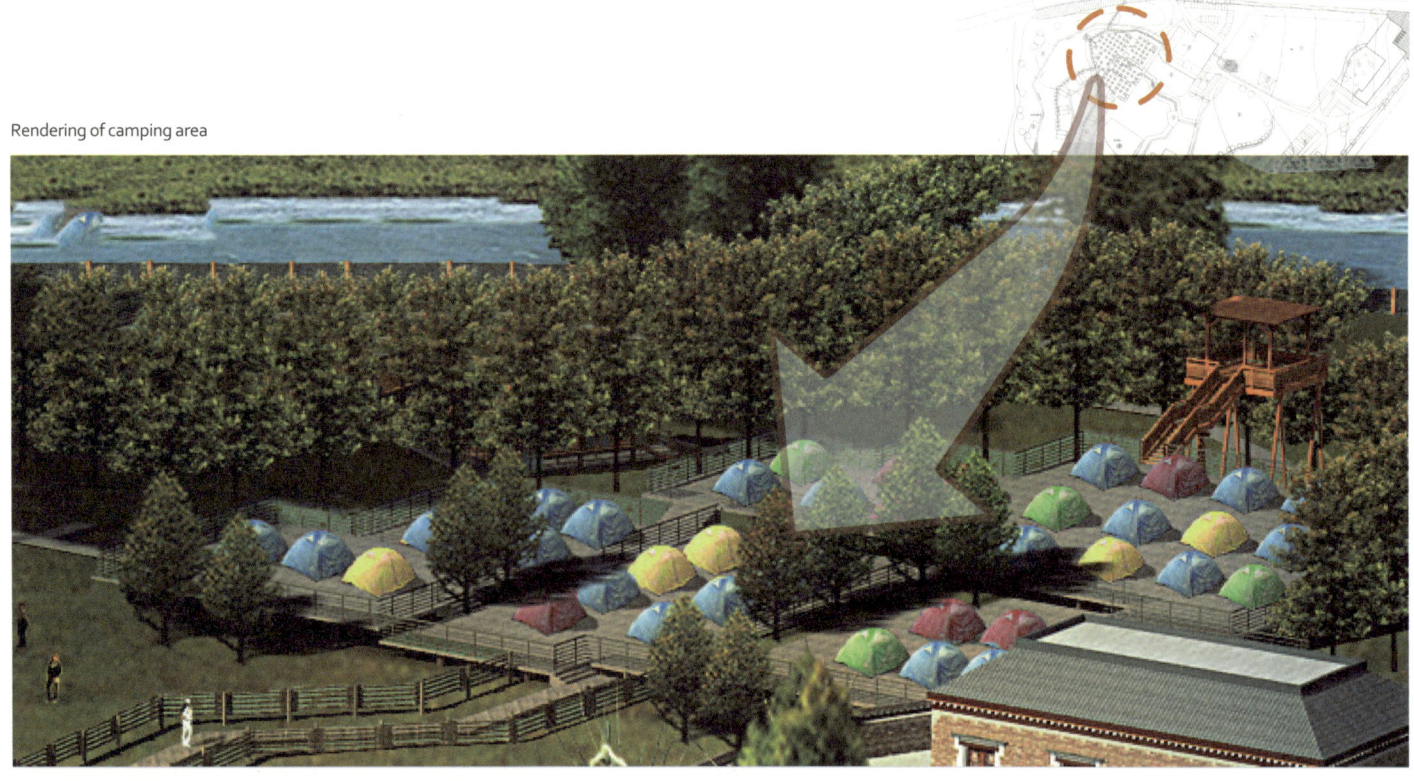

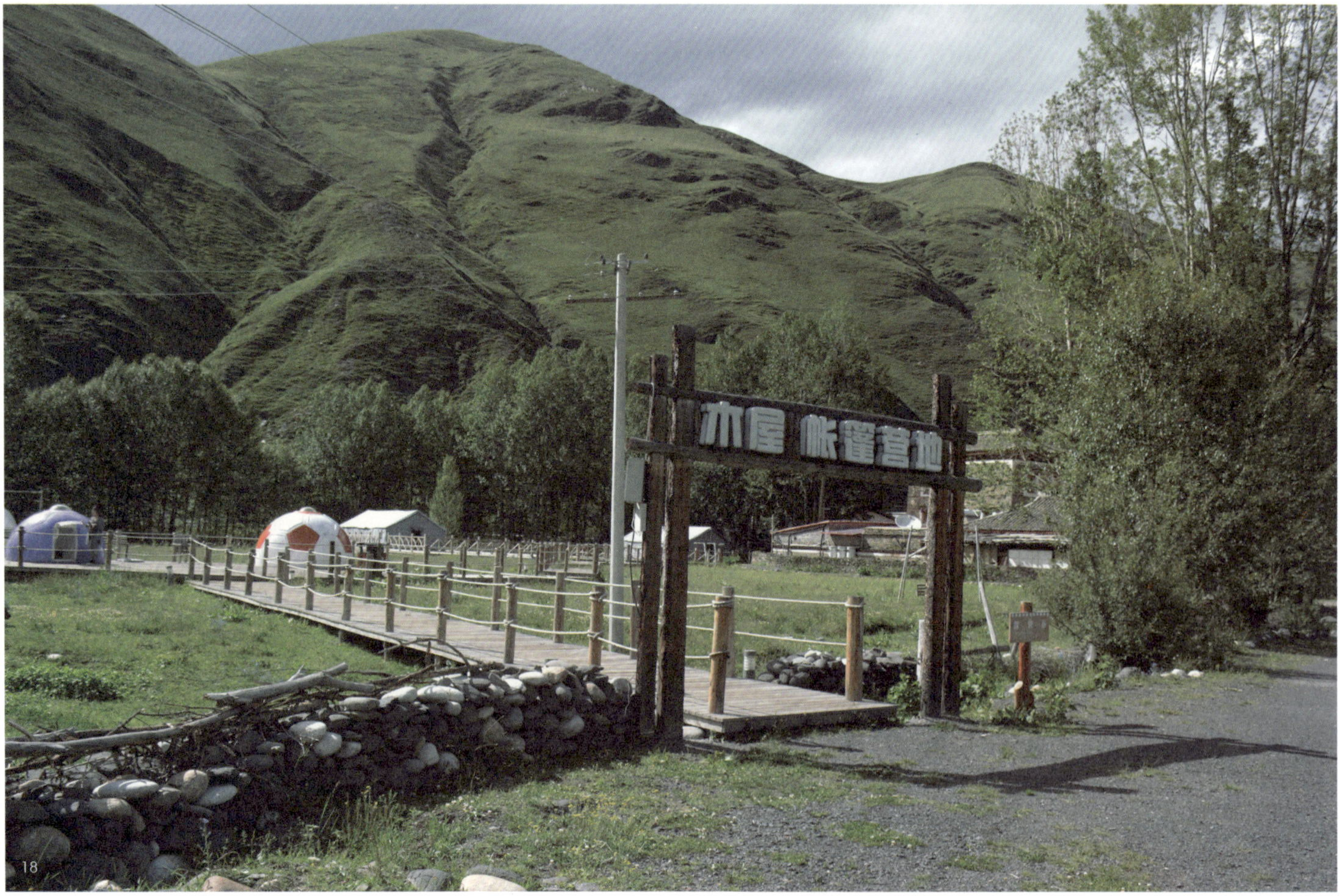

18

18-21 / Camping area

Rendering of RV area

22 / RV area
23-25 / Interior view of RV

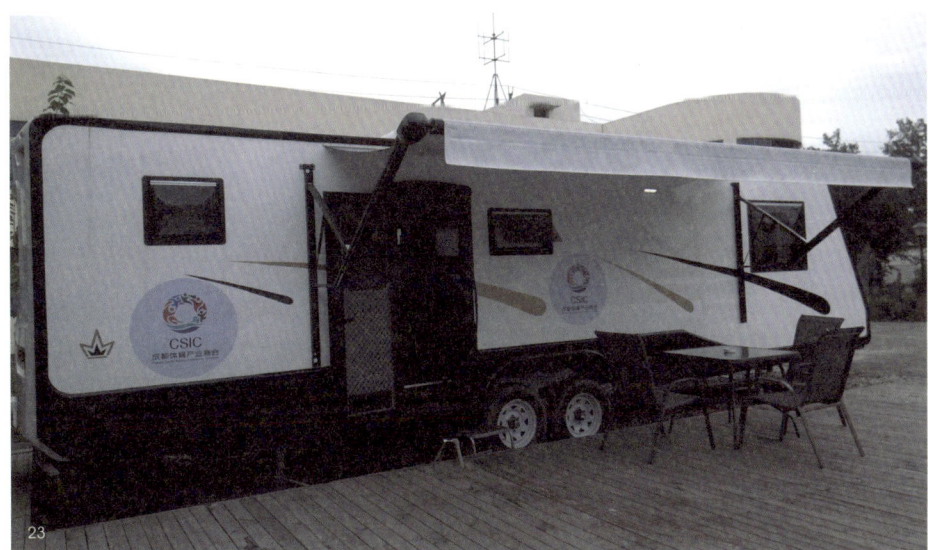

26 / Hotel exterior
27 / Hotel suite
28 / Hotel standard room

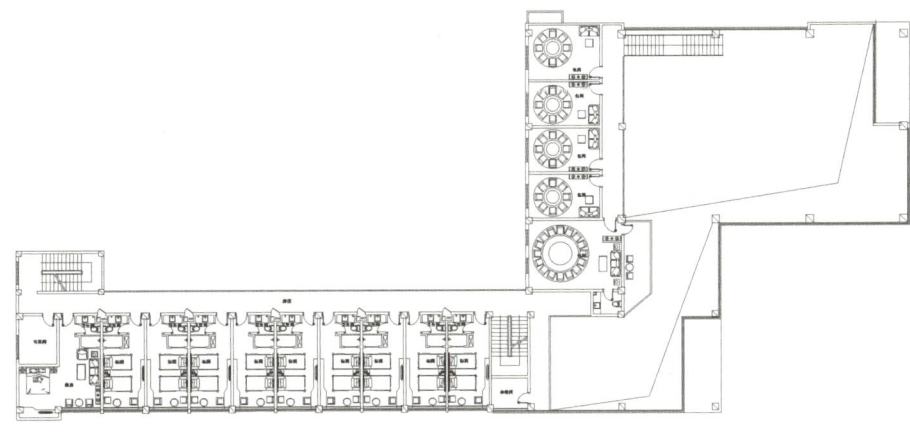

Second-floor plan

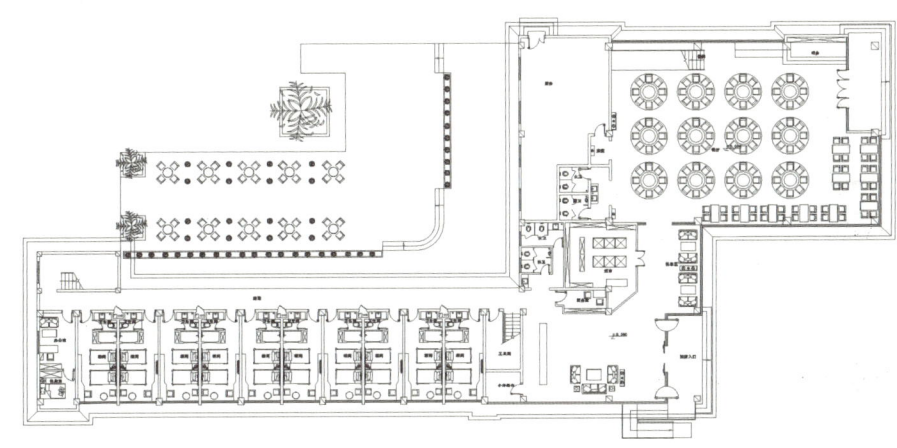

First-floor plan

Jiange Cuiyunlang RV Campground along No.318 National Road

Location / Sichuan, China
Area / 538,196 square feet (50,000 square meters)
Completion / 2015
Architect / China Building Technique Group Co., Ltd.
Photography / Louis Yao Cai

The campground, located at Guangyuan scenic spot in Sichuan, is a comprehensive tourism project integrated with RV campsites, tourism and recreation, recuperation and holidaying services. The design is around RV campsites, sightseeing of ancient Shu Road, experience of ancient Shu culture, holidaying in the forest and experience of agriculture and aims to create a new international RV resort campground with functions of 'eco-sightseeing,' 'holidaying in the forest,' 'campground experiencing' and 'agriculture experiencing.'

The campground consists of a compressive service area, a RV campsite area, a recreational resort area and a reserved buffer area. Grouping of RV campground holidaying is the feature of the whole area. It puts mainly self-driving travel to the center, highlighting eco-environment friendly and container-type house experience, capitalizing on cabins and camping tents which are closely related with nature and thus creating a resort environment for people to get close to nature and feel it.

Campground accommodation facilities include a module space hotel, cabins, RVs and tents. The visitor center and module space hotel are arranged into four container clusters which are formed with a total of 38 container modules.

The module space hotel in the campground has a reception hall and a container-like house experience area. This new experiencing living type has improved the living environment and visitors' traveling experience to a large extent. Container-type houses are easy to assemble and unassemble and transport. Through varied combination and overlay, they can form different living spaces, meet varied visitors' demands and enrich interests and experiences.

For the design of the comprehensive reception hall, the designers create a reception area, a chess and card room, toilets and baths and other functional spaces with containers. The roof platform of the 969 square feet (90 square meters) reception hall is tiled with anti-corrosive wood and provides an extra recreation space for visitors. The design of the reception hall integrates post-modernism style by using floor-to-ceiling glass at both front and back sides. It is simple and bright and its color is consistent with the dominant tone of the scenic spot. The reception area in it combines guest-welcoming, serving coffee and other comprehensive functions. The height of the hall is increased and the front and back French windows ensure sufficient lighting and ventilation for the inside space.

The campground hotel building, mainly in brown, white and timber color, blends into green cypress trees and has a well-arranged layout that is integrated with its natural environment and provides a space for people to get close to nature. Each hotel has a sunbathing platform and allows visitors to enjoy a sunbath.

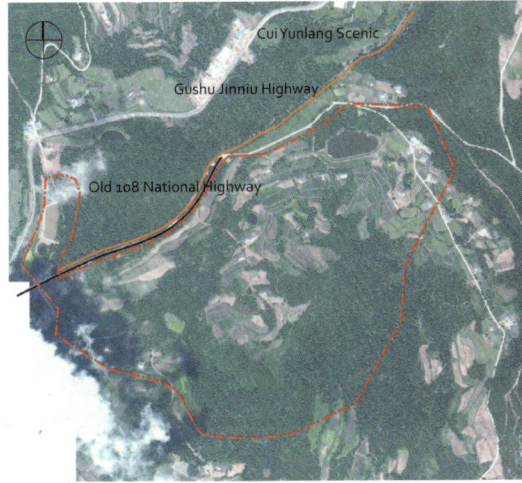

Outline of campsite's geography

Rendering of campsite

01 / Aerial view

Site plan of campsite

① Main entrance
② Entrance plaza
③ Reception area
④ RV area
⑤ Tent area
⑥ Wooden villa
⑦ Recreation plaza
⑧ Container house
⑨ Camp area for self-driving visitors
⑩ Restroom
⑪ Showers
⑫ Camping area
⑬ Children's play area
⑭ Restaurant

02 / Entrance
03 / Exterior of reception hall
04 / Reception hall

05,08 / Exterior of wooden villa
06-07 / Double room in wooden villa
09 / Standard room in wooden villa

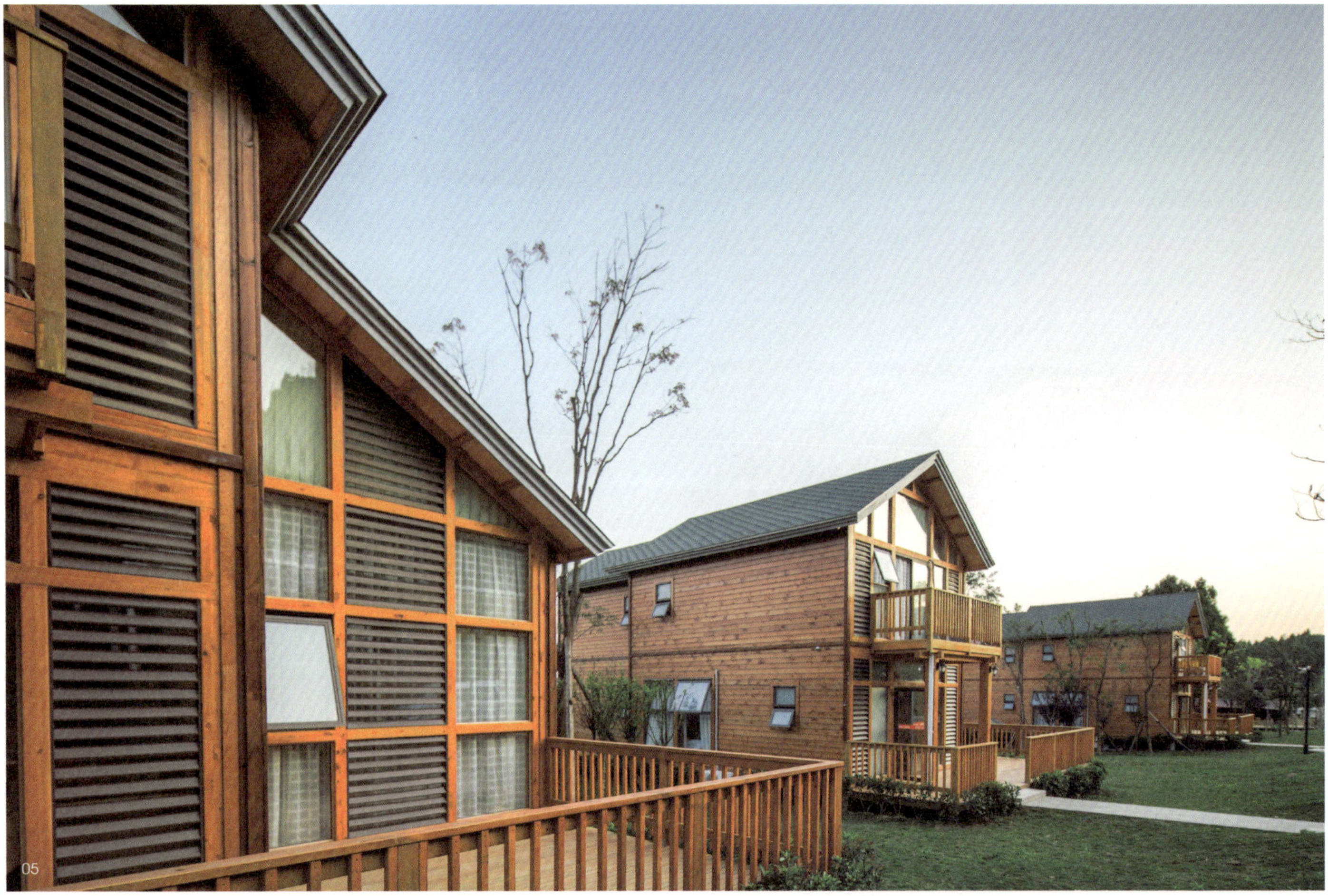

05

06

07

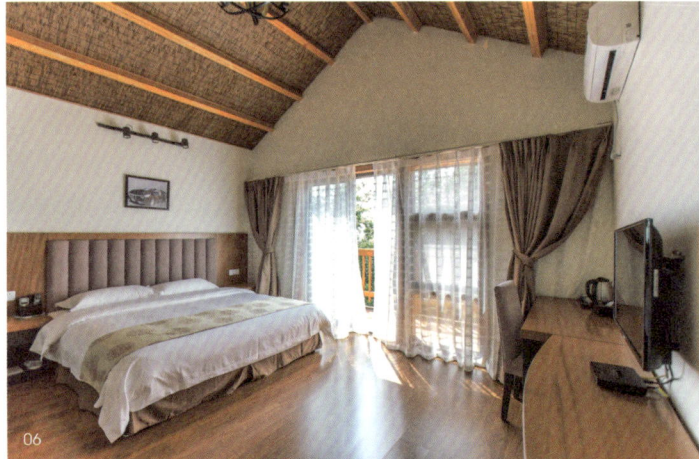

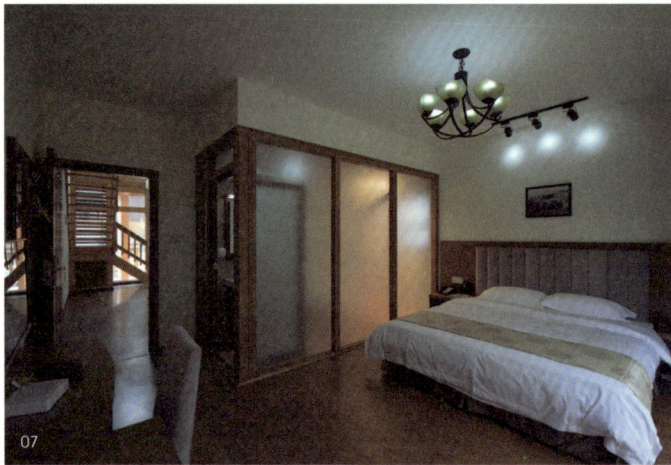

10-11 / Exterior of garden villa
12 / Recreational area on terrace
13 / Standard room in garden villa

14 / Exterior of tent suite
15 / Tent suite terrace
16 / Interior of tent suite

17-19 / Exterior of RV
20-22 / Interior of RV

Home of Freedom-Mount Huang Qiyun Campground

Location / Anhui, China
Completion / 2015
Architect / Qi Yunshan Investment Group, Ltd.
Photography / Qi Yunshan Investment Group, Ltd.

Home of Freedom, originated from the concept of 'family, health and recreation,' pays attention to family and healthy growth of children. It advocates an attitude of returning to nature, saving energy and protecting our environment and attempts to create a leading family resort in China. Home of Freedom campground consists of tree houses which are a unique cultural and architectural art feature, an exposition park which contains a variety of accommodation, clubs in rich outdoor sports themes and over 20 outdoor recreational activities.

In the exposition park, there are campsites with themes of special tree houses, RVs, containers, camping and others. In the shades of pine trees, a quiet and comfortable holidaying environment is created for guests. There are also more than 20 activities in the campground such as sky expedition, archery, strop ropeway, mini golf and etc., as well as theme clubs for parent-child interaction activities, outdoor training, recreational sports, and water sports.

Each tree house in the tree house world is unique and designed separately by Germany tree house designers or excellent Chinese designers. Fascinating interior design and personalized housekeeper service will bring extraordinary experience for visitors. Designers have much freedom in the design. What they keep in mind is what kind of house to build and for whom. They create a house based on their understanding and ideas of the campground. Finally, they set up their own scenes and design many excellent tree houses. The site selection and construction of tree houses shall take into account how to make the architectural form blend into the surrounding environment and how to create different visual effect and experience for their residents.

Each tree house in the campground has a story. For example, 'Building Blocks' gets inspiration from a father who plays Lego with his son. He wants to build a tree house with clean and transparent windows for his children in the waters and mountains. The tree house is constructed with over 500 pieces of glass and wood members and is a fairyland concealed among pine trees. On sunny mornings, the father will sit on the floor while the son will pillow his knees to hear him tell stories. They bathe in the sunlight shot in through the window and such quite and warm accompany is what the designer wants to give his son. Another example is 'Hamburger.' It has a outdoor wood structure rectangular corridor, French windows and a sunken living room. Randomly arranged cushions form a secret garden designed for gathering of friends. 'Bridal Chamber' is a tale of love. Such buildings create a feeling of identity which is also what the designer wants to express.

01 / Grassland
02 / Aerial view

Map of campsite

The mission of 'Home of Freedom' is to build a connection between human and nature. With low density and micro-ecology, it follows natural texture and design principle of blending into the environment. It is a theme outdoor recreational destination for self-driving travel and recreational tourism market.

03 / Grassland
04 / Park area
05 / Cabin
06 / Limin House
07 / Tree house
08-09 / Interior of tree house

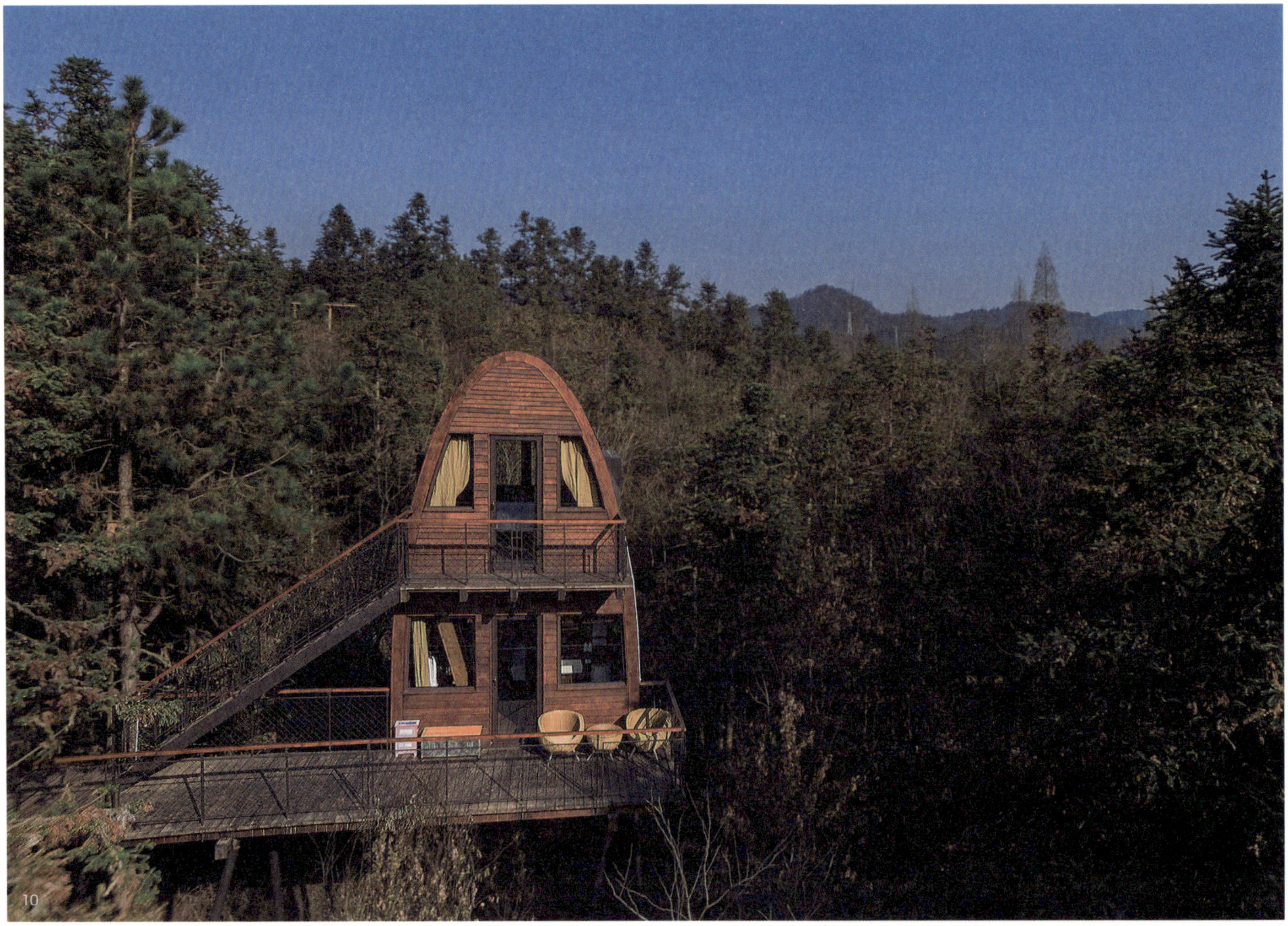

10 / Beacon tree house
11-12 / Tree restaurant
13 / Tree bag house
14 / Building block tree house

Plan of tree bag house

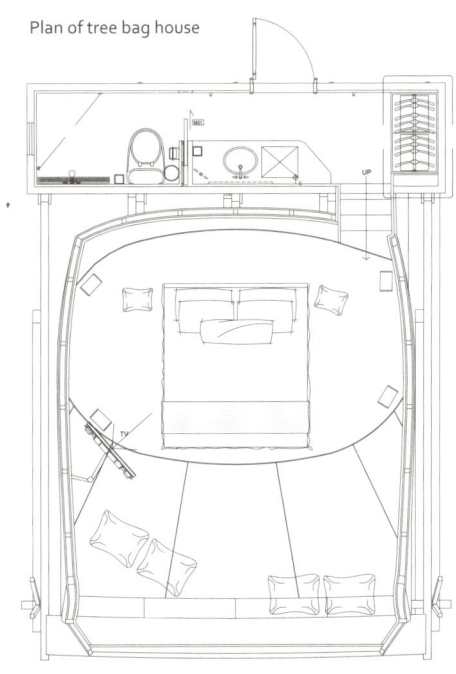

15 / Beacon tree house
16 / Steamer tree house
17-19 / Interior of steamer tree house

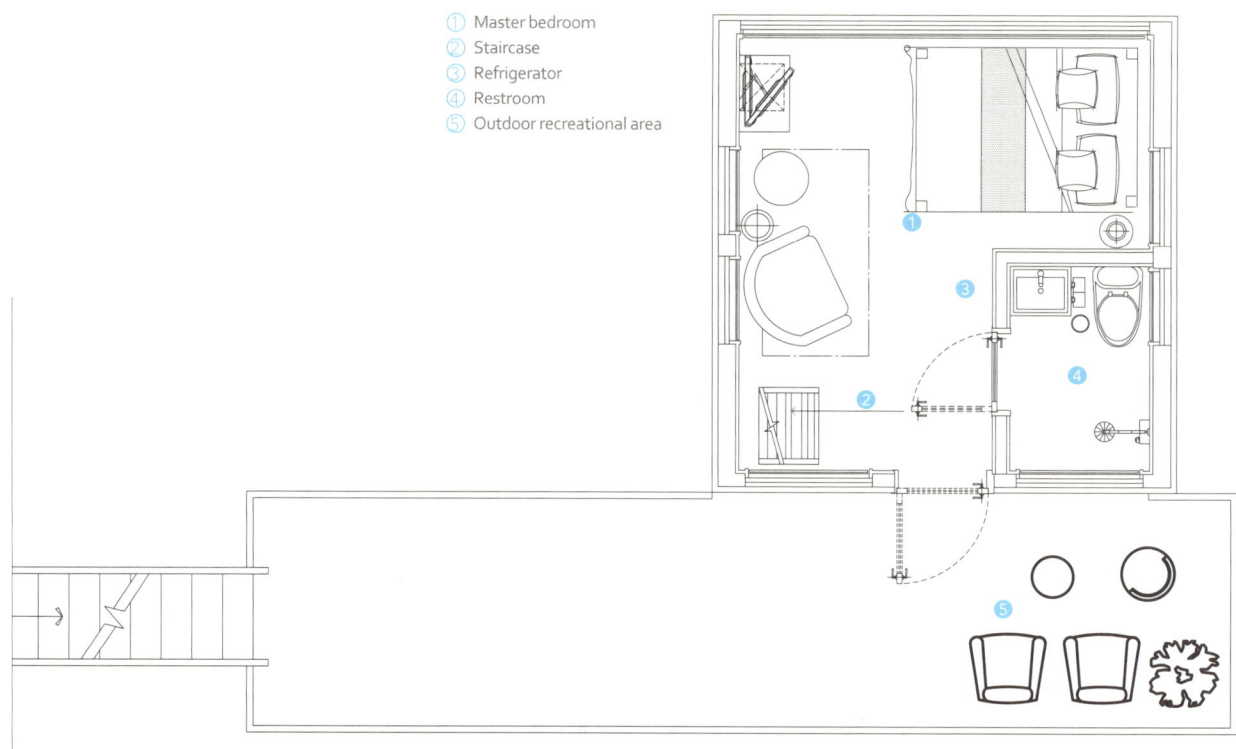

① Master bedroom
② Staircase
③ Refrigerator
④ Restroom
⑤ Outdoor recreational area

Floor plan of beacon tree house

15

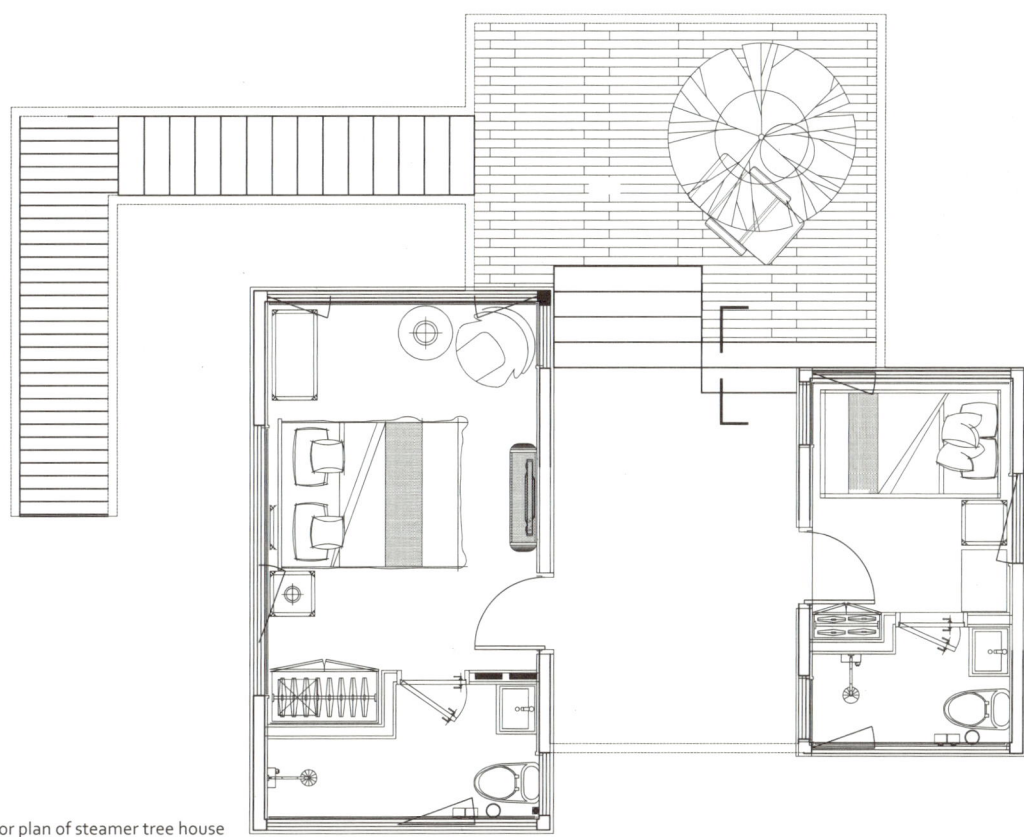

Floor plan of steamer tree house

20 / Hamburger tree house
21-22 / Interior of hamburger tree house
23 / Kaleidoscope tree house
24 / Cowboy tree house

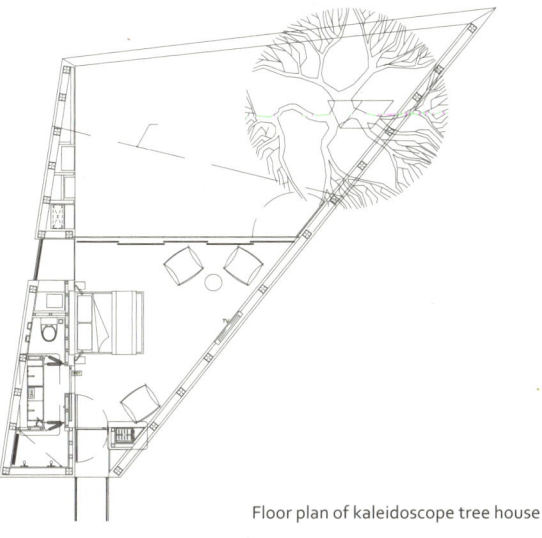

Floor plan of kaleidoscope tree house

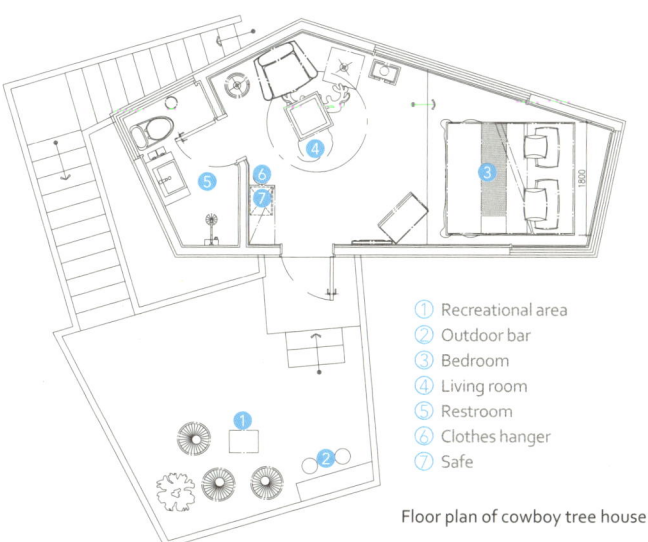

① Recreational area
② Outdoor bar
③ Bedroom
④ Living room
⑤ Restroom
⑥ Clothes hanger
⑦ Safe

Floor plan of cowboy tree house

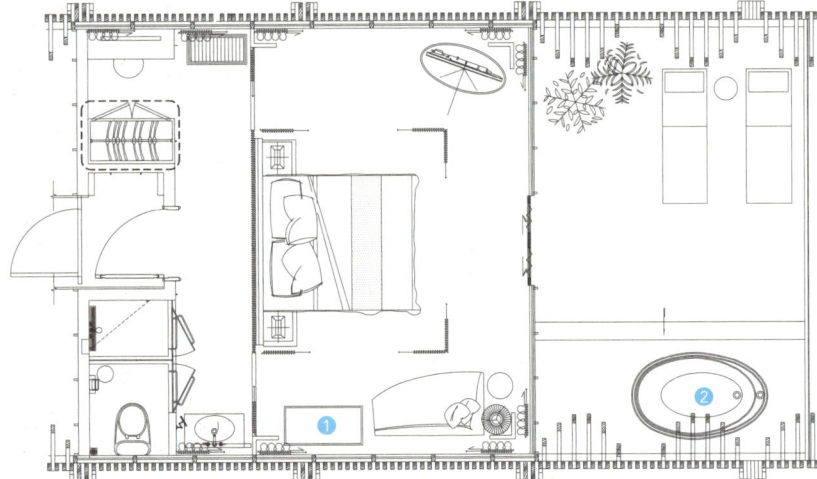

① Bathtub
② Mini-bar

Floor plan of girl's tree house

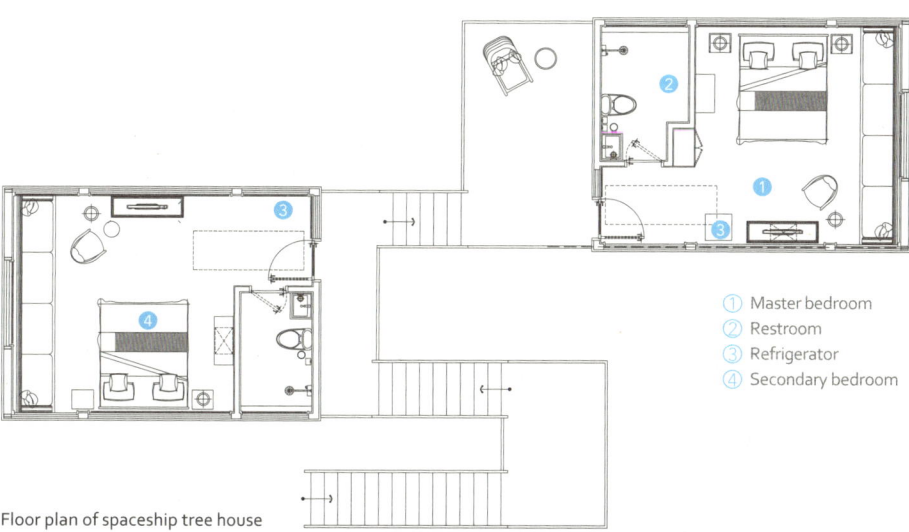

Floor plan of spaceship tree house

① Master bedroom
② Restroom
③ Refrigerator
④ Secondary bedroom

25 / Girl's tree house
26 / Interior of girl's tree house
27 / Spaceship tree house
28-29 / Interior of spaceship tree house

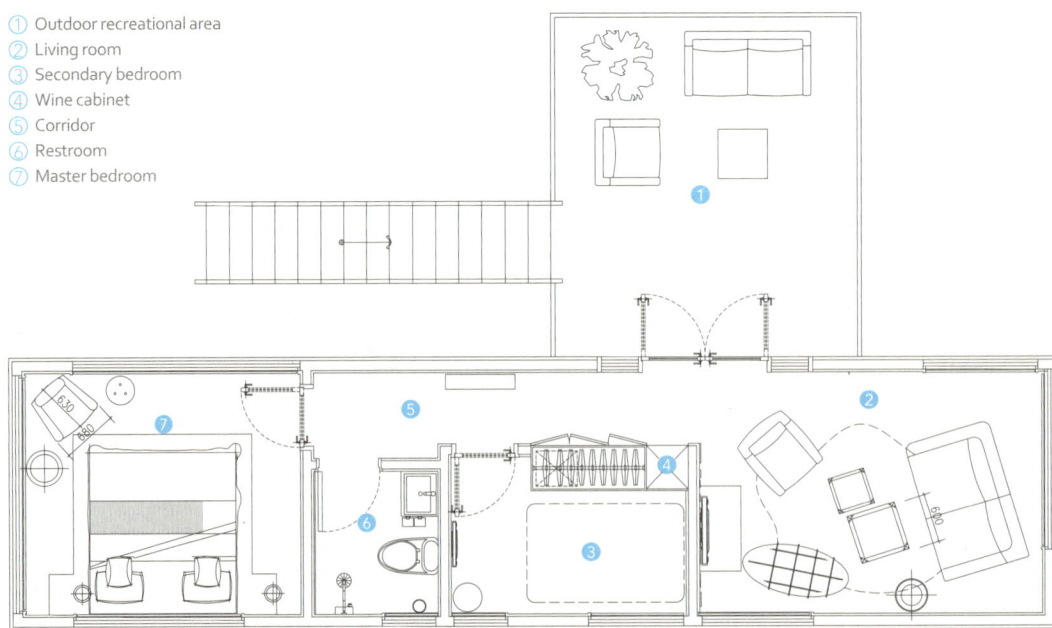

① Outdoor recreational area
② Living room
③ Secondary bedroom
④ Wine cabinet
⑤ Corridor
⑥ Restroom
⑦ Master bedroom

Floor plan of watcher's tree house

30 / Watcher's tree house
31-32 / Interior of watcher's tree house
33 / Cabin in woods
34 / Interior of cabin in woods

Floor plan of building block tree house

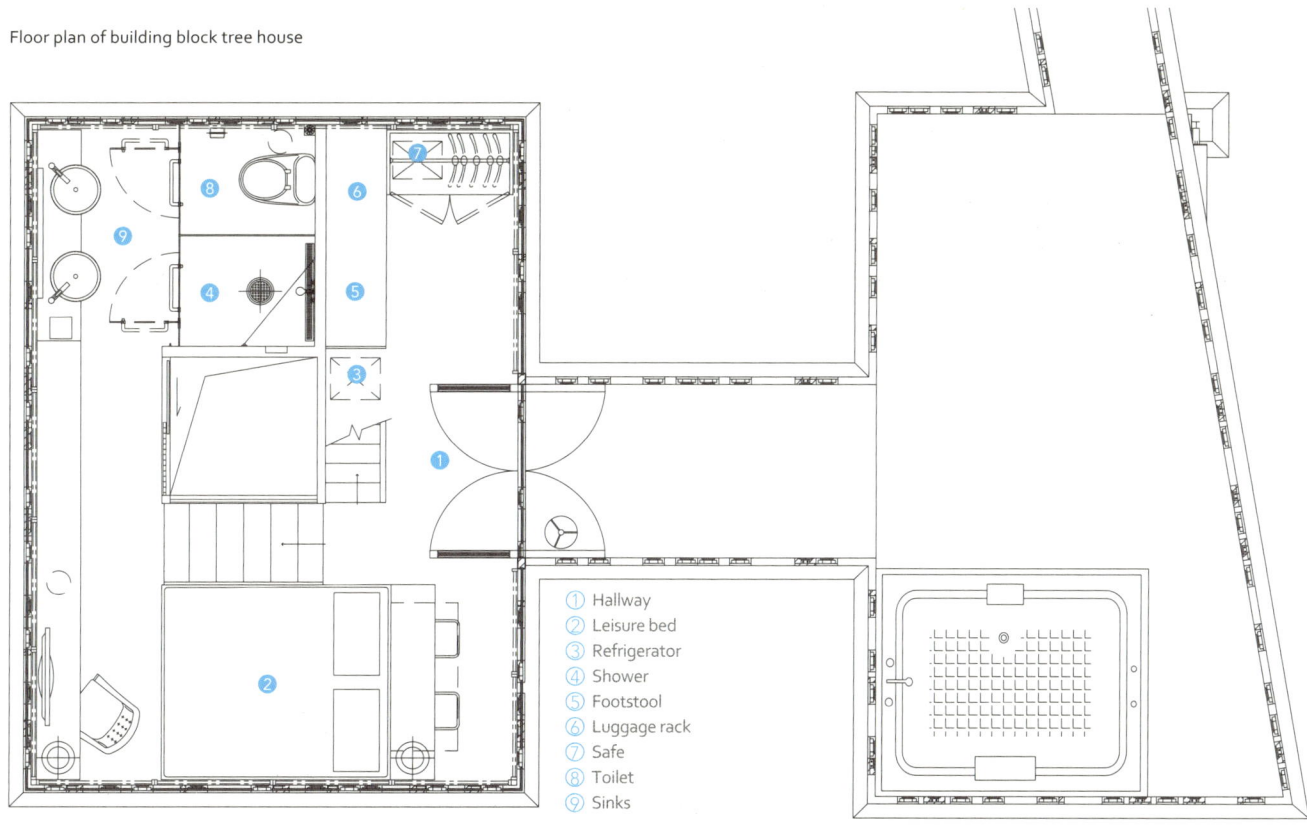

① Hallway
② Leisure bed
③ Refrigerator
④ Shower
⑤ Footstool
⑥ Luggage rack
⑦ Safe
⑧ Toilet
⑨ Sinks

35 / Cabin in woods
36 / Interior of the cabin in spruce woods
37 / Overhead view of park
38 / Cabin

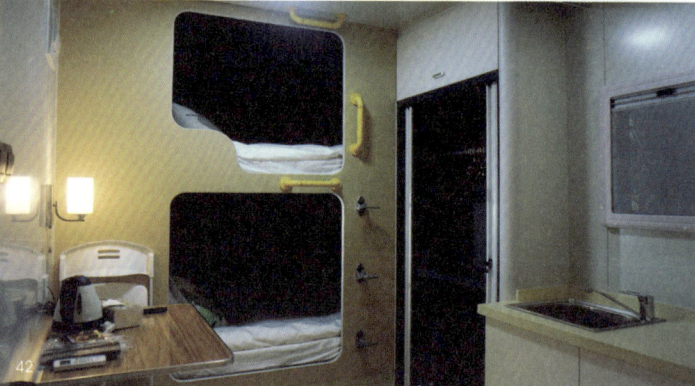

39-41 / Container house
42 / Interior of container house
43 / RV lot
44 / Cement pipe cabin

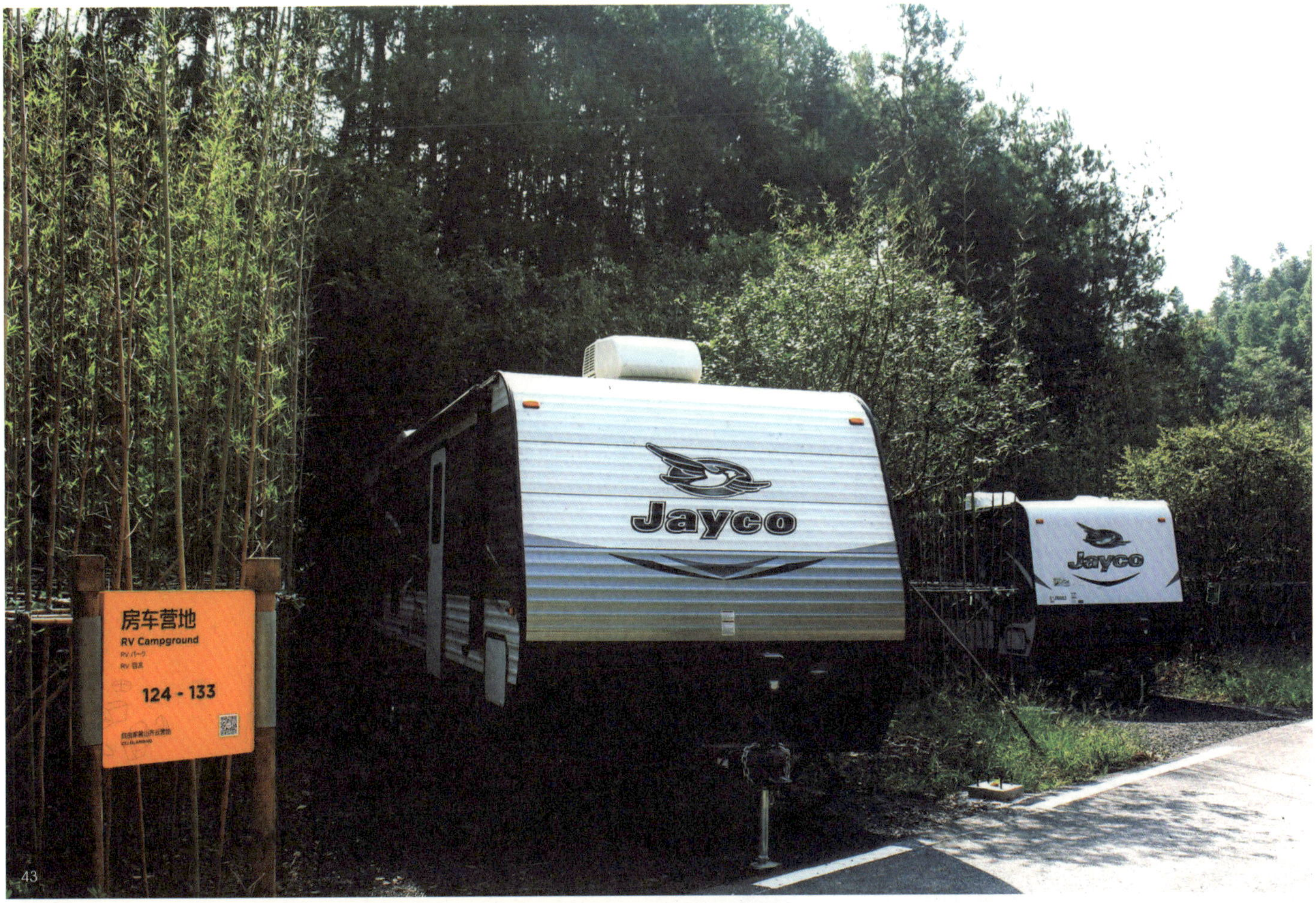

房车营地
RV Campground
RVパーク
RV 営地

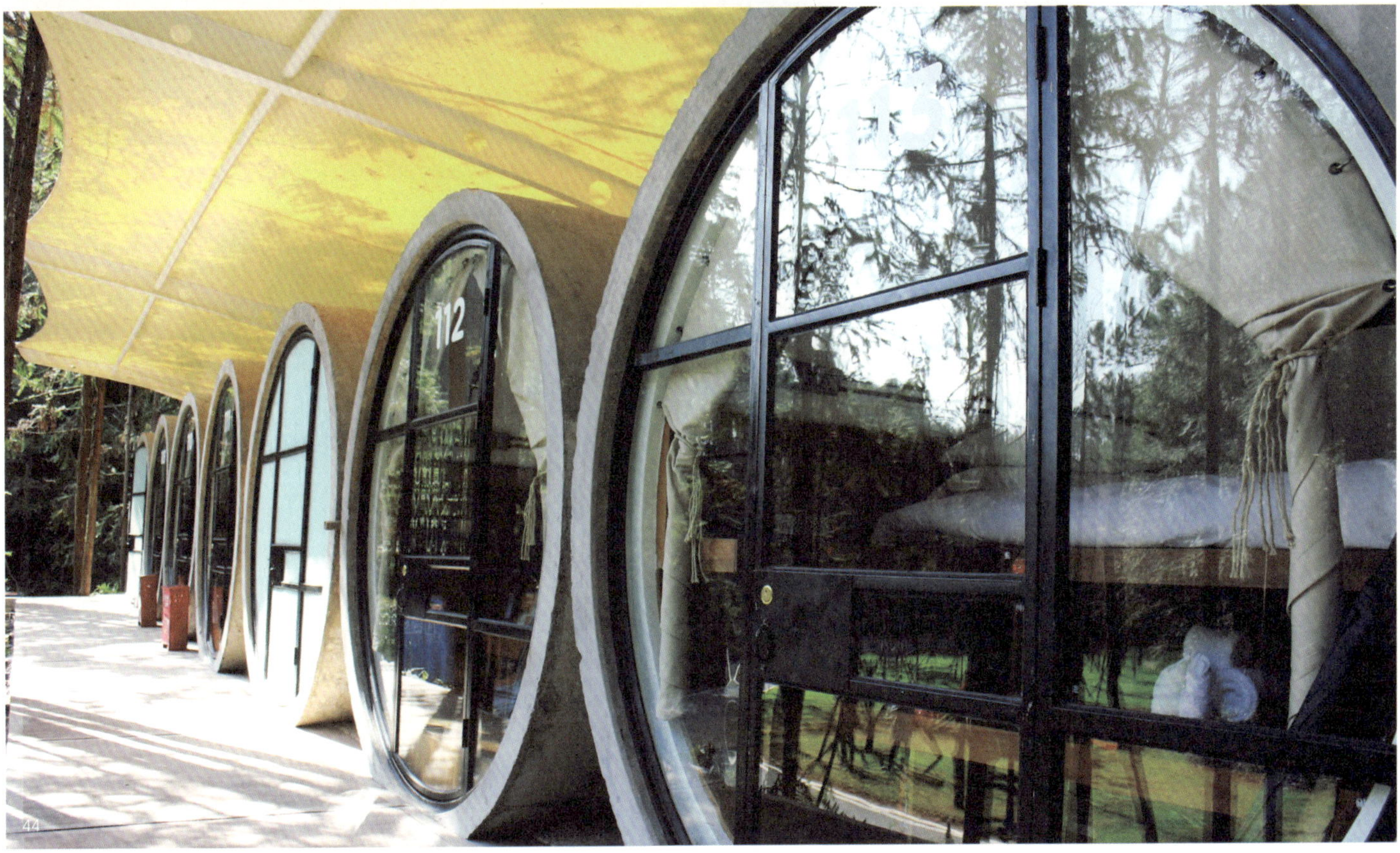

124 - 133

Ga-pyeong Glamping

Location / Ga-Pyeong, South Korea
Completion / 2016
Architect / ArchiWorkshop
Photography / June-Young Lim
Client / Glamping on the Rock

Ga-Pyeong region is located outskirts of Seoul. The site is famous for Arboretum, pine forest and mountains with rocks. The project embraces these characters of region. Likely, to other places, pine trees and large Rocks were easily found on the site. The architects pursue to express the atmosphere of the site character on its master plan. When people visit the site, they should experience the nature as itself and should not be disturbed by destructed nature.

The site is located on the edge of a pine forest, which has slope height difference of 82 feet (25 meters) from the south to north end. Area for glamping camping is on the nature side. The buildings are positioned on the road side, as if they protect the campground.

The buildings are divided into three volumes along the slope. The buildings are merging into the nature. The last volume on lowest side is used as welcome center. The façade of the building is combination of mirror and black cedar wood panels. The mirror panels embrace the surrounding nature.

In this project, we introduced two glamping designs. They are 'rock flower' and 'dynamic triangle.' Both the buildings and the glamping are positioned along the inclined slope.

The word 'glamping' was introduced over 10 years ago in Korea but its meaning was misappropriated in terms of quality and comfort. Instead of glamorous camping, low quality tents were installed and profiteered.

The designers came to a mind of creating Glamping, which gives people chance to experience the nature even closer, while providing place to experience uniquely designed architecture and comforts. The site should be a place, where nature, ecological values, comfort and modern design are equally balanced. This concept led to the creation of gamping architecture in Korea.

The glamping units are juxtaposed with a minimum change of the nature.

The designers developed the glamping units and named the design 'Rock Flower'. The basic concept of 'Rock Flower' was inspired by the rocks on the site.

Site plan

01 / Scenic view of site

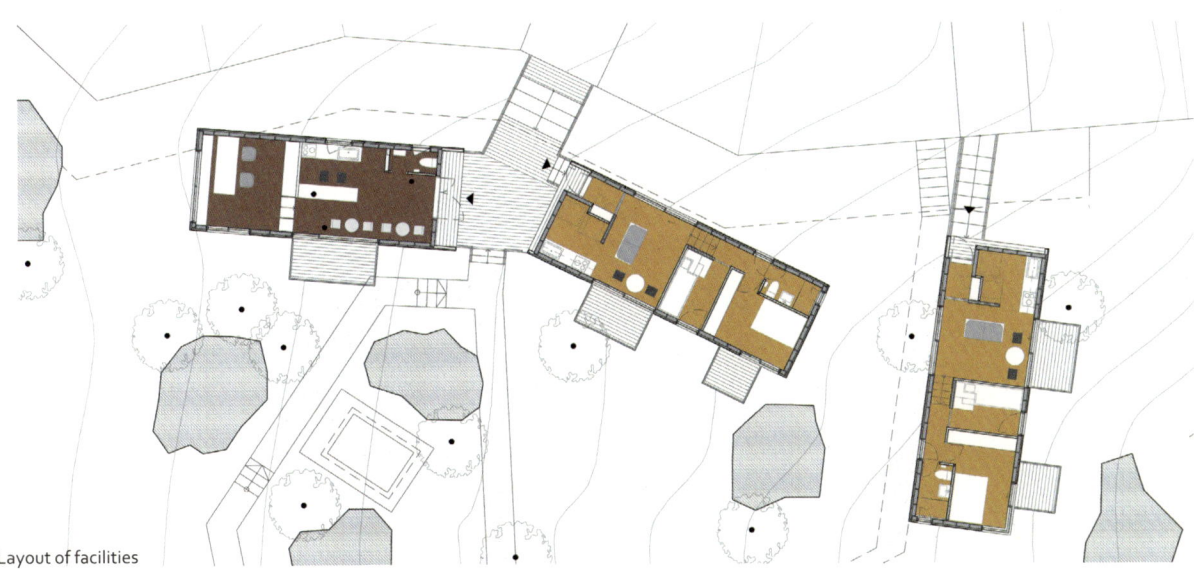

Layout of facilities

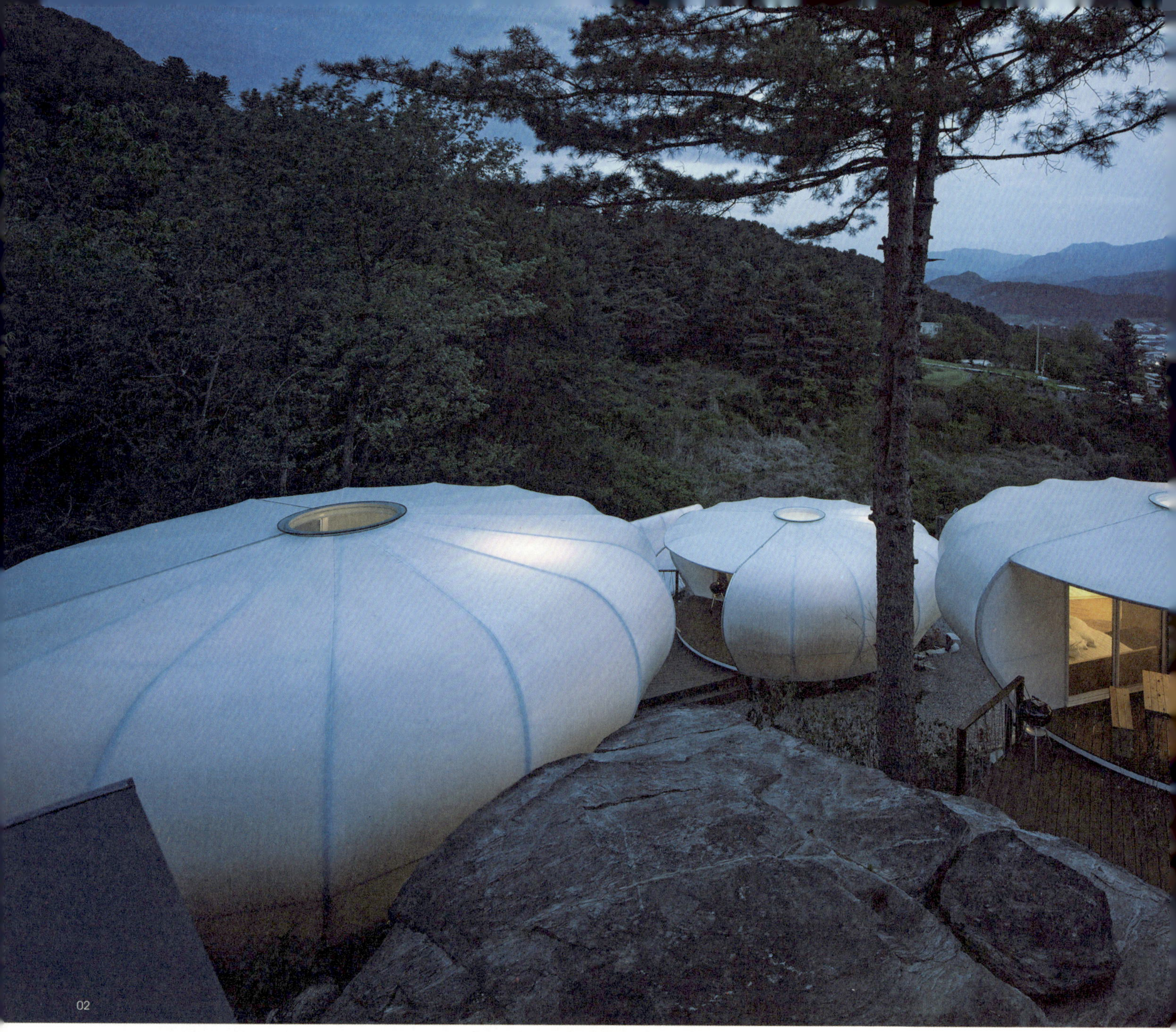

02

03

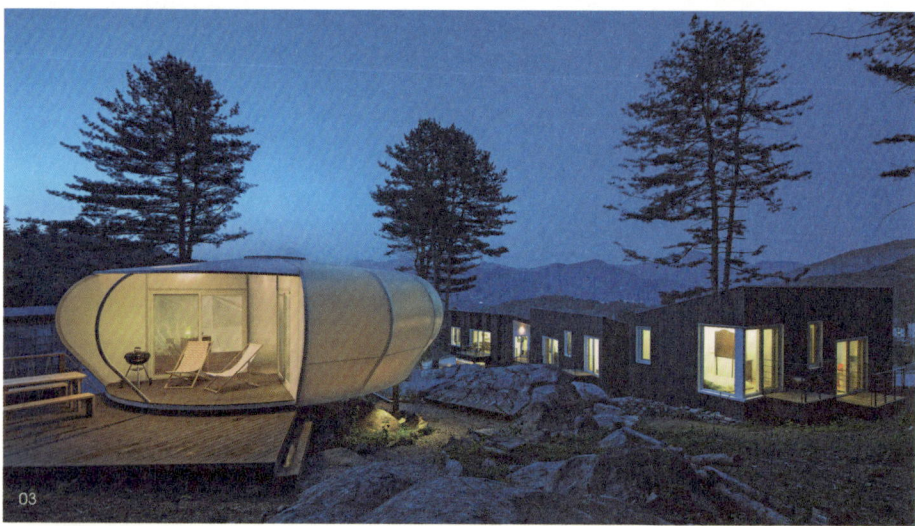

02 / Group of lodgings next to rock formation
03 / Lodging aglow at night
04 / Scenic nighttime view

There were number of large rocks on the inclined steep hill and the flowers were grown between gabs. The design intension is to express the glamping as flower buds on the rock.

The window with 1.5-meter-diameter on top of the glamping helps to bring the sun light as well as experience the nature closer.

The shape of the landscape/nature has highest design character and the designers reflected this while planning the master plan.

The shape and the position of the structures were carefully considered to give aesthetic emergence both during the day and the night time.

When the form was designed, the architects considered the vertical structure spacing not to exceed the maximum width of the standard membrane size. This helped to reduce the cost as well as better control over visual effect of the joints between the surfaces.

Because of the translucent character of the membrane, the shadow of the structure gave lantern effect, when projected on the surface.

05 / Private terrace
06 / View of scenery from outside lodging
07 / Interior of lodging
08 / Alternate view of terrace

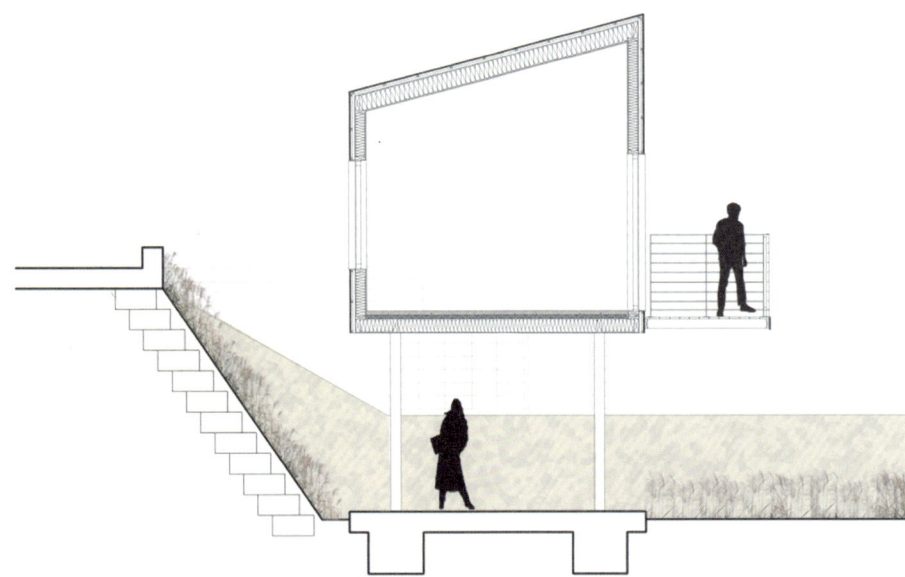

Diagram

09 / Welcome center
10 / Wooden houses positioned along slope
11 / Close-up of welcome center
12 / View from deck in lodging
13 / Site entrance
14 / Interior of welcome center
15 / Sleeping area inside lodging

Parque Tejo

Location / Rossio ao Sul do Tejo, Abrantes, Portugal
Area / 74,809 square feet (6950 square meters)
Completion / 2015
Architect / Atelier Rua
Photography / Miguel Manso, FG+SG Fernando Guerra
Client / CÂMARA Municipal De Abrantes

In Rossio ao Sul do Tejo village, the existing campsite with around 43,056 square feet (4000 square meters), is closed due to its advanced degradation and obsolescence. The existing constructions, mainly support facilities, are abandoned. Dense vegetation, mainly maple trees, confers the exterior areas an essential comfort for the desired new program.

A new plot of 31,753 square feet (2950 square meters) acquired by the Abrantes Municipality will be joined to the old campsite. In this area, the existing constructions are in a state of ruin and unworthy of rehabilitation except for two old warehouses that will be adapted to support facilities. According to the law, new constructions are forbidden in this site, and therefore, the footprints of the old ruins will be respected in the layout of the new campsite.

The extension of the campsite to a capacity of around 300 users, reinforces the need to undergo a deep restructuring.

The plot naturally establishes a border between the intricate layout of Rossio ao Sul do Tejo, with its small low-rise houses, and a broad and unobstructed Tejo riverfront and the city of Abrantes.

The proposal takes advantage of the morphology and irregular nature of wall that limits the plot to the north, with its attached pre-existing constructions and their footprint. A unifying, continuous structure, capable of aggregating the whole program, creates a fluid and organic front to the new constructions. This is a neutral element between the density of the houses and the broad riverfront. This open and permeable structure aims to establish a direct and permanent relation with the green areas throughout its whole length and in the areas of the program that are not enclosed (circulations, toilets, washing areas). For technical, functional, safety, thermic and hygienic reasons these two cores (reception/lounge and cafeteria) are enclosed, and because they are the only parts of the structure that are considered buildings, they

01 / Project surroundings
02 / Overhead view

Site plan

① Entrance
② Parking
③ Gatehouse
④ Reception/Lounge center
⑤ Terrace
⑥ Cafeteria
⑦ Washing area
⑧ Women's restroom
⑨ Men's restroom
⑩ Camper service area
⑪ Technical center
⑫ Service entrance
⑬ Caravan/Camper plots
⑭ Playground
⑮ Picnic area

respect the footprint of the demolished ruins. This solution allows the desired levels of comfort and functionality while preserving the informal atmosphere, in contact with the outside green space.

The program's dispersion throughout one of the sides of the plot allows the allocation the riverfront to the tent and leisure areas.

A new entrance to the west was made possible with the attaching of the new plot, allowing a direct access from the Marginal do Tejo Avenue, facilitating the arrival of users, campers and caravans, as well as emergency vehicles. The old entrance becomes a service access for loading and unloading.

From the main entrance, the program unfolds in a line but with hierarchy, establishing 4 nuclei of distinct uses. The entrance nucleus that comprises the night watch control point, the parking, and the reception, allows the control of users until the lifting gate. The second nucleus, the leisure area, comprises the lounge space, the cafeteria and its terrace. The third nucleus is constituted by the service areas like the toilets

03 / View of camping plots

and washing areas (laundry and sinks). The fourth nucleus is the support area, with a service station for campervans and caravans, a technical area for installations and the garbage and recycling container areas. This last nucleus is located next to the service entrance.

The whole structure is walkable along a gallery in direct contact with the exterior and that gives access to the different parts of the program. This gallery is defined by an elevation composed of several vertical elements that create a physical barrier, interrupted by openings accessing the camping area. The toilets (in spite of keeping the necessary privacy) and the washing areas are included in the same open nature. Due to prolonged people permanence, the reception (with its service counter, office, staff's toilets and changing-rooms and lounge space) and the cafeteria (with its service counter, pantry, storeroom, toilets and mini-market) are enclosed.

The designers opted for a lightweight construction solution, consisting of a slab [detached 8 inches (20 centimeters) from the ground and with occasional contacts to the soil to keep its permeability] and a lightweight roof slab with the necessary insulation and waterproofing. The metallic structure that supports the roof is anchored in the concrete wall that defines the whole south perimeter of the plot. All the pillars of this structure are placed along its northern edge, composing an elevation with a rhythm of vertical elements covered in prefabricated fiberglass white elements.

In general terms, the inner walls consist of plain water-resistant panels, applied on a light steel structure. Thicknesses vary according to the need of thermic insulation (enclosed areas). Concrete walls were used only in specific locations due to safety and equipment installation reasons.

For easy execution and maintenance, all the electric and communications infrastructures as well as the water supply (warm and cold) run visible, suspended from the ceiling.

The renovated existing warehouses were properly insulated, besides all the necessary reparations to the stone walls, plaster and painting. The roof in insulated

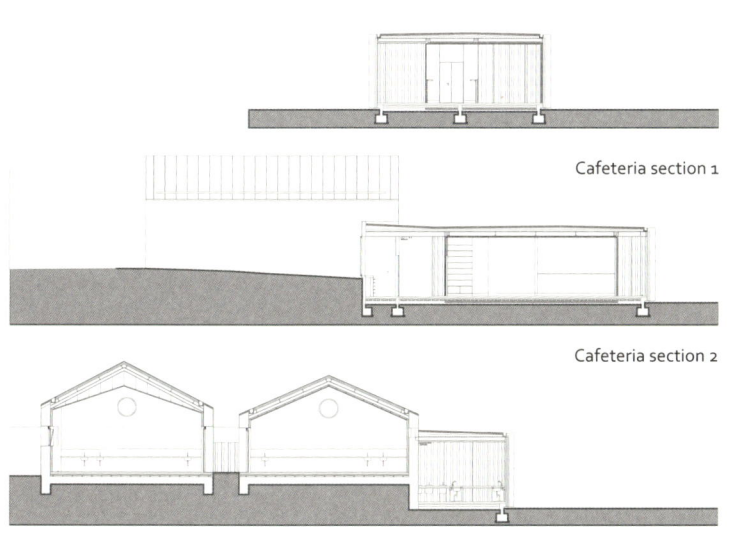

Cafeteria section 1

Cafeteria section 2

Interpretation center section

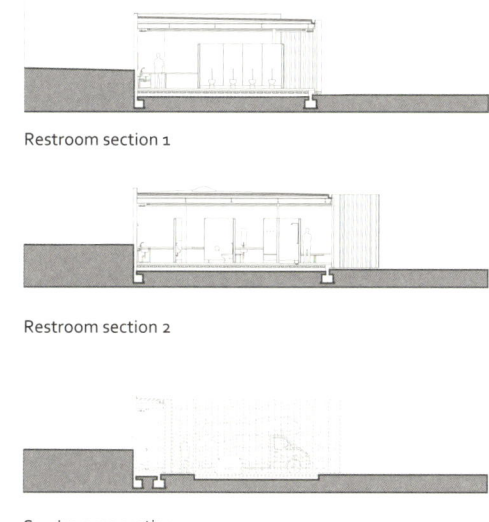

Restroom section 1

Restroom section 2

Service area section

04 / Camping entrance
05 / Reception area
06 / Cafeteria exterior

metallic 'sandwich' panels lays on a structure of metallic beams that are anchored to the stone walls. Sheets of acoustic panels cover the ceiling in order to unify the interior space.

The concrete paving lays on a structure of cement-wood composite panels, concealing a layer of thermic insulation

07 / Cafeteria exterior/Lounge area
08 / Cafeteria/Entrance

09 / Corridor
10 / Cafeteria interior
11 / Gallery

12 / Toilets
13 / Washing area
14 / Washbasin detail

Restroom section

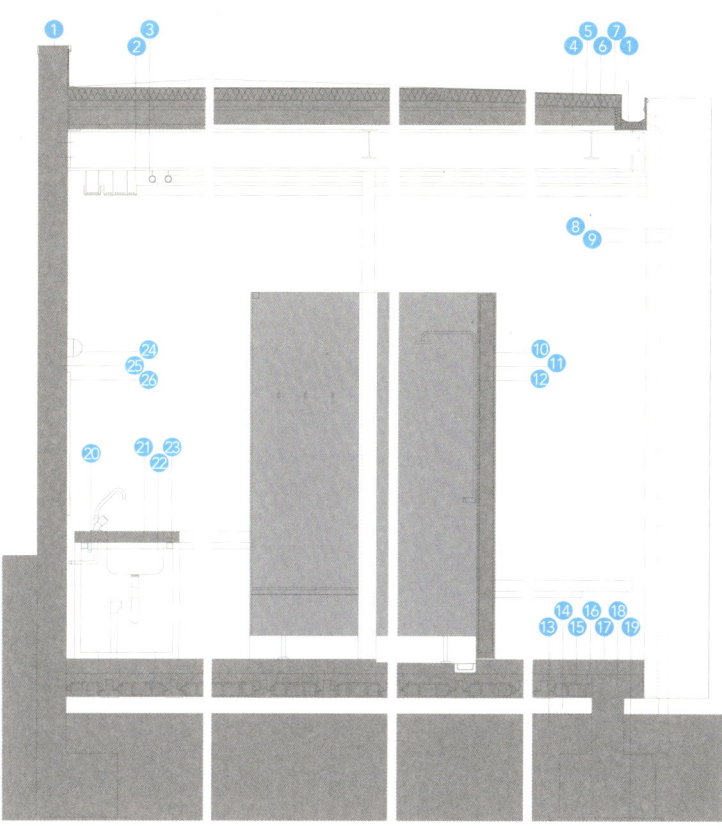

① Thin zinc gutter
② Metal ducts
③ Hot and cold water system
④ Composite slabs
⑤ Concrete filling
⑥ Thermal insulation - rockwool fiber panels
⑦ Waterproofing
⑧ Prefabricated white fiberglass façade elements
⑨ PVC tube within the façade element
⑩ Fiber-reinforced cement panels
⑪ Supporting steel structure
⑫ HPL panel
⑬ Hard soil
⑭ Ventilated air box
⑮ Reinforced smooth concrete slab 15cm thick
⑯ Concrete screed
⑰ Transparent satin varnish
⑱ Reinforced concrete strip footing
⑲ Concrete finishing
⑳ Hot and cold water supply attached to underside of bench
㉑ Worktop
㉒ Stainless steel sink
㉓ Round wall light fitting
㉔ Reinforced concrete wall
㉕ Silicon waterproofing
㉖ Mirror

Index

p114
Architype
Website / www.architype.co.uk
Email / london@architype.co.uk
Telephone / 0044 020 7403 2889

p286
ArchiWorkshop
Website / www.archiworkshop.kr
Email / office@archiworkshop.kr
Telephone / +82 2542 3947

p122
Álvaro Planchuelo
Website / www.alvaroplanchuelo.com
Email / estudio@alvaroplanchuelo.com
Telephone / 0034 91 447 4932

p294
Atelier Rua
Website / www.atelierrua.com
Email / info@atelierrua.com
Telephone / (+351) 217 959 316

p194
Avanto Architects
Website / www.avan.to
Email / surname@avan.to
Telephone / 358405773022

p104
Binario Architectes
Website / www.binarioarchitectes.com
Email / info@binarioarchitectes.com
Telephone / 0032 043 445 300

p188
BTE Architecture
Website / btearchitecture.com

p34
Carl-Viggo Hølmebakk AS
Website / www.holmebakk.no
Email / post@holmebakk.no
Telephone / 0047 2246 7600

p240
Chengdu Hengji Decorative Engineering Co., Ltd.
Website / www.hjzs.com.cn
Telephone / 86 028 85212907

p256
China Building Technique Group Co., Ltd.
Website / www.cbtgc.com
Telephone / 86 010 64517637

pp62, 68
de Leon & Primmer Architecture Workshop
Website / www.deleon-primmer.com
Email / office@deleon-primmer.com
Telephone / 001 502 582 6295

p200
Gjøde & Partnere Arkitekter
Website / www.gpark.dk
Email / johan@gpark.dk
Telephone / (+45) 2897 6538

p210
JDS Architects
Website / jdsa.eu
Email / office@jdsa.eu
Telephone / 45 3378 1010

p182----------------------------------

Joaquín Alvado Bañón

Website / joaquinalvado.wordpress.com
Email / mail@marthaschwartz.com
Telephone / Joaquin.alvado4@gmail.com

p176----------------------------------

Jorge Javier Andrade Benitez

Website / www.joregeandradebenitez.com
Email / jandradebenitez@gmail.com
Telephone / 0998 3231 52

p82-----------------------------------

K2S Architects Ltd.

Website / www.k2s.fi
Email / k2s@k2s.fi
Telephone / 00358 09 6831 3961

p50-----------------------------------

lab03

Website / www.lab03.nl
Email / lab@lab03.nl
Telephone / 0031 6 2470 3797

p76-----------------------------------

Laboratory of Architecture #3

Email / archlab3@gmail.com
Telephone / 995 322 22 5596

p104----------------------------------

L'Escaut Architectures SCRL

Website / www.escaut.org
Email / info@escaut.org
Telephone / 0032 2426 4815

p170----------------------------------

LAAC Architects

Website / Web: www.laac.eu
Email / office@laac.eu
Telephone / 43.(0)512 8903 350

p88-----------------------------------

Line and Space, LLC

Website / www.lineandspace.com
Email / studio627@lineandspace.com
Telephone / 001 520 623 1313

p98-----------------------------------

Lake|Flato Architects

Website / www.lakeflato.com
Email / marketing@lakeflato.com
Telephone / 001 210 227 3335

p166----------------------------------

Matteo Thun + Partners

Website / www.matteothun.com
Email / uinfo@matteothun.com
Telephone / 3902 6556 911

p158----------------------------------

Miró Rivera Architects

Website / www.mirorivera.com
Email / info@mirorivera.com
Telephone / 5124 7770 16

p42-----------------------------------

oto arquitectos

Website / www.oto.pt
Email / acs@oto.pt
Telephone / 351 21 383 0660

p104----------------------------------

PIGEON OCHEJ PAYSAGE

Website / www.dupaysage.be
Email / info@dupaysage.be
Telephone / 0032 472 35 39 85

p268----------------------------------

Qi Yunshan Investment Group, Ltd.

Website / www.sunriver.cn
Telephone / 86 0559 7523551

p152----------------------------------

Saunders Arkitektur

Website / www.saunders.no
Email / post@saunders.no
Telephone / 4755 3685 06

pp240, 256----------------------------

Sichuan 318 Motel Investment Management Co.Ltd

Website / 318h.com
Email / Hotel318@126.com
Telephone / 028-83321318

p132----------------------------------

Smith Vigeant Architectes

Website / www.smithvigeant.com
Email / info@smithvigeant.com
Telephone / 001 514 844 7414

p152----------------------------------

Wihelmsen Arkitektur

Website / www.tommie-wihelmsen.no
Email / kristian@twarkitektur.no
Telephone / 0047 95287158

p56-----------------------------------

X Architects

Website / www.x-architects.com
Email / info@x-architects.com
Telephone / 00971 4388 4611

p228----------------------------------

Xiaoyin Architectural Design Office

Email / panyoucai@qq.com

p268----------------------------------

Zi Youjia

Website / www.zyj.com
Email / service@zyj.com
Telephone / 86 023 63410070

Published in Australia in 2018 by
The Images Publishing Group Pty Ltd
Shanghai Office
ABN 89 059 734 431
6 Bastow Place, Mulgrave, Victoria 3170, Australia
Tel: +61 3 9561 5544 Fax: +61 3 9561 4860
books@imagespublishing.com
www.imagespublishing.com

Copyright ©The Images Publishing Group Pty Ltd 2018
The Images Publishing Group Reference Number: 1466

All rights reserved. Apart from any fair dealing for the purposes of private study, research, criticism or review as permitted under the Copyright Act, no part of this publication may be reproduced, stored in a retrieval system or transmitted in any form by any means, electronic, mechanical, photocopying, recording or otherwise, without the written permission of the publisher.

 A catalogue record for this book is available from the National Library of Australia

Title: Tourism Infrastructure Design
Author: Edited by Joaquín Alvado Bañón, Krizsán András, and Pan Youcai
ISBN: 9781864707816

Production manager | Group art director: Nicole Boehringer
Senior editor: Gina Tsarouhas
Assisting editor: Benjamin Sepsenwol

Printed by Everbest Printing Investment Limited, in Hong Kong/China

IMAGES has included on its website a page for special notices in relation to this and its other publications. Please visit www.imagespublishing.com

Every effort has been made to trace the original source of copyright material contained in this book. The publishers would be pleased to hear from copyright holders to rectify any errors or omissions.

The information and illustrations in this publication have been prepared and supplied by the contributors. While all reasonable efforts have been made to ensure accuracy, the publishers do not, under any circumstances, accept responsibility for errors, omissions and representations, express or implied.